INSURANCE AS GOVERNANCE

Richard V. Ericson, Aaron Doyle, and Dean Barry

Insurance as Governance is the first major sociological study of the insurance industry. It examines how the industry controls our institutions and daily lives in ways that are largely invisible, and how it thereby functions as a form of government beyond the state.

Drawing on extensive ethnographic research on industry practices, the work penetrates the complexities of the insurance industry and demonstrates why it is such a powerful and pervasive institution. The authors advance the concept of moral risk as they consider how insurance companies partner with governments and corporations in the negotiation of economic policy.

In effect, *Insurance as Governance* documents liberal theory at work. It offers a major case study of liberal governance beyond the state. The authors argue that insurance is increasingly liberal rather than welfarist in orientation, and that it is in fact the vanguard of liberalization in governance throughout postindustrial societies. Wide-ranging in scope and original in approach, the text provides a sophisticated integration of empirical data and theoretical approaches relating to insurance, risk, governance, and security.

RICHARD ERICSON is Principal of Green College and Professor of Law and Sociology at the University of British Columbia

AARON DOYLE is Assistant Professor of Sociology at Carleton University.

DEAN BARRY is Policy Research and Development Officer, Citizenship and Immigration, Government of Canada.

INSURANCE AS GOVERNANCE

Richard V. Ericson

Aaron Doyle

Dean Barry

UNIVERSITY OF TORONTO PRESS
Toronto Buffalo London

© University of Toronto Press Incorporated 2003
Toronto Buffalo London
Printed in Canada

ISBN 0-8020-3728-3 (cloth)
ISBN 0-8020-8574-1 (paper)

∞

Printed on acid-free paper

National Library of Canada Cataloguing in Publication

Ericson, Richard V., 1948–
    Insurance as governance / Richard V. Ericson, Aaron Doyle, Dean
Barry.

    Includes bibliographical references and index.
    ISBN 0-8020-3278-3 (bound).   ISBN 0-8020-8574-1 (pbk.)

    1. Insurance.   2. Risk (Insurance)   I. Doyle, Aaron   II. Barry, Dean
III. Title.

HG8026.E75 2003   368   C2002-905943-7

This book has been published with the help of a grant from the Humanities
and Social Sciences Federation of Canada, using funds provided by the
Social Sciences and Humanities Research Council of Canada.

University of Toronto Press acknowledges the financial assistance to its
publishing program of the Canada Council for the Arts and the Ontario
Arts Council.

University of Toronto Press acknowledges the financial support for its
publishing activities of the Government of Canada through the Book
Publishing Industry Development Program (BPIDP).

Contents

Acknowledgments

This book is the result of five years' involvement with people in many institutions, and we thank them most warmly for their generosity and support.

We are especially grateful to the organizations and individuals in the insurance industry who are the subjects of our research. It is only through them that we are able to pursue our scholarly interest in what they know and how such knowledge is used in governance. While their deep insights about insurance form the core of the book, we hope that in return our analysis has some value for them.

Financial support was provided by a number of organizations. Substantial funding for data collection and analysis was awarded through a research project grant of the Social Sciences and Humanities Research Council of Canada. Richard Ericson enjoyed the enormous leave privileges of a Killam Research Fellowship sponsored by the Killam Programs, Canada Council for the Arts. He also received generous support as a Visiting Fellow of All Souls College, Oxford, during the 1998–9 academic year. Substantial support has been provided by the University of British Columbia. This book also received a grant from the Humanities and Social Sciences Federation of Canada. We are deeply indebted to all of these organizations for sharing with us the value of independent scholarly inquiry.

The research was based at Green College, University of British Columbia. Green College is a most stimulating intellectual and collegial environment in which to pursue interdisciplinary research, and we thank colleagues there for many discussions that have influenced our work. We are especially grateful to Diana Ericson, Dene Matilda, Rosanne Rumley, and Lillian Yee for their research assistance.

Richard Ericson also derived exceptional intellectual stimulus for the research during his year as a Visiting Fellow of All Souls College, Oxford. In particular, he thanks Andrew Ashworth, Roger Hood, and Lucia Zedner for their friendship and support.

Many other scholars have influenced this work through conversations, debates, and their own research. In this regard, we are especially grateful to Tom Baker, Aditi Gowri, Ian Hacking, Kevin Haggerty, Carol Heimer, Pat O'Malley, Michael Power, Nicholas Rose, Violaine Roussel, and Jonathon Simon. Early formulation of ideas and research results was helped by critical response to talks given by Richard Ericson at All Souls College, Oxford, the University of Edinburgh, the London School of Economics and Political Science, City University of New York, the University of Connecticut, the University of Toronto, and the University of British Columbia.

As always, it is a pleasure to be associated with University of Toronto Press. Virgil Duff is an ideal sponsoring editor, offering a wonderful combination of enthusiasm, wisdom, advice, and support. We thank four anonymous readers – one for the Humanities and Social Sciences Federation of Canada, two external readers for the University of Toronto Press, and a member of the University of Toronto Press Manuscript Review Committee – for reviews that have led to substantial revisions and a much better book. We are grateful to Allyson May for her thoughtful copy-editing.

RICHARD V. ERICSON

AARON DOYLE

DEAN BARRY

INSURANCE AS GOVERNANCE

Introduction

Insurance is embedded in all aspects of daily life. Yet how the insurance industry operates is not widely understood. Most individuals have several insurance policies – some obligatory, others by choice – and appreciate that these policies are among the most costly necessities of life. Nevertheless, insurance remains in the background. It is something that people take for granted to meet exigencies they would prefer not to think about.

Insurance also remains in the background in social science. Except for narrow specialisms in law and economics, it has not been subject to extensive analyses. Although the insurance industry is among the most pervasive and powerful institutions in society, the sociology of insurance remains nascent. This book is therefore written as a seminal contribution to the sociology of insurance. It provides a theoretically informed and empirically rich analysis of the insurance industry as a vehicle for understanding present-day society.

The core of this book is an ethnographic study that documents how the insurance industry governs our lives. It is based on extensive interviews with 224 people in Canada and the United States, as well as observations of their activities and analysis of their documents. Interviewees include people with a wide range of responsibilities in the insurance industry, professionals in expert systems that serve the industry, representatives of consumer associations, members of the general public who were consumers, industry regulators, senior civil servants, and members of Parliament. Observational research included attending industry conferences, and observing sales operations, loss-prevention operations, and claims-related examination practices.

Since insurance is a multifaceted institution that operates on a society-wide basis, it must be analysed through several branches of sociology. Our research necessarily draws upon, and contributes to, the sociologies of institutions, consumption, governance, knowledge, and regulation.

The insurance industry is an important locus of research for the sociology of institutions. Insurance is an institution that should be central to sociological investigation because it is a key component of political economy. Insurance companies interlock with other powerful corporations and the state to negotiate political economy on all levels of society. Insurance also governs other institutions through its powers of transferring and distributing risks. It strongly influences how institutions structure their environment, how they produce, take, and manage risks. It has a similar influence on individuals regarding each of these dimensions. It is central to the political economy of the person, how each individual designs her own risk portfolio through efforts to learn from the past, manage the present, and provide for the future.

The insurance industry is also instructive for advancing the sociology of consumption. In spite of its significance for people's lives, insurance is a product that most buy with little appreciation. They spend large sums of money to purchase something they have little knowledge about and therefore cannot adequately assess with respect to price and features. The only material thing they obtain at the outset is a piece of paper: a legal contract that they rarely read and even more rarely understand. They do understand that embedded in the contract is a promise to pay if something goes wrong. However, the details are typically obscure and most hope that they will not have to collect on the promise, since they can only do so if a loss has been suffered. They are buying trust in an abstract system, a peace of mind and taken-for-grantedness that if the worst happens there will at least be financial compensation.

These features of insurance differentiate it from the consumption of material goods, which has been the predominant focus of sociological theories of consumption. Unlike Nike running shoes with which we 'Just Do It,' insurance is an expensive product directed at long-term, imagined futures. Because they are less consumer-driven, many insurance products must be sold proactively and aggressively by providing lucrative incentives to sales staff. Sales staff promote the product by marketing (in)security, the need to consume more because of dreaded futures. Marketing (in)security is substantially different from the marketing of material goods, which brands identities and cultivates 'coolness' through positive lifestyle images and a sense of immediacy.

Insurance is also unique because consumers are actually a part of the product: the product consists of all members of the risk pool that the insurance company differentiates, packages, and sells. The company and its agents, as well as the policyholders in the pool, have a great stake in each other's behaviour because that behaviour can affect the integrity of the risk pool. For example, company underwriters who fail to select good risks for the pool will cost the company in higher claims, which in turn are passed on to all policyholders via higher premiums and more stringent contract conditions. Claims agents who are not vigilant about false claims will likewise cost both their company and claims-free policyholders. The policyholder who fails to take preventative measures in the knowledge that she can collect insurance in the event of a loss, or who makes a false claim, again costs both the company and fellow policyholders in the pool.

As elaborated later in this introduction, and fleshed out in the research studies that follow, the reactive 'moral risk' aspect of the insurance product means that insurers devise elaborate technologies for designing, selecting, and policing the risk pools they sell. This activity begs questions about how the insurance industry governs. A defining role of all government – whether by the state, private corporations, or communities – is the maintenance of risk pools large enough to ensure that expected losses are reasonably predictable and thus subject to governance. Therefore a sociology of governance, and more broadly a political sociology, are indispensable for understanding how the insurance industry participates in the constitution of society.

In its ideal form, insurance governs through nine interconnected dimensions. First, it attempts to produce knowledge of risk by objectifying everything into degrees of chance of harm. Second, it makes everything it objectifies calculable and thereby subject to commodification. It uses actuarial techniques to convert the concrete facts of objective risks it produces into probability classifications. Each classification is then assigned its respective cost so that prices can be set and compensation for the effects of chance can be paid. Third, actuarialism creates a risk pool, a population that has a stake in the identified risks and the specific harms they entail. This stake transforms the population into a collective with an interest in minimizing loss and compensating those who have suffered loss. Fourth, insurance protects against loss of capital. What is actually insured is not the particular event that causes harm to a member of the risk pool, but the capital against which the insurer offers indemnification. Fifth, insurance is managerial. It manages risks on the basis of surveillance and audit for a population dispersed in space and time but nevertheless bound together by the collective interests noted above. Sixth, the population is also bound legally. Insurance objectifies risk by making it subject to contract and adjudication. At the same time, it helps the law to assign liability to the party most able to distribute the loss through insurance. Seventh, in providing a futures market in security, insurance offers a cultural framework for conceptions of time, destiny, providence, responsibility, economic utility, and justice. Eighth, insurance is a social technology of justice. It bridges individual and social responsibility through distributive justice (collective sharing of loss) and restorative justice (financial indemnification). Ninth, insurance is therefore political, combining aspects of collective well-being and individual liberty in a state of perpetual tension.

These economic, social, legal, cultural, and political dimensions of insurance as governance point to its significance for political sociology. Insurance systematically grafts morality onto economics and thereby perpetuates questions about moral citizenship and responsibility. Questions include whose risk and whose security are at stake, and who is responsible to whom in this regard? The welfare state model urges strong central government to create large and undifferentiated risk pools that foster social responsibility. The private insurance model makes risks the property of non-state organizations and individuals. It therefore urges differentiated risk pools, based on market segmentation and ability to pay, that foster individual responsibility. Its moral economy is to minimize welfare social transfers and maximize liberal risk transfers to the level of organizations and individuals.

There are political reasons to expect that the private insurance industry has become especially salient in recent years. The role of the state is changing rapidly, and with it the mechanisms of governance. In particular, there has been a downsizing of the state and a greater focus on governance through local knowledge of risk. Accompanying this trend is an increased emphasis on private corporate, community, and individual responsibility for risk. Each of these entities is to form their own liberal risk regime: a semi-autonomous program for taking risk and minimizing harm for which the entity is responsible in both decisions and effects.

In this era of governance through liberal risk regimes, one would expect the private insurance industry to take up some ground left by the downsizing of the state. It has similar, although in each case more limited, purposes to those of the state in forming governable risk pool populations and thereby providing security. People still need to insure their risk taking, and private insurance provides the market-based mechanism for doing so.

The state has not relinquished its hold on governance through mechanisms of risk and security. However, the state's grip is loosening as it also models itself as a liberal risk regime. This model promotes a discourse of responsibility and self-sufficiency among non-state entities. It also fosters practices that indeed make everyone more responsible for self-governance. In both discourse and practice, the state tries to foster the well-being of all and each through liberal risk regimes.

The state is thus entwined with the private insurance industry, helping to form the economic, social, legal, cultural, and political aspects of insurance as governance outlined above. The insurance industry is a significant contributor of investment capital in the political economy, and its investment practices are regulated by the state. The state also regulates the fairness of risk pooling practices, and the manner in which insurance policies are sold and claims are compensated, in order to shape how insurance functions as a social technology of justice. The state frequently collaborates with the insurance industry in joint ventures, for example, to form entire insurance markets or to partially underwrite specific risks. In these contexts the state is part of the insurance industry and a major contributor to its viability. In return for its involvement in all of the dimensions described above, the state receives enormous benefits. The insurance industry invests heavily in government bonds and other securities. It is also a major source of tax revenue and employment. Most significantly, private insurance relieves the state of having to compensate losses it might otherwise be politically compelled to cover.

We have already stressed that governance is based on local knowledge of risk. The formation of populations at risk and the distribution of risks among them are primary activities in all governance, including that which involves insurance. It follows that research on insurance as governance must include an understanding of risk. The sociology of knowledge as it pertains to risk is therefore another important field for our analysis.

Risk has become so central to contemporary governance that many sociologists now suggest we live in a risk society. One view of risk society is that its institutions, knowledges, technologies, and productive processes pose enormous risks as danger. Global warming, nuclear catastrophe, chemical spills, and other environmental disasters that result from the progression of science and technology lead to a focus on the long-term consequences of risk for the well-being of populations. However, efforts to ameliorate dangers are typically made within the framework of the very institutions, knowledges, technologies, and productive processes that give rise to dangers in the first place and, therefore, often compound rather than lessen them. Catastrophes are inevitable within the complex knowledge and technological systems we use for risk taking and mitigation. The thrust for progress and thirst for profits ensure a perpetual dance between the taking and taming of chance.

Insurance is a core institution in this risk society. On the one hand, it underwrites the ability to play with danger. It addresses the propensity of things to go wrong because of fallible institutions, people, knowledge, and technological capacity. Indeed, under the legal liability system, insurance is often directed to compensate simply because it has the deep pockets to do so. It may even compensate when catastrophes happen as a result of risks that were unknown at the time of underwriting. On the other hand, insurance is crucial for loss prevention and harm minimization. Through inspections and contract enforcement, it articulates standards of risk management that foster safety and security.

The insurance industry serves these functions by making claims regarding its own institutional knowledge, technological, and productive capacities. It has its own science, actuarialism, which claims an ability to assess risks with reasonable accuracy in order to commodify and distribute them. But the insurance industry also faces the limits of its own knowledge as a capacity for action. A crucial limitation is that actuarialism is dependent on other fields of scientific knowledge regarding any particular risk subject to underwriting. For example, if scientists are unable to predict the location and impact of earthquakes, insurers will have enormous difficulty underwriting them. If medical researchers are unable to agree on the diagnosis and treatment of whiplash following a car accident, then insurers will likewise operate in conditions of uncertainty. Actuarialism is further complicated by its entanglement in the complexities of financial risk, for example, how insurance premiums should be priced, claims compensated, and investments made.

These complexities make insurance an ideal institution within which to explore the nature and limits of knowledge capacities. Insurance is the quintessential institution of applied knowledge and social necessity. Insurers are forced to make knowledge count, literally. But they have enormous difficulty in doing so because of the fallibility of science and technology more generally: not every chance can be tamed; risk is only a probability statement; unanticipated consequences always loom; all institutions, including insurance, produce risks through the very processes by which they manage them.

Risk society theorists have advanced the belief that more and more risks are uninsurable. By this they mean that major risks, such as natural disasters and technological catastrophes, defy insurance logic because they are surrounded by uncertainty. Not having studied the insurance industry, they fail to appreciate that it will insure just about anything. Insurers gamble, trying to manage any fallout through a variety of pricing, claims control, financial risk redistribution, and investment strategies.

These considerations point to why risk society should be viewed as much more than a producer of danger. Risk society is composed of intersecting institutions that organize in relation to the production and distribution of knowledge of risk. Risk communication systems are now so fine-grained and pervasive that the risk society can also be conceptualized as one concentrating on the socialization of risks of everyday living. A significant proportion of the resources of all institutions is dedicated to risk communication, aided by increasingly sophisticated information technologies. Risk society is wired with closed-circuit television, smart cards, computerized databases, and other technologies of surveillance, for the production of knowledge useful in the administration of populations. For example, credit card systems provide an instant record of the time, place, and spending habits of the consumer. This knowledge is useful not only for immediate security purposes, but also for databases that can be used for marketing, assessments of creditworthiness, police investigations, and so on. Risk society is also networked through daily news, advertising, and other public media that make us hyper-reflexive about health, lifestyle, financial, and crime risks. Even sports media are framed by the barrage of probability statistics, serving as a metaphor for a risk society that cannot be transcended even in leisure.

The insurance institution is a hub and repository of the risk communication systems of other institutions. This positioning occurs because of its centrality to the practices of all institutions in defining, producing, taking, and managing risks. This consideration returns us to why research on insurance is crucial for sociological understanding of institutions. Research on insurance risk communication practices not only reveals a great deal about the insurance industry itself, but also about other institutions and how they coordinate in the constitution of risk society. Insurance-generated risk communications provide an elaborate technology for governance, helping to structure the institutional domains of politics, economy, business enterprise, health, justice, and so on. Two views of risk society – society as a producer of risks through its institutions, knowledges, technologies, and productive processes, and society constituted through the risk communication networks of institutions – are exemplified in how insurance operates as a technology of governance.

As a technology of governance, insurance defines how people should act. In this respect it is a moral technology. This brings us to the concept of 'moral risks,' which is central to our analysis. The risks that are defined, produced, taken, and managed by the insurance industry always include moral assessment of the people and harms involved. Insurance as governance is primarily focused on the regulation of moral risks.

Insurance produces and responds to moral risks through its actuarial practices of classification and probability calculation. All statistical knowledge of risk provides an objective standard of normalcy. It specifies what is normal about a population and who within it deviates from the norm and therefore poses a risk. At the same time, what is statistically normal functions to evaluate what ought to be. The statistical norm of what is usual or typical is always entwined with the ethical norm as restraint. In this respect, all actions that are classified and calculated by insurance occur under a description of moral risk. However, these descriptions do not pinpoint a single right answer, but rather pose questions of probabilities and possibilities that require moral assessment for action. Acting in this way, insurance classifications contribute to a broader discourse of moral responsibility. They effect moral regulation by making people think of risk objects in terms of their own ethical conduct with respect to those objects: being knowledgeable about risks and doing their part to prevent, minimize, and distribute them.

Insurance risks are also moralized and subject to attributions of responsibility through the ways in which they are posed as dangers. A risk as danger raises questions about the probable magnitude of its outcome. Answers to these questions inevitably entail moral evaluations of the probable outcome and how to mitigate it. Again a discourse of moral responsibility ensues. This discourse is invoked as a defensive mechanism to protect against the self-interested conduct of others by reminding them of their moral responsibility to minimize harm. To be at risk is to be sinned against by others, whether institutions, communities, or individuals. The risky individual is singled out to uphold the moral solidarity of the collective, but the sinning collective is also used to uphold the moral autonomy of the individual. Here risk morally codes danger as a threat to liberty.

In combination with the ways in which they are embedded in actuarial classifications and evaluations of danger, moral risks arise in the interactive dynamics of the insurance relationship. Here moral risk refers to the ways in which an insurance relationship fosters behaviour by any party in the relationship that immorally increases risks to others. For example, the insured may pose a moral risk because being insured reduces the incentive to avoid loss. This moral risk not only has negative consequences for the insurer, who faces higher claims costs, but also for others insured in the risk pool, who may face higher premiums and less favourable contract conditions as the insurer tries to recoup the loss. Moral risks are not limited to the behaviour of the insured. Insurance agents can pose moral risks to the insured if they sell them the wrong product or something they do not need at excessive rates. Insurance service providers – for example, lawyers, health care professionals, and autobody shop operators – may pose moral risks to the insurer, the claimant, and the pool of insured if they systematically overbill and provide unnecessary services. Insurance executives and their financial managers may pose moral risks to everyone else in the insurance relationship if they are imprudent in their underwriting and investment practices to the point of threatening the solvency of the company.

These interactive contexts of moral risk give rise to discourses of responsibility and regulatory practices. As citizens of the insurance relationship, all participants are directed to be highly responsible in their risk taking and management practices so as to minimize avoidable loss that will affect others. Everyone is to act as if there is no uncertainty, all chance can be tamed, and all risks are moral. The regulation of insurance on every level – the insured, company officials and agents, claims service providers, and industry coalitions – entails perpetual efforts to 'responsibilize' all and each regarding how moral risks are produced and distributed. This effort involves a substantial regulatory apparatus employing a variety of means: insurance contract conditions and incentives, surveillance technologies, engineering design for preventive security, education campaigns, policing crackdowns, and situational judgments of moral character.

If insurance simply responded to risks that are objective, in the sense that they are unrelated contingencies beyond individual control, then there would be no need to address individual responsibility for them. In practice the question of who can control a risk is determinative of whether it is insurable and on what terms. The need to determine individual responsibility for risk control is at the heart of moral risk detection and assessment. It turns insurers into agents of governance in all aspects of their operations.

In summary, we live in a society that encourages a downsizing of the state and governance based on local knowledge of risk. The insurance industry is a key institution in this society because it serves many of the same purposes as the state, and it is uniquely placed to foster governance based on local knowledge of risk. As *the* practical institution of applying scientific and technical knowledge of risk across all other institutions of society, the insurance industry runs up against intractable problems of knowledge as a capacity for action. Its limitations in this regard are addressed through another type of knowledge, knowledge of moral risk. While knowledge of moral risk is systematized through information technology, it is nevertheless based on situational, intuitive, and subjective assessments. As such it is potentially discriminatory, unjust, and a source of inequality.

The limitations of its knowledge and risk communication systems make the insurance industry a fallible institution. The irony of insurance is that in the very process of pooling risk it also constantly unpools it. Insurance sells good risk pools. In order to protect the integrity of a given pool it must deselect those who pose too great a moral risk. This process of deselection creates more and more specialized risk pools – with highly variable premiums, contract conditions, and surveillance mechanisms – and excludes a substantial number of people entirely.

In insurance, differentiation, segmentation, and exclusion are simultaneously processes of marketing and moral assessment in underwriting. Preferred risks are doubly desirable as insurance clients: they are seen to be affluent customers, on the one hand, and less risky in terms of claims, on the other. However, insurers also profit by pooling substandard risks, as insured in the resulting pool, with little market choice, are compelled to purchase insurance under the most substandard arrangements.

A private insurance company is not in the business of redistributing resources among the insured, but rather of discriminating in favour of those who contribute to the goodness of the pool and the prosperity of the company. It would be acting immorally if it did otherwise. Thus it constitutes communities of interest, user-pay communities into which entrance is purchased with cash, not collective sentiments. Instead of social solidarity and community as a moral binding of durable relationships, private insurance tends to fragment populations into selective risk-rated communities with a price tag. Again, this tendency marks the confluence, on the one hand, of niche marketing by insurers to survive in the marketplace and, on the other hand, of intensified efforts to cope with risks they produce themselves through ever more finely tuned assessments of populations.

These considerations raise questions about limits to governance beyond the state, and the nature of and need for state involvement in insurable forms of security. A great deal of what is attributed to the welfare state regarding moral risk creation, debt financing, and bureaucratic red tape can also be attributed to the insurance industry. The insurance industry both creates moral risks among its populations and poses moral risks to them. It speculatively finances its operations through debt in a manner that parallels national debt. Its myriad criteria of underwriting and claims processing, backed up by elaborate surveillance systems, can make it exceptionally bureaucratic, inefficient, and unjust.

Our project is to look inside this mysterious institution and explain how its approaches to governance illuminate contemporary society. The book is organized as follows.

Part I engages academic debates about the contemporary state, forms of governance beyond the state, and the role of the insurance industry as an institution of governance. This engagement is important for placing the research in sociological context and for establishing the analytical framework for the empirical investigations that follow. Nevertheless, readers who are primarily interested in our ethnographic analysis of the insurance industry can begin with Part II.

Chapter 1 depicts the contemporary state as fragmented into partnerships with private corporate institutions. In this respect the state is only one institution among others, albeit a special institution that acts for the general interest according to principles of public service. In the process of so acting, it not only shapes other institutions but is shaped by them. The state is itself 'governmentalized' through participation in the regimes of other institutions.

In chapter 2, we show how the fragmentation of the state into the regimes of private corporate institutions is exemplified in the operations of the insurance industry. Insurance is *the* institution of governance beyond the state. The insurance industry uses methodologies of law, surveillance, expertise, and policing in collaboration with the state. The insurance contract is a kind of legal bond to the territory, population, and sovereign authority of the insurance company, underwritten by state legal and regulatory processes. The bond is solidified through systems of surveillance and audit built by professional experts charged with making practical decisions about who and what to insure on what terms. The bond is cemented through a private policing apparatus that patrols its institutional boundaries, protects the well-being of its populations, and promotes the authority of its regime.

There is also collaboration at the level of ideology. As part of its efforts to downsize itself, the state actively promotes individual responsibility for risk. This promotion involves an attack on welfare, including the moral risks posed by state insurance systems and the malingering and dependency that result at the level of welfare recipients. Reconfiguring itself as but one player in the interinstitutional field of insurance, the state limits its role to turning people into responsible risk takers and managers who purchase private insurance, offering at best a temporary safety net when things go wrong.

In chapter 3, we consider how insurance systems both produce moral risks and govern them. The organization of insurance offers incentives to all parties in the relationship to engage in risky behaviour with immoral consequences. The insured, sales agents, claims service providers, and company directors and officers are often influenced in ways that encourage them to put others at risk. A given party is likely to pose a moral risk to others where there is a cushion from the consequences, high financial returns, low visibility, inadequate policing, and readily available justifications to morally neutralize their risky behaviour. Insurers respond with a wide range of governance mechanisms, which are the subject of our empirical investigations in Parts II and III.

Part II analyses governance of insurance practices. In chapter 4, we demonstrate that in many respects insurance underwriting is gambling, a decent bet made on the basis of existing knowledge and conditions. In some contexts it is highly speculative, creating financial risk exposure for everyone involved in the insurance relationship. This exposure can be partially addressed through prudent investment of premium revenue, which not only provides a reserve to manage claims but is also a primary source of company profit. However, prudence is always at issue because again the tendency is to gamble, in this case in the hope of higher investment yields. Cushioned by corporate limited liability rules and industry compensation schemes for policyholders, some insurers have speculated wildly on investments and run up huge deficits in financing them, knowing that most of the fallout will be borne by employees, policyholders, debtors, and creditors.

Reinsurance is another mechanism for hedging bets. The originating or primary insurer lays off its underwriting with other insurers in order to spread the financial risk. Reinsurance is fraught with moral risk judgments and implications. There is always suspicion that the primary insurer will be less attentive to underwriting and claims control if it is covered by reinsurance. Primary insurers are in turn suspicious of reinsurers, who have in some instances been unable to meet their obligations and even deceive partners about a risk exposure they have collectively underwritten.

Insurers also address solvency risks by organizing compensation schemes to provide policyholders with coverage up to a specific limit in the event that their insurance company fails. These schemes are supposed to make participating companies more vigilant about governing each other's underwriting, investment, and reinsurance strategies, on penalty of having to pay significant compensation in the event of failure by one of their members. However, this assumed basis of more responsible industry self-governance is weakened by the fact that the costs of the scheme are passed on to policyholders through an additional charge on premiums. Policyholders end up paying for their own insurance on the possible failure of the insurer's promise to pay.

The insurance industry is highly competitive. Solvency is an omnipresent issue, and mergers and acquisitions are commonplace. Competition as a threat to solvency is fuelled by over-capacity, the entry of other financial institutions into the insurance business, the proliferation of alternative self-insurance arrangements, more and more specialized insurance products, and new marketing and distribution channels to sell those products. These forces combine to encourage more risk taking in underwriting to gain or at least protect market share, posing substantial solvency risks in some cases.

In chapter 5, we address corporate governance. Management of the moral risks posed by insurers is effected through four interconnected mechanisms of corporate governance. First, state regulation occurs through the corporate licensing system, solvency risk auditing, and market conduct surveillance. State regulators are a valuable source of refereeing and rationalization beyond what industry associations can provide to members of a fiercely competitive industry. They help to self-moralize the corporation as the cornerstone of self-governance. The subjective and ethical aspects of corporate governance are increasingly the focus of regulation, on the principle that if corporations are to take more risks, their directors, officers, and agents must receive instruction about their moral responsibilities in doing so. Second, industry associations govern member companies through standards, rules, rate-setting, and sanctions. These activities not only shape industry practices, but also make evident the hierarchies and power relations among member companies, and the systematic means through which they 'governmentalize' the state. Third, actuaries are employed by insurance companies to discipline underwriting practices. Actuaries are management executives more than number crunchers. They give authority to the creative interpretation of actuarial data in the context of the company's culture and a competitive environment that urges speculation over precision. Fourth, an insurance company's directors, officers, and agents are also governed by fellow insurers who underwrite policies for errors, omissions and other employment liabilities. Analysis of how insurers rate their clients in other insurance companies is especially revealing of how the insurance industry governs.

In chapter 6, we analyse the structure and consequences of market misconduct. The selling of life insurance provides a case study of how insurers pose moral risks through their market conduct and their limited efforts to govern the problems that ensue. Life insurance agents regularly sell clients the wrong product and features that disadvantage them in the context of five sources of influence. First, agents have incentive to sell products with the most lucrative commissions, regardless of their suitability for the policyholder. Second, they are also pressured by job insecurity: they are recruited to exploit their network of family and friends, and when that network is exhausted so is the job. Third, many life insurance policies that depend on investment performance are highly risky. As a result, it is extremely difficult for anyone – even actuaries, let alone consumers – to assess the quality of products offered by an individual supplier among competitors. Fourth, there is increasing market segmentation, with more and more complex investment features and commission incentives that accentuate each of the above factors and also encourage the 'twisting' or 'churning' of existing policyholders into more risky policies. Fifth, the sales culture reinforces an aggressive buyer/seller relationship rather than a professional/client relationship, ensuring that life insurance sales continue to pose moral risks to consumers. Efforts to govern these risks through regulations, professionalization, surveillance, and alternative distribution arrangements do little to address, let alone change, these core structural and cultural features of market misconduct.

Part III focuses on how the insured are governed. In chapter 7, we document that, at the point of underwriting, everyone is suspected of having moral attributes that need to be taken into account in designing the terms and conditions of insurance. There is a direct relationship among such moral assessments, insurance market segmentation, and exclusion of the undesirable. We explore the way in which personal line insurers of homes and automobiles underwrite in these terms. Sophisticated data systems track and rate insured persons and their properties, functioning as authentification intermediaries to inform insurers in an instant whether the prospective policyholder is worth underwriting. Agents' field judgments feed the data system, as the interpersonal and technical dimensions of risk interface. The field agent engaged in 'front-line underwriting' is not a free-floating moral governor, but is herself governed through closed-ended forms and computer-based formats that embed underwriting criteria and review her decisions. Once the insurance applicant-as-suspect is turned into a viable prospect, moral risk data are used to assign her to the appropriate risk pool. Superstandard pools are formed for wealthy clients, who are offered superior claims service for expensive premiums. Substandard pools for poor customers are made profitable through high deductibles, exclusion of some standard policy features, and making other standard policy features expensive options. State regulation of unfair risk segmentation practices is sidestepped by creating subsidiaries or specialized companies that sell only to identified segments.

In chapter 8, we consider how, once insured, the policyholder is required to be an agent of prevention. Focusing on the fields of home, commercial, and automobile insurance, we show the dominant theme in the governance of loss to be that the insured are taking too many risks and therefore are justifiable targets for engineering, education, and enforcement efforts aimed at prevention. This theme plays off of wider political culture and social movements, in particular the victims' movement, which declares unequivocally that individuals who harm others are culpable, regardless of their ignorance, miscalculation, or mistakes. Ironically, a strong blaming the victim component results.

Everyone is suspected to the degree that they are deemed to be contributors to a more risky environment.

In chapter 9, we document that suspicion of the insured crystallizes in the claims process. There is a presumption that people will inflate the harms they have suffered and otherwise adjust their insurance claims story to suit their interests. The claimant's moral neutralization of fraud is seen as opportunistic. Since she has been paying premiums over time – which have swelled the investment coffers of the insurer and been distributed to others in the pool who have suffered losses – a payback of extra magnitude is justifiable in the event of a claim. Knowing that fraud is institutionalized in the insurance relationship, claims agents work on the assumption that everyone is capable of some larceny.

Insurers respond with a surveillance apparatus that scans for 'red flags' of fraud in the claimant's demeanour; insurance record; employment, income, and credit records; and race, ethnicity, and other signs of the claims culture the person participates in. Automated data systems 'trigger' red flags as soon as the client calls the claims centre to report a loss, indicating whether special investigation is necessary. Large insurance companies also have substantial in-house private police forces called Special Investigation Units. These units have expanded substantially in the past decade as competitive insurance markets and some state restrictions on underwriting criteria have tightened premium revenues and therefore led to a crackdown on claims fraud as an alternative means of capital protection. These units also contract with private investigators and cultivate informants as additional policing resources.

Prosecution and punishment of insurance fraud through the legal system is extremely rare. Summary justice is effected internally through denying a claim, cancelling the contract, or changing contract conditions. Moreover, a great deal of fraud is tolerated because of insufficient evidence, the efficiency of making 'nuisance payments' that are less costly than investigations, and the desire to maintain a relationship with policyholders who would be offended by allegations of fraud that are easy to visualize but difficult to prove. Overpolicing can be counterproductive to the smooth flow of social and economic relations in the insurance business, and expediency in governance results.

We now turn to the broader sociological framework and academic literature that inform our research. While our ethnographic analysis of the insurance industry in Parts II and III can be read separately, they took shape in the context of the ideas developed in Part I.

Part I

GOVERNANCE, INSURANCE, AND MORAL RISKS

1. Governance beyond the State

Individualities may form communities, but it is institutions alone that can create a nation.

Benjamin Disraeli (1866)

Everybody knows that government never began anything. It is the whole world that thinks and governs.

Wendell Phillips (1859)

Becoming a Top Dog State

The *Financial Times* of London regularly publishes a feature section on states. Each time this section appears, a particular state is surveyed through articles on its political economy and data on its economic performance. Also included are display advertisements paid for by the state that promote its favourable investment environment. These sections are comparable to inserts found in local newspapers where, for example, a car dealer or insurance agent pays for a display advertisement and then also obtains 'advertorial' space in the 'news' columns to write something in greater depth intended to create additional desire for the product. The difference in the present case is that the newspaper represents international finance, and the state is the corporate entity seeking competitive advantage and market share through advertising and advertorials.

On 25 May 1999, the *Financial Times* published a feature section on Canada. The most prominent advertisement in this section is reproduced in figure 1.1. This advertisement takes up the bottom half of the

"*Top Dog in the G7 performance race*"
Financial Times, May 12, 1998

Canada... You can't beat our track record

World's leading exporter to the United States
Daily Canada–US Cross Border Trade of 1.3 billion dollars

Lowest costs for manufacturing in the G7
KPMG G7 Business Cost Comparison 1999

Leading technology workers
First in higher education enrolment, third in computers. Global Competitiveness Report 1998

Best R&D incentives in the G7
Conference Board–R&D Incentives in OECD Countries, 1997

Best country in the world in which to live
United Nations Human Development Index 1998

For two years running, the OECD has predicted Canada will be "top dog" in the G7 for economic growth. With a track record like this, plus the best business costs in the G7 and preferred access to the NAFTA market, why invest anywhere else? For more information, fax your business card to 44-171-258-6384.

Government of Canada   Gouvernement du Canada   Canada

Figure 1.1. Canada as Top Dog in the G7 Performance Race, 1999.

front page of the section. The top half consists of a table with Canada's economic performance indicators, and a lead article headlined, 'Ottawa Takes Third Way Cue from Europe.' This advertisement reveals how the state of Canada wishes to be represented in the world of international finance. It is also indicative of the role of the state in supporting private corporations and business enterprise.

A state has three interrelated components (Offe 2000). It is a *country*, a fixed territory with borders recognized internationally that give it a material foundation. It is a *nation*, a population of people with recognizable identities who participate in collective processes and fulfil collective responsibilities. It is a *sovereign authority*, a regime that struggles in hegemonic processes to acquire and retain authority in relation to other formidable powers, including for example other states as well as private corporations without national borders.

The advertisement in figure 1.1 pictures the *country* of Canada as competing on a greyhound racetrack. It is not clear whether this racetrack is on Canadian territory, but that detail does not matter because this is the competitive world of international finance. The race involves finely honed competitors from other economic elite, Group of Seven states: the United States, Japan, Britain, France, Germany, and Italy. With no sense of place, these countries compete in a fast-paced environment of risk management, risk taking, and gambling. As in the world of dog racing, one can only imagine the future and take risks with data based on past performance. In this regard, according to no less of an authority than the *Financial Times* itself, Canada was 'Top Dog in the G7 performance race.' The advertisement continues: 'Canada ... You can't beat our track record. For two years running, the OECD has predicted Canada will be "top dog" in the G7 for economic growth. With a track record like this, plus the best business costs in the G7 and preferred access to the NAFTA market, why invest anywhere else?'

The *nation* of Canada is depicted in several pithy statements on the left-hand side of the advertisement. Its population is said to be happy ('Best country in the world in which to live'), well-trained for productivity ('Leading technology workers'), and committed to the collective processes and responsibilities of commerce ('World's leading exporter to the United States'; 'Lowest costs for manufacturing in the G7'; 'Best R&D incentives in the G7'). In a world of right-sized workforces, and diminished state social benefits, the population must be lean, mean, and sleek, like greyhounds. The federal Liberal government that placed this advertisement proudly declares that Canadians are top dogs.

The advertisement clearly represents the *sovereign authority* of Canada as being diminished. Canada is reduced to an agent of capital investment and expansion in fierce competition with other states.

The competition is so fierce that the advertisement represents the Canadian population as dogs, and shows them competing in a form of racing that is illegal in Canada. It is illegal because it is a form of gambling that is difficult to risk manage and distance from corruption. It is also illegal because it is inhumane: the dogs have no life other than breeding and training for the races, which consist of chasing a mechanical object they never catch. Moreover, those dogs who are not competitive enough, or who retire, are frequently destroyed. If not destroyed they are often neglected, or left to charitable agencies established to offer them a little contentment in their post-racing years.

The competition is so fierce that Canadian tax dollars are spent on advertisements placed in the international financial press that depict Canadians in such uncivil terms. In this context of global corporate finance, the individual state itself is an underdog, desperately struggling for recognition as 'world class.' In the world-class system, nations and their populations must strive harder and gamble more if they are to prosper and be happy.

The competition is so fierce that the state is forced to reduce its own call on resources to participate in collective processes and fulfil collective responsibilities. Thus an article accompanying this advertisement informs the international financial community that 'Canada's [social] programme spending as a percentage of GDP has declined from more than 16 percent in 1993 to 12.6 percent this year and will continue to fall to 12 percent, the lowest level in 50 years.' In the current financial times, this rightsizing of the state is good news. The new collective responsibility is to participate in one's own *social* diminishment, both on the corporate level of the state and private sector companies and on the personal level of the individual. The state ends up promoting its diminished responsibility for collective welfare, and rightsizes its health, education, and welfare workforce as part of this responsibility. Similarly, the private corporation seeks ways of cutting benefits to employees, and of making them redundant. This process is exemplified by the bank teller who is required to ask customers why they are using her services rather than the bank machine or Internet. The more successful she is in persuading the population of bank customers to pursue the mechanical object, the sooner she puts herself out of a job and into the hands of the diminished state.

Governance

In this advertisement and the associated advertorials, the Canadian state promotes its willingness to partner with non-state institutions in the pursuit of mutual prosperity. The promotion suggests it has recreated itself as a leaner and more competitive entity in conjunction with partners in investment risks. As such, the promotion exemplifies contemporary governance. The state decentres its sovereign authority by mobilizing private corporations to govern at a distance. It helps them to establish their own regimes of population risk management that will simultaneously serve collective well-being and individual enhancement.

Liberal governance has always been dedicated to state collaboration with other institutions. The liberal state is to meet the demands of other institutions for conditions that make economy, culture, and society workable. As Rose (1999, 2000) observes, the state is itself governmentalized through its participation in the regimes of other institutions. It cannot be captured as an essence, but only seen as a kaleidoscope of myriad practices of governance in relation to other social institutions. Far from standing alone or in binary opposition to civil society, the state helps create a civil society in which it is one of many institutions:

> Institutions – familial, commercial, professional, political, religious – make up the empirical texture of civil society. In each institution there is a partial source of social right; the seat of a *de facto* founding authority; a certain task or enterprise; and a postulated, *a prior* consensus. The durability of the institution contrasts with the ephemeral life of its individual members; the individual only becomes a citizen and subject of right through and thanks to the institution; the citizen's obligations to it are logically exterior to his or her rights. But the state, too, figures here only in a relativized role, as one institution among others, the special institution which acts for the *general interest* and according to the principles of *public service* (Gordon 1991: 32).

Taking the example of governance of market economies, the state joins with private sector institutions to structure market 'freedom.' The 'free' market is certainly not free from the state and is in many respects a creature of the state (Dandeker 1990: 221–2). As Slater (1997: 60) remarks, 'the free market as an institution is not a sphere of freedom from the state but a mechanism encouraged by the state to allow it to manage "at a distance" a complex process it cannot directly govern.'

Market economies require a number of state-backed regulatory mechanisms (Lowi 1990). First, there must be provision for law and security. The rule of law and preventive security devices create predictability about risks and how to deal with them. Law and preventive security devices bring order to the markets so that market regularities can in turn contribute to social order. Second, the state provides a legal framework for the institution of property. Property 'is a synthesis word for all the laws against trespass ... a residuum of the things that the state does to permit me to call something my own and to have a reasonable probability of making it stick' (ibid.: 21). The state's role is to minimize the risk of property ownership so that there can be markets for the exchange of property. Third, the state must establish a legal framework for contracts and their enforcement. Contracts manage the risks in property exchanges through agreements to regulate specified aspects of the future. They are crucial in both structuring markets and in allowing participants to take risks in the market. Fourth, the state establishes legal, scientific, and technical standards for market operations. The standards function of the state on behalf of private sector institutions in the market economy is enormous, consuming a significant portion of the gross domestic product (GDP). Fifth, the state provides for the conveyance of particular aspects of the public domain into private market hands. This conveyance includes not only the privatization of spheres like public health and public policing, but also privileges such as licensing of professional services and corporations. 'The corporation itself is a form of license, and it has been sought as a privilege – that is, "limited liability," which is a governmentally protected limit on the risk of all stakeholders' (ibid.: 23). Sixth, the state provides social overhead capital – for example transportation, communication, military, policing, and workers' compensation and welfare infrastructures – as public goods. While everyone benefits from social overhead capital, particular benefit is derived by private market entrepreneurs. 'Those with the biggest incentive to take risks in society – e.g. entrepreneurs – are the ones with the greatest incentive to governmentalize these capital functions, in order to guarantee their provision at all and in order to force even the most casual, sporadic, and unlikely users to share the costs' (ibid.: 24).

In all six of the areas outlined above, state involvement in providing for market economies is plural, equivocal, and in flux. As represented in Canada's top dog advertisement, the state as country is fragmented into territories largely controlled by other institutions that include and exclude according to their own peculiar requirements. The state as nation is fragmented into populations largely constituted by other institutions that seek members in terms of consumption preferences and habits. And the state as sovereign authority is fragmented into the risk management systems of other institutions that make the consuming liberal subject more responsible for her own risk taking and security provision.

Institutional Territories

The very effort of the state to institutionalize private property relations for market economies requires the state to relinquish significant aspects of its own territorial jurisdiction. Enclaves of private activity into which the state can intrude under limited conditions – corporate settings, retail complexes, entertainment centres, residential structures, and so forth – have their own physical borders, surveillance technologies, private police, private insurance, and other mechanisms for population control and risk management (Davis 1990; Ericson and Haggerty 1997; Hannigan 1998; Loader 1999). Through these mechanisms each institution is able to establish private spaces and places in which to act in relative privacy and confidentiality, and thereby to strategize, mobilize, and transact with other institutions, including the state. In doing so, each institution claims some territory for corporate sovereignty.

The state's boundary troubles do not end with the territorial limitations of private property that the state itself creates. The state is also exposed to the boundless energy and movement of capital, with significant implications for control of institutional territory. Greater domestic state control of capital was available in the tight regulatory period between 1930 and 1970. The current period rivals the situation before the First World War, when international capital flows were even larger than now (*Economist*, 7 October, 1995; Hirst and Thompson 1996).

Since 1970 institutionally managed money or disconnected capital – for example, pension funds, mutual funds, investment funds, and endowments – has increased elevenfold worldwide in proportion to other forms of capital (Giddens 1998: 30; Gates 1998). At the same time a frenzy of mergers and acquisitions has created increasingly powerful multinational corporations, some of which rival or surpass the GDP of mid-size Western hemisphere states. Held (2000: 46) records that 20,000 multinational corporations account for up to one-third of output, 70 per cent of trade, and 80 per cent of direct foreign investment worldwide.

The effect of this dominance on the state is that macroeconomic policy is subservient to the corporate governance strategies of multinationals. For example, multinational corporations raise finance in the most favourable capital markets, shift employment to places with lower costs, and create centres for technological development that are most efficient. Moreover, institutional money managers and multinational financial institutions conduct trade in foreign exchange markets that far exceeds the trade in goods. Daily trading in foreign exchange increased almost sevenfold between the mid-1980s and mid-1990s, reaching $1.2 trillion in 1995 (McQuaig 1998: 157). Most of these foreign exchange transactions are very short term, with heavy involvement of financial institutions in swap transactions based on inside information (ibid.: 158).

Advances in information technology have created a more integrated financial system for the international flow of capital. The technology allows capital allocation decisions to be made on the basis of real-time, abstract, quantitative assessment of risk and returns rather than consideration of place and populations affected. As such the flight of capital from one institution to another – including from one state's territory to another – is simply a reflex of the quantitative abstract system.

The fact that the international financial system is more integrated through sophisticated information technology means that it is also potentially subject to more sophisticated surveillance and regulatory capacity. However, tighter regulation is at the same time more difficult, given a lack of internationally coordinated political will to regulate. As figure 1.1 represents the situation, countries are figuratively competing on a dog racetrack and constantly trying to attract private sector institutions as customers to gamble with them. In this territorial dominion run by *pari-mutuel* machines, the greatest fear is that institutional investors and multinationals will place their bets elsewhere.

Giving ground to other institutional territories at home and abroad has serious consequences for the state. The territory of democratically elected government is circumscribed by private corporate sources of unrepresentative economic power. The democratic promise to make collective life willed and chosen is compromised. The exercise of will and choice transpires in terms of the criteria of private institutions the individual manages to access. State 'sovereignty as an illimitable, indivisible and exclusive form of public power' dissipates to the extent that 'the locus of political power can no longer be assumed to be national governments' (Held 2000: 52).

Globalization has arisen as an ideology to simultaneously express fears about loss of sovereignty and to rationalize decisions that are an escape from the state's political responsibility. State sovereignty over its dominion is unravelled as the state perpetually is forced to 'legitimize what it cannot control for fear of forfeiting what control it has' (Magnusson 2000: 87; see also Stehr and Ericson 2000).

Consuming Populations

The governance of the state as nation involves many populations beyond those the state counts as citizens. Each private corporate institution develops its own criteria for recruiting and selecting who it counts as members, and for de-selecting and excluding those who do not count. It also devises a range of strategies and techniques to motivate, mobilize, and manage its population. For example, financial institutions such as banks, credit card companies, and insurers decide whom to accept as risks, how to segment them into risk pools, and what incentives to give them to enhance their risk ratings and therefore benefits. They use their own private corporate techniques of what Foucault termed 'biopower,' 'discipline,' and 'sovereign power' (Foucault 1991). These techniques operate in conjunction with and beyond the population management strategies and technologies of state government. While Foucault focused on state-based techniques of making up populations, the same techniques are part of private sector institutions. Indeed, as the state concedes institutional territories in market economies, the population-forming and disciplinary strategies of private corporations expand and in turn become models for state governance as well (Power 1994). In both market segmentation and risk-pooling strategies, private corporations fragment the citizenry into consuming populations who will choose to spend freely and take risks with them (Gandy 1993, Turow 1997).

Each private institution produces detailed knowledge about the populations under its jurisdiction. This knowledge is produced in applications for acceptance into institutional membership, during each transaction with the institution, and in the accumulation of aggregate data. For example, a bank customer makes an application for an account that is screened, has each transaction with a bank card and credit card electronically recorded, is subject to being risk pooled for various preferred customer ratings and services, and is subject to having financial information about her sold to other institutions. In this governance beyond the state, as in state-based systems of population management (Hacking 1990; Ericson and Haggerty 1997), people are 'increasingly held to others not by a few iron bonds,' such as religious and political affiliations, 'but by countless gossamer webs knitting together the trivia of their lives' (Boorstin 1973: i). The development of sophisticated risk communication technologies for recording human transactions and aggregating knowledge about them means that 'a relatively thinly populated country with well developed means of communication, [such as Canada], has a denser population than a more numerously populated country, with a badly developed means of communication' (Karl Marx, *Capital*, quoted in Poster 1990: 1)

A wide range of both state and private sector institutions create special communities of interest through the techniques of risk selection and population management. As Hacking (1990: 6, 7) demonstrates convincingly, 'even the very notion of an exact population is one which has little sense until there are institutions for establishing and defining what population means.' The necessary institution was science and, in particular, the development of probability statistics. Now all institutions create their own special populations of consumers using probability statistics and the risk communication systems that generate those statistics. Institutions individually and in networks comprise 'what a society is' and have been integral to 'the western concept of community' (ibid.; see also Castells 1989, 1996, 1997, 1998).

Private corporate institutions beyond the state fragment populations. Fragmentation occurs across institutions, as each sector, and each institution within a sector, competes for consumers of its own products and activities. This effort to consume consumers is paralleled within each institution, as a given organization further segments its consumers in terms of their contribution to the well-being of the enterprise. Each organization engages in the politics of 'choice, identity and mutuality' (Giddens 1998: 44) to attract and retain consumers within its own fragmented community.

These institutional communities of interest are alien to traditional imaginings of community as based on sharing, tradition, quality face-to-face relationships, and local organization, combined with a sense of immediacy and the opportunity for direct results. They are also distant from the communitarian promise of a 'third space' located 'between the authority of the state, the free and amoral exchange of the market and the liberty of the autonomous individual subject of rights' (Rose 1997c: 3; 1999: chap. 5; Etzioni 1993, 1997). These institutional communities of consuming populations are created for peculiar habits of consumption and particular contributions to political economy. It is community in this sense that some economists have become interested in (Thompson 1997), as they modify their neoclassical, natural economic actor models towards models that emphasize local economic exchange networks and interpersonal trust as important marketing ingredients.

Each institutional community creates means of governing its own liberal subjects. In particular, it devises 'technologies of the self' which integrate subjects into 'its structures of coercion or domination. The contact point, where the ways individuals are driven by others is tied to the way they conduct themselves, is what we can call, I think, government' (Foucault 1982: 38). In this view, subjectivity, will, and freedom itself are not antithetical to power but the result of power configurations and the technological inventions that produce them. Freedom is an instrument and objective in governing populations. As Rose (1999: 72) expresses it, population management within each institutional territory is the art of creating practices that govern through freedom. At the same time, institutions objectify the attributes and practices of their consuming populations to create realities about them that are more than the sum of their individual actions. 'There is no such thing as "the governed," only multiple objectifications. Practices of governing are not determined by the nature of those who they govern: practices determine their own objects' (Rose 2000: 151–2).

The individual experiences not freedom as absence of restraint, but rather agency as a capacity to act within the parameters of the institution concerned. The individual learns self-governance, how to operate within both state and private corporate institutions in an enterprising manner to become her own political economy (Gordon 1991: 44–5). All institutions now instrumentalize the autonomy of their consuming populations by emphasizing the sovereignty of the choosing individual. Individuals are left with no choice but to choose (Giddens 1991).

While consolidation of sovereignty in private corporate institutions may entail more agency and choice, it does not follow that it therefore involves less disciplinary power and restriction. Consumer sovereignty still embraces sovereign power: the power of each corporate institution to constitute its own peculiar consuming population (Magnusson 2000). There is no escape from consumer sovereignty and the ways in which it compels each member of a consuming population to conduct herself. 'Everyone *must* be a consumer. This particular freedom is compulsory' (Slater 1997: 27). The citizen as consumer is itself a form of political subjectivity, although this subjectivity, the choices upon which it is based, and the means by which it is regulated vary substantially across institutional territories (Hunt 1996, 1997).

The citizen as consumer is sensitized by a discourse of rights pertaining to her choices. As Dandeker (1990: 53) following Giddens (1985) remarks, 'in modern capitalist societies, a crucial area of citizenship rights are "beyond" the state and anchored in an organization based on private property.' In the present period, citizenship formation itself has shifted to private corporate institutions to a substantial degree. 'Individuals are now to be linked into a society through acts of socially sanctioned consumption and responsible choice ... Citizenship is no longer primarily realized in a relation with the state, or in a single "public sphere," but in a variety of private, corporate and quasi-public practices from working to shopping' (Rose 1999: 166). A discourse of consumer rights, as these relate to the practices of each institution concerned, is imbedded in this construct of citizenship. The state itself elides the language of citizen rights and freedoms with that of consumer choice to the point where they coincide (Slater 1997: 37).

In any institutional regime, the rights of citizenship are selectively granted and always conditional on proper conduct. The individual is perpetually monitored regarding her consumption behaviour to evidence her credentials for citizenship on a continuous basis (Rose 1999: 246). On the principle that 'with expanding individualism should come an extension of individual obligations,' there are to be 'no rights without responsibilities' (Giddens 1998: 65). In the private corporate sector, any given member of the consuming population who proves to be irresponsible can simply be excluded from further consumption, or downgraded to less preferred consumer status with attendant lessened access to goods and services. The discourse of individual rights itself ends up being disciplinary because it only allows interrogation of the ethical valence of individual actions within a framework of institutional sovereignty (Gowri 1997).

The discourse of rights is also ascendant at the corporate level. Corporations develop their own charters of rights to delineate the regimes of choice to which they subscribe. They also endorse the rights declarations and legislation of state-based institutions, especially when they themselves have previously been in flagrant violation of rights (Giddens 1998: 49). At the same time they seek state legislative support to be viewed as corporate personalities with rights entitlements because they are subject to victimization. They also want state legal endorsement of their trade and protection rights regarding the flow of international capital. The Multilateral Agreement on Investment (MAI), for example, has been described by Richard Gwyn as 'a charter of rights for absentee landlords' (McQuaig 1998: 23).

Liberal Risk Regimes

We have shown that the sovereign authority of the state is entwined with many institutional regimes beyond the state, each of which constitutes its own sovereign authority. These institutional regimes, like the regime of the state, coordinate their activities and constitute their authority through the production and distribution of knowledge of risks. We live in risk societies in which substantial resources of institutions are dedicated to ascertaining risks and communicating knowledge about them to secure the institutional environment and those who people it (Beck 1992a, 1992b, 1999; Douglas 1986, 1990, 1992; Douglas and Wildavsky 1982; Giddens 1990, 1991; Ericson and Haggerty 1997; Lupton 1999; Ericson and Doyle 2003).

Risk refers to external danger, such as a natural disaster, technological catastrophe, or threatening behaviour by human beings. The system for communicating risk – its rules, formats, and technologies – is also part of the social meaning of risk. For example, a risk communication system regarding a population to be managed, such as bank customers, actively constitutes that population and the meanings of their activities. It is an instrument of surveillance, defined simply as the production of knowledge about a population useful in its administration (Dandeker 1990). The risk communication system for surveillance is not merely a conduit through which knowledge of the population is transferred. Rather, it has its own logic and autonomous processes. It governs institutional relations and circumscribes what individuals and their organizations are able to accomplish. Events are called into being, made visible, and responded to through the rules, formats, and technologies available in the risk communication system. That is, the risk communication system makes things real, a social fact.

Knowledge of risk is embedded in statistical laws of probability. Probability statistics have had a fundamental influence on social, political, economic, and cultural understanding and behaviour (Hacking 1990). Probability statistics make it possible to imagine underlying structures to institutions and the wider world, which in turn create a sense of certainty upon which action can be taken. Chance is made real, a form of knowledge that provides a capacity for action. As such, probability statistics provide knowledge of risk not only for 'the taming of chance' (ibid.), but also for the taking of chance.

Because they provide knowledge of risk for action, probability statistics are entwined with liberal conceptions of choice, freedom, and liberty. In their early development two centuries ago they were understood as precluding free will, because they were used to suggest deterministic explanations of human behaviour. However, as Hacking shows, they are actually productive of indeterminism. Indeterminism breeds an incessant quest for more and better knowledge of risk in the hope that chance can be further tamed and that risks can be taken more profitably. The result is 'rational choice theory, the fantasy according to which a utility of preference function, plus a probability function over beliefs, determines what a person will do' (ibid.: 150). This fantasy has become ecstasy in present-day liberal risk regimes. Risk communication systems proliferate on the compelling promise that more will work where less has failed (Ericson and Haggerty 1997; Haggerty and Ericson 1999, 2000). But a greater sense of choice is not liberty. Human agency remains a product of institutional regimes. 'The erosion of determinism and the taming of chance by statistics does not introduce a new liberty. The argument that indeterminism creates a place for free will is a hollow mockery. The bureaucracy of statistics imposes not just by creating administrative rulings but by determining classifications within which people must think of themselves and the actions that are open to them. The hallmark of indeterminism is that cliché, information and control. The less the determinism, the more the possibilities for constraint' (Hacking 1990: 194).

The population classes created by risk communication systems are not simply abstract entities but real people to be managed. As Hacking observes, 'we obtain data about a governed class whose deportment is offensive, and then attempt to alter what we guess are relevant conditions of that class in order to change the laws of statistics that the class obeys. This is the essence of the style of government that in the United States is called "liberal"' (ibid.: 119).

On the other hand, precisely because they generate knowledge of risk and with it, 'radical doubt' (Beck, Giddens, and Lash 1994), liberal risk regimes provide for critique and alternatives. 'It is in the name ... of particular risks we may face ... that we both revoke and invoke the power of the state' (Burchell 1991: 145). It is also in the name of risks that we 'revoke and invoke' the sovereign authority of private corporate institutions. It is in the name of liberty regarding the more costly forms of state welfare regimes that liberalism has advanced. Liberalism favours more governance beyond the state as a check on the inflationary logic of state-centred regimes through which consuming populations have escalating expectations about the state's responsibility for social problems (Donzelot 1991: 174ff).

In contemporary liberal risk regimes there is a strong movement towards governance beyond the state. State social insurance, welfare, and security provision are substantially reduced in favour of private sector alternatives. Recall the *Financial Times* article in which it is proudly declared that the percentage of Canada's GDP dedicated to social program spending declined by almost one-quarter in the late 1990s to 'the lowest level in 50 years.'

Strong state welfare regimes favour state-wide pooling of risk, where participation in the pool is both a prerogative and duty of citizenship rather than a private market choice. Indeed, collective pooling of risk in the name of well-being and solidarity is the hallmark of citizenship in strong social democracies. Obviously this collective pooling of risk entails loss of liberty (Berlin 1969: 125). Basic elements of social insurance, welfare, and security provision are not to be left to private market choices and to the inequality, unfairness, and loss of solidarity that inevitably results.

The movement towards private market alternatives for insurance and security provision is accompanied by a discourse that calls for 'embracing risk' (Baker and Simon 2002). This discourse is embedded in institutional routines, classification systems, information systems, and other forms of governance. It fosters the demarcation of institutional territories beyond the state, and the rights, responsibilities, and practices of the consuming populations who inhabit each territory.

This discourse of embracing risk provides a set of six principles for liberal risk regimes. First, there is to be a minimal state. People are presumed to have enough self-restraint, willingness to share, and capacity for self-governance that civil society can be a self-generating basis of social solidarity. Second, market fundamentalism is stressed. A 'free market' is supposed to provide security and prosperity by encouraging fragmented individuals and collectivities to participate in market relations that stimulate economic growth and manage risk. Third, emphasis is placed not only on risk management but also on risk taking. As participants in fast-moving and fluctuating markets, people must become educated, knowledgeable, reflexive risk takers who are adaptable to transitions in their lives. Fourth, individual responsibility is underscored. Each individual is to be her own political economy, an informed, self-sufficient consumer of labour markets, personal security markets, and other consuming interests. Fifth, within a regime of responsible risk taking all differences, and the inequalities that result from them, are a matter of choice. Conceived as choice, inequality becomes seen as inevitable. Sixth, the state is posed as a risk. The state is a necessary but uneasy partner that must itself be viewed as a problem subject to vigilant monitoring and active reform.

The state actively promotes these principles through its participation in the liberal risk regimes of other institutions. This promotional activity is exemplified in the *Financial Times* material analysed at the beginning of this chapter. The state rightsizes its own social program excesses, provides terrains on which competitive races can be held, and helps stock the races with healthy, competitive, risk-taking populations.

As an active promoter of freedom, the state is constantly articulating its own limits and arguing that other institutions can do things better. Even the welfare state, which offers various freedoms from economic hardship, unfairness, and injustice, can also thereby foster confidence in self-sufficiency among its consuming populations that begins to work against its own purposes (Broadbent 2000).

The welfare state is now seriously eroded. Erosion has transpired over several decades, although its timing and degrees vary substantially among states (Atkinson 1999, 2000; Goodin, Heady, Muffels, and Driven 1999; Culpitt 1999). Resources are finite, and the fiscal costs of welfare have placed heavy deficit and debt burdens on states that put them in dependency relationships to the multinational community of financial institutions.

The industrial work environment in which welfarism developed has changed substantially. Fordist production has declined and with it the solidarity of workers whose culture was embedded in it. As mentioned previously, economic globalization entails the flight of capital and associated employment opportunities to the most favourable contexts, which is a real threat to workers and therefore a vehicle for lessening some of their employee benefits and disciplining their work habits. The information revolution has also altered the work environment in many ways. It has produced a neo-Fordism in office settings, for example, call centre operations where workers are under constant surveillance. This discipline is furthered by the fact that many information economy jobs can be located anywhere. Thus call centre operations are often located in more remote and less expensive jurisdictions: the American Express information centre is in Ireland, and the Canadian province of New Brunswick has attracted many call centre operations as part of its movement from a resource-based economy into the information economy.

While workers have a new sense of economic risks, so do ageing populations who once enjoyed the security of the stronger welfare state but now face new insecurities as they reach retirement and the possibilities of a longer life. Baby boomers are at the vanguard of being encouraged by the state, in partnership with financial institutions, to provide for their own financial futures (Foot 1996; Rayher 1998; Clarke 1999). A sense of financial security is in turn related to other security concerns. Protection against environmental, health, and property crime risks all become the subject of state and private market partnerships. Private insurance – especially the preventive security arrangements it enforces through contracts and surveillance – becomes an especially important institution of governance beyond the state.

The fragmentation and individualism fostered in wider consumer culture (Slater 1997; Turow 1997) is now brought home more forcefully in the consumption of security products. People look beyond the collective welfare possibilities offered through the state to individual and specific group solutions: personal insurance; employer group insurance; personal protection locks, sprays, alarms, and cellular telephones; gated communities; private policing, and so on. This new individualism regarding security products is also related to a new politics of identity. Just as they choose to pay a large premium to buy a name brand and to wear its symbol of corporate identity everywhere they go (Schor 1998; Klein 2000), so consumers identify themselves with their participation in various institutional territories and consuming populations of privatized security (Loader 1999; Haggerty 2003; Rigakos 2002; Huey, Ericson, and Haggerty forthcoming).

The subject in liberal risk regimes requires knowledge of risk in order to be an active consumer. This knowledge is increasingly available in the risk-centred stories in mass media, in more specialized publications such as the financial press, and in the promotional material of companies that market security products. The mass media themselves have become much more dominated by knowledge of financial risk. Newspapers devote special sections to individual wealth accumulation. Cable television stations do the same. For example, CTV's NewsNet runs real-time financial market trading indices over cheap, wire-fed disaster news items from anywhere that augment both a sense of insecurity and the need for security. Among the primary advertisers on this channel are mutual fund and insurance companies communicating to a specialized audience of equity market investors. This environment of reflexivity about financial risk suggests that ours is an era not of postmodernity but hypermodernity, in which risk is embraced and life is lived more contingently (Baker and Simon 2002).

In liberal risk regimes, the taking of chance is emphasized as much as the taming of chance. This sensibility is evident in the major news stories about health and the environment. Human scientific and technological processes with a probability of contributing to potentially disastrous health problems (e.g., genetically modified foods in the context of geonomics) and environmental problems (e.g., fossil fuel emission in the context of global warming) are nevertheless bet on because they promise well-being in other senses, such as profitability, efficiency, employment, and convenience. 'What might be called a society's threshold of modernity is reached when the life of a species is wagered on its own political strategies' (Dillon 1995: 154).

The 'casino economy' (Clarke 1999: 46) is also transparent in the hypermarketing of financial security products. There too the knowledgeability of the players is limited and speculation is characteristic. In the United Kingdom, the state actively promoted individual purchase of equity in those of its own corporations that were undergoing privatization; of investment-oriented private life insurance and annuity schemes; and of transfer of funds from state and company pension schemes to individual investment schemes, without due regard for how financial institutions feed off naïve clients (ibid.).

Casinos, lotteries, and other forms of gambling are also characteristic of liberal risk regimes. They too are encouraged by the state in partnerships with private corporations, especially as the state becomes more desperate for revenue in the process of rightsizing itself. In Canada, for example, all casinos and lotteries were illegal until 1969. By 1997, Canadians were spending more than $20 billion a year on gambling and 'provincial governments [were raising] $4.5 billion a year, or an average of 2.7 percent of their revenues, from gambling' (Laframboise 1998). By 2001, net annual gambling revenue for governments in Canada was $6.3 billion, accounting for 3.41 per cent of all government revenue (Parker 2002). In spite of advertising claims to the contrary, only a tiny fraction of the state's revenue from gambling is earmarked for social services or charities. In Ontario, for example, only 6.5 per cent of government lottery proceeds go to charity, and only 1.7 per cent to social services, with declining shares since the early 1990s (Laframboise 1998). Ontario has experienced substantial reduction in welfare provision and stringent moral regulation of welfare recipients through 'workfare' and other programs that emphasize that good people should work hard. At the same time, the Ontario government spends millions of dollars a year on 'the selling of hope' through lottery advertising. The target market is poor Ontarians who gamble because they cannot afford insurance and other financial products that promise future security. Lotteries with odds as high as one in fourteen million of winning the jackpot are advertised with slogans such as 'Go Hog Wild' and 'Don't Think for an Instant' (ibid.). In this sector of the casino economy, reflexivity about known risk is to be abandoned in favour of embracing the thrill of impossible odds. Risk taking is all there is to it.

Liberal risk regimes are committed to the production and distribution of knowledge of risk not only to inform their consuming populations but to regulate them as well. Contrary to red-tape commissions ostensibly aimed at the reduction of bureaucratic regulation (Ontario Red Tape Commission 1997), liberal risk regimes entail greater regulation as they develop new forms of expertise, surveillance, and audit to manage risk environments (Booker and North 1994; Power 1994). As Dandeker (1990: 210) remarks about contemporary 'post-industrial' societies, while they 'may rely more and more on professional expertise or knowledge workers ... any suggestion that we are witnessing the decline of bureaucracy should be viewed with as much skepticism as should claims concerning the trend towards "disorganized capitalism."' Regulatory bureaucracy expands not only in state institutions but in private corporations as well. For example, the more health insurance is transferred to private insurance systems the greater the costs of administration and regulation. Thus the United States has exceptionally high administration costs in its largely private health care system.

Strong liberal risk regimes, exemplified by the United States, try to achieve collective welfare through the maximization of market-based

TABLE 1.1
Relative poverty rates (%)

	Post-tax/transfer	Pre-tax/transfer
Australia	6.4	21.3
Belgium	2.2	23.9
Canada	5.6	21.6
Denmark	3.5	23.9
Finland	2.3	9.8
France	4.8	27.5
Germany	2.4	14.1
Ireland	4.7	25.8
Italy	5.0	21.8
Netherlands	4.3	20.5
Norway	1.7	9.3
Sweden	3.8	20.6
Switzerland	4.3	12.8
United Kingdom	5.3	25.7
United States	11.7	21.0

Source: Kenworth (1999: 1130)

economic growth and wealth accumulation. They accept inequality and considerable poverty as inevitable. As indicated in table 1.1, with the three notable exceptions of Finland, Germany, and Norway, the relative poverty rate in most Western countries is 20 to 25 per cent prior to the intervention of the state in the form of tax concessions and social transfers. After tax and social transfer measures have been applied, the United States stands out as having more than double the average of the other countries in relative poverty. In their analysis of the United States as a 'liberal' regime, the Netherlands as a 'social democratic' regime, and Germany as a 'corporatist' regime, Goodin and colleagues make the following observation for the mid-1980s to mid-1990s:

> Post-government poverty [post-tax and social transfers] ... varies dramatically across these countries. Even just on an annual basis, the proportion of the population of post-government poor in the US is on average around 18 percent, whereas it is less than half that in Germany and less than half that again in the Netherlands. Significant though they are, these differences are magnified further still over time. Dutch poverty rates drop to around 1 percent over a five-year period, whereas American rates remain around 15 percent and German ones around 6. And whereas post-government poverty virtually disappears (dropping to 0.5 percent) in the

Netherlands over a ten-year period, it remains stubbornly stuck at just 6 percent in Germany and 13 percent in the US. (Goodin, Heady, Muffels, and Driven 1999)

Furthermore, Goodin and colleagues, and Atkinson (1999, 2000), conclude from their research that there is no strong evidence to show that liberal state meanness and leanness produces a more productive and growing economy compared to social democratic states. All Western countries produce roughly similar levels of well-being and prosperity for most citizens, but liberal risk regimes with more partial state insurance and security systems are clearly more productive of poverty.

There is ample evidence that states which embraced the liberal risk regime most fully in the past twenty years – for example, the United States, the United Kingdom, and New Zealand – have also experienced the greatest wealth inequality (Wolff 1995; Giddens 1998: 106; Keister 2000). One consequence is a growth in populations at the extreme margins, who effectively exit full participation in civic life. As just mentioned, poverty is one extreme. In the United Kingdom, for example, the liberal risk regime has created 'a growing pool of economically inactive families' with compounding problems of health and deprivation (Association of British Insurers 1995: 18–20). Elite exclusion is another extreme. The elites insulate themselves in spatial, social, cultural, and political as well as economic terms, giving another meaning to governance at a distance (Reich 1991, 1999). In the middle are people who spend beyond their means because their reference group is a more wealthy consuming population (Schor 1998). In some recent periods in the United States, national-level spending has exceeded incomes. Hyperconsumption is fuelled not only by this 'spending up' to the level of more wealthy reference groups, but also by burgeoning wealth available to some through participation in investment markets.

As noted previously, liberal risk regimes develop in the context of new electronic communication economies, globalized cheap labour markets, fear of flight of capital, and fear of statelessness. Many of those not left unemployed and economically inactive are nevertheless working poor, because the only jobs available to them are in minimal wage service sectors. These jobs are often uninteresting and sometimes dehumanizing, and welfare assistance may indeed be an unattractive but necessary option for many. Thus it is not surprising that liberal risk regimes cut back on welfare and develop, for example, stringently regulated welfare-to-work programs and work-hardening regimes for people on disability insurance compensation (Ericson and Doyle forthcoming).

In strong liberal risk regimes, the mindset becomes one of welfare as poor relief (McMahon 2001; Petrou 2001). It is a reactive security measure to protect otherwise selfish people who are better off, rather than a proactive well-being measure expressing collective solidarity. In this sensibility, welfare is only an 'effort to solve the ancient and perennial problem of how to save people from starvation without lowering their incentive to work' (Lowi 1990: 25). When poverty is accepted as a necessary cost of doing business, the corollary is that the best way out of it is to have people help themselves. The market will normally provide enough options for people to make responsible choices. Thus, unfulfilling employment, unemployment, and poverty are seen only in terms of bad choice by individual members of the consuming population.

Liberal risk regimes use figurative language (Ortony 1979) to ensure their discourse is embedded in practice. Contrary to the evidence that strong liberal risk regimes are characterized by high levels of poverty, the language they use persistently suggests that economic hardship, and the broader loss of well-being that results from it, are only temporary (Gusfield 1989: 45). An example of the shift in the moral language of liberal risk regimes is that from 'welfare' to 'safety net.' In turn there are many new concepts within the discourse of 'safety net' to encourage people to see state support as only very temporary relief from their efforts to get ahead by taking risks. For example, in Canada the state unemployment insurance scheme has been relabelled 'employment insurance' to indicate that one must always be working, even when the work is seeking work. State political discourse, as well as private marketing of (in)security, perpetually reinforces the need to insure, save, and invest for the possible (dis)abilities of life. Abilities are fostered to a limited extent by the 'social investment state' (Giddens 1998), but its only promise is to commodify people as 'human resources' within the utilitarian morality of liberal risk regimes. New Labour in the United Kingdom even suggests that the trope of 'trampoline' is better than 'safety net' because people become entangled in nets whereas what they should be doing is bouncing back immediately (ibid.). Of course this view ignores how exhausting trampolines are even for the most fit, as well as the possibility that the less fit will miss the mark and become seriously disabled when they fall through one of the holes on the edge. Vertical life on the trampoline is likely to be even worse than horizontal life on the dog racetrack.

2. Insurance as Governance

We especially protest against insurance being included in the category of dry subjects. Of course, we at once admit, that a volume of insurance tables is not calculated to beguile the general reader ... But behind the scenes of every office a dozen little dramas are enacted daily.

Insurance Monitor (1863)

One of the clearest evidence of the faith of our people in free institutions and the future of America is the fact that millions of our citizens own life insurance policies.

Dwight D. Eisenhower

Take Harlem, for example. They don't need any insurance because they don't have anything valuable to insure.

Chief Actuary, New York Department of Insurance (1977)

Insurance as Governance beyond the State

Governance beyond the state is widely discussed and analysed in academic literatures, such as those that address globalization, postmodernity, and knowledge societies. It is the subject of even more pervasive attention in mass media and public discourse, as different approaches to governance are rationalized and implemented. The institution of insurance is an ideal locus for researching governance beyond the state. Yet, except for narrow specialisms in law and economics, with their preference for rational choice models, social scientists have paid little attention to insurance. As Slater (1997: 51) and Schor (1998: 212n9) remark, economics rarely examines social and especially cultural dimensions, for example, through research on product consumption. But Slater and Schor themselves pay no attention to insurance consumption as exemplifying the intersection of economic, political, cultural, and social dimensions.

The insurance industry has been largely neglected by sociologists, who prefer to elaborate the minutiae of other institutions such as education and criminal justice. One reason for this neglect is the fact that sociology has traditionally drawn legitimacy from being part of the *social* apparatus of the state, and therefore tends to research state institutions. While this focus has resulted in sociological research on some aspects of state insurance and welfare, it has not extended to the private insurance industry. More generally, sociologists have conducted comparatively little empirical research on private corporate institutions and business enterprise, and rarely address this sector thoroughly in their theoretical exegesis on the relation between the state and other institutions. Transformations in governance are analysed with regard to changing relations among states (Hindess 2000), or regarding new constellations among state, community, identity politics, and social movements (Rose 1999). Even essays on the shift from the welfare state to liberal risk regimes fail to address private insurance (e.g., Giddens 1998), although it is obviously *the* institution beyond the state most responsible for risk assessment, population management, and security provision. An exception is Strange (1996), who includes a short chapter on insurance in a book addressing economic globalization and the diminishing state. Strange opens this chapter with a lament that she has little to go on:

> The business of insurance plays a growing and important part in the world market economy. Those who supply it are not seeking power over outcomes – but they exercise it nonetheless. And increasingly so. Yet it is hardly mentioned in texts on world politics; and in economics, the study of insurance is dominated by a few informed specialists, most of whom are ideologically committed to the value judgments of economic liberalism, putting the pursuit of free trade and untrammelled competition above all other possible policy objectives.
>
> How and why the insurers and risk managers exercise such power over outcomes, and with what consequences for the world market economy and for the allocation of values among social groups, national economies and business enterprises is a fundamental question for contemporary international political economy. For fifteen years I have waited, in vain,

for someone to write a definitive analysis – not just a descriptive account – of this highly transnational business. (Strange 1996: 122)

In this chapter, we outline the importance of studying the private insurance industry as an institution of governance. We make five basic points. First, the private insurance industry has many of the same goals as the state. It seeks forms of social security and solidarity by pooling risks. It pursues preventive security arrangements for loss reduction and minimization of harm to citizens. It is an important facilitator of choice, liberty, and freedom, making risks the property of persons through contracts even while it also pools them. In this respect, it helps to articulate the relationship among individual ethical conduct, moral community, and social responsibility.

Second, the private insurance industry has many of the same methodologies as the state for achieving these goals. It uses surveillance – the logics and technologies of population management – for governing at a distance. It has sophisticated information systems for selecting risks (underwriting) and compensating loss (claims). It mobilizes professional knowledge in risk management and restorative processes: legal, medical, financial, material, and so on. It has a substantial private policing apparatus in all forms – technologies, investigators, and inspectors – to address fraud, and to effect preventive security and loss reduction. Because it functions at a distance in terms of abstract expert systems, it devotes resources to fostering trust in its systems.

Third, the private insurance industry is subject to many of the same social forces as those faced by the state. It is the quintessential institution of risk society, constantly anticipating and monitoring the changing risk environment with enormous financial and other consequences at stake. Many risks are difficult to insure because of, for example, environmental changes (e.g., pollution liability), advances in medicine and health (e.g., increasing life expectancy), property crime patterns (e.g., a shift to vehicle-related crime), political crime (e.g., terrorism), and a more litigious society (e.g., employment liability, products liability). There is also a changing environment of risk regarding insurance business operations, especially in relation to processes of economic globalization. The four relatively autonomous pillars of financial institutions – banks, insurance companies, trust companies, and credit unions – are collapsing. For example, banks are making incursions into the insurance industry. The rapid acceleration of mergers and acquisitions in all industries also characterizes the insurance industry. Multinational insurance companies have demanding shareholders, and one response is cost-cutting measures based on information technology development and employee rightsizing. The contractual basis of insurance company employment is being rewritten, as is the insurance company relation to broker and agency operations. As major players in capital investment markets, insurers are part of the new geography of money that has no sense of place other than where it might temporarily alight to maximize capital gains.

Fourth, the private insurance industry partners with the state in a society-wide system for regulating insurance practices. The private insurance industry is a significant contributor of investment capital in the political economy, and its investment policies and practices are regulated by the state. In turn the state benefits enormously from the political economy of insurance. For example, it receives substantial tax revenues and avoids having to compensate losses it might otherwise be required to cover. The state also regulates the market conduct of private insurers regarding sales, underwriting, and claims. Insurers often seek profitability by aggressive sales techniques that are unethical, and state regulatory mechanisms attempt to modify such practices. Insurers use underwriting criteria that segment policyholders into many different risk pools with highly variable premiums and contract conditions. The irony of private insurance is that it unpools risks in the very act of pooling them, often using rating criteria that are unjust. State regulators govern these rating criteria to achieve a more even-handed insurance system. Insurers also try to minimize what they have to pay out in claims. Claims adjustment and investigative practices are subject to state regulation. Part of the regulation of claims is directed at professional service providers who make their living from insurance claims. For example, there is regulation of managed care systems in health service provision, of autobody repair shops with respect to vehicle accident claims, and of the legal profession involved in liability claims.

Fifth, the private insurance industry partners with the state in developing technologies that make individuals responsible for their own well-being and that of others in their immediate environment. It constitutes the individual as the decision making economic subject who is responsible for the risks she faces. This is not the free subject, but one subject to liberal risk regimentation and discipline. The individual's identity as a responsible risk manager and risk taker is shaped by the technologies of insurance, which are often relied upon more than other forms of community cooperation.

State and Private Insurance Industry Goals

The private insurance industry shares with the state the goal of providing security and solidarity through the pooling of risks. Collective security needs are imagined and addressed through discourses of insecurity (Beck 1992a; Dillon 1995; Davis 1998). Insecurity is based on knowledge of risk as danger and on the fears generated by that knowledge. Moreover, the rational knowledge of probability calculation not only allays fears but also accentuates them because risk is always surrounded by uncertainty. 'Don't ask what a people are, the genealogist of security might say, ask how an order of fear forms a people' (Dillon 1995: 158). Fear leads to the prosecution of order in the name of security, and in so doing ends up proving itself.

The state has an interest in fostering security mechanisms in private institutions that protect property and populations. The private insurance industry is crucial in this respect. It provides technologies and social arrangements for allocating risks across pools of risk takers. It provides for a sharing of the risks of misfortune through financial compensation of loss. It is also active in the formation of preventive security arrangements that try to minimize loss. As such, the private insurance industry exemplifies the role of all private corporations: to govern through their powers of transferring and distributing risk, involving the state when necessary (Zwiebach 1975). In this respect, what is public territory, and therefore the responsibility of state institutions, arises out of risk management practices in private institutional territories.

Insurance systems share basic properties for providing security and solidarity through the pooling of risks (see especially Ewald 1991; Ericson and Haggerty 1997: 108–10). First, insurance objectifies everything into degrees of chance of harm. Each classification is then assigned its respective cost so that compensation for the effects of chance can be paid. When objective risks are classified in this way accidents become normal, and in that sense not accidents at all.

Second, insurance tries to make everything it objectifies calculable. It uses actuarial techniques to convert objective risks into probability statements. Based on the law of large numbers, it seeks to create large enough risk pools that the mathematical expected value of losses is relatively predictable and thus subject to governance.

Third, it is the creation of large risk pools through actuarialism that makes insurance collective and a basis of social solidarity. The population formed in an insurance pool has a stake in the identified risk and the specific harms it entails. This stake leads to collective efforts to protect against eventualities that are known to cause those harms. The insurance company promotes preventive security through contract conditions, inspections, and education campaigns in an effort to minimize harm to everyone, including itself.

Fourth, insurance protects against loss of capital. There is a collective goal of offsetting the harmful consequences of loss as these can be calculated financially. Indeed, what is actually insured is not the particular event that causes harm to a member of the population concerned, but the capital against which the insurer offers indemnification. Insurance cannot directly address the actually lived and suffered loss: the effects of the loss of a loved one, limb, or property of sentimental value are indeed incalculable. But insurance can at least provide some certainty that capital will be there to repair whatever damage can be expressed in monetary terms. This means that everything, whether person or property, is commodified for insurance purposes. Put most simply, insurance is the exchange of money for the promise of money in the future if a loss occurs. The conditions of this exchange vary. It is a consumer choice in private individual insurance. It is a condition of participation in some risky activities (e.g., compulsory insurance for drivers). It is a condition of membership (e.g., employment) in some private group insurance plans. It is a condition of citizenship via taxation or compulsory premiums in state social insurance plans.

Fifth, insurance is managerial. Insurance offers governance through surveillance and audit. It manages risks on a technical basis and at a distance, for a population dispersed in time and space but bound together by the collective interests noted above. The insurer's interest is in protecting these common interests, but also in loss minimization for the maximization of its own capital. These interests drive the expansion of surveillance and audit.

Sixth, insurance is legal. It objectifies risk by making it subject to contract and adjudication. At the same time, it helps the law to assign liability for loss to the party most able to distribute the loss through insurance.

Seventh, insurance is cultural. As a template for rendering the world in objectified, calculable, collective, capital, managerial, and legal terms, insurance transforms cultural mentalities and sensibilities. For example, in providing a futures market in security, insurance alters conceptions of time and destiny. In making risks collective and commodified, insurance alters notions of providence, responsibility, and justice. In propagating the 'managementization' of the world, insurance ensures that life is experienced as a perpetual round of calculations of economic utility. By objectifying the world, insurance forces the individual to look at herself in the hall of mirrors of her risk attributes.

Eighth, insurance is a social technology of justice. It offers distributive justice in the form of collective sharing of burdens. It also offers restorative justice as indemnification, whereby the loss of one is suffered, at least financially, by all. Insurance thus bridges individual and collective responsibility. Depending on other political rationalities it intersects with, insurance can favour a conservative, rational choice model of justice and individualism as much as social justice and collectivism.

Ninth, insurance is therefore political. It is central to liberal risk regimes because it combines aspects of collective well-being and individual liberty. This combination can lead actuarially constituted groups of policyholders to become effective collective actors in the struggle to secure benefits they were promised or to which they feel entitled. It can also lend itself to more extreme forms of libertarianism and necessity for self-governance. This result occurs in particular when insurance unpools risks by disaggregating people into increasingly specialized market segments according to their differences from others in the population.

Private insurance helps form the individual liberal subject by perpetuating the view that risks are the property of persons. Even though risks are socially imposed, it is the responsibility of the individual to take action to manage them and the effects of their consequences. For example, the automobile, and the road and traffic systems on which it depends, are socially imposed, but the individual is legally required to purchase insurance that will indemnify her against the consequences of this imposition.

Insurance is based on a contract model of society in which the individual becomes social by paying premiums to participate, and by agreeing to rules of participation. As such, it entails both a loss of freedom – financial costs and conformity to the rules – as well as a source of freedom for risk taking. It gives individuals control of their own destiny regarding what they wish to secure against, and what risks they wish to take. The individual liberal subject has a will to secure. This will is in turn related to wills for knowledge, truth, and virtue regarding risks: how to gain enough certain knowledge of risks to take appropriate action. On the other hand, as we have already pointed out, security is also associated with insecurity and restrictions on freedom. The will to knowledge of risk for life preservation can hinder or negate life because it circumscribes self-enhancement and growth. As Defert (1991: 215) emphasizes, 'each new measure of protection makes visible a new form of insurable insecurity ... security can become an inexhaustible market, or alternatively an impulse toward a motive for ever more interventionist political action.'

To the extent that it targets preferred markets and thereby unpools risks and excludes people from its populations, insurance entails loss of freedom. '"Territory" is derived not only from "terra" or land but also from "terror" or terrorize, to frighten and exclude' (Rose 1999: 34). In classifying populations into myriad rating categories for different premiums, deductibles, exclusions, and protections, insurance excludes some from its institutional territories altogether, while those included participate on widely divergent terms. Thus insurance, as part of the will to security, is centrally involved in the politics of identity and difference, and of fear and indifference. The 'politics of security are always already politics of identity/difference and desire by virtue of being a politics of fear ... Fear is also an education in what we are not, what we do not have, what we are supposed to care for and care about, whose lack, or fear of it, is expressed by the articulation of security ... not only a discursive economy of danger ... also a discursive economy of the absence that involves desire' (Dillon 1995: 174).

Insurance can be made to work for democracy, in Macpherson's (1973) sense of establishing a more egalitarian regime in the interstices of economic and social life. This egalitarianism is what state-based insurance systems promise, and what the state hopes private insurances will also provide. Broadly pooled insurances can work beyond legal discourses of freedom through rights by instituting freedom through well-being in knowing that there will be material support for losses suffered. Indeed, while it is based in law, especially the law of contract, insurance operates beyond the law of contract. Insurance operates beyond the law because its systems affect the minutiae of everyday routines across society. In this respect, insurance exemplifies what Foucault (1977) called 'counter-law,' in that it provides a basis for social organization that simultaneously underpins and escapes legal regulation. 'Insurance arrangements form a material constitution, one that operates through routine, mundane transactions that nevertheless define the contours of individual and social responsibility. For that reason, studying who is eligible to receive what insurance benefits, and who pays for them, is as good a guide to the social compact as any combination of Supreme Court opinions' (Baker 1996: 291).

As a moral technology of responsibility, private insurance differs from state insurance. It is not grounded in the generosity of redistributing wealth but rather in protection of specific economic interests. Nevertheless, private insurance offers an ongoing articulation of moral community, responsibility, and ethical conduct. Insurance company officials who design policies as well as state officials who regulate them are concerned with how private insurance operates ethically and contributes to moral community.

pvt insurn diff moral technology

Ethical concerns about private insurance focus in particular on the problem of unpooling risks (see especially Gowri 1997, Baker 2003). Insurance tends to 'open up a population to indefinite analysis into more and more finely detailed sub-classes of risk' (Defert 1991: 219). One reason for this tendency is that private insurers want to sell consumers a good risk pool that will keep premiums at a reasonable level. The insurer manages funds pooled from the group of insureds and has a fiduciary responsibility to them. Consumers are buying the security of the risk selection process and resulting pool. Because it is unfair for lower risk insureds to be heavily subsidizing higher risk insureds, discrimination among risks is necessary. Thus private insurers seek not equal treatment of all policyholders, but equitable treatment within a given rated class. Without such discrimination the goal of mutual aid can unravel (Stone 1993).

unpooling risks

discriminating among risks necessary

On the other hand, unpooling raises a number of ethical dilemmas. Categories that discriminate actuarially can establish differences in cost related to risk. However, they may be socially discriminatory. Common examples are insurance rate discrimination by gender, and by socioeconomic standing measured through credit ratings or place of residence. Private market forces create the problem of anti-selection. An insurer who decides not to divide a risk class will quickly lose preferred risks to competitors who do, and thereby end up with a substandard pool of high-risk policyholders who are still paying standard premium rates. *PRIVATE COMPETITION PROBLEM HERE*

Market forces therefore drive all companies in the direction of finer risk rating. This results in more money being spent on surveillance for knowledge of risks, which escalates administrative costs and therefore premiums, leading to further unpooling (Heimer 1985: 5). The much greater administrative costs incurred in the more private insurance-

surveillance = greater admin costs

based U.S. health care system, compared to the more public insurance-based Canadian health care system, is a case in point. The U.S. system has led analysts to observe that it costs more to deny coverage, and to provide a broad menu of specialized coverages, than it would cost to cover the entire U.S. population through a state-based system (Gowri 1997: 162–3). Ironically, the more the risk classification system is refined, the more the product may cease to resemble insurance. It fragments the wider community into highly specialized segments of risk and security and perpetuates insecurity among the excluded as well as those who aspire to a better class rating.

Insurance as Governance at a Distance

The insurance industry shares with the state many of the techniques for governing at a distance. It uses risk communication systems to develop knowledge of the populations under its jurisdiction. These systems include information technologies for obtaining knowledge about populations useful in underwriting decisions and claims processing. Also included is expert knowledge from a range of professionals who advise on underwriting and provide services related to claims. Insurance companies also have a substantial policing apparatus to address underwriting and claims fraud as well as loss reduction through preventive security.

Surveillance through information technology, expertise, and private policing is based on suspicion and mistrust, and yet ironically it is underpinned by trust in the abstract systems of insurance. Trust cannot be taken for granted, thus it is not surprising that insurance companies, like the state, devote considerable resources to marketing their enterprise as trustworthy. The selling of trust in abstract systems is characteristic of governing at a distance, whether by the state or private corporate institutions (Heimer 2001).

Insurance practice is based on surveillance. Insurers must decide who should be insured, and how those selected for insurance should be rated for specific premium levels and contract conditions. The underwriting decision cannot be made solely on the basis of knowledge from internal company records, and insurers therefore turn to external sources such as state institutions, other financial institutions, medical institutions, and so on. Insurers also require detailed knowledge about the populations they insure to make judgments about claims for compensation. Such knowledge is used to ascertain the legitimacy of a claim, the level of compensation that should be offered, and how the claim paid should alter the conditions of future contracts with the policyholder. Here too insurers must look to outside sources of knowledge – experts on health, property damage, environmental conditions, crime, and so on – as well as to their own records.

In order to govern in this way, an insurance company must be proactive in both constituting risks and the populations it sells to. Its main technology is quantification, a calculus of probabilities that brings a risk into being and provides a conception of what is normal. Normality refers to the statistical average for the population and activity concerned. But that average in turn values normality as virtuous, an ideal towards which members of the population should strive (Hacking 1991: 168). Everything that is other than normal in fact and value is suboptimal and subject to differential ratings as well as governance mechanisms for moral improvement.

Insurance exemplifies how a great deal of contemporary governance is organized around quantification and probability statistics (Hacking 1990, 1991; Porter 1995). Yet, because it is governance at a distance through abstract systems, much of its organization and effects remain sub rosa. People do not reflect on how they are governed through insurance arrangements, except situationally when they are deemed not normal and have to undergo extraordinary tests to qualify for insurance, or when they make a claim that is subject to dispute. A regime based on probability statistics regarding risk provides a kind of 'anti-rhetorical rhetoric' of governance, suggesting that things are being done objectively and therefore normally (Porter 1995: 78). Insurance is experienced as technical, standardized, subtle, perhaps mysterious, if it is experienced at all (Reichman 1986; Simon 1987; Ewald 1991; O'Malley 1992). Its abstract system constitutes a 'surveillant assemblage' (Haggerty and Ericson 2000), governing through institutional territories of electronic data systems and probability calculus as much as by disciplinary regimes bounded in physical space.

Insurance practices exemplify the tendency of liberal risk regimes to widen and deepen surveillance as a normal part of operations. First, the search for better knowledge of risks and the populations subject to them is incessant and perpetuates itself. Knowledge of risk is like a kaleidoscope, displaying new patterns with every technological scan and institutional classification. The calculations are perpetual and immediately feed back into the risk environment, altering practices which in turn affect probabilities and insurance rating. While the process of refining surveillance technologies for better knowledge of risk is highly rational, reflexivity means that reason is actually subverted in the sense that certain knowledge is not possible and doubt is institutionalized (Giddens 1990: 39, 176–7). Doubt fuels more surveillance.

Second, expertise is a key component of insurance surveillance systems and their capacity to govern at a distance. Experts working for insurers constantly invent new technologies of risk assessment. For example, the insurance industry has driven the development of medical technologies. An early example is urinalysis blood testing, while a recent example is genetic testing (Lemmens and Bahamin 1998; Novas and Rose 2000). Major areas of scientific and professional knowledge in medicine have arisen around specific fields of insurance. For example, there are approximately 740 journals that address occupational health and safety, a field directly linked to workers' compensation insurance (Adams 1995: 210).

Experts are also crucial to the ways in which insured populations are taught to be self-governing. Insurance experts teach insureds the habits of prevention, for example, providing them with regimes of preventive health care and of preventive security for their property. Insured populations are also taught how to be financially self-sufficient through insurance practices, for example, how to use life insurance as an investment vehicle and for tax advantages. When insureds have suffered a disability and are costing insurers substantial claims benefits, they are taught how to become better and self-sufficient more quickly. The insured subject is treated as a kind of 'proto-professional' (de Swaan 1990: 14) about risk, as someone who is her own risk manager but at the same time takes advice from the experts as necessary.

Insurers are also vigilant in governing experts. For example, they use surveillance to enforce accountability of insurance service providers. Service providers are increasingly audited not only in relation to their billing practices, but also in every step of their professional judgment concerning diagnosis and treatment (Power 1994, 1997; Rose 1999: 147). Whether it is managed care systems in the human body shops of physicians, or managed car systems in the autobody shops of mechanics, insurers treat the expert as subordinate and 'mere executant' (Castel 1991: 281) of the risk management system. In this process, professional knowledge is commodified for insurance purposes and professional jurisdiction is eroded. As Abbott (1988: 146) observes, 'forms of esoteric expertise can easily be reduced to keystrokes.' In this world of surveillance for the governance of professional practice, a given profession is best understood in its interinstitutional relations with other professions regarding questions of jurisdiction and control. Abbott (1988: 320) points out that 'the state of modern medicine has more to do with the state of modern nursing, pharmacy, law and accounting than with that of nineteenth century medicine.' He should also have included insurance.

Third, liberal risk regimes use insurance technologies as part of their effort to equalize social conditions. This effort too depends on the extension of surveillance (Dandeker 1990: 214). The development of workers' compensation schemes, whether provided primarily through state or private insurance systems, is a case in point. The commodification of the worker's entire working life as a valuable entity requires surveillance for detailed knowledge not only of all and each member of the worker population, but also of populations of professionals in finance, health, and employability who operate this system of insurable well-being (Defert 1991: 222; McClusky 2002).

Fourth, surveillance also proliferates because risks as dangers are tolerated economically, politically, culturally, and legally, but then are regulated through insurance-driven systems as an alternative form of control. For example, tobacco is legally available over the counter, but tobacco consumption is restricted through insurance provisions. Employers prohibit tobacco consumption on their premises in part because of insurance liability requirements regarding a healthy working environment. Smokers applying for life insurance are subject to self-reporting and medical examination requirements and pay substantially higher premiums than non-smokers. In the United States, guns are also dispensed routinely over the counter, but surveillance devices such as metal detectors and security guards are then required as a condition of insuring the premises in which possession of guns poses danger.

Fifth, when scientific and professional knowledge is unavailable or limited in its capacity for risk management, surveillance expands in the form of private policing. The handling of some disability insurance, such as soft tissue injuries following accidents, is a case in point. When it is extremely difficult to diagnose, measure, and treat the problem, it is also extremely difficult to know what level of professional service is required. In this absence of expert knowledge, there is a surveillance crackdown on insured claimants, and on the professions who try to address the loss, to provide some certainty for the efficient management of the system.

Governance at a distance through risk management systems must include the deployment of trust management systems. Liberal risk regimes foster distrust. It has been widely documented and lamented that trust in government by the state has declined markedly (Nye, Zelikov, and King 1997). Giddens (1998: 51) cites survey evidence that citizens' confidence in the trustworthiness of the U.S. federal government declined from 76 per cent in 1964 to 25 per cent in 1994. Such evidence is used to argue the need for institutions that facilitate trusting self-government at levels of organization beyond the state (Fukuyama 1996). However, many non-state institutions, including insurance companies, also have difficulty establishing trust.

A major reason for distrust in large institutions is that they themselves operate on the assumption of distrust. As we have seen, because they govern at a distance, institutions rely on surveillance systems to risk manage their populations. The hyper-reflexivity about risk engendered by these systems institutionalizes distrust (Porter 1995: ix; Luhmann 1979: 92). There is a decline of innocence, as every member of the population is suspected to the degree that they might contribute to risk (Priest 1990; Ericson 1994; Staples 1997). The reliance on risk communication systems 'in effect promotes suspicion to the dignified scientific rank of a calculus of probabilities. To be suspected it is no longer necessary to manifest symptoms of dangerousness or abnormality, it is enough to display whatever characteristics the specialists responsible for the definition of preventive policy have constituted as risk factors' (Castel 1991: 288–9).

Ironically, even as they use their technologies of distance and distrust – for example, swiping peoples' identities as they process their applications, credit cards, passports, and other documents of identity, and recording their every movement on closed circuit television – institutions must encourage people to trust these technologies and the abstract systems in which they are embedded. An institution's electronic communication systems, expert knowledge, and symbolic currencies (e.g., credit cards, access cards, money, frequent flyer points, etc.), as well as the bureaucracies that organize it all, must be trusted to the extent that routine transactions can be taken for granted and the parties involved can feel secure (Giddens 1990: 26).

This trust is cultivated in part through face-to-face relations with employees of institutions, such as bank tellers, insurance agents, tax officers, health care workers, sales clerks, and so on. However, institutions cannot rely entirely on these interpersonal contacts to routinize trust. Most institutional transactions are not face-to-face, and even when they are the agent or official of the institution concerned is usually not known personally by the customer and is often seen as an executant or cog within the bureaucracy. There must be trust in the abstract system itself, for it is the knowledgeability of the system that produces the capacity to act and desired outcomes.

Trust fills gaps in knowledge so that confidence can accrue and action can take place. The gaps can exist because of time-space distance in the transaction, a lack of expertise, failure to comprehend systemic processes involved, and the fact that knowledge of risk is always probabilistic. Trust reduces 'social complexity by going beyond available information and generalizing expectations of behavior [replacing] missing information with an internally guaranteed security' (Luhmann 1979: 13). As such trust at once facilitates the tolerance of uncertainty and the rationality of risk taking.

Knowledge of risk structures trust (Simmel 1950, 1978; Luhmann 1979; Giddens 1990; Misztal 1996). In dealing with the fact that knowledge of risk is probabilistic, trust helps in making the transition from probabilities to possibilities for action. Trust is based on whatever awareness of risk is provided by the technologies, expertise, and symbolic currencies of the abstract system itself, but also provides the inferential leaps required to move from that awareness to decisions and behaviours. Moreover, those decisions and behaviours may prove to be troublesome, wrong, or bad, at least in retrospect. Thus trust has an evaluative and moral dimension with respect to risk taking. We trust that the results of a person's or institution's risk assessment, and intended actions based on that assessment, are appropriate for our purposes. When it is institutionalized in the abstract systems of risk management, trust secures risk communication and habitualizes risk taking. Most people do not routinely think of the things we have been describing here when they use their credit cards.

The complexities of abstract systems of risk *force* trust in institutions. One simply has no choice but to trust them if one wants to participate in social life at all. This creates a bias towards the centre, that is, towards the capacity of central authorities in the state and other major institutions to manage things on our behalf. 'If the selection of risk is a matter of social organization, the management of risk is an organizational problem. Since we do not know what risk we incur, our responsibility is to create resilience in our institutions. But by choosing resilience, which depends on some degree of trust in our institutions, we betray our bias toward the centre' (Douglas and Wildavsky 1982).

However, liberalism is always suspicious of the centre. Trust is something that cannot be coerced (Mistzal 1996: 21), and when it seems too forced, liberal critique will emerge to cultivate distrust. For example, in the name of privacy, there is increasing distrust of the growth in surveillance (Bennett and Grant 1999). Ironically, one result of this distrust is that the authorities themselves become subject to increasing surveillance through audits (Power 1994, 1997). In contemporary surveillance systems, trust is always in dialectic with intensive distrust.

Institutions respond by addressing trust at a different level. They sell trust as a symbolic good. Thus the state is the largest single advertiser in Canada, followed by a few large entities in the private corporate sector, including financial institutions. Indeed, one traditional pillar of financial institutions in Canada is called, simply, a trust company. The word trust appears frequently in mission statements, logos, and letterheads of corporations. Insurance companies in particular sell their products through advertising that underscores their trustworthiness (Stone 1994). This advertising uses moral language and images to suggest that abstract systems can be trusted: State Farm Insurance is 'Like a Good Neighbor'; 'You're in Good Hands with All State'; the rock of Prudential. But just as trust cannot be coerced, it may also prove difficult to buy it (Mistzal 1996: 21). Trust must be nurtured in ongoing relationships where familiarity, mutuality, and keeping promises bring peace of mind and a feeling of security. Thus the selling of trust through advertising is also embedded in the counter-knowledge of distrust. Whether in the abstract systems of surveillance or in public advertising, trust is 'fragile with respect to its substitutes, such as insurance, monitoring, rewards or sanctions' (Arrow 1974: 23).

Contemporary Insurance Regimes

Private insurance markets have always been encouraged by the state as a crucial means for ensuring the well-being of all and each. Life insurance, for example, was supported because it alleviated the state from having to care for the dependents of deceased persons, provided a source of charitable income for additional social relief, contributed to the political economy through employment, and provided the state with tax revenue (Zelizer 1979: 17). In workers' compensation schemes, the authority of private institutions is integrated with the state's public service preoccupation with the health and well-being of citizens.

At the beginning of the twentieth century, insurance companies in Canada promoted their enterprise as crucial to the building of nationhood itself. This self-portrait was similar to that of other major private corporate institutions of the time, such as the railways. This point is illustrated by the advertisement of the Citizens Insurance Company reproduced in figure 2:1. The advertisement is headed, 'To Build Up a Nation, Support Its Institutions.' The name 'Citizens' identifies the company with nation-state citizenship. The company's directors, officers, and chief agents are listed as upstanding citizens. The company's financial strength as a contributor to the well-being of Citizens' policyholders, citizens of the state, and the national political economy is displayed as a promotional feature INSURANCE + NATION

While state and private insurances have always been mixed, the composition of the mix and its ramifications for political economy *Political* vary according to prevailing rationalities. State and private insurance *Rationalities* concepts, techniques, and practices are perpetually reconfigured in *of time* relation to changes in the social, economic, managerial, legal, cultural, moral, and political contexts. Insurance concepts 'emerge as governmental concepts shaped by political rationalities, not simply as objective descriptors of the nature of insurance schemes or institutions. Each is variously constituted, distinguished and valorised over time, bestowed diverse capacities, characteristics or potentials that make it difficult to assign terms such as "private insurance" and "state insurance," let alone the relationships between them, without reference to the political rationalities of the time' (O'Malley 1997: 29–31).

We mapped the contemporary rationality in chapter 1. Governance is fragmented into multiple institutional territories of consuming populations managed through liberal risk regimes. This constellation for governance is not only the subject of abstract political theory and protracted public debate. It is also addressed in the discourses and practices of insurers themselves. The following statement is not by Ulrich Beck (1992a, 1992b, 1999), but from an insurance company's annual report:

> The nature of risk itself has changed and will continue to do so. The relationship between business, the communities it serves, its employees and the environment (immediate and remote), is immeasurably different from what it was a few years ago. Concern about, for example, the health

\Governance fragmented
\Multiple territories of consuming population
\liberal risk regimes

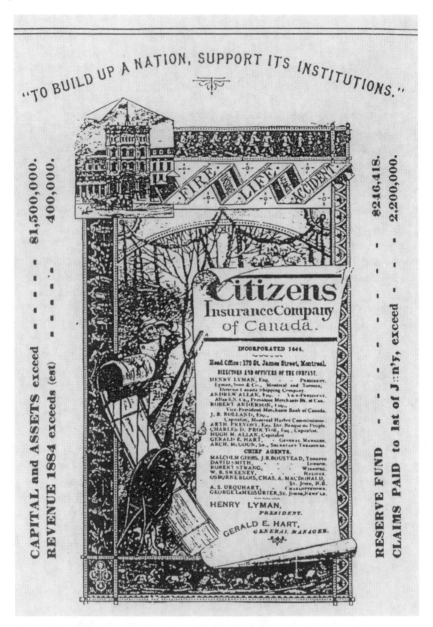

Figure 2.1. Advertisement for the Citizens Insurance Company of Canada, 1884.

implications of industrial pollution, or the environmental implications of oil spills is now commonplace and extends from that for the immediate problem to that for the long-term effects, which are often unquantifiable.

In a period in which demographic structure, too, is changing, and one in which formerly underdeveloped countries are emerging as the world's new centres of industry, the biggest change of all has been in people's expectations and in governments' ability, or willingness, to meet them. The implied responsibility for individual's welfare is, to a large extent, being transferred from the state to corporate entities and, in many instances, to the individuals themselves.

The outcome of all this is that, today, conventional insurance cover, traditionally relied on to mitigate risk, can no longer provide the only answer: conventional cover for some risks may simply not be available or may have become so expensive as to be unviable.

Sedgwick is not immune to these shifts in social structure ... [One response has been] extending our traditional transaction-based core business to include a consultancy role in which we devise innovative means of identifying, mitigating and managing risk. Our long-established and primarily wholly-owned global network gives us an unparalleled ability to do this on a worldwide basis. (Sedgwick Insurance 1996: 6)

SEDGWICK INSURANCE.

As this statement indicates, insurers are practical analysts of social structure and change. Their applied social science moves from the most general macro levels of globalization to the finest-grained detail of actuarial tables. This is knowledge that counts, literally. Fundamental aspects of political economy and the well-being of populations are at stake.

NB

Private insurers, especially multinationals such as Sedgwick, participate in the regulatory and economic management process. They do so, for example, by helping other multinationals control investment risk, enhance business stability, extend their credit, and finance major projects. In 1996, Chubb Insurance, a major multinational, had as a client the multinational aircraft manufacturer Boeing. Boeing insured $22 billion in assets with Chubb, which in turn involved two hundred other insurers and reinsurers worldwide, organized through global insurance broker Johnson and Higgens. This broker had fifty-nine full-time employees based in Boeing's Seattle headquarters (Chubb Insurance 1996). JOHNSON and HIGGINS / CHUBB INSURANCE.

CORPS control others MNC risk stability credit finance

The state can control some aspects of the economy more effectively than others. For example, it can control cash directly, but has less hold on cash equivalents (Zelizer 1997: 15). Canadian Tire money does not bear the head of the Queen, but rather that of a frugal Scot. Private insurance is a form of money as contract, a promise to pay the bearer under specified conditions. A piece of paper just like 'hard' currency, the insurance contract as money may be purchased from a local neighbourhood agent in an act of personal trust, but once possessed, it signifies trust in the abstract systems of the insurance company. It is a bond to the institutional territory, consuming population, and liberal risk regime of the insurance company, albeit also underwritten by some state regulatory processes. As such, the insurance contract can be seen in the same light as currency or other forms of economic credit, as analysed by Simmel (1978). It is based on and prompts a belief that the insurance institution 'will assure the validity of the tokens for which we have exchanged the products of our labor ... the feeling of personal security that the possession of money gives is perhaps the most concentrated and pointed form of manifestation of confidence in the sociopolitical organization and order' (ibid.: 179).

This trust in money instruments, such as insurance, as a vehicle to trust in 'socio-political organization and order' more generally, is entwined with liberal conceptions of freedom. The promises of personal security made through the insurance contract provide a space of regulatory freedom to take more liberal risks. Money instruments in general are widely experienced as a source of freedom and autonomy. The capacity to spend freely is a kind of speech act about identity, liberty, and democracy. Thus it is not surprising that in the supreme territory of money, the United States, a Supreme Court decision equated spending with speech and declared that both are equally protected by the First Amendment of the American Constitution (Rueschemeyer 2000: 255–6; Dworkin 1996).

Of course, money in the form of insurance contracts or any other instrument is not a source of unchecked power and inevitable freedom. Many money instruments, including insurance, are regulated through the formal legal apparatus of the state. They are regulated even more pervasively through the practices of financial institutions. The social meaning of money differs markedly according to the forms it takes and the contexts of its use (Zelizer 1997). It can exist outside markets, be noninstrumental, and be shaped by political, social, and cultural structures rather than determinative of them. Money can be a great source of 'unfreedom,' alienation, and misery, especially when the moral economy of the relationships involved is not reciprocal and compromises the very freedom that money promises. Simmel (1978: 403–4) captures this aspect when he remarks that the alienating effects of money mean 'our age ... certainly possesses more freedom than any previous one [but] is unable to enjoy it properly ... the freedom of liberalism has brought about so much instability, disorder and dissatisfaction.'

These features are evident in insurance as a money instrument that differentiates socio-economic hierarchies and institutionalizes inequalities. The aforementioned tendency of private insurers to market segment their products into preferred risk pools, and the resultant unpooling of risk that leaves many underinsured or uninsured, is seen as an inevitable outcome of market forces in liberal risk regimes. In the United States in 1999, such processes left about 44 million citizens without any health insurance whatsoever. The trends in private insurance in Canada point in the same direction (Ericson, Barry, and Doyle 2000).

In contemporary liberal risk regimes, the social welfare role of the state and economic well-being 'are now seen as antagonistic: the social is to be fragmented in order to transform the moral and psychological obligations of economic citizenship in the direction of active self-advancement' (Rose 2000: 159). Lost in this view is the fact that in welfare state regimes, social benefits play an important role in economic growth, ease structural change, and encourage risk taking (Abramovitz 1981; Atkinson 1999, 2000). Indeed, multinational corporations encourage state insurance programs as an important component of their decisions on where to locate production facilities and employment. State insurance schemes relieve employers of having to pay more expensive benefit packages to employees, and also allow them to shift some responsibility for the general well-being of their employees. For example, long-term care insurance financed through an employer's payroll tax can be more expensive than contributions to a scheme organized through the state (Atkinson 2000). Multinational vehicle manufacturers find Ontario an attractive location for production in part because of that province's state health care infrastructure (Broadbent 2000). Chrysler Corporation at one point estimated that its employee health insurance benefits added $500 to the price of each vehicle manufactured in the United States, and that this cost placed them at a disadvantage relative to foreign competitors (D'Arcy 1994: 172).

There are state vehicle insurance systems in four Canadian provinces. In British Columbia, the system was developed because private insurers could not organize a market that was priced reasonably and operated fairly, and because the insurers were not local companies and therefore moved large amounts of employment and capital out of the province.

Redlining

In the United States, there have been significant ongoing problems in the private home insurance market in poor areas. Insurers 'redline' these areas as unacceptable risks and a private insurance market is not formed. Redlining is the term for unfair discrimination, not based on real differences in risk or cost, against a particular geographic area. This problem has led to a number of remedial efforts organized by the state, voluntary community organizations, and insurance companies. The state backs the Fair Access to Insurance Requirements (FAIR) Plan as a residual market facility 'where homeowners must obtain coverage if they cannot find an insurer who will sell them coverage voluntarily. Typically, FAIR plan coverage is more limited and can cost relatively more than purchasing coverage through the voluntary market' (Klein 1997: 51). Therefore various community-based programs have arisen, such as MAPS (Market Assistance Plans), which broker between local neighbourhoods and insurers by, for example, helping to screen and qualify consumers (ibid.: 76). Some of these programs are initiated by insurance companies themselves, who also work through municipal governments to obtain better police and welfare services for the neighbourhoods concerned (Knight 1997). While insurance generally encourages reliance on governance through the abstract systems of distant institutions, rather than interpersonal mutual support and community cooperation, such examples indicate that there can be active mobilization by state, private insurance, and community organizations to address the more serious problems of unpooling.

Unique blends of state and private sector insurance are created to meet specific exigencies in organizational life. Heimer (1985: 189–90) describes how an organization for ex-prisoners had its own fund to secure fidelity bonds, but if these funds became exhausted the excess was covered by an insurance policy with a private insurer. The premium for this insurance policy was in turn paid for by a state welfare agency.

Walker and McGuiness (1997) describe state and private commercial insurance company collaboration in the face of terrorism against the political economy itself. After IRA bombings of City of London financial institution facilities, insurers no longer included terrorism in their standard commercial property policies, and reinsurers excluded terrorism from their contracts. The solution to this crisis was the Reinsurance (Acts of Terrorism) Act 1993. The U.K. government set up an insurance company called Pool Re with commercial insurers in the City market. A special pool was created to allow in effect the commercial insurers to reinsure themselves. The state insurer agreed to cover 90 per cent of claims not met by the pool, with unlimited liability. The state thus committed to a potentially enormous reinsurance liability without a corresponding premium, except for that available through compulsory taxation of all citizens. As Walker and McGuiness argue, this scheme was still consistent with the governance beyond the state ethos of the U.K. government at the time. There was minimal state intervention beyond establishing and administering Pool Re. Responsibility remained with consumers to purchase terrorism coverage, and private insurance companies remained liquid. Various state, private insurance, and private industry collaborations in terrorism insurance coverage are developing in the context of the September 11, 2001 attacks on the World Trade Center in New York (Ericson and Doyle forthcoming: chap. 5).

In this chapter, we have introduced ways in which the private insurance industry serves as a system of governance. It does so in various forms of collaboration with state governments: sharing similar goals of security and solidarity through the pooling of risks; using similar techniques for governing at a distance; and collaborating in insurance regimes. We now turn to consideration of the specific mechanisms through which insurance as governance is accomplished. These mechanisms are organized through the concept of moral risks.

3. Governance through Moral Risks

To carry life insurance is a moral obligation incumbent upon the great majority of citizens.

Franklin D. Roosevelt

You're not just selling insurance. You are merchandising the concept of responsibility.
Program Calendar for Agents, Life Underwriters Association of Canada (1998)

Risk and Morality

The relationship between risk and morality is the subject of fervent debate across academic disciplines (Ericson and Doyle 2003). Some scholars view the concept of risk and practices of risk management as not being morally principled. For example, Giddens (1990, 1991) argues that the ascendency of abstract systems of risk entails the 'evaporation of morality,' as people increasingly focus on pragmatic knowledge of risk in their immediate environment to routinize their activities and feel secure. 'Moral principles run counter to the concept of risk and to the mobilizing of dynamics of control. Morality is *extrinsic* so far as the colonizing of the future is concerned' (Giddens 1991: 145). Garland contends that risk management systems are 'forward-looking, predictive, oriented to aggregate entities and concerned with the minimization of harms and costs, rather than with the attribution of blame or the dispensation of individual justice' (Garland 1997: 182).

The risk management systems of insurance have been used as a case in point. Lowi (1990: 32) observes that in the social insurance systems of the welfare state 'the very concept of risk had already taken the morality out of responsibility and had made the consequences of risk – injury – a merely instrumental matter.' The same is said about private insurance systems. Simon (1987: 62; 1992: 44) and Reichman (1986: 151–2) believe that insurance systems disempower the individual as a moral and political subject, creating instrumental communities of interest rather than ones based on collective conscience and moral solidarity. At a different level, the tort liability system in civil law has shifted responsibility to the party in the best position to prevent injuries or, failing that, to spread the costs of them. There is lessening regard for the moral intentions of litigants, and more emphasis on insurance as the primary institution of prevention, risk distribution, and indemnification. While this use of the tort liability system for risk management does not result in 'the evaporation of morality' (Giddens 1991: 145), 'the moral foundation of the new regime is relentlessly utilitarian' (Priest 1990: 215).

Other scholars do not see risk discourse and practice as antithetic to morality. Risk discourse is used in public culture as a synonym for danger, in order to imagine moral orders, solidify moral boundaries, and strengthen moral regimes. Risk management practices are in turn integral to moral regimes. They effect moral regulation by making people think of risks in terms of their own ethical conduct with respect to them. Ethical conduct includes being knowledgeable about risks and doing one's part to prevent, minimize, and distribute them.

Douglas (1990, 1992) analyses risk as a political vocabulary of moral responsibility and accountability. The moral dimension of risk arises in particular from the fact that 'risk is not only the probability of an event but also the probable magnitude of its outcome, and everything depends on the value that is set on the outcome. The evaluation is a political, aesthetic and moral matter' (Douglas 1990: 10). Thus risk is connected to moral assessments of threat or danger. It is used in political culture to mobilize moral communities for dealing with danger in particular ways, and to force accountability. The word 'danger' sufficed in the past, but in liberal risk regimes trying to respond to globalized culture, the scientism of risk analysis has greater rhetorical effect. The word 'sin' also sufficed in the past to translate dangers into moral and political issues, but sin like danger is becoming obsolete as a mobilizer of moral community compared to 'the modern, sanitized discourse of risk.' 'A neutral vocabulary of risk is all we have for making a bridge between the known facts of existence and the construction of a moral community ... Risk, danger and sin are used around the world to

legitimize policy or to discredit it, to protect individuals from predatory institutions or to protect institutions from predatory individuals'
(ibid.: 4–5).

Douglas argues that risk as a rhetoric of moral responsibility is especially strong in the individualistic culture of liberal risk regimes. Risk
is invoked as a defensive mechanism to protect individuals from
encroachment by others. To be at risk is to be sinned against, vulnerable to the threats of imposing institutions, communities, or individuals.
Rather than singling out the sinning individual as a suitable enemy to
uphold the moral solidarity of the community (Durkheim 1964), the
sinning community is used to uphold the moral autonomy of the individual. Risk codes danger as a threat to liberty. In so doing, it slips easily into enhancing liberty for some at the expense of others. In this
capacity, risk discourse provides 'automatic, self-validating legitimacy
to established law and order. We see their punitive or deterrent function. But that is only half of what is happening. Those who fear the
taboos see dangers and their connection with morality as part of how
the world works' (Douglas 1990: 8).

The embeddedness of morality in risk is not limited to public political discourse. As Hacking (1990: 160ff.) shows, risk and morality are
also entwined at the level of probability calculations and risk management practices. Statistical knowledge of risk provides a discourse of
moral normalcy. With the advent of probability statistics, the word
'normal' was used to connote objectivity about human beings. Probability statistics describe what is normal about a population, who within
it is normal, and who poses a risk. However, the word 'normal' functions simultaneously to evaluate what ought to be. 'It uses a power as
old as Aristotle to bridge the fact/value distinction, whispering in
your ear that what is normal is also all right ... The norm may be what
is usual or typical, yet our most powerful ethical constraints are also
called norms' (ibid.: 160, 163).

No one can escape being subject to risk discourse and risk management practices. All actions are under a description of risk (Hacking
1986). As such, everyone takes risks (Adams 1995: 16), including the
risk of inaction (Giddens 1990: 32). Knowledge of risk, probability, and
normalcy is used in action, and the action taken in turn feeds back into
the risk management system. Furthermore, because risk is entwined
with morality, all actions and the risk assessments that result from
them are simultaneously given a moral description. These processes
are captured in Hacking's concept of the 'looping effects' of knowledge

of risk: 'Such social and personal laws were to be a matter of probabilities, of chances. Statistical in nature, these laws were nonetheless inexorable; they could even be self-regulating. People are normal if they conform to the central tendency of such laws, while those at the extremes are pathological. Few of us fancy being pathological, so "most of us" try to make ourselves normal, which in turn affects what is normal' (Hacking 1990: 2).

Statistics of risk are produced on the basis of moral classifications (Douglas 1986, 1992). Quantitative risk assessments do not offer a unique rationality that pinpoints a single right answer, but rather pose questions of probabilities and possibilities that require moral assessment for action (Adams 1995: ix). 'Risk management decisions are moral decisions made in the face of uncertainty' (Adams 2003). Similarly, efforts by state regulatory agencies or insurers to commodify risks also entail moral preferences and reveal relative values (Adams 1995: ix). Insurance is a technology of responsibility that quantifies and commodifies moral commitments in every detail of underwriting, preventive security, and indemnification (Ewald 1991: 206–7).

Moral assessment is also part of risk taking in everyday life. As the individual takes action under a description of risk, she often blames herself because, in the reflexive light of incoming knowledge, the action taken disappoints and an alternative action seems preferable in retrospect. This self-blaming is a key aspect of how people give significance to their lives and carve out their autonomy in morally responsible terms. Risk taking confirms moral autonomy, liberty, and individuality. Thus efforts to make people more responsible through risk management strategies of normalization are always subject to the looping effect of risk compensation: that the person will then take more risks because of the new level of security provided, in part because the assertion and confirmation of individual autonomy is a major reward for risk taking in individualistic cultures. The individualistic interplay of normalization, security, restraint, and risk taking is an engine of liberal risk regimes:

> The ethics of lifestyle maximization, coupled with a logic in which someone must be held to blame for any event that threatens an individual's 'quality of life,' generates a relentless imperative of risk management not simply in relation to contracting for insurance, but also through daily lifestyle management, choices of where to live and shop, what to eat and drink, stress management, exercise and so forth. Of course, this

inaugurates a virtually endless spiral of amplification of risk ... these arrangements within which the individual is re-responsibilized for the management of his or her own risk produces a field characterized by uncertainty, plurality and anxiety, thus continually open to the construction of new problems and the marketing of new solutions. (Rose 1996: 343, 346)

In keeping with the 'logic in which someone must be held to blame for any event that threatens an individual's quality of life,' the contemporary trend is to construe all events as a product of human agency and therefore controllable through attributions of responsibility. Institutions such as science, law, medicine, and insurance participate in the search for human causes of events that will show them to be motivated, and therefore subject to attributions of individual responsibility for indemnification after the fact, and to be predictable, and therefore subject to attributions of responsibility for prevention before the fact. For example, backed by medical science (Evans 1993), vehicle insurers have erased the word accident from their moral vocabulary and substituted 'collision' or 'crash.' This new moral language is accompanied by claims that over 90 per cent of all 'crashes' are the result of individual driver actions rather than, for example, road conditions, vehicle conditions, or the view that accidents just happen (Insurance Corporation of British Columbia 1996).

Gusfield (1981) points to these trends in his brilliant analysis of how impaired drivers are represented in American political culture. He shows that the cultural organization of vehicle accidents is predicated on the view that they result from individual driver performance. This view is underpinned not only by the strongly individualistic character of American culture, but also by scientific research and legal discourse that individualize social problems in order to attribute responsibility and justify intervention. 'Multicausality weakens the capacity and purposefulness which make control seem possible' (ibid.: 74). Thus, when alcohol is involved as part of an accident it becomes *the* cause regardless of other factors. The attribution of a primary cause is crucial to pinpointing responsibility and taking punitive or remedial action.

In a section entitled 'Accident, Risk and Certainty,' Gusfield (1981: 47) observes that not only do attributions of causal responsibility lead to political responsibility and accountability, but that the reverse is also true. The political culture gives selective credence to particular causal theories that form the preferred knowledge for taking action. Liberal risk regimes prefer knowledge that reduces the multicausal world into a simple cause that in turn allows attributions of responsibility and performances of accountability. For example, 'although studies of alcohol-involved accidents find approximately two-thirds of them are single-vehicle ones, such studies of responsibility as have been done study only multiple-vehicle crashes. Thus they substitute an insurance oriented view of responsibility for a research oriented one of "cause"' (ibid.: 72).

One major consequence of this framework of political and causal responsibility is blaming the victim. The person who might otherwise have been seen as the victim of an accident is now seen as a contributor to the crash because her driver performance is faulty: she has failed to take adequate preventive measures by learning and acting upon knowledge of risk. 'As responsibility is divorced from motivation, all victims of accidents are potentially culpable. Culpability arises not from the motivations of the victim or other agents, but from their miscalculation or ignorance of risks' (Green 1997: 199).

This logic of seeing accidents as a product of individual failure is extended to other areas of risk management. For example, the victim's movement regarding crime has succeeded in responsibilizing potential victims to reduce their exposure to risk (O'Malley 1998). Potential victims are treated as suspects: they are suspected of not doing enough to prevent criminal victimization in the first place. Actual victims are treated as offenders: they are responsible for the security breach that allowed criminal victimization to occur. Similar trends are evident regarding individual responsibility for health risks. As we will see, this moral regulation is effected in particular through insurance as an institution of governance.

Moral Risks in Insurance Relationships

The relationship between risk and morality has always been a preoccupation of the insurance industry. Indeed, the concept of 'moral hazard' has been used for more than two centuries, both within the insurance industry and in public policy debates about insurance (Heimer 1985; Baker 1996; Moss 2002). Within the insurance industry, moral hazard is a practical concept used to understand and act upon risks in moral terms. In particular, the focus is on how to detect, categorize, and govern those who seek to take advantage of the insurance relationship to the detriment of the risk pool and the insurance company. In public policy debates, the focus is on using moral hazard arguments to object to government involvement in insurance schemes. Such objection has been especially salient in recent years. Moral hazard arguments have been mobilized to attack the welfare state and argue for more mechanisms of governance beyond the state, including those available through the private insurance industry. The fundamental assumption is that state insurance schemes inherently create greater moral hazard at the level of insured persons compared to private insurance schemes (Moss 2002).

Regardless of whether it is organized through state or private industry schemes, insurance is a moral technology of governance, constantly articulating how people should act. The risks that insurance defines, produces, takes, and manages always include moral assessment of the people and harms involved. This infusion of moral risk assessment into insurance as governance occurs through three interconnected processes.

First, insurance responds to and produces moral risks through its actuarial practices of classification and probability calculation. As discussed in the last section in reviewing the ideas of Ian Hacking, statistical knowledge of risk specifies what is normal about a population and who within it deviates and therefore poses a risk. This specification of normalcy and deviancy evaluates what ought to be, so that the statistical norm of what is usual or typical also bears an ethical norm as restraint. In this respect, all actions classified and calculated by insurance occur under a description of moral risk. Furthermore, these descriptions pose questions of probabilities and possibilities for further action that require moral assessment and contribute to a broader discourse of moral responsibility. They effect moral regulation by making people think of risks in terms of their own ethical conduct with respect them: they must become knowledgeable about risks and do their part to prevent, minimize, and distribute them.

Second, as discussed in the last section in reviewing the ideas of Mary Douglas, risks are also moralized and subject to attributions of responsibility through the ways in which they are posed as dangers. An insurance risk as danger raises questions about the probable magnitude of the outcome and how to mitigate it. Answers to these questions entail moral evaluations, including attributions of moral responsibility. These attributions remind others – institutions, communities, and individuals – of the need to minimize harms in order to uphold the moral autonomy of the individual. Here insurance risks morally code danger as a threat to liberty.

Third, in combination with the ways in which they are embedded in actuarial classifications and evaluations of danger, moral risks arise in the interactive dynamics of the insurance relationship. Here moral risk refers to the ways in which an insurance relationship fosters behaviour by any party in the relationship that immorally increases risk to others (Ericson, Barry, and Doyle 2000). This definition of 'reactive' moral risk is broader than the one typically used by insurers themselves, as well as by some researchers (e.g., Heimer 1985; Reichman 1986; Giddens 1998). It is usually only the insured who is seen in terms of moral risks. Being insured is said to reduce the insured's incentive to avoid risky behaviour or to minimize loss through preventive security, with negative consequences for insurers. For example, moral risk influences on the insured party will increase if the insurer is seen as distant and anonymous, or if there are discrepancies between sales stories and claims stories that create a sense of bad faith; if there is an opportunity for fraud created because of inadequate selection of the insured population and/or inadequate policing of the claims process; and if the insured is able to neutralize morally her fraudulent behaviour as just in the circumstances.

Our broader definition stems from the fact that the social organization of insurance offers incentives to other parties in the insurance relationship to engage in risky behaviour with immoral consequences (Baker 1996; Ericson, Barry, and Doyle 2000; McClusky 2002; Heimer 2003). Insurers themselves are often influenced in ways that encourage them to put others at risk, including their policyholders, employees, competitors, and state governments. Moral risk at the level of insurance companies and their employees and suppliers can occur for the same reasons it occurs among insureds: the cushion provided against the consequences of risk, very high economic stakes, low visibility and inadequate policing, and readily available justifications to morally neutralize risky behaviour.

In public statements, insurers sometimes fall back upon the rhetoric of science and appearance of neutrality to claim that they do not engage in moral risk assessment. For example, a representative of the National Association of Independent Insurers, appearing before a U.S. Senate Committee investigating insurance redlining practices, made the following statement: 'The insurance industry refrains from moral pronouncements about its customers. We measure risk as accurately as we can, applying experience and objective criteria refined for more than two centuries. We leave it to others to speak of discrimination and other such moral terms' (cited by Squires 1997: 1). However, an excursion into the world of insurance company policy manuals and practices reveals that the enterprise is constituted by knowledge of moral risks (Powers 1997; Glenn 2000).

Moral risks are posed by motivated and intentional acts. For example, an insured desperate for cash might commit arson in order to collect insurance on her property. She might also exaggerate the value of household effects destroyed in the fire to inflate the value of the claim. Moral risks can also be more systemic. For example, morally blameworthy contribution to loss can occur systematically when health insurance makes medical treatment effectively free or very inexpensive at the point of consumption. Insureds have an incentive to use health services even when it is not medically necessary, sometimes to the point of dependency and iatrogenesis. They may also spend less on prevention measures that would lessen the need to seek medical treatment.

As if rational choice regarding money is all that matters, economists Arnott and Stiglitz argue that moral risks can only be reduced by an open market private health insurance system that prices according to ability to pay for levels of consumption. The moral risks of 'nonmarket insurance' are

> illustrated by what happens if an individual catches pneumonia as a result of going on a hiking trip with inadequate rain gear. His employer gives him compensated sick leave; part or all of his medical expenses are reimbursed by his insurance policy or the state; uncovered medical expenses may be partially deductible from his income tax; and family and friends rally round to provide other forms of support. Such extensive support, while directly helpful, deleteriously affects individuals' care to avoid accidents. In terms of the example, had the individual borne all the costs of the accident himself, he might have taken the trouble to carry adequate rain gear. (Arnott and Stiglitz 1991: 179)

This imaginative illustration by economists writing in a leading scholarly journal exemplifies how moral risk is depicted in liberal risk regimes. The thrust is away from conceptions of accident and negligence, and towards treating every event as if it resulted from intention. This treatment allows the actors involved to be judged as morally responsible for losses incurred. This rational choice/moral responsibility framework constitutes *the* myth of liberal risk regimes.

In the contemporary depiction of moral risks, nothing is beyond human capacity for harm reduction. Even extreme physical risks such as natural disasters are deemed manageable. Rock slides onto highways can be predicted and contained; storm clouds can be seeded by aircraft to turn hail into rain (Brun et al. 1997); earthquakes can be predicted using timelines of several centuries and the human environment altered to lessen the impact (ibid.). On the level of individual responsibility, people can be educated and warned to take precautions that reduce harm. Signs on the roadway warn of rockslides; weather forecasts suggest when expensive property should be protected from impending storms; schools and workplaces educate on how to secure property and person against the impact of earthquakes. In insurance-driven systems of governance, people must act *as if* there is no uncertainty, all chance can be tamed and all risks are moral.

The question is not whether there will be moral risks, but the source of such risks and who will bear the losses resulting from them. If fire insurance agents are on commission to sell full replacement-value insurance, they have an incentive to sell policies above the property value and then to deny the property is worth that much when a claim is made. Valued-policy laws that regulate this problem shift moral risk to insured, who have an incentive to commit arson when the market value of their property falls below the insurance policy value (Heimer 1985). If employers have the greatest capacity to prevent workplace accidents, then the limited liability for such accidents that employees concede to employers through workers' compensation insurance will pose a moral risk among employers greater than that which occurs among workers seeking compensation for workplace accidents (Baker 1996: 280). In the field of products liability, a stricter liability regime fosters greater moral risks among consumers, while a loosening of liability shifts moral risks to manufacturers (ibid.: 274).

These examples suggest that regulation of insurance entails perpetual efforts to transfer and distribute moral risks. Moral risks derive from reactive risk, the capacity to react to something that alters the probability of loss or gain (Heimer 1985: 3, 11, 19). Reactive risk varies, for example, by the time and space distance between the policyholder and those who actually can control losses; the extent of volitional control over loss-producing actions; incentive systems built into insurance contracts; a sense of trust and justice beyond the mechanics of the contract; systems of audit and accountability for placing control in the hands of those who are not the policyholders; and regular alteration of contracts in response to changing risk environments. The more indirect the control over the loss, the greater the likelihood of insurance on reasonable terms. The person who is totally in control of the potential for loss and gain – and in that sense is autonomous or free – is deemed uninsurable because she poses too great an individual moral risk. Thus ironically the very efforts to make the insured subject more directly responsible for harm reduction can reach a point where her moral risk amplifies.

The same situation applies to other parties in the insurance relationship. Suppliers of insurance-related services who are given too much autonomy over their expertise and what it is worth pose serious risks to other parties in the insurance relationship (Dornstein 1996; Weisberg and Derrig 1991, 1992). Similarly, insurance company employees induced to sell policies and manage claims competitively will pose moral risks to insurance consumers in the short term, and to their companies in the long term (Clarke 1999). And insurance company directors and officers given too much fiduciary control, especially incentives to maximize return on capital through investment, will jeopardize policyholders, employees, suppliers, and creditors (McQueen 1996).

The fact that moral risk is structured into the insurance relationship means that it can be positive and functional for some parties but negative and dysfunctional for others. From the viewpoint of the insured, insurance is often purchased precisely because the person wants to take more risks. For example, vehicle insurance allows the driver and her passengers to engage in a risky activity with less regard for the consequences of a crash. Directors and officers insurance for company executives and errors and omissions insurance for company employees allow considerable risk taking with lessened personal consequences of costly negative outcomes. Indeed, the corporate limited liability system is an insurance-like means for risk taking that protects the entrepreneurialism and investment speculation of the company operatives. Where a significant harm results in the company no longer having net assets, the costs of entrepreneurialism are shifted onto shareholders, creditors, and other victims.

The entire liability insurance system can be seen as fostering some desirable moral risks. The fact that a party has liability insurance enables the person who has suffered a loss at the hands of that party to acquire financial compensation for the loss. Thus it is not surprising that where liability insurance is available it will change behaviour in ways that sometimes cause substantial losses for insurers. Liability insurance crises, for example, regarding environmental liability and vehicle tort liability, have weakened many insurance companies to the point where they are taken over or cease to conduct business. Nevertheless, the losses of insurers are gains for others in particular and for society in general. This is a system of compensatory justice that serves at least a partial redistributive function through the operation of moral risk.

Moral risks in health insurance can be viewed in a similar light. If people have comprehensive health insurance coverage with little or no penalties for higher levels of consumption, they will consume more and there will be higher financial costs at the level of health expenditure. However, this moral risk effect may constitute an overall social gain in terms of population health and well-being that in turn creates other benefits, including economic productivity.

Moral risk can also be functional for insurers (Baker 1996). First, moral risk provides a means through which insurers argue against state regulations that affect their autonomy. Insurers have often contended that immoral insureds will take advantage of a proposed regulation to the detriment of the moral members of their population and the strength of the private insurance institution more generally (ibid.; Moss 2002). Second, insurance industry efforts to regulate problems of moral risk signify the morality of the insurance enterprise itself. Third, if the insurance-buying public is depicted as immorally providing false information to secure policies on more favourable terms, then stricter governance of the underwriting process is seen as legitimate. Fourth, if claimants are suspected of routinely padding their claims and often committing fraud, then stricter governance of the claims process is also seen as legitimate. Fifth, if both applicants for insurance and claimants are depicted as moral risks for insurers, then higher insurance rates are more justifiable.

Moral Risks and the Welfare State

The welfare state shifts moral risks to the level of less fortunate citizens. This shift is at the progressive taxation expense of more fortunate citizens. It also costs business enterprises that could profit more from better taxation and investment conditions which allow *them* to be more morally risky at the expense of the less fortunate, including their own working poor employees.

The welfare state systematically grafts morality onto economics in order to combat poverty and other major risks to the well-being of the population (Procacci 1991). It thus constitutes a moral citizenship of social responsibility. It takes for granted that some aspects of life are above and beyond the marketplace and incorporates them in its regime of governance as an aspect of citizenship (Ignatieff 1995). In so doing it seeks equality of social rights over and against the economic inequality that is built into the marketplace. Even if people have unequal wealth and money incomes, they are to enjoy equalized social incomes through entitlements to basic standards of living and decency. As such, 'the welfare state is the high point of a lengthy process of the evolution of citizenship rights' (Giddens 1998, referring to the vision of T.H. Marshall).

Research demonstrates that citizens are more likely to participate socially (e.g., in voluntary organizations) and politically (e.g., in political parties and voting as well as community politics) as state social provision grows (Rueschemeyer, Huber-Stephens, and Stephens 1992). Such social and political participation creates a non-commercial space of cooperation, yielding public good and happiness. This ideal contrasts sharply with liberal risk regimes where emphasis on equality of opportunity fosters competition and a self-regarding form of happiness in which the individual keeps looking at himself or herself in the hall of mirrors of the commercial marketplace (Turow 1997; Schor 1998).

Recent efforts in the United Kingdom and the United States to advance a 'third way' alternative to welfare state regimes (first way) or liberal risk regimes (second way) remain embedded in the second way. This embeddedness is related to the fact that we are now citizens of liberal risk regimes in which the main focus is the socialization of the risks of everyday living rather than the socialization of property (Beck 1992a, 1992b; Beiner 1992, 2000; Ericson and Haggerty 1997). Indeed, risk itself has become a form of property. In this form, risk is increasingly seen as the responsibility of the individual, whose main citizenship right is choice about how to take it and mitigate it at once.

Privilege and underprivilege remain a matter of how moral risk is differentially distributed (Giddens 1990: 125–6). For example, the relationship between wealth and health is clearly established (Sullivan, Stainblum, and Frank 1997). Making the less fortunate more responsible for paying for their own medical service needs ensures that they will be formed into a population with poor nutrition, greater susceptibility to illness, and earlier death. The only way out of the regressive unpooling for individualized well-being is collective pooling of certain risks fundamental to the well-being of all. This requires commitment to normative public goods that are not separable into private property (Gowri 1997; Reich 1999; Loader and Walker 2001).

It currently seems difficult even to imagine more collective pooling, because the structural framework of risk society, and the frameworks of each liberal risk regime within it, have solidified. One result of this solidification is conventional wisdom about what is wrong with the first way, the welfare state. The welfare state is discredited because it is seen as generating intractable problems of moral risk at the level of consumption.

First, state welfare systems are said to create cultural relationships of dependency on social security. Instead of the desirable emphasis on risk taking and enterprise, risk minimization, avoidance, and aversion create human and institutional inertia.

Second, there is an economic relationship in which people pay substantial 'premiums' (taxes, social security payments, etc.) and expect returns over time. The welfare state not only offers substantial and generous benefits, it is the ultimate deep pocket. The population on state benefits inevitably overconsumes. While in consumer society the private market alternatives of any commodity, including insurance, are to be consumed voraciously, welfare consumption as habit must be tenuated.

Third, the cultural and economic relationships in the welfare state lead people to take advantage of bureaucratic inefficiency and situational opportunity. Often the risks insured do not fit the need, the wrong groups are insured, and claims are not policed adequately. Bureaucratic inefficiency is compounded by professional interests: professionals in the system receive very substantial salaries and benefits, and have iatrogenic effects. The welfare state's strong emphasis on social justice, with its values of welfarism, trust, and the promise of security, make it easy for professionals and claimants alike to morally neutralize a questionable benefit claim.

Extreme arguments about the moral risks of the welfare state suggest that people might be better off with no state insurance provision at all. In these arguments, welfare provision involves several ironies that defeat its purpose and sometimes compound rather than correct the risks it is supposed to offset.

First, there is the irony that while the welfare state lavishes money on scientific and technical knowledge to improve the well-being of its population, there is no accepted scientific knowledge of the limits to this social improvement activity. There is 'no internal principle of limitation' (Foucault 1988: 169), no objective threshold for saying that needs are satisfied. The lack of a principled rationale to ration state benefits results in political efforts to control benefits. These control efforts create legitimacy problems for the welfare state, as they are arbitrary and uneven. Legitimacy problems are compounded because control efforts include the intensification of surveillance in a desperate effort to impose discipline. As Foucault observed regarding state health care benefits systems:

> A machinery set up to give people a certain security in the area of health has, then, reached a point in its development at which we will have to decide what illness, what type of pain, will no longer receive coverage – a point at which, in certain cases, life itself will be at risk. This poses a political and moral problem not unrelated, all things considered, to the question of the right enjoyed by a state to ask any individual to go and get himself killed in a war. If it is given a voice, even in the form of a more or less acceptable rationality, it becomes morally unbearable. Take the example of dialysis machines: how many people are being treated in this way, how many others cannot benefit from them? Supposing the choices by which one ends up with this inequality of treatment were revealed: the exposure of such guidelines would cause a scandal. In this area a certain rationality causes a scandal. (Foucault 1988: 171–2)

Second, state welfare systems can ironically end up making people less self-sufficient and less responsible for self and others. Foucault has also commented on this irony of dependency. While welfare state provisions are supposed to produce more autonomy, they produce dependency of two types: too much integration (which leads to loss of autonomy, including less scope for risk taking); and, alternatively, too much marginalization or outright exclusion for the recalcitrant who cannot be integrated (ibid.: 160).

Third, taken too far, state insurance schemes might ironically reduce safety and security. This logic suggests that the less the welfare provision, the more there will be a responsible workforce above the poverty line; the less workers' compensation for disabilities incurred at work, the greater the workplace safety; the less the availability of disability insurance in general, the greater the availability of an able, responsible workforce. As Baker (1996: 238–9) observes, this sensibility that less help to the unfortunate yields more resources also 'helps deny that refusing to share these burdens is mean-spirited or self-interested.'

Fourth, and embodying these other ironies, the welfare state is said to work against its own purposes of collective responsibility and welfare. In arguing that liberal risk regimes offer greater well-being than the welfare state, Marsland says, 'We shall look back on the welfare state with the same contemptuous amusement as that with which we now view slavery as a means of organizing effective, motivated work ... [The welfare state] wreaks enormous destructive harm on its supposed beneficiaries: the vulnerable, the disadvantaged and the unfortunate ... cripples the enterprising, self-reliant spirit of individual men and women, and lays a depth charge of explosive resentment under the foundations of our free society' (Marsland 1996: 197; quoted by Giddens 1998: 13).

The third way argues the same way. Giddens (1998: 114–15) observes that 'welfare prescriptions quite often become sub-optimal, or set off situations of moral hazard. It isn't so much that some forms of welfare provision create dependency cultures, as that people take rational advantage of opportunities offered.' Giddens then proceeds to argue that dependency cultures are created by welfare state insurance systems. For example, he argues that 'Benefits meant to counter unemployment ... can actually produce unemployment if they are actively used as a shelter from the labor market' (ibid.). He cites Lindbeck's (1995) work on Sweden to assert that 'the higher the benefits, the greater will be the chance of moral hazard, as well as fraud [to the point where] serious benefit dependency is no longer seen as such but simply becomes expected behavior ... Once established, benefits have their own autonomy' (ibid.).

All of these arguments about the moral risks of the welfare state are exercises in truth, power, and virtue. The truth is that there are limits to knowledge, for example, the inability to provide a principle of limitation that specifies when state-provided welfare needs have been satisfied. The truth is that people sometimes act in rational choice terms: rules and dollars and cents are at the very core of common sense. Therefore power should be exercised to change the rules and monetary incentive structures of welfare provision to impose limits on the state's redistributive activities. These changes are virtuous because in the long term and the aggregate they will bring well-being to a greater number of individuals and therefore to the population as a whole. Perfected, this redistribution of moral risk does not seem to be an exercise in power, but only a search for truth, and a virtuous one at that (Baker 1996: 239–40).

Moral Risks and Liberal Risk Regimes

The welfare state forms a moral citizenship of social responsibility. In contrast, liberal risk regimes constitute a moral citizenship of individual responsibility. In liberal risk regimes the relationship between risk taking and risk control is made increasingly interdependent. A key question is who assumes the 'responsibility for the unintended consequences of risk taking in ordinary economic activity?' (Lowi 1990: 26). The primary answer is that the individual is responsible for the misfortunes as well as the fortunes of risk taking. Life becomes more of a gamble.

In participating with business enterprise in the formation of this citizenship of individual responsibility, the state abandons welfare as its raison d'être and downgrades it to but one dimension of its population management activities (Giddens 1998: 116). Emphasis is placed instead on the social investment state, which works to make citizens into '"responsible risk takers" ... people need protection when things go wrong, but also the material and *moral* capabilities to move through major periods of transition in their lives' (ibid.: 100). In other words, they are to understand that the moral burden of risk taking and risk control is falling more directly on them, and they themselves are to deal with the difficult transitions that result.

The state replaces welfare social transfers with liberal risk transfers. The American financial institution environment in the 1980s is a clear case in point. As part of Reaganomics, financial institution speculators were able to set up savings and loans companies or 'thrifts' with clearly inadequate capital requirements. These companies attracted thrifty commercial security investors and individual depositors with inflated interest rates, and sometimes with deception. The lure to depositors was made even more attractive by an increase in federal government deposit insurance (FSLIC) on each account from US$40,000 to $100,000. The companies were not similarly thrifty with their investments. They gambled with abandon, especially on property markets, and lost several hundred billion dollars. As Adams (1990: 22) reports, this moral risk transfer 'unleashed a horde of habitual risk takers without subjecting them to any risk ... The new owners had every incentive to be as ruthless as possible ... In the words of one regulator, "Heads they win, Tails, FSLIC loses." Insurance professionals have a term for it, "moral hazard." The policy offers too much temptation to cheat.'

The availability of enhanced deposit insurance lessened the pressure on investigators and prosecutors to criminalize fraudulent behaviour, and, on policy makers and legislators to use criminal law in restructuring the industry after the fact. Instead, the U.S. government accepted responsibility for creating this criminogenic environment. It used taxpayers' money to meet billions of dollars in deposit insurance claims, as well as other financial consequences of the fallout. As stated by the chair of the Federal Deposit Insurance Corporation who led the government bailout, 'If you combine a credit card on the United States with no limits, the chance to invest that money just about any way you wanted, and then call off supervision because you decide you have deregulated the industry, you create almost an entrapment – a fatal attraction or whatever they call it in law' (quoted by Zimring and Hawkins 1993: 282).

This is socialism American-style. The federal government ended up forcing each taxpayer to participate in paying off several hundred billion dollars in debt over time. On average, the tax burden of this debt to an American family of four was greater than the cost of ordinary property crime victimization that family would experience in a lifetime (Zimring and Hawkins 1993). Such direct experience of moral risk transfer undoubtedly makes individual citizens reflect differently on the meaning of thrift in liberal risk regimes. 'The sermons of the rich are not very meaningful to the poor as long as the rich are themselves so well protected against risk. Successful people do take risks in America, but in a very carefully constructed, minimax framework. Dramatic examples of governmentally sponsored risk management for the well off are as recent as the $500 billion cost of the savings and loan safety net' (Lowi 1990: 32–3).

The poor do receive some compassion in liberal risk regimes, but it is 'compassion with a hard edge ... a kind of moral rearmament' (Rose 1997c: 22), as exemplified in George W. Bush's 'compassionate conservatism.' Moral rearmament begins with work and the enterprising self. There is a reassertion of the Benthamite principle that good people work hard. Where people are not working, they are to be taught skills and given temporary subsidies to make them work worthy. There is a belief that most people will derive their sense of worth from the work/consumption nexus, and therefore respond favourably to this 'government through the calculated administration of shame' (Rose 1999: 73). If they are recalcitrant, they are subject to punitive measures, including increasing exclusion from the moral community (ibid.: 263ff). If they choose criminal career options, they will be 'governed through crime' (Simon 1997), meaning their participation in illegal drug and property crime economies will also be audited (Ericson and Haggerty 1997). In this regard, it is not surprising that states with the most liberal risk regimes have the highest levels of incarceration (Zimring and Hawkins 1991).

Liberal risk regimes for the work worthy resonate with some of Bentham's (1962) other principles regarding how benefits to the poor must be tied to good work. The 'self-liberation principle' holds that there is to be 'no relief ... [without] working out the expense – till then no enlargement.' Where the self-liberation principle fails, the 'earn-first principle' is invoked: 'when ability adequate to the task is certain, and laziness apprehended, no meal given, till the task by which it is earned has *first* been performed.' In all cases, 'the principle of less eligibility' is to ensure that the unemployed person does not receive welfare that makes him as well off as the person in the lowest rung of the working poor. 'Every penny bestowed that tends to render the conditions of the pauper more eligible than that of the independent laborer is a bounty on indolence and vice.'

For citizens with decent incomes, liberal risk regimes provide endless possibilities of security product consumption. From personal and property security protection devices to insurance and other financial products, the individual is able to consume according to her wealth. This security products consumption certainly grants powers of freedom for the individual. However, it also poses her as a moral risk and subjects her to governance on each institutional territory in which she participates.

For example, the working individual faces her employer's regime for making her a responsible subject. Employers have compulsory insurance requirements with attendant assignment of moral risks. In the United States in particular, employers are developing 'wellness centres' that simultaneously encourage workers to keep fit and monitor their efforts in doing so. For example, the Coors brewing company has a

23,000-square-foot wellness centre devoted to keeping workers healthy with exercise programs, on-site medical personnel, and a counseling center. Coors estimates that by providing this 'benefit' to employees the company saves $2 million a year by cutting sick leave and medical costs. But it also offers management a detailed source of medical information about their workers ... the biggest saving ... comes from using the data to identify costly benefits that can be reduced, or to shift costs to employees ... [At] Hershey Foods Corporation ... workers now pay an extra $30 a month for health insurance if they have high blood pressure, $10 for high cholesterol, $10 if they don't exercise, $50 if they use tobacco, and $30 if they are overweight. Hershey caps the total of such charges at $840 a year per employee; the testing is mandatory ... A New York electronics firm began charging ... [highest risk] workers higher premiums, instantly shifting $232,000 of health care costs to employees. The 20 per cent who refused to take the wellness test were charged the highest premium. (Staples 1997: 114–15)

Greater freedom from the state's governance of work and consumption places the individual into the governance regimes of employers and insurers. In these institutional territories, consuming populations are constantly assessed as moral risks and made responsible for their own decisions. The insurance logic of these regimes constitutes individual moral risk in strictly rational choice economic terms: '1) money compensates for loss; 2) people are rational loss minimizers; 3) taking care requires effort; 4) taking care is effective; 5) people with insurance have control over themselves and their property; 6) insurance payments are not conditioned on a given level of care' (Baker 1996: 276). Erased is the individual's personal understanding that many losses are only partially compensated by money; action is motivated by purposes beyond loss minimization; reflexivity about risk has limits in relation to both effort required and effects accomplished; and individual control is limited in a world of complex institutions and their abstract systems.

The individual is bound to experience the contradiction between the liberal risk regime emphasis on her individual choice and the fact that risk is usually so multifaceted that even experts cannot isolate one or a few risk factors on which to make a choice. She is thereby also bound to appreciate why *she* is posed as a moral risk and forced to make her own choices:

The mistake of equating insurance and redistribution results in a disproportionate focus on the hazards of compensating injured consumers and workers as opposed to the hazards of not compensating them. The mistake of assuming that money compensates for loss and that the insured is in control of his situation results in the exaggeration of the hazards of that compensation. And, the mistake of ignoring institutions leads to the conclusion that the only solution for these exaggerated hazards is less protection for the sick or injured (which, of course, means less liability and lower insurance premiums for manufacturers and employers). (Baker 1996: 283)

Governance through Moral Risks

Quantitative evidence regarding specific moral risks and their effects is often rudimentary or missing altogether (Baker 1996). For example, in cases where homes and their occupants are redlined as unacceptable risks, the insurance companies engaging in such practices often have no hard evidence to support their decisions. An American home insurance company subject to litigation regarding redlining had underwriting guidelines addressing the insurance applicant's credit history, the condition of the adjacent home, the age and value of the home to be insured, and the property's market value compared to its replacement cost. Yet it could not produce hard evidence regarding the relationship between these criteria and its claims-paying experience (Lynch 1997: 164–5). There is no publicly available data to substantiate the theory that homeowners will commit arson when the market value of their property falls below the insured replacement value. Many agencies do not maintain up-to-date records on market value compared to replacement value, and even the initial determination of this ratio by underwriting agents 'is frequently subjective or determined without uniform procedures or guidelines' (Ritter 1997: 196–7). The insurance system ideal is 'that the odds be known, that numbers be attachable to the probabilities and magnitudes of possible outcomes. In practice, since such numbers are rarely available, they are usually assumed or invented, the alternative being to admit the formal treatments have nothing useful to say about the problem under discussion' (Adams 1995: 25).

Regardless of their quality, the invention of numbers, and the classifications and probabilities to which they refer, are an important basis upon which insurers recognize and respond to moral risks (Hacking 1990; Porter 1995). '[I]t is enough to create new names and estimations and probabilities in order to create in the long run new things' (Nietzsche 1974: 121–2).

Insurers invent the realities of moral risks through three interconnected processes. First, they embed surveillance of moral risk in the organizational arrangements of the insured population. Second, as an extension of this surveillance, they develop a number of means by which insured populations participate in the governance of their own moral risks. Third, when surveillance fails to provide formal criteria for moral risk assessment, insurers substitute situational, intuitive judgments of moral character to make decisions.

If insurance simply responded to risks that are objective, in the sense that they represent unrelated contingencies beyond individual control, there would be no need to address individual responsibility for losses (Reichman 1986: 151–3). In practice, the question of who has control over a risk is crucial in determining whether the risk is insurable and the conditions under which it will be insured. The need to determine individual responsibility for control is at the heart of the moral risk detection and assessment enterprise. Insurers become micro-managers of moral conduct as a crucial component of their efforts to allocate risk across a population of risk takers.

Insurer surveillance of the insured intensifies according to the degree of knowledge asymmetries, and the extent to which the potential for loss reduction lies in the hands of policyholders (Heimer 1985: 182). Surveillance is embedded in ordinary functions of the organization concerned in order to facilitate governance at a distance. Ships at sea provide a clear example of a risk at a physical distance from direct insurer surveillance, and therefore subject to complex arrangements within the ship's rank structure to report on potential risks and to control actual losses (ibid.). Surety and fidelity bonds regarding the honesty and performance promises of employees are another case in point (ibid.: 153–4). The failure of ciminological knowledge to predict individual honesty, and of other social science knowledge to predict performance, means that surveillance must be embedded in work organizations to audit workers' honesty and performance. Requirements may include, for example, employment screening with lie detectors and drug tests; probationary reputation-building periods of employment; electronic surveillance of employees; scheduled audits and spot checks; and, deposits of collateral.

Reactive risk is always part of such insurance-driven surveillance practices. That is, the perception of moral risk is affected by how it is managed through the surveillance technologies. The moral risk itself is in flux because surveillance alters 'that which is predicted as it is predicted' (Adams 1995: 13–14). As with social objects more generally, moral risk 'is just the continuous possibility of the activity' (Searle 1995: 36), used as a basis for action but changed in the process of that action.

A key aspect of surveillance systems for governing moral risk at a distance is to make the insured self-governing. The ideal is to make each policyholder a watcher as well as watched and a bearer of her own control. Self-governance is accomplished through a number of interconnected mechanisms of creating individual responsibility for risk control.

Insurance builds control into the environment of everyday activities. The built environment is governed through insurance contracts, inspections, and incentive programs that require policyholders to keep their properties up to standard and secure from potential liabilities and losses. Insurance also builds control into the organizational environment. Fidelity bonds, surety bonds, errors and omissions insurance, employment liability insurance, and workers' compensation insurance demand rigorous auditing procedures to the point where in many work organizations there is continuous surveillance. The individual insured for specific activities is similarly made responsible for preventive action that reduces harm. For example, some vehicle insurance policies are void if the insured is impaired by alcohol at the time of an accident.

Direct surveillance is backed by education campaigns that make the insured aware of risks in relation to insurance standards and security precautions to be taken. As Adams (1995: 16) documents, there is an enormous proliferation of both expert and lay literatures on risk, and these literatures have a particular bias towards individual responsibility for risk management. For example, human error is overwhelmingly portrayed as the cause of accidents of all kinds (Reason 1990). The upshot is that these literatures favour risk management solutions that focus on the individual. They also favour risk reduction rather than a balancing of costs with the benefits of risk taking. 'Most of the literature on the subject is inhabited by *Homo prudens* – zero risk man. He personifies prudence, rationality and responsibility' (Adams 1995: 16).

There is a long history of moralistic discourse in the selling of life insurance (Zelizer 1979, 1997; O'Malley 1997). British friendly society insurance agents went door-to-door weekly to collect life insurance premiums, effecting prudentialism through a regularity of time and place. The contemporary emphasis on more private life and health insurance purchases, and on self-administered pension plans, is also based on a discourse of prudentialism. Prudentialism emphasizes the moral earmarking of money for future unanticipated as well as planned needs of self and significant others. People are coaxed and cajoled into financial product purchases by portraying money itself as 'a meaningful symbol of attitudinal feelings such as personal inadequacy, loss of control, shameful failure, security, or a need for social approval' (Zelizer 1997, referring to the work of Lane 1991).

Insurers also effect control through their rating systems for underwriting insurance policies. Insurance sales prospects are initially treated as suspects until they are qualified according to rating criteria. The contemporary trend is towards finer and finer ratings, market segmentation, and unpooling because of the acceleration of moral risk assessment at the underwriting stage. Policyholders are also treated as suspects, suspected of not doing enough to control moral risks on behalf of the insurer. They are subjected to inspections, surveillance, and changed contract conditions regarding ongoing assessment of their conformity to insurance standards of care of their property and persons. Claimants are treated as offenders, as having failed to implement sufficient control measures to prevent the loss from occurring.

Insurance offenders are punished in ways parallel to punishment in the criminal justice system. The policyholders may have their premiums increased (a fine); they may be asked to participate in loss recovery (restitution); they may be subject to more stringent insurance contract provisions (conditional sentences); they may be required to purchase additional insurance warranties (bonds); and, they may have their insurance withdrawn altogether (banishment). While this blaming the victim approach is punitive, it also has a criminal corrections or rehabilitation element. 'The argument is that rewarding meritorious or healthy forms of behavior through a risk rating system might produce behavior change for the better in some of those seeking to qualify for lower insurance rates – a form of "doing good" towards those who at first glance appear to be the losers' (Gowri 1997: 153).

Moral risk is also governed through the civil law system for tort liability. Civil damage awards that enforce liability rules, statutory rights, and insurance practices are a very powerful regulator of moral risk. They internalize the costs of risks to the parties that generate them, thereby serving to reallocate control to the party in a position to deal with the underlying conditions of risk. Legal responsibility is imposed for the miscalculation of the risk. The punishment is a damage award that will not only compensate the loss but force the responsible party to undertake new calculations for risk control. Priest (1990: 214–15) views this legal system for responsibilizing risk control as being so pervasive and penetrating that everyone is imprisoned by it. No act is solitary, it always takes place in a matrix of responsibility for risk:

> Such a regime aspires to impose legal controls on all activities in the society that contribute to loss in any way. Thus, every action by every citizen becomes subject to potential legal review because every action will increase the risk of loss in some way ... [T]his represents a vastly expanded commitment to standards of individual responsibility ... An individual is responsible not only for intentionally or maliciously harmful behavior, but for all behavior that increases the risk of loss, though the loss itself may be remote ... The law charges each citizen to carefully monitor every action for its potential contribution to loss ... The centrality of risk effectively prevents all efforts of social escape. (ibid.)

The formal regime for governing through moral risk is based on a complex interinstitutional system of law, actuarialism, surveillance technologies, and professional expertise. However, this system still requires insurance operatives to make it work. Studies of insurance practice indicate that 'character underwriting' and intuitive social judgments about the insurance client are commonplace (Heimer 1985; Baker 1996; Glenn 2000). There is little that is new in this regard. Consider the following characterization of the good underwriter from the *Monetary and Commercial Times*, 27 May 1870.

> There is no post of duty, in the elaborate organization of forces by which mercantile operations are wrought out, that requires more skill and experience than that occupied by the fire underwriter ... A cool judgment, decision of character, and a good knowledge of human nature, are qualities that are constantly being called into play. He must be enterprising, without being rash; cautious, but self-reliant and energetic; while keeping his rate-book in view he should not fear to experiment in a direction which general principles and intuitive knowledge seem to indicate a wise course to follow. To adhere strictly to the rates and rules on every occasion, is to play the part of a mere machine; the business of a true underwriter is to say when these guides shall and when they shall not be followed – when the ordinary routine shall be departed from in order to effect a particular object ... This he ought to do with special reference to

the 'moral hazard' of insurance, which the underwriter should learn to weigh with precision, for on his ability to do this depends, more than anything else, the success of his company. (Cited by Hives 1985: i)

The informal criteria which underwriters use are in part derived from the moral understandings embedded in the formal system. However, where necessary, criteria are also situationally invented to help address problems with implementing that system. Among the problems are limited knowledge; the need to move from aggregate population data to each particular case; the need to generate business competitively in spite of formal criteria; and the moral character of all factual construction. The smooth flow of insurance business requires continually changing criteria of moral assessment according to the pragmatic exigencies of everyday practice.

Situational assessment, surveillance, and contractual sanctions to make the insured bearers of their own control do not address the structural problems of which they are a symptom. All are based on negative logic. As Baker (1996: 282–3) concludes, 'the success of insurers in managing insurance incentives may well mean that the most important "moral hazard" effect is not increased loss, but rather increased social control.'

Researching Insurance as Governance

In Part I, we have conceptualized the insurance industry as an institution of governance. We have argued that insurance practices in defining and responding to moral risk are key loci for understanding how risk society operates. Risk is a neologism of insurance (Ewald 1991), and our understanding of risks and how to respond to them is embedded in the institutional templates of insurance (Giddens 1991: 111).

We take the view that the regime of insurance practices, and the subject-positions and subject-functions it fosters, are best understood from the viewpoint of its practitioners and consumers. As Douglas (1986) emphasizes, risk taking judgments are rational from the cultural perspective of those making the judgments. While the cultural perspective of people articulates with the risk logics of the wider institutional systems in which they participate, the meaning of risk is negotiated in each social transaction where a risk is being addressed. This negotiation means that there is no direct translation between a regime's rationalities and programs and what people do in relation to risk. For example, people take unusual risks for profit and fun, and for expressions of consumer preference, style, and identity (Lupton 1999: chap. 5, 6–8; Simon 2002, 2003). It is crucial to understand how people perceive and respond to what is possible within the governing practices of liberal risk regimes.

A focus on the perspectives and actions of participants in the insurance system also allows sociological appreciation of the 'value rational' (Weber 1964) or 'emotionally-driven and morally-taxed' (Garland 1997: 202–3) aspects of insurance as governance. Insurance is marketed and consumed not only in terms of actuarially based risk calculus, but also in relation to fear and other emotions regarding security. It is therefore an important vehicle for researching 'ontological security ... [as] the confidence that most people have in the continuity of their self-identity and the constancy of the surrounding social and material environments of action' (Giddens 1990: 94). On the one hand, ontological security depends crucially on how people integrate their routines with the abstract systems of insurance. Everyday life entails 'an active complex of reactions to abstract systems, involving appropriation as well as loss' (ibid.: 150). On the other hand, ontological security is based on emotions and often 'rooted in the unconscious' (ibid.: 113). People buy insurance for peace of mind regarding imagined futures, and both they and the agents who market insurance products to them in these terms hope that there will be no need to actually use it.

A focus on the perspectives and actions of participants in the insurance system also allows us to address questions about risk and human agency. Moral risk assessment involves interpretive judgments about human agency. Always at issue is whether the individual event, process, or state of affairs to be insured is within human control and therefore subject to attributions about human responsibility for the loss.

The insurance determination of human agency and the attribution of responsibility is in turn an instructive vehicle for understanding how freedom is governed in liberal risk regimes (Rose 1999). Insurance provides enormous freedom for people to take risks without having to fear the full burden of negative outcomes. It therefore serves as a technology of empowerment for those with the means to acquire it and to use it to advantage. On the other hand, those unpooled from the preferred insurance populations, or excluded from obtaining insurance altogether, are likely to experience insurance as but another institution that keeps them relatively powerless. This dialectic of empowerment/powerlessness is characteristic of liberal risk regimes.

In governing through moral risk, insurance perpetually links human agency to the management of consuming populations and the structure of the political economy. Research on insurance as governance is therefore a means of analysing the relation between agency and structure: how the micro, meso, and macro levels of society constitute each other (Giddens 1984; Archer 1988). Rose (1997b: 3), for example, identifies as a research priority the need to analyse how the macro level of regimes relates to the myriad programs, technologies, and human activities that transpire in their jurisdiction.

Research on how insurance governs through moral risk also provides a means of analysing social solidarity and moral community. Strict moral risk control of insured persons unpools populations. This unpooling contributes to the fragmentation and dispersal of populations characteristic of liberal risk regimes. The result is a loosening of social solidarity and a lessening of moral community to the point where established ways of thinking about these terms requires revision. As Foucault (1988: 166) recommended, there is 'considerable conceptual work to be done in renewing the conceptual categories that dominate the way we approach all these problems of social guarantees and security ... We completely lack the intellectual tools necessary to envisage in new terms the form in which we might obtain what we are looking for.'

Insurance commodifies all risks, including moral ones, in terms of money. It is therefore an especially instructive vehicle for understanding the relationship between moral regulation and money (Zelizer 1997). Liberal risk regimes place renewed emphasis on money and freedom. Individual financial risk taking rather than state social security is now to provide social guarantees and security; guarantees develop outward from the liberal subject rather than downward from the state.

This last point brings us to where we began Part I. Insurance is the central institution of governance beyond the state. Its liberal risk regimes make up populations on its own institutional territory. Insurance thereby helps to constitute new conceptions of citizenship, participation, social solidarity, and moral community.

Some general questions about governance posed by Rose (1999: 58) apply to the specific case of insurance as governance: 'How have we been made up as governable subjects? What kinds of human beings have we come to take ourselves to be? What presuppositions about our nature are operationalized within strategies that seek to act upon our actions?' The prescription here is consistent with that of Burke (1989).

Sociology teaches us to see how we see. This visualization is accomplished by a relational approach to knowledge in which multiple perspectives are sought and juxtaposed in analysis (Mannheim 1936). The cacophony of voices is not to be molded into a consensus and simple conclusions, but rather seen as itself the answer. It is the incongruity of seeing how we see through multiple lenses that yields critical insight. This is an approach of negation, which includes the trope of irony, seeing something as its opposite. Irony provides critical understanding of what is taken for granted in institutions, which in turn reveals the limits of those institutions.

This approach to sociological understanding requires triangulation as a research strategy (Miles and Huberman 1994). Triangulation allows multiple perspectives to be articulated and engaged in the pursuit of negation and irony. There is to be triangulation of data sources (e.g., persons, times, places), methods (e.g., observations, interviews, document analyses), researchers (e.g., a team field research approach), and data types (e.g., qualitative texts, tape-recorded interviews, observations, quantitative data).

So informed, we entered the practical world of insurance operations. Our focus is on how participants in the insurance institution – for example, company executives, officials, agents, adjusters, expert service providers, consumers, and regulators – govern through moral risks. All three of the book's authors participated in extensive field research, to which 276 researcher days were devoted in 1997, 1998, and 1999. Most field research was conducted in Canada, but we also collected data in the United States.

We conducted 224 open-focused interviews with participants in the insurance institution. All but a few of these interviews were tape-recorded and transcribed. A summary of the types of persons interviewed is presented in table 3.1. Interviewees were selected on the basis of theoretical sampling according to the triangulation approach discussed above. Interviewees were involved in a broad range of life, health, property, and casualty insurance systems.

We interviewed fifty-nine employees of private insurance companies. At the corporate level these interviewees included chief executives, sales executives, claims executives, and specialists in public relations, underwriting, and reinsurance. At the operations level we interviewed employees who specialized in loss prevention, underwriting, marketing, sales, and claims. We also interviewed officials in private insurance industry associations who lobby the state on behalf of the industry, and who provide a number of information and regulatory services to member companies and consumers.

We interviewed thirty people who work in expert systems that serve the insurance industry. These included operators of surveillance data systems for underwriting, claims processing, and fraud investigation. Also included are actuaries, marketing information specialists, and representatives of medical and legal professional associations whose members are governed through insurance systems.

We interviewed ten insurance broker representatives. Three represented large, multinational corporate brokerages whose capitalization exceeds that of many insurance companies. Three were small independent brokers operating their own local agencies. Four represented brokers' associations that try to maintain the interests of brokers in relation to both insurance companies and state regulators.

We interviewed forty-eight employees of state-run insurance operations. Among these, twenty-five were involved in vehicle insurance, eleven in health insurance, ten in workers' compensation insurance, and two in employment insurance. There were seven senior civil servants at the corporate executive and policy levels. Others managed public relations (three), underwriting (two), marketing (two), loss prevention (nine), and claims operations (eleven). A third group was field-level claims adjusters (ten) and fraud investigators (four).

We interviewed twenty-one state representatives who were involved in the regulation of private insurance. Included are four officials responsible for the regulation of how insurance companies invest and manage their assets. Also included are fourteen regulators responsible for the market conduct of private insurance operations, for example, regarding the professional training and standards of sales agents, deceptive sales practices, claims services, and systems for dealing with consumers' complaints. Three elected members of legislatures were also interviewed because of their direct involvement in the legislative process pertaining to insurance industry regulation.

We interviewed fifty-six insurance consumers. Among these, fifty-one were recruited as visitors to Science World in Vancouver. While people stood in line to purchase tickets for Science World, they were asked if they wished to participate in a study of insurance consumption. They were offered the incentive of immediate admission without queuing or charge, as well as a ticket for a future visit. These interviewees were selected entirely on the basis of their willingness to participate in this context. We also interviewed in other contexts two corporate risk

TABLE 3.1
Persons interviewed

Interviewee type	Interviews conducted	
	N	%
Private insurance companies		
Chief executive officers	5	2.2
Public relations	4	1.8
Reinsurance/corporate risk	2	0.9
Underwriters	5	2.2
Loss prevention	4	1.8
Marketing executives	15	6.7
Marketing managers and agents	9	4.0
Claims executives	4	1.8
Claims managers and adjusters	4	1.8
Industry association officials	7	3.1
Subtotal	59	26.3
Private insurance expert systems		
Underwriting information services	6	2.7
Actuarial experts	4	1.8
Marketing information services	4	1.8
Claims information services	4	1.8
Fraud investigation services	8	3.6
Claims service provider associations	4	1.8
Subtotal	30	13.5
Private insurance brokers		
Corporate brokers	3	1.3
Independent agency brokers	3	1.3
Broker associations	4	1.8
Subtotal	10	4.9
State insurance programs		
Policy and planning executives	7	3.1
Public relations	3	1.3
Underwriters	2	0.9
Marketing managers	2	0.9
Loss prevention programs	9	4.0
Claims operations managers	11	4.9
Claims adjusters	10	4.5
Claims fraud investigators	4	1.8
Subtotal	48	21.4

TABLE 3.1
Persons interviewed (*concluded*)

	Interviews conducted	
Interviewee type	*N*	%
Insurance regulation by the state		
Financial regulators	4	1.8
Market conduct regulators	14	6.3
Elected members of legislatures	3	1.3
Subtotal	21	9.4
Insurance consumers		
Individuals	51	22.8
Corporate risk managers	2	0.9
Consumer association representatives	3	1.3
Subtotal	56	25.0
Total	224	100.0

managers who were responsible for deciding on insurance purchases as well as self-insurance (retention) levels. Finally, we interviewed three representatives of consumer associations who had taken on particular cases of advocacy on behalf of insurance consumers.

We observed insurance practices in a variety of contexts. We attended insurance conferences that addressed the future of the industry, corporate management, reinsurance, marketing, and insurance fraud. Selected conference sessions were tape-recorded and transcribed, and we also talked informally with conference participants. We observed insurance sales practices in various contexts: regional sales meetings between managers and agents, call centre operations, and agent-client meetings. We observed claims-processing operations regarding vehicle, health, and workers compensation insurance.

During our interviews and observations, we were given several hundred documents that proved useful for our analysis. From insurance companies, we obtained training and operations manuals for sales agents, claims adjusters, loss prevention inspectors, and fraud investigators; underwriters' rating manuals; marketing research and strategy documents; and sales promotional material. We obtained documents from expert service providers to the insurance industry, for example regarding data systems used in marketing, underwriting, claims processing, and fraud investigation. Insurance brokers provided us with sales material as well as policy documents regarding the rapidly changing sales distribution system. State regulators of insurance practices provided us with documents pertaining to policy, standards of insurance practice, the training and licensing of sales agents, and consumer complaint systems. Corporate risk managers gave us documents on policy and procedures. Consumer association representatives provided material on particular cases of complaint or actions against insurance industry practices. A few individual consumers gave us material pertaining to their specific complaints or actions against the insurance industry.

We are now ready to proceed with our analysis of how insurance governs through moral risks. In Part II, we examine how insurers are governed. In decisions about investment, reinsurance, corporate strategy, and market conduct, insurers pose moral risks to each other, their consumers, and the political economy. These moral risks are governed through a nexus of state regulators, industry associations, insurance company procedures, and expert services. In Part III, we analyse the ways in which the insured are governed. In applying for insurance, engaging in loss prevention efforts, and making claims, the insured pose moral risks to each other, their insurers, and the political economy. These moral risks are governed through myriad surveillance and policing mechanisms.

Part II

GOVERNING THE INSURERS

4. Negotiating Political Economies

Money is indeed the most important thing in the world; and all sound and successful personal and national morality should have this fact for its basis.

George Bernard Shaw, *The Irrational Knot* (1885)

The difference between a little money and no money at all is enormous – and can shatter the world. And the difference between a little money and an enormous amount of money is very slight – and that, also, can shatter the world.

Thornton Wilder, *The Matchmaker* (1955)

Economy is distributive virtue, and consists not in saving but in selection.

Edmund Burke, *Letter to a Noble Lord* (1796)

Insurers have a unique responsibility to remain solvent in order to make good on what they have sold, their promise to pay. In this regard they differ from other inefficient businesses that go bankrupt, which have at least distributed most of the goods paid for by consumers.

Insurance solvency cannot be left to the unfettered effects of the market. The political economies of insurance operations must be negotiated among members of the insurance industry and state regulatory agencies. Negotiation focuses on risk management of loss ratio security. The insurer's loss ratio consists of the following calculation:

Premium revenue
Minus administrative expenses
Minus loss prevention expenses
Minus reinsurance premiums

Minus claims paid
Plus reinsurance claims
Plus investment returns

Although there are many complexities and subtleties, the basic elements of loss ratio security are as follows. The insurer competitively markets its policies to attract premium revenue. Expenses must be paid to administer all aspects of the insurance company operation, for example, marketing, claims processing, expert services (legal, accounting, actuarial, medical), and so on. Expenses are also paid for inspections, surveillance, policing, and educational programs that help to prevent the losses insured against and therefore reduce insurance claims costs. By far the largest potential call on premium revenue is actual claims, which must be kept to a manageable level in order to retain some money for investment. One crucial mechanism for managing the claims level involves the primary insurer taking out its own insurance with other insurance companies: these reinsurers are paid premiums and then become responsible for claims above an agreed-upon level. The money remaining after all of the above expenses have been addressed is invested across a range of products – bonds, equities, real estate, and so on – hopefully allowing the insurer to increase capital and turn a profit.

In this chapter we address, at a general level, the way in which loss ratio security and solvency are achieved through the governance of underwriting, investment, reinsurance, policyholder compensation schemes, and competitive markets. The subtleties of the processes involved, as well as the management of loss prevention and claims, are addressed in subsequent chapters. Every aspect of achieving loss ratio security entails both risk taking and risk management of the insurer's capital. The focus is on who and what to insure on competitive terms; what to invest in; how much of the financial risk to retain or redistribute through reinsurance; how to manage policyholder compensation schemes to cover for failures; and how much to undercut the competition in order to attract business. In each of these decision areas insurers pose substantial moral risks to other parties in the insurance relationship.

Underwriting

One crucial aspect of loss ratio security is the selection and rating of risks to insure. Insurers are not just selling widgets; they are selling the risk selection process itself, that is, the security a good risk pool brings to the consumer (see chapter 7). 'The purchase of insurance is buying the prerogative of entering into a risk pool with (appropriately screened and rated) similar persons ... For the insurer, taking responsibility for an insurance company's solvency means making judgments about the risks or persons who shall be allowed into this community of support' (Gowri 1997: 84–5). Moreover, the insurance consumer as a moral risk is herself a part of the product, because her prevention efforts and claims behaviour affect the nature of the product. 'The insurance product must be kept affordable and viable by ensuring that each participant in a pool is metaphorically pulling her own weight. Higher risks vitiate the product by raising the rates for all' (ibid.).

Underwriting involves uncertainty (Ericson and Doyle forthcoming). New risks arise for which there was no knowledge at the time of underwriting. Moreover, once known, these risks can initially be responded to only in a tentative and speculative manner. For example, environmental liability underwriting was initially conducted in the dark. Insurers wrote occurrence-based policies that meant they were responsible for a pollutant that was there but unknown at the time of underwriting. The eventual payment of billions of dollars in asbestosis liability claims is a case in point. Such long-tailed environmental liability caused many insurance companies to go bankrupt or be taken over. As a result, a 'hard' liability insurance market developed in the 1980s, in which premiums escalated, contract conditions became more stringent, and some insurances were unavailable (Ontario Ministry of Financial Institutions 1986).

An underwriter explained in interview that all underwriting is 'a good bet at a certain time under certain conditions and under certain knowledge.' After discussing a recent incident in which he paid a large claim that would take ten years to recover through premiums from all clients in the book, he said that he would nevertheless keep underwriting in that field. 'Because I think a good creative person as an underwriter is going to find a way to write a deal if they're good. Bad underwriters and inexperienced underwriters decline.' When asked for an example of something he would decline, he said that he draws the line on illegal activity. He recently underwrote an Internet company whose operations included gambling, but excluded the gambling side of the business from the insurance contract. 'You've got to play with what you know and make the bet, and if it's something that really bugs the crap out of you [you drop it].' He said he declined to gamble on gambling in this case because he had read in a Sports Illustrated article that Internet gambling may be illegal. On the other hand, his company was willing to underwrite legal gambling, such as state-run and charitable lotteries. For example, insurance policies were sold to cover lotteries that do not sell enough tickets to meet prize obligations or that experience errors or omissions by their employees and agents. His company once paid a claim to a lottery that experienced a ticket printing error whereby everyone was declared a winner!

Everyday language in the occupational culture of underwriters reflects the gambling aspect. Policyholders in a particular field of insurance constitute a 'book,' they are 'bet' on as risks, and bets are 'laid off' with other bookmakers through reinsurance.

Even fields of insurance that seem most actuarially sound from the viewpoint of experience tables nevertheless contain various elements of gambling in underwriting. Life insurance underwriting is illustrative (for detailed analysis see Ericson and Doyle forthcoming: chap. 2). Life underwriting involves four basic elements of speculation. Mortality rates instruct on normal age-of-death for populations with different characteristics. Persistency rates provide data on how long people hold life insurance policies before allowing them to lapse. Administrative expenses data inform about how much should be charged for the administration of the life insurance policy, especially regarding the high front-end load of paying agents' commissions and setting up contract administration. Investment return projections relate to both policy value, where the contract includes an investment component, and the company's ability to profit from the investment of premiums received.

The actuarial science of mortality tables is well established. Indeed, it was a flagship of early efforts to tame chance (Zelizer 1979; Hacking 1990; Clark 1999). Lifespan for a population is predictable, and insurance rates can be established accordingly. While an individual buys life insurance as a gamble that she will die abnormally, life insurers sell the product in the knowledge that populations die normally.

Insurers have always gambled in the writing of life insurance contracts. Indeed, life insurance was sold long before mortality tables were invented (ibid.). In the present era, the primary speculation is in selling life insurance with investment value. Insurers must make good political economic guesses about the future rates of investment return. They also gamble on various aspects of peoples' medical condition that are subject to the limitations of medical knowledge. AIDS has affected life underwriting, as has the development of drug testing and genetic testing (Novas and Rose 2000). There is even gambling on already under-written policies in this context. For example, there are companies that buy investment-based life insurance policies from people in the AIDS community at less than face value, giving clients money up front and gambling that they will not live too long.

Life companies also gamble on persistency rates. On the one hand, they need to retain policyholders over time to collect premiums, especially over the first few years in order to recover and go beyond front-end sales commission and administrative charges. On the other hand, they sell policies for which premiums become fully paid up after a specified period (but the policy remains in force afterward) as well as policies with fixed premiums. Depending on the investment environment, it is necessary to have predictable lapse rates on these policies. They also sell term life insurance policies to young people, especially those with families, which pay only death benefits. It is profitable to have these people retain these policies during their early and middle years of life by paying premiums, and then drop them as they enter their later and riskier years. The premium structure becomes increasingly steep as people grow older, and there is a strong incentive to terminate the policy and leave the insurance company with years of premiums collected but no benefits paid.

Miscalculation of lapse rates can be costly to companies, although the costs can be spread to higher premiums for new insureds. For example, Canadian life insurers sold a 'Term-to-100' policy with a fixed premium for the policyholder's lifetime. Actuaries guessed wrongly on lapse rates, as relatively few policyholders decided to terminate their contract. Combined with a declining interest rate and investment return environment for life insurance investments, and demands from state regulators for higher reserves on these products, insurers significantly increased premiums for new consumers of these products (*Globe and Mail*, 6 July 1998).

Life underwriting also entails charging various administrative expenses to cover off contract risks, including lapses. These charges are quite steep in the case of more complex investment products. For example, one life insurance company we studied had a range of what it called 'risk charges' associated with its universal life investment products. It increased a number of these 'risk charges' to new policyholders. Previously there was a special charge if the client terminated the policy within three years; this period was extended to nine years. A new 'lapse prevention premium' scale was also introduced, along with a scale for increasing policy value at a proportionately greater level as each year passed. Various additional and new administrative charges were also added, including a steep increase for the costs of insurance coverage which protects policyholders in the case of company bankruptcy. Ironically, unknown to many of them, insureds are compelled to pay for insurance on their insurance company in case it gambles wrongly and fails.

Life insurance gambling also transpires in investment markets. This topic is taken up in detail in the next section, and in chapter 6 where we examine various misselling scandals that have plagued the industry. Apart from their high-rolling activities in various speculative investment markets, life insurers have frequently made bad guesses about basics such as future interest rates. For example, life insurers in the United Kingdom offered guaranteed annuity rates to people buying contracts between the 1950s and 1980s. Miscalculating both mortality and interest rates, they thought they would never have to honour most of their guarantees. They were wrong. In 1999, they faced an estimated £11 billion cost of paying these contracts. One effect has been fundamental weakening of some companies and further consolidation of the industry. The industry has turned to government to help finance this crisis, as well as to legitimate increased charges to policyholders with guaranteed annuity options. A critic of the government's decision to allow insurers to impose charges to policyholders retroactively in order to correct their earlier bad gambling habits observed, 'It is like a car company offering free airbags for drivers and passengers and then at a later date, when a crash occurs and the airbags inflate, to suddenly levy an additional charge' (*The Times* (London), 2 January 1999, p. 22).

Investment

While insurance companies manage their loss ratios through underwriting, administrative cost control, loss prevention initiatives, the policing of claims, and reinsurance, their capacity to absorb large losses as well as to make substantial profits is derived from investment of the money remaining from these activities. Their investment risk taking is both facilitated and cushioned by various mechanisms that effectively insure them. These mechanisms include industry-funded regulatory regimes and policyholder compensation schemes, as well as corporate liability rules that protect some (e.g., directors and officers) more than others (e.g., creditors). Such mechanisms are sources of moral risk to the extent that they reduce insurance company incentives to avoid more risky investments.

In making investments, insurance companies are to operate as prudent persons. A senior civil servant responsible for financial industry regulation told us that the prudent person rule means the investor must treat other peoples' money as if it was her own, 'presuming that you would handle your money competently and wisely and not gamble it away.' Regulators largely assess prudence not in terms of a given single investment, but how that investment relates to a company's investment portfolio and to its wider practices in financial risk management. However, as another senior financial industry regulator observed, the problem is that prudence can only be assessed by experience, and experience often proves wrong in retrospect. 'How do we know the future? It is like horse racing, you can go on past performance, but there are regular examples of how probability statistics based on the past fail to foretell the future.'

Since gambling is endemic to the enterprise, the key to solvency, and to the hope of profits, is how the bets are spread. A regulator of insurance company solvency said her assessments are based on 'the way that a company off-loads the risks that it cannot handle or chooses not to handle.' The allowable risks vary in relation to the specifics of each insurance company.

Capital management involves a range of interrelated practices that trade off risks and returns (see for example Canadian Life and Health Insurance Association 1997b). Insurers must hedge their bets to control their exposure to something that may be too risky, but this hedging may in turn pose additional or alternative risks. There are significant exposures regarding, for example, the management of securities portfolios, real estate portfolios, credit risks, interest rate risks, and foreign exchange rate and settlement risks. One single element in this constellation can cause serious problems if not managed properly, as we will see shortly in our analysis of insurance company failures. For example, there are substantial risks simply in the arrangements by which foreign exchange transactions are settled. In its 1996 *Annual Report*, the Canadian Federal Office of the Superintendent of Financial Institutions noted that in April 1995, worldwide daily foreign exchange trades were estimated to be $1.23 trillion. This level 'combined with the global interdependencies of FX market and payment system participants, raises significant concerns regarding the risk stemming from current arrangements for FX trades.'

The management of these various fields of financial risk is in turn related to the proper management of underwriting, financial liabilities, and liquidity of assets. Underwriting and liability management entail controlling the risk of exposure to financial losses resulting from obligations to policyholders. Liquidity management involves means to ensure that funds are available when needed to pay claims and other major expenses, including certain investment losses. Operating liquidity is required to meet short-term needs. Strategic liquidity is required for political economic change regarding economic and market conditions, regulatory and political environments, consumer preferences and confidence, product design and administration procedure, and forms of concentration of insurable risks.

In order to juggle all of these aspects of risk spreading, insurance companies require systems of corporate governance that articulate with state regulation. These systems are analysed in chapter 5. There is a need for internal control procedures regarding the everyday practices of directors, managers, and employees, as well as independent audits that provide external control.

There is a need to manage insurance companies that are part of conglomerates in relation to the possibility of contagion risk: one of the companies in the conglomeration may be imprudently exposed to investment or insured risks in a manner that drains resources from the others. Contagion risk was a problem, for example, in the aforementioned environmental liability crisis, where some companies suffered from their partners' exposure to perpetual environmental claims and were eventually forced to drop their ties to them.

The investment practices of an insurance company play back on its underwriting and claims practices. The financial strength of an insurance company affects the very definition of certain kinds of losses, for example, catastrophic losses, which in turn affects how risks are rated, how claims are paid, how coverage will be altered after a loss, and so on. Investment and underwriting are inextricably related.

An example of how much investment-related risk a major insurance company is willing to pose to other parties is provided by the case of Confederation Life. The following account of the Confederation Life failure relies heavily on the excellent analysis by McQueen (1996).

As of the mid-1990s, Confederation Life was the largest-ever North American insurance company failure, and the fourth largest financial institution failure worldwide. However, its failure was not unique in the Canadian context. Both Sovereign Life and Les Coopérants Mutual

Life Assurance Society collapsed in 1992, and for many of the same reasons, relating especially to imprudent real estate market investment and financing. At the point of collapse, Confederation Life faced unmet liabilities to life and health insurance policyholders of $450 million in Canada ($275 million of which was covered by the industry compensation scheme, CompCorp), and $800 million in the United States. Trade creditors and bond and commercial bond holders faced unmet liabilities of $1.3 billion.

Confederation Life diversified enormously in the 1980s, exemplifying Milton Friedman's (1988) view that 'the social responsibility of business is to make profits.' For example, it developed a wide range of new insurance products, operated both a trust company and a lease financing company, and invested in derivatives and real estate. The contagion risk among some of these operations spread rapidly and unchecked, and that risk proved fatal.

The major problem was Confederation Life's participation in speculative real estate markets and the way in which its trust company operation was used in this regard. Rather than being encouraged to manage money conservatively, company officers were given strong incentives to be aggressive in an area they knew little about. For example, executives of the trust company were paid multi-million dollar bonuses to lend aggressively at the height of the real estate market, and they and their wives also profited from the 'flipping' of condominiums sold to them by the trust company's largest borrower. The federal government's Superintendent of Financial Institutions observed in retrospect that real estate investment was 'fashionable' at the time and '"I do not believe there were many well articulated strategies that reflected a real understanding of the risks involved in real estate lending ... little of this dealt with what could happen if the inflationary assumptions about resale prices and rental rates did not pan out"' (Superintendent McKenzie, quoted by McQueen 1996: 66).

By 1989, 74 per cent of Confederation Life's assets were tied up in real estate-related investments (compared to 30 to 40 per cent for other major Canadian life and health insurance companies), and these investments were debt financed to exceptional levels (141 per cent of surplus, compared to, for example, 4 per cent in the case of Sun Life of Canada). Moreover, in the very high interest rate environment of the time, they were paying around 12 per cent interest on this debt and therefore required ongoing investment returns of at least 15 per cent to be profitable. When the capital value of their real estate holdings dropped 40 per cent by 1994, they were holding properties and debt that proved too much to bear. As a regulator indicated to us in interview, Confederation Life had a self-made 'mismatch problem': too much investment in commercial property mortgages without proper expertise, financed with short-term commercial bonds. 'And that is something you don't do! A management problem. Way too aggressive. They thought they would just keep receiving those commercial rates and people would just come in. It doesn't happen. They are downgraded and no one wants to touch this anymore.'

This very aggressive investment stance was part of Confederation Life's effort to become a diversified financial services company. The four relatively autonomous sectors of the financial services industry in Canada were converging. Banks were especially aggressive, acquiring trust companies, establishing insurance operations, and expanding discount stock brokerages and mutual fund sales operations. These institutional shifts in the financial services marketplace also entailed the proliferation of new products, and of the means of distributing them. For example, Confederation Life eliminated its 'captive' (career) sales agent system and distributed through various broker and agent commission sales networks. These new sales agents, inexperienced with the company, were asked to sell new products they were also unfamiliar with. Seventy-five per cent of the products were new, and sensitive to the interest rate environment. Forced to be aggressive in fields they knew little about, agents participated in various forms of misselling. Their misselling was underpinned by sales documents in the United States that misrepresented the sources of consumer protection available to policyholders. Not surprisingly, class action suits followed in a number of states, including Georgia, New York, and New Jersey. Company employees also suffered. While they may previously have trusted the company and felt secure in its employ, they eventually lost jobs, insurance benefit packages, and a sense of worth. Retired employees on company pensions also lost some benefits.

While the risk regime of Confederation Life was liberalizing, there was little regulatory control within its own corporate governance system, the industry, or the state. Many corporate governance mechanisms were weak or side-stepped. Some financial transactions among internal units were so complex that efforts to audit them were dropped. McQueen (1996: 108) describes an internal system for borrowing and transferring funds as just a mockery of a legitimate creditor-debtor relationship. CTSL [Confederation Treasury Services Ltd.] would not pay off any loans; it had no funds other than what it borrowed. All it could do, was expected to do, and did do, was shuffle money from one pocket to another and roll over the notes that came due. The system CTSL had created was rather like the national debt. Just as governments and society became addicted to spending, so did Confed. Just as governments thought for a time that deficits could pile up to the sky, so did Confed think that it could consume its internal funds and create new businesses without worrying about the cost or eventual repayment of those funds.

The CEO of Mutual Life Assurance Company of Canada concurred with this view that insurance companies behaved just like the state during this period. "'We created the illusion of increasing prosperity, while actually creating a sharply increasing debt. Asset values rose, creating the illusion of profitability and increasing capital, which enabled companies which were in fact eroding their real capital base to publish results which appeared to be buoyant'" (ibid.: 121).

The illusions of grandeur about profitability blended with illusions of invulnerability. Within the corporate culture, serious problems could be denied with reference to company tradition, status, and size. Of course such illusions become realities: participants in the system think and act as if their regime is invulnerable.

Regulators did not intervene in the liberties being taken by Confederation Life. There were clear signs that gambling was rampant. Annual company growth was 25 per cent over one period. As U.S. insolvency expert Victor Palmieri observed in retrospect, with a growth rate of that magnitude, "'you sense that management is on a game of its own, that's all you have to know. You don't have to look at the financial statements. All you have to know is you've got the typical autocratic leader selling you his vision of the future, and there is no tomorrow. That was the time to bail out'" (ibid.: 250).

Some games escaped the notice of regulators. For example, some of the mortgage deals made by Confederation Trust were so complex that they escaped regulators' attention entirely. However, regulators made it clear that it was not their job to micro-manage companies. Imprudence is commonplace, and the state's responsibility is limited to the protection of policyholders. Since CompCorp arrangements were in place, as well as industry plans to acquire the profitable sides of Confederation Life, policyholders would receive most, if not all, of the protection and benefits promised. As a regulator explained in interview, Confederation Life 'wasn't prudent ... and that's exactly what happens. You get this situation in financial institutions and it happens over and over again ... there's a lot of subordinate debenture holders that are going to lose everything, but no policyholder will have lost anything and gee, you know, in our business we call that regulatory success. And it would appear, given that, the federal government entered the situation at the correct time.'

In a crisis of capital, Confederation Life could not sell more insurance to raise capital because it no longer had a sufficient capital reserve base. The company could not be sold because it was a mutual rather than a stock company. In conjunction with an industry consortium, a federal government loan was sought to help with a buyout. However, the federal government did not want to add further moral risks to its relationships with the industry and refused to assist in the financial restructuring of Confederation Life. The regulators only brokered selected arrangements after the fact, such as deals with liquidators and rehabilitators. As a regulator stated in interview,

> the government didn't even think for one minute ... about the request for a bridge loan to help the consortium to actually buy Confederation out. They didn't take forty-five seconds to decide – 'No bloody way!' – and with that we closed the third largest insurance company, basically the biggest international insurance insolvency, on an assessment. It was manageable in a public, political kind of sense. And so, I happen to think that fact of increasing public, political, parliamentary acceptance of insolvency is a good thing, because ultimately if people – yeah the regulatory system has got a responsibility to prevent undue loss – but undue loss doesn't mean no loss. And if people in the system think that everything is going to be saved, behaviour is going to be perverse.

This regulator said that the federal government's response marked a substantial shift in its approach to financial service industry failure. In the early 1980s 'two tiny, miniscule Western [Canadian] banks' had cost '$1.6 billion of real money – not deposit insurance charged back to the industry money – real money from taxpayers in an attempted bail out.' The new approach shifted responsibility to the companies – for example, requiring them to finance policyholder protection programs such as CompCorp – and to consumers who, more than ever, must respect caveat emptor. As the Superintendent of Financial Institutions declared in the wake of the Confederation Life failure, risk and responsibility must reside in the liberal risk regimes of the corporations themselves. 'Failure is a fact of life in the United States ... In Canada, we have difficulty coming to terms with it. In Canada, when people lose money there is a need to search for a villain who is always by definition not the person who loses the money. We have to mature as a country and part of that maturity is to allow failure of financial services companies' (quoted by McQueen 1996: 258).

Other companies demonstrated little inclination to protect Confederation Life, or indeed their own image. Instead the major industry players jostled, negotiated, and then circled like vultures to acquire the profitable areas of business that remained in the Confederation Life portfolios. Great West Life insurance company was given the lead role in a possible restructuring arrangement. This company was given liberal access to Confederation Life documents and processes, and it therefore acquired greater knowledge of operations than either government regulators or Confederation Life executives themselves. This knowledge positioned Great West Life to acquire profitable areas of the business. Thus, 'the due-diligence process was more like rape than prelude to marriage' (McQueen 1996: 182–3). The minister responsible for financial regulation of the insurance industry observed, 'The Canadian government and Department of Finance were far more concerned with the reputation of Canadian insurance companies than were the Canadian insurance companies. If they had been concerned with their reputation, they would have made sure that Confed did not fail, and they would have taken a much more active interest in developing a solution' (ibid.: 219–20).

The $275 million industry payment to policyholders under the CompCorp scheme was in effect a business expense for the companies participating in the acquisition process (ibid.: 231). Besides, as we have seen, policyholders are required to pay premiums to CompCorp as insurance on their insurance, so that this business expense was also at the expense of policyholders. None of the Confederation Life directors and officers faced sanctions beyond the shame of what was seen in retrospect, by some, as too much risk taking. The president of Confederation Life could offer nothing more than a farewell dinner speech in which he in effect echoed the Superintendent of Financial Institution's statement that consuming populations in liberal risk regimes must accept responsibility for failures in those regimes. 'As I look into the new century, I sense a return to those older values that drove people to be self-reliant, to take responsibility for their own future and that of their families' (ibid.: 158).

Reinsurance

Reinsurance is a key ingredient in loss ratio security. A given company may decide to reinsure because it does not have sufficient capacity to take on a given risk itself, or because it wants to further distribute the risks in its overall portfolio. Industry-funded compensation schemes for policyholders, such as the CompCorp scheme, also constitute a form of reinsurance in that they provide for the indemnification of the policyholders of a company that is unable to meet its contractual obligations.

The world of reinsurance and compensation schemes is ripe with moral risks. Insurance companies involved in reinsurance contracts want to lay off risks with companies that are prudent, have good contractual practices, are well managed, and work with other reinsurers of high standing. To this end, they inspect and audit each other and work through reinsurance brokers who provide ongoing intelligence about companies. With large premiums and claims stakes involved, there is often distrust of other insurance companies as policyholders, just as there is regarding individuals as policyholders.

Reinsurance is an arrangement in which an insurance company contracts to indemnify another insurance company for losses sustained under policies it has issued. The first company is the primary or ceding company and the second company is the reinsurer. Some reinsurance agreements are 'facultative,' protecting specific individual risks on a contract offer and acceptance basis. Other agreements are based on a reinsurance 'treaty,' protecting a block of the primary company's business rather than giving the reinsurer the right to reject on a per risk basis.

The portion of the risk insured by the primary company is the retention level. For example, on a $20 million insurance exposure, the primary company may keep only $2 million coverage and spread the remaining $18 million among various reinsurers. In the event of a claim, the primary company covers payments up to $2 million, the first reinsurer covers losses in excess of this amount up to its specified limit, and so on.

Small insurance companies reinsure most of their policies, and at very high levels. Reinsurance is the price of loss ratio security and solvency because a single catastrophe would ruin them. As an actuary said in interview, 'That is what the farm mutual is doing by reinsuring, is laying it off like a bookie does at a racetrack.' In contrast, large insurance companies have high retention levels, similar to the large bookmaking firms in the racing industry. Not laying off the risk is also a bet, but one that large companies are usually able to take without fear of insolvency.

A multinational insurance company we studied was in the process of reducing reinsurance. As explained by a senior underwriter, 'We've been treating out too much, we've been impairing our growth and profitability.' A senior executive explained the company's approach: 'Unlike some other companies, which will lay a lot off to reinsurance, we've differentiated ourselves in the market by being an underwriting company making an underwriting profit consistently. And in doing so, we have very strict underwriting guidelines that *we force our underwriters to take the bet on*, as opposed to laying a lot of it off to reinsurers.'

The scale of retention can be very substantial. For example, in its 1996 Annual Report, the Chubb Insurance Company recorded a retention level for each catastrophic event of $US100 million. In the previous three years, it paid out catastrophic losses of $US375 million, with no single incident being above the retention level.

Large companies can also decide to 'go naked' and not carry any reinsurance in significant areas. A senior actuary told us in interview that this was the approach taken by a large British multinational company in the mid-1980s regarding certain fields of catastrophic insurance. In 1987, they suffered approximately £300 million in claims following a storm in Britain. A storm resulting in claims of a similar scale was repeated two years later. 'Even at that, they didn't regret it ... over the next decade they saved well over the amount of money they would have got out of a reinsurance claim.' This interviewee said that his company was currently 'going naked' with respect to potential losses resulting from an earthquake in British Columbia. 'We haven't had an earthquake yet ... and, if we do, it is only $80 million [in projected losses].'

Large companies can also afford reinsurance exchanges with each other. At one time Sun Alliance Group and the Chubb Group had a reinsurance exchange regarding their respective property and casualty blocks of business. The Chubb proportion was reinsured with the Sun Alliance Group on a quota share basis (i.e., reinsurers share the same portion of the losses as they do the premiums of the ceding company).

A subsidiary of Chubb in turn assumed a portion of the Sun Alliance Group's property and casualty business on the same basis (Chubb *Annual Report* 1996).

The decision to lay off bets with other insurers is related to the primary insurer's expertise in the insurance product concerned. We studied a large company specializing in disability insurance. A company official said, 'We keep virtually all of the risk because we feel that we're even more sophisticated in our actuarial experience than the reinsurers are. We might use reinsurers for audit.'

When the primary insurer is specializing in a niche market, there may be parts of the market that it can retain and profit from greatly, while other parts are best spread and pooled through global reinsurers. We studied a company that specialized in accidental death and dismemberment insurance. Some aspects of this market were subject to actuarial knowledge and control by the primary company, for example, policies for school children. Other aspects were too specialized for sufficient knowledge and reasonable pooling, for example, accidental death and dismemberment insurance for executives who face war zone risks while travelling. In these cases, Lloyd's of London took all of the risk and the originating company was simply the agent.

Multinational reinsurance companies have become more involved in direct underwriting. This greater involvement is linked to more specialized risk pools and insurance products. Such market segmentation, and involvement of reinsurers in it, has characterized the life and health insurance industry in particular. Speaking at a conference of insurance brokers, a reinsurance company representative said, 'In the old days, usually reinsurance means you spread around the risk on large cases ... [Today, using reinsurance on specialized life and health insurance products] you get better pricing, you can deal with all kinds of risks, you can leverage your capital much better, you get better return on your investment, you can get coverage in broader areas. More and more insurance is being reinsured. Say twenty to thirty years ago it was only about 6 or 8 per cent of insurance in Canada was later reinsured. Now it is over 30 per cent, probably closer to 35 per cent.'

A colleague from the same reinsurance company noted a related competitive trend. As banks and other direct sellers of term life insurance move into the market, adverse selection problems arise because the healthier members of the population switch to the direct sellers and the less healthy higher risks remain with the traditional companies. Reinsurers then move into the traditional market, and primary insurers lay off the higher risks of these remaining policyholders with them.

While direct underwriting from reinsurers is invited in some cases, it is unwelcome in others. A significant component of the fiercely competitive insurance market is that 'reinsurers are coming direct to brokers looking for business that might not find its way to them otherwise, offering unusual programs to draw premium from the traditional markets' (Sedgwick 1997: 10). Many insurance company officials we talked to addressed this trend and how it was being resisted. For example, a commercial insurance underwriter identified one of the world's largest reinsurers as 'specifically going directly to brokers and sometimes to clients and saying, "We want to underwrite your insurance." And they'll cut a deal directly with them, cut out the companies ... Most insurers are refusing to deal with them because of that.'

These comments illustrate the tensions that characterize reinsurance relationships. Reinsurance involves a complex blend of trust and moral risk assessments in underwriting decisions. On treaty contracts, the reinsurer is underwriting the primary insurer as a company. It therefore assesses the company itself as a moral risk and looks for signs that the company is trustworthy. We interviewed the vice-president of a primary insurance company who was in charge of managing reinsurance arrangements for his company. He observed that reinsurers 'Underwrite the company ... [and there is] a moral hazard in underwriting the company ... If you have a treaty with a reinsurer, a group of reinsurers, they're essentially giving you their pens. You have the authority to underwrite business and to give a part to them ... And they don't see the individual policies or risks that are in there ... [So] we have to keep a certain amount before we can involve them. We have to have a financial interest in it as well ... that reinsurer has to have *faith* in the company.'

As this interviewee stresses, the first sign of trust is the level of risk the primary insurer is willing to retain. If the primary insurer accepts a significant portion of the risk, it is seen as having a commitment to careful underwriting, effective loss prevention, and vigilant claims control that protects reinsurers. In this respect the retention level is similar to the deductible in an insurance policy held by an individual.

Second, reinsurers audit primary insurers to ensure that they have acceptable underwriting, loss prevention, and claims processes in place. The audits include random selection and scrutiny of the primary company's files, and sometimes questioning of the parties involved in the cases represented by the files. Audits also scrutinize the primary insurer's financial status in relation to its competitive position in the industry.

Third, reputation through association with other good companies is a basis of trust. If the primary insurer has ongoing collaboration with other good companies that underwrite large, complex, and profitable reinsurance, its own reputation is cultivated. Good associations indicate that the primary insurer has an expert network to draw upon in underwriting risks it may not be familiar with itself. Reinsurers are more likely to agree to participate in a marginal case if they know that both expertise and financial risk is spread across a network of other good companies.

Fourth, experience is a related basis of trust in reinsurance relationships. Profitable collaborations over time fuel confidence and lead to more elaborate and risky arrangements on marginal cases.

Fifth, because substantial moral risks always linger, informal networks among primary insurers, reinsurers, and reinsurance brokers are crucial to making deals. In major 'transactions, everyone looks beyond the financial statement, auditing, and procedural criteria to discover details of the corporate cultures of partners. The subjective aspects of who the key players are in each company, and the specifics of recent deals they have made, are key forms of knowledge in reinsurance risk taking.

Many of the dimensions described above are revealed in a case recalled by an interviewee whose company was working on a 'stop loss' reinsurance deal. Stop loss reinsurance is coverage initiated when a primary insurer's loss ratio rises above a pre-established percentage. For example, a primary insurer may reinsure the dollar value of all claims that are above 75 per cent of the premiums it has received. This form of treaty typically offers protection only when the primary insurer has exhausted all of its other reinsurance in relation to the specified product. Stop loss is in effect insurance on the primary insurance company's underwriting.

The moral risks entailed in stop loss reinsurance are obvious. The primary insurer may take less care in issuing policies and increase the riskiness of the pool. It may also be less concerned about governing the moral risks of its policyholders, and thus loosen contract conditions and surveillance mechanisms that force policyholders to participate in loss prevention. It may also loosen its policing of excessive and fraudulent claims if it knows that its loss ratio is protected above a pre-established level.

The interviewee working on the stop loss reinsurance deal was employed by a large property and casualty insurer. He explained that the greatest concern was the company's vehicle insurance loss ratio, which might be adversely affected by an upturn in the economy. In effect, the company was seeking protection against economic change, 'the one in one hundred chance of an economic upturn and the rating we have set being inadequate ... [an estimated] $200M deviation from the expected value of claims.' With an upturn in the economy, vehicle accident claims increase significantly because more people buy cars, most of which are newer and more expensive; these people drive greater distances; and many of them are inexperienced drivers. This combination of factors entails an increase in the accident rate, which in turn creates the deviation from the expected value of claims and the need for reinsurance.

The company had been out of the reinsurance market for five years, choosing to 'go naked' instead. The interviewee said that it was not a problem to cover a major catastrophic loss, such as the crash of a school bus resulting in $90 million in claims, or an earthquake resulting in $80 million in claims. These claims could be covered by, for example, a 2 per cent premium rate increase across the board over a period of two years. But a $200 million deviation from the expected loss ratio was of greater concern.

The problem was that since the company had been out of the reinsurance market for five years, it had lost much of its good association, experience, and networking credentials with reinsurers. In order to regain standing it might have to buy catastrophic accident risk reinsurance and earthquake risk reinsurance at premiums of, say, $2 million each annually, in order to obtain what it really wanted, namely, stop loss reinsurance. The interviewee estimated stop loss reinsurance would carry an annual premium of $15–$20 million to cover the 1 per cent chance of $200 million in extra claims brought on by an economic upturn.

> We have no 'bank' in the marketplace ... We have no exposure in the marketplace, and therefore the trust of the marketplace. Reinsurance is a business built on trust. Believe it or not, a bunch of thieves trusting each other ... The trust that is developed from being involved in the marketplace, showing your hands. Because every time you go into the reinsurance market, you have to take your company's position with you, your claims record and all that stuff, them getting to know you and you know them.

And they say, 'This chap is OK. We'll sell him this coverage for $2 million rather than $2.5 million.' Or, 'We don't like that guy. We don't trust him. We won't even sell him this reinsurance coverage.'

Stop loss reinsurance requires particular trust and credibility because the relationship carries substantial moral risks. 'If you buy reinsurance that is associated with your operating ... just through sheer sloppiness and not paying attention, your claims can grow ... They could examine [underwriting data] and put their spin on them. What they can't do though is determine whether we will be, having bought this, whether we will then lapse into carelessness ... There is a moral hazard attached to it. So they cannot tell that ahead of time, unless they begin to trust you ... by knowing you ... and knowing the company.'

The interviewee felt that building a record with catastrophic accident and earthquake reinsurance would mean that

you are exposing yourself to the marketplace and allowing the marketplace to judge you and be comfortable with you ... [By 'going naked' without reinsurance we] wiped out this trust. If we kept up [catastrophic accident and earthquake reinsurance] for the sake of a couple of million dollars a year – or maybe less actually ... we'd have been able much more readily to be back to the market to buy it [stop loss reinsurance] for $10 million rather than $15 million because they trust us. When you go back to the market now after all of these years, not having been near the market, then the price is going to be more like $15 million to $20 million because they don't know us and don't trust us ... The trouble is, insurance people are just as much thieves and robbers as anybody else in this world [laughs] ... and there is a genuine moral hazard attached to this.

This interviewee emphasizes that reinsurers treat the primary insurance company as a moral risk in the same manner as the primary insurance company treats the individual policyholder. Premiums are steep. Another property and casualty primary insurer we studied paid $12 million each year for $400 million in catastrophic reinsurance coverage, the main concern being earthquakes and major storms. Over several decades, it had paid out hundreds of millions of dollars in premiums without any claims at higher levels of reinsurance. Its only significant claim followed a hailstorm in which reinsurers at lower levels paid out about $8 million, after the company itself had paid out to its retention limit of $15 million. As is the case with insurance claims by individuals, reinsurance claims are met with higher premiums. The head of reinsurance for this company stated, 'It's not like you can pass the risk on to them ... If you have losses that hit [above] that [retention] level, you're going to be paying them back essentially over a period of years.'

The interviewee employed by the company seeking stop loss reinsurance also emphasized that repeated claims, or a single claim indicating the primary insurer is a serious risk, result in a cancellation of reinsurance. Cancellation bears stigmatization, which makes it difficult to obtain reinsurance elsewhere. As in other business enterprises, the inability to obtain insurance signals the company's demise. 'There is no need to go to court, the reinsurance people just pay the case and walk away from it. And they assume that in the [reinsurance] marketplace that that insurance company will get nothing in the future. And that insurance company will be out of business pretty shortly. That's the way of dealing with it.'

Given what is at stake with premiums and the moral risks of the reinsurance relationship, primary insurance companies are also careful about their partnerships. One sign of systemic risks is the fact that primary insurers provide contingency reserves for reinsurance that is not recoverable. For example, the annual report of a life and health insurer notes,

> Reinsurance ceded does not discharge the Company's liability as the primary insurer. Failure of reinsurers to honour their losses could result in losses to the Company; consequently, allowances are established for amounts deemed uncollectable. A contingent liability exists should an assuming company be unable to meet its obligations ... The Company evaluates the financial condition of its reinsurers and monitors concentrations of credit risk arising from similar geographic regions, activities, or economic characteristics of the reinsurers to minimize its exposure to losses from reinsurer insolvency. (Seaboard 1996: 17–18)

We interviewed a corporate risk manager for a property and casualty insurance company who was responsible for maintaining the intelligence system on reinsurers. He described his task as 'assessing the long-term financial state of the reinsurers that we're dealing with. Because reinsurance is a longer-term transaction, especially in some lines ... we do an annual review of all the companies that are in our program, we get current financial information ... Standard and Poor's or Best's ... minimum criteria, certain size, profitability ratings, growth ratings.' He said that these reviews provide some confidence, but that additional intelligence is necessary. To this end he contracted with four reinsurance brokers to obtain 'back room' and 'street' knowledge of 'what is behind the figures.' The use of four brokers is an effort to spread the risk further, because they each have strengths and weaknesses in their reinsurance intelligence networks. He said that these brokers have

> very large back shop operations ... [for example] a team in New York that does nothing but analyse the companies. And they get a lot of street information that isn't available from just looking at the numbers, intangibles. Yes, this number looks like this, but it's because so-and-so is doing this. So-and-so has left the company and gone to this company. And this company is really owned by this company. And in the background, even though this subsidiary's number may not look as good, in the background there's a parental guarantee that its massive parent will bail out if something goes wrong ... I can give these guys a call if I've got concerns and say, 'OK, here's what isn't really apparent' ... If we're looking at a parental relationship, or say a massive European holding company actually owns all of these subsidiaries, the existence or absence of a guarantee of the subsidiary liabilities would be crucial. If we get word that there is one we would normally ask for a copy of it just to see how iron clad it is. Some of them aren't worth the paper they're printed on, because they'll say we'll guarantee the liabilities, unless we change our mind and say not [laughs] ... You want something that's irrevocable, definitely guaranteed. And again we're dealing with things that may not show up for twenty years, on some of the liability areas specifically ... some of the claims don't show up for a decade.

This type of surveillance and documentation is necessary not only because of the assumption of distrust, but also because of the complex system of global reinsurance. Reinsurers spread their own risks by taking out further reinsurance, a practice called retrocession. A retrocession assemblage may be so complex that few if any parties know its full extent and details. Therefore, although a primary insurer may investigate its immediate reinsurance partners, its knowledge of how they in turn spread their risks is minimal or non-existent, first and foremost because the reinsurers themselves often do not know. We interviewed an earthquake insurance underwriter for a multinational property and casualty insurer. As someone responsible for reinsuring the company's earthquake exposure, he observed,

> I've never asked a reinsurer who they're sharing risk with around the world because as it gets further and further away from the initial transaction, if it's diluted so much, who knows where the dollars come from and go to? Similarly it's not really my business to ask them who are my competitors they're working with ... We're a close enough industry that when ABC Reinsurance comes to town, I'll say, 'What have you been doing for the last couple of days?' 'Well, I had lunch with Commonwealth, and then I went over to Lombard and I'm visiting Zurich this afternoon.' You get a *feeling* for who your competitors are dealing with in terms of reinsurance.

A vice-president in charge of reinsurance for a property and casualty insurer said that this inability to penetrate the abstract system of retrocession is why reserves must be held in case of system failure. He pointed to the well-publicized Lloyd's retrocession debacle in the 1980s as a case in point (see Luessenhop and Mayer 1995; Mantle 1992):

> LMX, London Market Excess ... where different Lloyd's syndicates would buy protection from other Lloyd's syndicates on their book of business, and that Lloyd's syndicate would buy it from another one, and it could come all around a circle so that the original person that ceded off that risk got it back again. After having gone through five or six other syndicates, each of them taking their own position or a little bit off of it, at the end of the day they were not able to tell how much risk they had ... They were all going in these big circles and circling back [laughs] ... they wouldn't necessarily know what was in the basket because it was a treaty.

Another example is provided by the Unicover Pool case (*Financial Post*, 17 July 1999; *The Times* (London) 14 July 1999; *BestWire*, 22 June 1999; *BestWire*, 8 March 1999). A group of workers' compensation insurers in the United States worked through reinsurance brokers, including Lloyds and their LMX syndicates, to create a reinsurance pool called Unicover Managers Inc. Initial reinsurer participants in the pool included Sun Life of Canada, Phoenix Home Life Mutual, and Cologne Reinsurance, who in turn involved several other companies in a spiral of retrocession that in some cases was four or five layers deep.

According to allegations by Sun Life of Canada (*Financial Post*, 7 July 1999), the primary workers' compensation companies sold policies at a rate that was fifty-two times the original estimate of premium revenue. Unicover told reinsurers it would underwrite US$150 million worth of policies in three years, but after one year it had generated US$7.8 billion in premiums! The primary insurers were able to obtain this level of premiums because they sold at prices that discounted expected losses at 30 to 40 per cent, then ceded their risk to the fronting reinsurer. The companies brought in at successive layers of reinsurance were unaware of the levels of premium and policy commitments and did not cover the risks assumed. Eventually they became swamped by claims for which they had not financed coverage, and Unicover closed to new business. The losses suffered by the reinsurers were estimated to be up to US$2 billion. Sun Life of Canada said its expected losses were US$700 million, or about 10 per cent of surplus, but assured the public this amount would not have material impact on the company.

Sun Life of Canada charged Unicover Managers Inc. with 'deliberate misconduct,' saying it 'grossly underestimated the volume of business of the reinsurance pool' (ibid.). Meanwhile, retrocessionaire Allianz initiated lawsuits against Sun Life of Canada, claiming it duped them. An expert in a securities firm was quoted by *BestWire* (8 March 1999) as stating, 'The pool participants all knew, or should have, that [Unicover] pool was playing reinsurance arbitrage, or "pass the trash."' The *Financial Times* (17 July 1999) also observed that 'In the industry, it's called "pass the trash," and the idea is to pass the risk to someone else and hang on to as much of the premium as possible. Said one analyst: "The problem is everyone thinks they have ceded the risk, and it's not clear where the thing ends, it's just a bowl of spaghetti."' As in the Lloyds debacle in the 1980s, 'Analysts say the pool's structure may have been a spiral with so many layers that some companies assumed risk they originally passed on to someone else' (*BestWire*, 8 March 1999).

The fraud can be even more blatant. For example, in another swindle involving Lloyds (*Sunday Times*, 14 March 1999), fronting offshore insurance companies were able to entice unsuspecting commercial firms as well as developing countries with discounted prices. They used a trick called 'asset-rental' in which they borrowed or rented assets from legitimate companies to demonstrate the viability of their financial statements. They bolstered credibility further by paying small claims. However, when a large claim was made, the offshore insurance company was put into liquidation and the swindlers escaped with their money. Other insurers were left to pay the bill, estimated as high as £100 million, through industry compensation schemes and reinsurance treaties. Ultimately they would have to pass the costs on to policyholders through higher premiums (for additional case studies, see Tillman 2002).

Compensation

The risk of insurance company insolvency is also addressed through compensation arrangements for policyholders. In this section, we consider the example of CompCorp, established by the Canadian Life and Health Insurance Association (CLHIA).

In negotiations over the formation of CompCorp, life and health insurers wanted the government to provide a state insurance scheme for policyholders similar to the Canadian Deposit Insurance Corporation (CDIC) scheme for individual account holders with banks, trust companies, and credit unions. CDIC compensates an individual account holder up to $60,000 in the event of failure of a deposit-taking institution. Among the industry arguments was the fact that about one-half of their revenues were derived from annuities and life policy investment products that compete with bank and trust company deposits. They estimated that about $100 billion in Canadians' savings were with insurance companies (Daw and Ferguson 1995: 34).

The federal government rejected industry arguments in this regard. A member of Parliament told us in interview that the CHLIA lobby for CDIC-like protection was opposed because the consequences of an insurance company collapse are not nearly as significant as a major bank's collapse. A federal government regulator of financial institutions concurred, saying that CDIC is more directed at 'systems stability' in the deposit-taking sector. The life and health insurance sector has the capacity to take over a weak company, or to liquidate the best parts of a failed company's business to competitors, as happened with Confederation Life.

The most fundamental argument, however, was that the government did not like CDIC but could not get rid of it for political reasons. They did not like it because it is morally risky at the level of both deposit-taking institution directors and officers, and at the level of individual depositors. At the corporate level, CDIC encourages excessive risk taking. A regulator explained that

with a 100 per cent deposit insurance, there's not sufficient incentives for institutions and their boards of directors to adequately manage the institution. There's an incentive for them to put the costs of their excessive risk taking back to the government ... [like] savings and loans in the United States ... As a private owner, you bear virtually no cost of the downside if the gamble doesn't work because the costs of that gamble on your customers are covered by the government through the deposit insurance system. On the other hand, if the gamble works and you do find the upside, you as the private owner benefit ... As a result you will encourage excessive risk taking and the corporate behaviour by the private market is protected by consumer deposit insurance ... That kind of moral hazard problem exists because of deposit insurance.

Deposit insurance is also a moral risk at the level of depositors. Investors are attracted to higher yielding investments with less prudent deposit-taking institutions if they know that any losses are covered by a government insurance scheme. Government-backed insurance for life insurance policyholders would create a similar moral risk situation. People would speculate more on life insurance as an investment knowing that, if they are unsuccessful, they still win and the government and its taxpayers lose.

The federal government has tried on three occasions to terminate or at least significantly alter the CDIC system, but without success. It has therefore taken the alternative route of not raising the $60,000 limit created at the inception of CDIC in 1967. The effect of inflation has meant that the level of insurance available now is only about $10,000 in 1967 dollars. This contrasts with the situation in the United States, where the deposit insurance limit is $US100,000. As we saw in the case of the U.S. savings and loan debacle, this remarkable act of socialization by the U.S. government has cost its taxpayers several hundred billion dollars.

Prior to the establishment of CompCorp, there was no mandated protection for policyholders. The more powerful companies in the industry would collaborate in trying to manage the fallout of failing companies by taking them over, or at least vying to purchase the more successful blocks of business. A CompCorp official explained in interview that 'with the old boys' network, if a company was in some difficulty ... the large companies would get together and say, "Come on guys, we've got an image to protect here, who's going to take over this sucker?"'

When CompCorp was established the large companies continued to dominate, for example, through a board that was largely composed of their CEOs. This board could control how failed companies would be dealt with and compensation given. A federal regulator of financial institutions told us that the way things were originally structured, pol-icyholder protection for even a mid-size company failure could not be adequately funded. Eventually the federal regulators pressured Comp-Corp into establishing a more independent board, which the industry agreed was better for optics.

At the outset membership in CompCorp was voluntary. This created the peculiar possibility that the board could terminate the membership of a company when it became known that the company was failing. The federal regulators again pressured CompCorp, this time to make sure that there was no opting out clause once a company had decided to join. Over time, provincial-level laws and regulators have mandated CompCorp membership, and about 90 per cent of life and health com-panies had become members by the late 1990s.

A CompCorp official informed us that in exchange for these various requirements of governments, CompCorp was given greater access to the regulators' information about companies. Unlike CDIC, Comp-Corp has no auditing authority of its own and can only ask a company for information. However, it has developed a relationship with the fed-eral regulators through which it receives certain confidential informa-tion about companies, as well as some standardized data, for example, data pertaining to minimum continuing capital surplus requirements. The official said that the information sharing at least allowed Comp-Corp to spot some signs of trouble, which in turn could be used as a basis for 'moral suasion' with the government regulators regarding seemingly high-risk companies. However, she noted that the warning signals were often distorted, not least because the standardized audit-ing methods themselves are limited. For example, the minimum con-tinuing capital surplus requirement (MCCSR) is 'a very complicated risk assessment, and the biggest problem with it is that it's sufficiently complicated that people think it's right [laughs]. And it's not. The MCCSRs for Confederation Life and Sovereign Life were not too bad at the time they failed.'

CompCorp assesses member companies in proportion to the level of premiums they collect. The maximum annual assessment is .5 per cent of premiums up to $100 million. CompCorp also has the ability to 'borrow' from member companies against assessments for future years. As noted previously, the companies in turn charge policyhold-ers. A company we studied lowered the interest payable on life insurance investment policies by .5 per cent to cover its CompCorp assessment, and later changed its approach to simply charging .5 per cent against the policy premium. Thus, while a CompCorp official said in interview that industry members see the process as 'a mandatory passing of the hat after the event,' the act of compensation is not as charitable as he suggests. The cost is shifted to the policyholder as a mandatory insurance on her insurance.

CompCorp is designed as an incentive for member companies to be vigilant about each other as moral risks, on penalty of having to pay significant sums of compensation in the event of failure. However, these incentives are weak when considered in light of the fact that the costs of CompCorp are passed on to policyholders. Moreover, as we saw in the case of Confederation Life, when a failure is imminent, the leading industry players circle like vultures to buy the best blocks of business from the failing enterprise, and the CompCorp payouts to policyholders become part of the takeover costs. Indeed, CompCorp Life Insurance Company has been established as a wholly owned subsidiary of CompCorp to manage this process. Its purpose is to take on the remaining bad assets as a bidder of last resort. The strategy is to avoid having the assets sold at distressed prices. The book of business is run over time in the hope that the value will strengthen to the point of attracting another company to buy it.

CompCorp and other industry officials are sensitive to the moral risks of their scheme at several levels. The scheme was originally opposed within the industry because it was seen as having moral risk similar to any welfare safety net strategy. It continues to be seen in this manner, as a kind of incentive to morally weak companies who would otherwise be more concerned about the quality of their management, the prudence of their investments, and the honest marketing of their products. A CompCorp official expressed this view as follows: 'Why should we subsidize our competitors? We're strong ... All we do by setting up the safety net is encourage people to fail. Was CompCorp a self-fulfilling prophecy? In the 100 years preceding the commencement of the CompCorp, no policyholder had ever failed to receive 100 cents of the dollar at death upon maturity of the contract. No one. When CompCorp came in, since that time, we've had three failures.'

CompCorp officials also perceive a moral risk in the way that their organization provides an 'out' for the federal government. One official said that Confederation Life would have been saved by the government without CompCorp. In the absence of compensation for policyholders, both the government and industry would have faced too much loss of legitimacy in the 'absolute chaos' of Confederation Life's failure. Of course, this is precisely why the government pressed the industry to establish CompCorp in the first place and refused to provide a scheme similar to CDIC. They did not want to be the insurer of last resort, using taxpayers' money to bail out gamblers who guessed wrongly.

CompCorp is also considered a moral risk at the level of policyholders. Just as depositors may be less concerned about where they have their savings account in light of CDIC coverage, life and health policyholders are presumed to be attracted to aggressive, low-cost insurance operators whose lack of prudence is covered by CompCorp. This sentiment was expressed by the first president of CompCorp who, ironically, was at the same time the CEO of Confederation Life during the process of it's failure! 'We are indirectly encouraging the buyer to consider price and return over quality of product. We are flogging a $200,000 limit and creating unease in the mind of the consumer who may now be afraid to buy insurance for more than $200,000 with one carrier. We are also placing the weak financial organization on an equal footing, in a marketing sense, with those companies that have acted prudently and conservatively' (quoted by McQueen 1996: 72). These comments from the high-rolling CEO of Confederation Life are remarkable. They prove once again that it is not the existence of moral risk somewhere in the system that is at issue, only who is authorized to take the risk, and who is left to bear the brunt of it.

Life insurance agents we studied concurred that CompCorp coverage is a consideration in decisions about coverage. An agent told us that when he has a client looking for 'cheap insurance,' such as a term life policy, 'I want to keep it under that $200,000 CompCorp limit [and] I don't care who I go with. On the other hand, when the coverage is significantly higher, I'm going to be a little bit more cautious about where I'm going to place that and I know we're going to pay a higher premium for it.'

The industry in fact downplays the role of CompCorp to consumers. CompCorp coverage is not marketed as a feature of the life and health insurance policy because it is seen as a negative sign that a policyholder has to take out compulsory insurance on insurance. CompCorp brochures, a hot-line, and a website are available to consumers, but these are not highlighted as part of the sales process. A CompCorp official said that for sales agents in particular, CompCorp is 'partially a bad news story.' At the news conference that launched the plan, 'I said to the press person that we want a good page six story [laughs]. Anybody who is concerned can find it, and anybody who is not won't.'

Competition

The insurance industry in Canada is characteristic of the competitive business environment fostered by liberal risk regimes. The highly competitive environment means that solvency is an omnipresent issue, and mergers and acquisitions are commonplace.

Competition as a threat to solvency is fuelled by six interconnected processes. First, there is overcapacity, with a large number of companies chasing business, especially in the property and casualty industry. Second, this overcapacity is compounded by the entry of the major banks and other financial institutions into insurance company ownership and cross-selling. Third, new information technologies and direct selling techniques are being used to substantially alter sales distribution systems. Fourth, there is a parallel competitive environment in other branches of the financial services industry, for example, regarding the sale of mutual funds and other investment products that compete with investing through life insurance. Fifth, this situation in the financial services industry leads to internal competition within the insurance industry to develop more and more specialized products for segmented markets. Sixth, there is also a trend towards various forms of self-insurance.

The Canadian insurance company environment is fundamentally shaped by globalizing trends in the industry. For example, with the exception of the Cooperators, the largest players in the Canadian property and casualty industry are part of multinational corporations. These companies participate in merger and acquisition activity internationally, and this activity has a substantial impact on both their Canadian operations and their positioning in Canada with each other. For example, in 1998 two U.K. insurance companies, Commercial Union and General Accident, merged. The new company became the top property and casualty insurer in premiums written, at 11.7 per cent of the Canadian market. This company and four others – ING Canada (6.1 per cent), the Cooperators (5.9 per cent), Royal (5.6 per cent), and AXA (5.0 per cent) – controlled over one-third of the market among over a hundred property and casualty companies operating at the time. If the next five companies are added to this total, the top ten controlled one-half of the market (*Globe and Mail*, 26 February 1998). Trend data reveal that the top fifteen property and casualty companies controlled 32 per cent of the market in 1960, 38 per cent in 1980, and 47 per cent in 1995 (Insurance Bureau of Canada 1996: 20).

The CEO of a property and casualty company we studied said that the established ways of attracting business through brokers and service to consumers are no longer sufficient. The new sensibility is to either 'gobble' or be 'gobbled up' as the key to survival. '[Traditionally you would] teach your staff to be very good at servicing, to build a good reputation and in turn stay close to the brokerage community and invite and encourage brokers to place more business with you. That's the normal way of doing it, but these are anything but normal times. Today, buy [another company] as fast as you can ... too many players on the field and so it's survival of the fittest ... gobble up as many as you can, get as big as you can, and there's a lot of people who think big is the only way to survive.'

The same sensibility prevails in the Canadian life and health insurance industry. We attended a conference for insurance brokers at which a speaker addressed consolidation in the industry. The speaker reported on a survey of ninety company CEOs in North America in which they were asked the most likely sources of future growth. The acquisition of blocks of business or entire companies was ranked first among Canadian CEOs. The drive to grow through acquisition is one force behind the transformation of mutual life insurance companies into stock companies. Stock companies are better able to finance growth via acquisitions. They offer more flexible financing (preferred shares, regular shares, various kinds of debt), the profit discipline of the stock market, and stock option profit incentives to executives.

There is a parallel consolidation in the brokerage industry. On a grand scale, in 1997 Marsh MacLennan bought Johnson and Higgins, which at the time was the largest privately owned brokerage in the world. The takeover eliminated competition for lucrative corporate clients and also provided better economies of scale, especially regarding information technology services. On a small scale, a Canadian property and casualty company we studied acquired a share in a brokerage company whose outlets were largely in more remote areas and therefore not competing too directly with its own captive agents. The acquisition of this brokerage, which also sold the products of other insurance companies, was seen by a company official as a way of 'diversifying our distribution system, so if the exclusive agents got "booked out" [i.e. were no longer competitive] at least we have a foothold with our partners in [the brokerage].'

The CEO of another property and casualty company said his previous 'middle-size' company was taken over by the present company because its traditional business was not profitable. It was only attractive for takeover because it had niche markets in selected areas which were profitable. 'You just cannot afford as a medium-size company to be a general player in the market. And as a medium-sized company you are too big for the niche markets in this country.' He concluded that the middle-sized generalist companies would not survive, only the niche specialists and the large multinationals. A few months after making this statement his present company merged with another multinational to grow bigger still.

Competition from banks is also changing the Canadian insurance market. Bank insurance operations offer cheaper, competitive products through direct selling and other efficiencies that reduce administrative costs and provide economies of scale. An accounts manager for a major international insurer stated in interview that the market niche is not specialized products or claims service, but a 'selling machine' playing on 'the magic of large numbers ... 50 cents here and 50 cents there, but you multiply that by millions of people that are involved and it amounts to a heck of a lot of money.'

The market for bancassurance is the lower end, for example, people who want modest term life policies and home policies. Speaking at an industry conference on bancassurance, the CEO of a bank's insurance arm observed that 'traditional players' will service 'affluent markets' while the banks will reach 'less affluent Canadians [who] will have improved access to insurance products and services.' He went on to say that the target included the 'under-served segment of the Canadian population' who have no insurance at all, for example, the 25 per cent with no private life and health plans.

The vice-president for marketing of one of the big, traditional life insurance companies spoke at another industry conference and confirmed that such market segmentation is indeed the trend being forced by bancassurance. He said that until 1997 his company was multi-distribution, but 'the result was that we were average across the board everywhere, and the end result of all this is that we were starting to lose significant market share to niche players.' The company then developed a plan to focus on three niches: business planning, affluent family estates, and individual wealth accumulation, which were estimated to constitute about 31 per cent of current company business. He said, 'we have to know absolutely everything about that target customer we're going after,' and to that end the company was developing a 'financial stewards' concept whereby each agent would have about a hundred special clients, 'servicing them very intimately ... the shift is going to come at the expense of our face-to-face channels.'

The banks' approach is more 'nibbling' than 'gobbling.' They do not seek direct head-to-head competition with large global insurers, but to make small acquisitions and to partner with smaller companies in a process of planned growth. One insurance company we studied formed a partnership with a bank and established a direct selling call centre. This company had no previous direct selling arm, but decided to take an 'if you can't beat them join them' approach with the bank. This approach signals the fact that insurance companies do not see themselves as having a great deal of choice in the matter. Indeed, they experience a number of competitive disadvantages with bancassurance, and Canadian financial institution regulators have struggled with these issues over time.

Proprietary information about consumers is one advantage available to banks. Through their account, investment, and credit card systems, banks possess substantial information about the wealth and habits of their consuming populations. Moreover, people seek financial products (e.g., mortgages, mutual funds, business loans) from banks at key points in their life course, and the cross-selling of insurance with these other products gives the banks a potential monopoly position on individual wealth accumulation and management.

Many interviewees indicated that in spite of restrictions on cross-selling and tied selling, such practices are routine. Banks routinely sell mandatory insurance on mortgages, and often try to link other insurance purchases with their extension of credit. A life insurance broker referred to a client who received a letter from a bank saying he would not be given credit without life insurance. The CEO of an insurance company said in interview that creditor insurance is so much a part of the bank-consumer credit transaction that it is 'almost an assumed consent type of product.' The banks profit a great deal from these products, which are often more costly and carry fewer benefits than the same products available from other insurers.

These perceived competitive threats from bancassurance are amplified by insurance industry views on how the federal government has given banks structural advantages in the Canadian political economy.

From the insurance industry viewpoint, the legislative and regulatory boost to the banking industry proves once again that there is no such thing as market fundamentalism, only market favouritism. For example, a CLHIA (1995) document addressing a financial institution review by the federal government does not mince words. With the collapsing of the four pillars, banks are said to resemble 'firms in an oligopolistic industry' that 'exhibit a tendency to maximize collective profits, to approximate the pricing behaviour associated with a price monopoly, and to compete primarily on a non-price basis once a "stable" price level has been reached' (ibid.: 93). Bank 'concentration' is said to pose various risks in which both the government and banks are agents: 'increased systemic risk, higher prices, reduced innovation and less choice,' all of which are 'not the result of free market forces.'

The document specifies a number of legislative and regulatory advantages of banks. Banks have had the federal Bank Act 'modernized' six times since 1927, whereas federal insurance legislation of 1922 was not overhauled again until 1992. Unlike insurers, banks are in certain cases given access to liquidity support from government with respect to failed loans. Regarding the federally regulated payments system, insurers must bill and pay through banks or other deposit-taking institutions, which carries not only a financial transaction cost but also an information transaction cost, because the bank can then obtain and use consumer information 'to generate a list of customers for targeted marketing purposes' (ibid.: 20–1). One-half of the life insurance industry premium revenues are from products that compete directly with banks – for example, annuities compete with retirement savings plans and investment funds – but they are not backed by CDIC. 'According to a January 1995 COMPASS Research study, 73 per cent of respondents would choose the CDIC-backed product over the CompCorp-backed product given a choice between two otherwise identical products. This greater level of confidence in a government-backed entity versus the private sector consumer protection plan exemplifies the competitive advantage' (ibid.: 24).

The development of information systems on consuming populations is also a threat to the solvency of smaller insurance companies and therefore a source of mergers and acquisitions. An increasing number of companies are unable to compete because they cannot afford the information system costs associated with the new segmented marketing and customer management techniques used in the insurance industry. The CEO of a multinational property and casualty company said that IBM was developing a new system 'built around the types of distributions that are developing worldwide. And the entry price for companies in that system is going to be immense. So if you are not large you are not going to be there ... that is one of the things that is going to drive this consolidation probably more so than almost anything else.' An executive with a capital markets firm said that even for major players, information technology partnerships and outsourcing are necessary. For example, the five largest banks in Canada established two companies to collectively manage bank office systems, and four of the largest life and health insurers established the Shared Health Network to manage pharmaceutical benefits. This executive drew an analogy between this trend and Nike as a 'pure brand name marketing organization but everything else is outsourced.'

Another competitive dimension that affects solvency is pressure to offer attractive returns on insurance investment policies and annuities. When the inflation rate is high, life insurers compete for business by offering rates of return on their products that reflect the inflation rate. As we have seen, Confederation Life tried to do this by investing in shorter-term, higher yield investments. The problem is that life investment products bear long-term commitments when the company's own investments mature. The new investment market does not offer the same high rates of return, but high yield commitments to clients remain.

Problems also occur in low inflation environments. The interest rates are low for safer investments, and there is pressure to move into riskier investments. For example, in the 1990s the stock markets were bullish for an unprecedented length of time, creating expected rates of return that could not be matched by conventional life insurance products and annuities. Products were sold against the perception that the markets would rise continuously, and they splintered into myriad exotic investment options.

A federal pensions regulator we interviewed sketched the following scenario in employer group pension schemes, which are a significant segment of Canadian life insurance company operations. The low interest rate environment places pressure on employers to increase their contributions to employee pension plans. Employers, in the spirit of cutting benefits that is characteristic of liberal risk regimes, refuse to increase contributions in an effort to force life company investment managers into higher yielding investment portfolios. 'And that is when the risk is going to start coming in pension funds, getting into high placement and more in the real estate just like the insurance company [e.g., Confederation Life] did ten, fifteen years ago.'

These competitive pressures create what insurance marketers call 'feature creep': the proliferation of specialized products with complex investment options and incentives. We interviewed the sales director of a life insurance company, who explained feature creep as follows:

> For example, a Term to 100 product that is basically supposed to be a level premium, payable to age one hundred, if you die anytime, we pay the death benefit. Simple stuff, right? But then you start to have [insurance company] people say, 'Well, if you pay premiums for twenty years, we'll give you a little bit of cash value if you want so that you could borrow it, or you could surrender it, or you can have a reduced paid-up value if you want to stop paying premiums' ... When you think about the universal life product ... you talk about how many investment fund options you have for your fund value, your cash value, and 'Gee, do you want to have a guaranteed interest rate? Do you want to participate in an index that's linked to the Toronto Stock Exchange? Do you want to have something that's linked to Fidelity Growth Fund? Do you want to have a term deposit? Do you want a daily interest?' I mean the multitude of options that become available just start to grow. And you talk about your death benefit options. Do you want to have a Level 1? Do you want to have your fund value paid out on death? Do you want to have fund value that increases to about age 80, then it starts to taper off so that you can sort of be careful about your mortality costs as you get older that you didn't have that erode your value?' ... Maybe I'm overwhelming you!

The marketing actuary of a life insurance company said in interview that feature creep is driven by competitive demand rather than sound actuarial practice. A company that does not match or better a competitor's latest feature risks losing its preferred consumers to that company. If this loss widens, the company may be left with too much substandard business, ultimately driving premiums up and reserves down.

Another source of competition with insurance companies is various forms of self-insurance that are being encouraged in an era of greater risk taking. Wealthier consumers invest in financial markets themselves to avoid the high fees and administration expenses of life insurance products, while among organizations there is a trend towards various forms of self-insurance that prove cheaper and better. For example, public institutions, such as a consortium of large Canadian universities, collaborate in self-insurance pools that cover most of their property, casualty, and liability risks. Private corporations increasingly maintain high retention levels, organize self-insurance operations, or form captive companies. We interviewed a broker who specialized in creating captives for private corporations. He said that his fee for doing this was much less than for arranging a commercial insurance contract with a traditional insurance company. However, he recognized that some fee is better than no fee because the corporate client's logic is simple: 'if you're going to pay a million dollars to the Royal Insurance Company ... why not pay that million dollars to your own subsidiary down in the Caribbean?'

The alternative market for commercial insurance in the United States rivals the traditional market (Sedgwick 1997: 36). It was estimated that in 1997 the commercial insurance market had $153.8 billion, or 55.7 per cent, of premiums, while the alternative market had $122.2 billion, or 44.3 per cent of premium equivalents. The alternative market included qualified self-insurance ($40.8 billion or 14.8 per cent), private retentions ($40 billion or 14.5 per cent), captives ($25.7 billion or 9.3 per cent), pools and trusts ($14.1 billion or 5.1 per cent), and RRG ($1.6 billion or .6 per cent). 'Corporate retentions in the US have increased, and despite the continued soft commercial insurance pricing and companies' aversion to the risk, the ability to gain control and capture underwriting profits is still an attractive option for risk managers worldwide' (ibid.: 37).

One response of large commercial insurers such as Sedgwick is to creatively finance risks above the retention and self-insurance levels that companies have established for themselves. These schemes also entail a kind of feature creep, this time for high-end commercial insurance customers. Sedgwick refers to this evolving area as Alternative Risk Transfer, or ART. The art of underwriting these niche markets

> may consist of finite insurance or reinsurance; catastrophic futures or options on catastrophic futures; multi-year insurance policies that limit the aggregate losses from several lines of exposure; combining funding from a capital market instrument with an insurance policy; and other similar approaches to loss funding. These programs entail substantial premiums and the possibility of a return of premium for favorable loss experience and perhaps an additional premium for unfavorable loss experience ... [T]he insurance limits are typically high and the exposure severe

such as environmental liability, asbestosis, products liability and products recall to name a few. In some areas nontraditional exposures such as exchange rates, interest rates, or raw material prices may be insured in the contract (ibid.).

In this chapter, we have explored the negotiation of insurance political economies through processes of underwriting, investment, reinsurance, compensation insurance, and competitive relations. We have documented how each of these processes bears moral risks to various parties in the insurance relationship. In the next two chapters, we consider additional moral risks posed by insurers and the governance mechanisms used to address them. Chapter 5 examines the mechanisms of corporate governance that are supposed to make directors and officers morally responsible in managing insurance political economies. Chapter 6 analyses the mechanisms for governing the marketing of insurance that are supposed to make sales agents morally responsible. While the goal is to embed self-governance in insurance practices, moral risks always percolate.

5. Corporate Governance

The smell of profit is clean / And sweet, whatever the source.

Juvenal, *Satires* (c. 100)

Society is produced by our wants and government by our wickedness.

Thomas Paine, *Common Sense* (1776)

You never expected justice from a company, did you? They have neither a soul to lose, nor a body to kick.

Adam Smith, *The Wealth of Nations* (1776)

Corporate governance mechanisms respond to and shape the moral risks of insurance relationships. They are designed to make each component of the insurance system self-governing. In this chapter, we examine four corporate governance mechanisms that intersect to foster self-governance. First, state regulators are active participants in corporate governance. They not only conduct audits and enforce rules, but also work on subtle dimensions of corporate culture to cultivate moral responsibility. In turn, the state's agents are governed by insurance company officials as they participate in the regulatory process. Second, industry associations have their own governance system. This system manages collective risks by providing information services, enforcing rules, and promoting industry values. Third, actuaries assemble numerical information, enforce rules, and foster a sense of responsible risk taking. Fourth, insurers insure their own directors, officers, and agents. Analysis of how insurance companies insure their own members provides unique insight into their corporate criteria of moral risk and responsibility.

State Regulation

State and insurance industry regulators are part of each other's liberal risk regimes. The state governs corporate governance, and corporations in turn govern the state.

The starting point for state regulation of any corporation is the licensing system (Lowi 1990: 23). A licence allows a corporation to do something that is otherwise illegal. Licensing is a key instrument for negotiating risks to the political economy. The state grants corporate business licences selectively to control who participates in particular markets and the terms of their participation. Such control regulates price stability at a higher level than would be likely in an unrestricted market. Licensing is also a mechanism for governing the qualifications and reputation of players in the market, to ensure that the moral risks they pose are within tolerable limits. This screening is especially important because the corporate licence grants the enormous privilege of limited liability, allowing directors and officers to take substantial financial risks in the knowledge that they will be cushioned from the consequences.

The state grants licences to insurance companies based on corporate analysis of what they will add to the political economy, and whether their contribution will be made in a morally responsible manner. We interviewed a state regulator in charge of corporate analysis for licensing. He said his job was to assess whether the insurance company applying for a licence will 'add value to the economic regime of the country.' The assessment of adding value was depicted as 'how you keep the scoundrels out. That's how you keep the quality of what's going on in place, and that's where you set the first standard of performance expectations with the owners and management of companies.' On the other hand, the assessment of economic contribution is not made in terms of responsibility to those who might suffer from the added competition, such as employees of existing companies who might lose their jobs. In liberal risk regimes, a key licensing consideration is a competitive environment that favours both consuming populations and capital expansion, even if it is at the expense of some existing companies:

> We could allow somebody into the country who might in our view add value from the consumer's point of view by adding competitive products, better quality products, better pricing, better managed operations, that

could in fact drive somebody who's already in the country out of the business because it could be a shallow market ... That may sound like it's at odds, that we're supposed to be maintaining public confidence in the insurance business ... We would be more interested in the safety and soundness of the operation than in the body count of employment. So, a very strong contributor to safety and soundness is good earnings. And a big, big proportion of the expenses incurred by any financial institution is actually salaries and wages. And so we would probably be more prone to try to see people operate efficiently, fewer people, lower costs, bigger earnings, bigger capital positions than we would be pushing them to maintain employment losses.

Licensed insurance companies are regulated actively and continuously through state governance mechanisms. The type and degree of state involvement varies substantially by insurance line, and whether the line is made compulsory by the state.

Private market vehicle insurance is the most heavily regulated because the state has made it compulsory and therefore cannot be a spectator. The product is compulsory because it is crucial for distributing the enormous liability risks associated with driving. The state structures private market vehicle insurance by, for example, making insurance contracts statutory so that they cannot be changed without state approval; requiring all premiums to be subject to regulatory approval; and undertaking systematic audits of company investment, sales, and claims practices.

Private life and health insurance companies are becoming more regulated in some areas. A number of prominent company insolvencies, misselling scandals, and downsizing of government health and social security insurance programs has prompted increased regulation.

State regulators focus on decision processes as they relate to the rules and values of the company. A regulator said his office was responsible for scrutinizing and shaping 'the way by which decisions are made in the company that polices its own activities in accordance with the direction of the board, or the value system within the organization.' This control of an insurance company's own controls is justified in terms of the state's obligation to protect consumers. While state regulators deem the company responsible for its own financial success or failure, the state imposes obligations designed to enhance public confidence in the company and in financial institutions more generally. Public confidence in an insurance company is based largely on fair marketing practices and on meeting promises to pay policyholders in the event of legitimate claims.

As we documented in chapter 4 regarding insurance company investment practices, the implementation of this state regulatory mission is elastic. State regulators are involved in a perpetual process of negotiating the political economy with each insurance company and the industry as a whole. A solvency regulator remarked in interview, 'What's an undue loss [laughs]? I don't know what an undue loss is [laughs]! I suspect, depending on how many calls the members of Parliament are getting, the definition of undue loss could change!' One of her colleagues emphasized that there is as much potential for undue loss from investment decisions that are too conservative as there is from those that are too risky. In the shifting investment markets of liberal risk regimes, there is an urge to move to whatever option might build assets for policyholder protection and company profit. The task of the state regulator is to educate, monitor, and negotiate with company investment managers in this regard. 'The last thing we want to do is to prevent an investor or an owner of an asset from making a better return. So you have to provide the tools, you have to provide the environment ... [to] get the most out of the buck ... There's bad managers, but there's no bad assets. Because an asset is always balanced with the risk ... The guiding principle here is what you are trying to match.'

The insurance industry not only accepts state regulation but actively invites it. State regulators are a source of expertise which an insurance company may lack and be too reluctant to seek through its industry association of competitors. A regulator said in interview that his staff was consulted regularly by the regulated 'rather than turning to their lawyers and the actuary, who often don't know anything about their business anyway and they may give the wrong advice.' In his expert role the regulator is much like the management consultant who provides an external source of expertise and legitimacy for the rationalization of corporate risks.

Insurance companies also want state regulators to patrol the border of their industry's position in relation to other financial institutions, and the border of each company in relation to various competitive pressures that might precipitate failure or unwanted mergers and takeovers. As expressed by a federal solvency regulator, 'They all want a strong cop on the beat ... Because at the end of the day, through their guarantee corporations [e.g., CompCorp,] they pick up the costs of failure in another way.'

Insurance companies 'pick up the costs' of state regulation itself. In Canada, the full costs of state regulatory operations are covered by a levy charged to each company according to the scale of its operations. At the federal level, there has been discussion of changing the basis of levy to include a penalty structure for companies that pose greater risks and therefore require more intensive supervision. In this 'modified user-pay' system, the more heavily regulated company would receive an additional bill for the privilege.

Just as an insurance company benefits from an audit by a prestigious management consultant firm (Thompson 1997), so it can profit from demonstrating compliance with state audits. The display of good management practices and ethical conduct becomes a 'good' for reputation, public confidence, and profits (Power 1997, 2003). An official of a large property and casualty insurance company said that his sole task was to work both within the company and in external media and government relations to foster the view that the company had a good management culture. A good management culture was seen as a valuable commodity. 'In terms of the merger and acquisition question ... I think one of the things that is going to make us attractive is this corporate culture.'

The actual mechanisms through which the state regulates corporate governance have both objective and subjective dimensions. In this section we will focus primarily on the subjective dimensions, as there has been a decided move in this direction in recent years. However, the objective dimensions are also salient. We will address them briefly here, and in more detail in the subsequent section on actuarialism.

State regulators of insurance company solvency use various quantified measures of solvency risks. A simple example is monitoring industry growth and profit levels to ascertain which companies are the outliers and should be subject to questioning as to why they are over- or underperforming. A federal solvency regulator described his job by giving the example of the industry average premium income increase being 5 per cent while a particular company is averaging 20–30 per cent year after year:

> You may find that their compensation packages for the agents and brokers is way out of line with the industry so they are effectively buying the business, the moment they reduce their compensation packages the business could disappear ... What may on the surface be looking like very good results may in fact not be good results. Growth in business could in fact impair their ability to maintain capital levels, for example. So you'd

have to look and see what their access to capital rates were like. Could they raise money on the market? Do they have an owner that's capable of putting in money?

The objective data provide the basis for asking questions and initiating investigations. However, objective data alone do not provide a basis for regulatory action, which is always grounded in the local peculiarities of the company involved (Lowi 1990: 38–9; Porter 1995: 102). The gap between aggregate data on solvency risk and the need to address local peculiarities is filled by the negotiation of trust (Heimer 2001). Subjective expertise embodied in moral actors steps in to deal with objective risks embedded in abstract systems. 'The validation of expertise meant that standardization was unnecessary. If the key entities at issue resisted precise measurement, then trust, or intrusive regulation, was required to fill the gap' (Porter 1995: 112). The chief actuary of a large property and casualty insurance company observed in interview that over his long career it had always been a

struggle to get my colleagues even in the insurance business, let alone government people or other hangers on ... to understand the financial dynamics ... And because they don't understand, it has been a [matter of] trust ... And ... they don't trust ... [Even our present chief financial officer] hasn't got that *touch* yet, that *feel* for financial dynamics ... There really isn't anybody in claims who understands these financial things ... The president doesn't understand ... He hasn't got this grasp of fundamental accounting rules on the one hand or the actual dynamics of the place on the other.

This chief actuary indicates that the financial risk environment of his insurance company is based on 'touch,' 'feel,' 'dynamics,' and so on. It is precisely these subjective elements that state regulators emphasize in their work of governing corporate governance. They want insurance executives and managers to be more in touch with their company's culture because, as elusive as it may seem, such knowledge provides a firmer basis for corporate risk management than the probability calculus of the abstract system. A solvency regulator observed in interview that 'governance of risk cannot really be measured objectively, it is more like a feeling ... the way they conduct their day-to-day business, the way they make their decisions, the way they set up controls ... subjective assessment. And it is done partly by having our analyst being on top of things ... [and our] examiner going on site – and having a feeling with the people they are actually dealing with – seeing the controller in place, seeing how they handle the business and that sort of thing.'

This solvency regulator said that character analysis of company directors, officers, and managers is a key aspect of his job:

> No institution is an expert in knowing whether their cast of characters that are running their company are actually better than the cast of characters running any other company. We happen to be able to look at any number of companies and ... actually determine this guy is the president, he's actually better than this president; this financial officer is not as good as this financial officer ... [We may] tell a company their management team needs strengthening. Can I prove it? No. Can I score it on a score of 1 to 10 against somebody else's? No. But I *know* this is a weak link in the organization. There just isn't enough talent there to pull off what they're trying to pull off.

Another solvency regulator emphasized that character analysis is crucial because conflicts of interest and blatant dishonesty are the core problems faced. 'A lot of failure that we find is that there is self-interest involved, conflict of interest. Dealings behind closed doors. Things we didn't know at the time, things that you cannot assess objectively, with a computer, with numbers ... What we are finding is, in most cases when there are failures, it is because there is some hanky panky going around, and we didn't know about it and often the [company] board doesn't know about it.'

The regulatory effort to 'self-moralize' (Werner 1992; Power 2003) the corporation as the cornerstone of self-governance is indicative of the emphasis on ethical conduct in liberal risk regimes (Rose 1999). If corporations are to take more liberal risks, their directors, officers, and agents must receive instruction about their moral responsibilities in doing so. The instruction takes place on the job, as corporate governance processes force decisions to be reflected upon in terms of the moral risks they pose.

Quantitative analyses of risk are also relevant to this process. As introduced previously, such data articulate standards – statistical normalcy – which also provide moral norms that shape decisions. As such, they are part of the system for disciplining corporate employees as moral actors. They instill an ethic which, when combined with subjective audits, self-moralizes the employee. At the same time, they self-moralize the corporate entity and provide legitimacy for actions in the name of the corporation. The effort to provide more self-governance through self-moralization requires an intensification of state regulation. While the rhetoric of liberal risk regimes may express a desire for less state regulation, it is actually directed at changing the nature of regulation.

As participants in state regulation of their activities, insurance companies are not passive recipients of top-down enforcement. Rather, they actively shape the state and its forms of legislation and regulation. Their governance of state governance transpires in the same contexts we have analysed with respect to state regulators.

Insurance company directors and officers serve on industry association and government committees that involve them with state regulators in ongoing negotiations of political economy. We interviewed a CEO who served on several industry committees dealing with regulatory affairs. For example, he co-chaired a government steering committee on a particular line of insurance with the head of a provincial government insurance regulation agency. He said in this capacity they were working 'on behalf of government ... making sure that if there are issues that are identified the government can act.' He gave as one example the negotiation of protocols and fees with health care providers regarding personal injuries arising from vehicle accidents. He stressed that regulation is inevitable because a licence to operate as an insurance company is a privilege that bears obligations:

> When you start from the presumption that at least some of our products are mandatory ... [and others], although they're voluntary purchases, they're purchases where there's a reasonable degree of trust – and there are substantial negative consequences if that trust is misplaced – it strikes me that there's a very logical reason why governments should want to regulate. And the industry would and should want governments to look at our solvency, to ensure that we actually can honour the commitments that we're making, and then to the extent that the purchases are actually obligatory purchases, that our market conduct and our rate levels are appropriate ... It's like a quid pro quo, if you will, of a very privileged position.

This CEO stressed that the regulatory apparatus can enhance the industry. He had participated actively in restructuring a provincial government insurance regulation agency because he saw its usefulness for his company and the industry as a whole. He gave the example of a major legislative change in which the government let the industry both define the problem and set the parameters of the solution, to the point where the legislation was '90 per cent' in accordance with the industry's framework. He used this example to illustrate how the state's liberal risk regime was enhancing the industry by, in effect, allowing it to govern government.

Industry executives and state regulators interchange positions on a continuing basis. State regulators are often former private insurance industry executives and managers. Many insurance company senior executives spend a great deal of their time on state and industry association regulatory committees. They also move among various insurance company, consultancy, and government positions. For example, an insurance executive we interviewed had in the past served as a policy adviser to the government's insurance commission; taught a university course on regulation; worked for a multinational consulting firm; worked for a firm that lobbied government on insurance legislation and regulation; served on industry association committees; and served on government committees dealing with the private insurance industry.

A state regulator of insurance company solvency said in interview that the move to more subjective assessments and self-regulation by insurance companies made his agency more dependent on those companies. While insurance companies were required to establish more internal governance mechanisms, and to disclose how those mechanisms were operating, this in turn gave the companies an opportunity to shape the state regulatory agency to the point where one meaning of 'self-regulation is reliance by entities like us on participants in the system.' A state regulator of insurance in another jurisdiction made the same point. He illustrated by saying that his agency used to develop a position paper and send it out to the industry for response, but the practice changed to have industry associations participate in developing these papers from the outset. He said this approach is best because 'if people are not prepared to comply with the standards, it's just like trying to enforce a speed limit on the highway, it just won't happen.'

In Canada, the insurance industry has been active in reform movements aimed at reducing unwanted restrictions by government and fostering desired restrictions. For example, the Ontario Red Tape Commission (ORTC) (1997) had substantial input from insurance industry sources. 'Red tape' sets up state regulation as a 'boo word' (Bay 1981): regulation is presumptively negative unless it can be shown otherwise.

It is negative because it does not serve the moral utilitarianism of private industry. 'Red tape impedes Ontario's economic growth and our ability to compete in a global economy ... diminish[es] our economic competitiveness by adding unjustifiable requirements, costs or delays to the normal activities of business and institutions' (ORTC 1997: iii, 1).

The task is not to get rid of regulation, but to have industry play a more prominent role in governing government. The ORTC (1997: 1) cites the *De-regulation Task Force of Great Britain* (1994–5: 1): 'All governments, left to themselves, tend to over-regulate.' The solution is to not leave government to government. Industry is to become active in 'changing the culture. Over many decades, a regulatory culture has developed that seeks to solve all problems by spending taxpayers' money and making new rules ... Just like spring cleaning of your home helps keep junk from piling up in your basement, an annual clearing out of government rules will help prevent unnecessary red tape from accumulating' (ORTC 1997: vii–viii). Private industry is to help foster this liberal government against government, one that incessantly pursues its own minimalization. Of course, the government's red tape commission itself is integral to this liberal discourse of government against government.

We interviewed someone who had held senior positions in both the insurance industry and government, and who was involved in a red tape review process. She made it clear that the insurance industry was seeking to regulate the state in terms of industry criteria of moral risk and responsibility.

> Why do you have to license an insurance company annually? Is Manulife going out of business? Why are you regulating everybody like they're all incipient failures? ... [Insurance companies] used to keep so much of their money locked up in bonds. Wait a minute, this is 1999. The game has changed, so you can still have security, but don't prescribe where you can put your money... The biggest problem with bureaucrats is that they haven't been given enough clear directions. I find that a good bureaucrat given clear direction is a wonderful piece of equipment and a wonderful asset to have ... So one of the things we're trying to deal with ... is the cultural aspect ... [As a] small businesswoman ... if I had to mind all of my employees, I wasn't going to be much of a businesswoman, was I? All I wanted around me were people who would think and do, weren't lazy. And that's what government should be about. There should be rewards for them taking their responsibility.

Not surprisingly, the ORTC had specific things to say about the reform of insurance systems. For example, it recommended allowing a controversial viatical insurance industry in the province. Viatical insurance involves the discounted sale of benefits of a life insurance policy to a third party by a terminally ill person. It is legally prohibited in most jurisdictions because of the explicit moral risks involved in gambling on time of death.

Several features of the insurance industry give it the upper hand in the regulatory dance with the state. As private entities, insurance companies are entitled to secrecy and confidence regarding much of the information they produce, including their governance processes. Secrecy and confidence is necessary to maintain competitive position and fiduciary responsibilities. It is also necessary because, as one regulator stated pithily in interview, 'The primary product of an insurance company is providing confidence to its policyholders.' Disclosure about solvency problems, morally risky governance structures, or the subjective nature of regulatory decisions could undermine the product.

This regulatory dilemma is articulated in the *Annual Report* of the federal Office of the Superintendent of Financial Institutions (OSFI) (1996: 8–9). The report stresses that confidentiality is vital to public confidence. Public awareness of a state regulator's investigation of a company could create a self-fulfilling prophecy of failure that would harm consumers along with other parties. Confidentiality is necessary to gain insurance company compliance with routine requests for information and on-site examinations. It is also necessary because publicity would force state regulators to reveal the subjective basis of their judgments, which would have the effect of forcing them back into more objective tests that are less effective from their viewpoint.

It is probable that if OSFI were required to publicize its own supervisory judgments, it would be forced to place heavier reliance on more objective and less judgmental tests in forming its evaluations. This would be a retrograde step because many of the emerging risks to which financial institutions are exposed are not readily susceptible to purely objective evaluation. The important supervisory challenge with respect to emerging risks is to evaluate the quality of the institution's controls over these risks. Such evaluations are, of necessity, somewhat subjective. If OSFI found itself forced to defer judgments until subjective concerns about weak controls were supported by objectively measurable financial deterioration, the result would be more cautious supervision and later rather than earlier intervention. (OSFI 1996: 9)

State regulators' access to information about an insurance company's operations is especially limited when the company is a multinational based outside Canada. The International Association of Insurance Supervisors has developed some de facto international rules and standards, but the rules have little sanctioning power beyond moral suasion. A Canadian representative on this body said in interview that its main function is to foster 'the power of consensus building, and the power of being seen to be stepping out of line by the private marketplace ... The reality of ... legal structures, and all public and political expectations, and indeed most compensation schemes too, is that they're nationally based in the case of failure.'

The international situation is complicated further by the fact that in the United States, there is a separate regulator for each state. A National Association of Insurance Commissioners considers common regulatory issues but can commit to very little regarding uniform standards, rules, and sanctions.

When a failure occurs, regulators in the insurance importing country have little clout if most of the remaining company value lies in the exporting country. Regulators are left to patch a deal with liquidators and rehabilitators, and to cool down litigious policyholders. For example, in the Confederation Life failure, most of the remaining value of the company was in Canada, but most of the losses on closure were in the United States (McQueen 1996). A Canadian solvency regulator involved in this case said the fact the remaining value was in Canada 'allowed it to be possible for us to do a deal with U.S. liquidators and rehabilitators to share things in exchange for them not going to tie us up in courts for years.'

The multinational dimensions of reinsurance arrangements pose additional problems for nationally based regulators. Federal solvency regulators in Canada told us that they had intensified their scrutiny of reinsurance arrangements. Intensification was attributed to the Confederation Life failure, problems with earthquake insurance underwriting and capital reserves, and the new emphasis on corporate governance structures as the key to solvency. One part of this effort was an attempt to convince offshore multinationals to provide more internal reinsurance to their Canadian subsidiaries. Insurance company executives and managers in charge of reinsurance told us that federal regulators scrutinized their guidelines and the way in which they were assessing the risk of reinsurers they chose. A continuing problem is that there is unsufficient reinsurance capacity among Canadian licensed companies to meet reinsurance needs. Consequently, reinsurance must be sought from offshore companies that are unlicensed in Canada and that do not have Canadian-based assets that can be regulated or seized if necessary. The federal regulator's response is to try to limit the amount of reinsurance that can be held with unlicensed companies compared to licensed companies and affiliates of the primary company.

Industry Associations

Industry associations serve three major functions in corporate governance. First, they provide a systematic means of governing governments. Second, they create information systems about insurance consumers and insurable risks. Third, they develop standards, rating criteria, rules, and sanctions. These mechanisms regulate not only at the level of everyday insurance practices, but also at the level of articulating hierarchies and power relations among member companies.

Industry associations see themselves as governing governments. For example, the website of the Insurance Bureau of Canada (IBC) promotes association membership as follows: 'More and more, governments are seeking constructive partnerships with private industry, especially if industry speaks with one voice and in the broad public interest. Membership in IBC generally improves the odds that government will hear and understand industry positions when it counts, *before* laws are enacted and regulations drafted' (IBC website 1997: 2–3).

Industry associations have legal staff to monitor the government's policies and legislative initiatives. We interviewed a legal staff member of an association who said that her unit's main activity was 'legislative watch' and 'court watch.' In using the term 'watch,' she was making a direct comparison to 'watch' programs in general, such as Neighbourhood Watch. 'Watch' has become the guiding trope expressing the need for vigilant surveillance. It addresses not only what is feared (in the present case, unwanted interference from governments), but also what might be a source of favour (in the present case, how governments might serve industry interests). As with all watch programs, 'legislative watch' and 'court watch' are proactive and preventive. They are based on continuous, close relationships with all branches of government that influence the insurance industry. The interviewee said that 'legislative watch' entails close association with government 'attorneys, the superintendents of insurance, the legislative counsel, the registrars for motor vehicles. Anybody that's got anything that affects insurance, we try to stay close to these people in the hope if there is legislation in the offing that they may speak to us beforehand.' 'Court watch' involves monitoring of legal actions in process as well as judicial interpretations of insurance contracts and legislation. The association sometimes seeks standing as an intervenor in a case in progress, or funds an appeal of a lower court decision that affects the industry negatively.

Associations also maintain databases to support their vigilance of legal processes. For example, the Life Underwriters Association of Canada (LUAC) has a database indicating which association members have relationships to specified members of federal and provincial parliaments, and are therefore the best conduits through which association issues can be addressed with legislators. Called the 'government contact program,' the database is used to filter important issues through LUAC members to the decision makers for those particular issues (Life Insurance Marketing Research Association 1997: 26). This lobbying information system is directed at proactive negotiation of legislative outcomes. It illustrates how the industry is part of the political process, negotiating political economies at every step of the way.

Industry associations negotiate political economies with governments on broad topics of insurance coverage. In some instances, they lobby governments to maintain or enhance state insurance schemes. For example, CLHIA is a strong advocate of public health insurance in areas that compliment private insurance coverage, or that are too risky for the private insurance industry to take on.

A state solvency regulator said in interview that all significant policies evolve through industry associations. 'We're going to always do what the association says we should do ... The art and science and theory of consultation ... [involves] power sharing, and sharing and development of policy.' In effect, this allocates controlling influence to the largest and most powerful insurance companies, because they dominate the associations and also have the biggest stake in issues being addressed. This interviewee made it clear that his regulatory agency was therefore also primarily governed by these powerful companies. He figures out the distribution of power among the insurance companies that control the association, and uses that power to achieve the regulatory outcome at issue. The key industry association players, in turn, use state power to achieve the regulation they want, which includes control of each other. None of this is to suggest that everything goes as planned or that desired outcomes are invariably achieved.

An example of failure was a proposal in the late 1990s to form the Ontario Life Agents Council for life insurance sales people to govern themselves (Ontario Insurance Commission 1997). In the spirit of self-governance promoted by the Ontario government at the time, the life and health insurance industry proposed to incorporate this council to license and discipline life insurance agents. These functions would thereby be removed from the direct responsibility of the government's regulatory agency. Among the aims stated in the draft constitution was 'to encourage through self-discipline and self-regulation a high standard of business conduct among agents' (ibid.).

The Ontario government eventually rejected this proposal because insurance brokers and consumer associations effectively argued the council would have been overly dominated by the largest insurance companies. It was decided that this dominance would disadvantage independent insurance agents and brokers and do nothing to advance the power of consumers (*Globe and Mail*, 24 May 1997). An official of an insurance brokers' association said in interview that in any discourse of self-regulation, one must always question who is the 'self,' and who holds the upper hand in regulation. He said, in this case, the self was the selfish large insurance companies, and the regulatory power was effectively retained by them through the state. For example, the council was to have twelve board members: four life company representatives, four members of 'the public,' and four life insurance agents. Since agents were in the minority it was not an *agents'* council, as the title might suggest. Moreover, the members of the public were explicitly not to be 'consumerists.' Instead, various proposals were made to have the public represented by former insurance industry employees. This interviewee observed, 'Self-regulating means you have the ability to make the rules ... The Insurance Act made it clear that the purpose of this organization would be to enforce the Insurance Act and its regulations ... It was totally under the control of government ... they were downloading the responsibility but they weren't downloading any authority.' A representative of a consumers' association that also opposed the council said in interview that the second draft of the proposal 'neatly removed the only clauses in the code [of agent's conduct] that had anything to do with the protection of consumers ... what he bought and how much it was going to cost him over the years ... They wiped all that out ... [in favour of] their duty to the company and their duty to the association.'

Industry associations collaborate with member companies and governments in managing risk communication systems. For example, the Insurance Bureau of Canada was formed in 1964 at the urging of the Federal Superintendent of Insurance. Several property and casualty companies were experiencing difficulty in meeting their claims liabilities, and it was felt the IBC could provide better information systems that would improve underwriting practices. The IBC has evolved into a risk communication agency that sells information to member companies. For example, it sells data on trends in insurance claims for various product lines and how these trends vary by province. In the six provinces and two territories with private vehicle insurance markets, it is the official statistical agency authorized by government to produce data about vehicle insurance risks. In Ontario, it is also the official statistical agency regarding commercial liability insurance.

Control of propriety information is always at issue in the operation of risk communication systems by industry associations. This issue is evident even in public declarations of policy, such as the one on the CLHIA website, which states, 'as an independent organization representing competitive interests, the Association cannot provide information that would be of competitive advantage to any company; discuss or set prices; or assist members in any direct way in their normal commercial activities' (CLHIA 1997c). A representative of a company that supplies risk communication services to the insurance industry observed in interview that major banks in Canada have been successful in their cooperative efforts to develop information system architecture and infrastructure. In contrast, insurance companies have been uncooperative with each other, investing in political lobbying efforts against banks rather than gearing up their collective risk communication systems to be competitive with banks.

> There's still as much distrust of each other and as much fear of each other as there is of the real competitors who are competitors outside the channel, like banks. You can sit around the table and say, 'That's a wonderful idea. The industry should do that for the benefit of the broker distribution channel.' And then they go away and say, 'Now how can I outsmart that son-of-a-bitch?' ... The industry needs to put away its own Machiavellian little struggles, saying one thing and doing another, and actually work together for their own survival. [But instead] it's going to be a lot more cut-throat ... [smaller] companies are either going to be disadvantaged technologically, or they're going to be amalgamating to get into econo-

mies of scale, or they're going to get gobbled up by the big guys, or they are going to find a niche way of surviving.

This interviewee points to the fact that, while an industry association may be effective at governing governments, it has difficulty regulating member companies that are highly competitive and constantly positioning themselves for mergers and acquisitions. A government regulator said, 'the industry is just so competitive that there's only minimal cooperation from the companies in their own trade association.' She said that in spite of the information system function of the association, individual member companies sometimes produce their own data to argue against the industry position. 'What they're doing is representing their own corporate interests ... That becomes very problematic in trying to reach a consensus; it's sometimes next to impossible because they don't want to ... take a back seat to their association.' She said that if, say, 10 out of 120 companies do not like a regulation agreed to by the government and industry association, they will each lobby government ministers and politicians to revisit the issue.

Another government regulator concurred, saying that this association was not an equal partnership of all member companies but rather is 'controlled by eight or nine big companies ... when the chips are down the guys who are paying the bills are the guys who are calling the shots.' A third government regulator said that this control by the largest companies meant that his agency sometimes side-stepped the association. For example, his agency developed an alternative dispute resolution system for dealing with personal injury claims arising from automobile accidents. Regulators who managed this system created a 'companies forum' consultation group with the alternative dispute resolution coordinator in each insurance company, side-stepping the association because it is 'CEOs and the CEOs have the broad perspective that is not very helpful.'

A few CEOs themselves decided not to belong to this association. One CEO we interviewed said her company did not join because 'they're a do-nothing organization. They'll often cause more problems than they solve ... There isn't unity in the insurance industry and it's largely controlled and run by members from large companies.' She said that the power of the top companies extends to how 'they interpret different things, the way *they* think it should be as opposed to what the law would call for.' She gave the example of a court ruling saying that if a car strikes a wild animal, the collision section of the vehicle insurance policy applies. However, influenced by the largest companies, the association continued to recommend that the optional comprehensive section of the policy should apply, thereby excluding the possibility of claims from the many drivers who choose not to have comprehensive coverage. 'They should not be in a position of ruling on situations like that. That should be left up to the courts. This is where I feel that they often interfere, trying to make decisions for the insurance industry whether you're a member or not.'

Some interviewees felt that although the largest companies effectively controlled regulation through this association and their relations with government, their power was diminishing. A manager for a company that was not among the elite group said this association had been 'a cartel' of the largest companies that was 'disgraceful frankly. They used to set the rates ... If they didn't like the way the market was going they'd change the whole market.' However, he felt that resistance by other companies as well as the entry of new companies was changing the power relations somewhat. The CEO of another company that was outside the top group said that companies used to cooperate more because there was one basic distribution channel through brokers. The fragmentation of marketing channels results in fragmentation of cooperation through industry associations. 'As you see the new entrants and as you see the differences and approaches on the distribution side, the degree of cooperation is actually breaking down on the regulatory activity.' In 1998, nine property and casualty insurance companies that sold through direct marketing channels formed their own association. Among the purposes of this association is to bring about legislative and regulatory changes that are directly relevant to their mode of marketing. For example, they sought changes to existing rules regarding the need for a signature on an application for an insurance policy and prohibition on part-time agents (*Globe and Mail*, 20 May 1998).

In spite of their power hierarchies and fragmentation, industry associations do structure corporate governance. A property and casualty company that wants a major exclusion condition in their insurance contracts needs to work through the association to obtain an agreement from other companies. For example, a unilateral exclusion in commercial underwriting on long-term liabilities, such as pollution or information system failures, may lead the company to lose substantial business and also create adverse selection problems. It is necessary to have other companies agree to similar exclusion clauses, or at least adjust their risk management practices to take into account what the company is doing.

Associations also structure claims processes to facilitate corporate governance across the industry. The IBC administers five different claims agreements that facilitate settlements and reduce or eliminate legal and court costs (IBC 1996: Appendix D). These agreements address, for example, the standardization of claims forms and practices and the settlement of claims.

Actuaries

We have already introduced the fact that actuaries participate with state regulators in solvency testing and the setting of standards for the rating and pricing of insurance products. In this capacity, they have formal bureaucratic and legal standing. For example, every insurance company requires an appointed actuary who is assigned statutory responsibilities, including determination of policy liabilities. The appointed actuary must report to the company's board, but also to OSFI, the federal solvency regulator. Responsibilities to OSFI range from formal protocols, such as capital adequacy testing, to whistle blowing. Actuaries employed by insurance companies also have an important place in corporate governance structures. They are management executives more than number crunchers, overseeing the loose interpretation of actuarial data in the context of a company's culture and competitive environment.

The motto of the British Institute of Actuaries is 'Actuaries make financial success of the future.' This is a bold claim, declaring that actuaries have the expertise to help everyone in the insurance relationship meet their 'financial success' goals. Actuarial science is indeed a sophisticated means of classifying populations and their environments for quantitative analyses helpful in deciding how to consume the future. The problem is that the classification system can only capture data about past performance, and the data analyses can only provide a basis for speculation about future contingencies. Moreover, the classification systems tend to be conservative and unimaginative, reducing populations and their environments to what is measurable, however crudely, and what is practical for deciding on insurable risks. More sophisticated mathematical modelling techniques are rare. When they are used – for example, in efforts to predict the effect of disasters such

as earthquakes or hurricanes – they are so replete with imagined scenarios and dummy variables that, when actual disaster occurs, they
collapse along with many of the buildings and insurance companies
involved (Ericson and Doyle forthcoming). For example, following the
unpredicted earthquake in Northridge, California, all existing probable maximum loss models of earthquake prediction were discarded
(Brun et al. 1997)

The obvious problem for the insurance industry is that it must price
its products before actual costs are known. Insurance companies do
not know in advance whether in the specific case they will be called
upon to actually provide the claims service that has been paid for in
advance. If they are called upon, they do not know when they will
have to pay for the claims service, nor how much it will cost in, for
example, health care bills or car repair bills. We interviewed a marketing manager for an insurance company who stressed, 'We're the only
industry that does not know the cost of its product when we sell it.' He
went on to say that while actuaries, like their science, may seem conservative, 'the business of insurance is not conservative. It's highly
speculative and it's very volatile. It is cyclical in nature.'

A senior executive of an institute of actuaries elaborated on the same
point. He said that, while actuarial science has all the trappings of science, for example, formal classification rules and quantitative analyses,
it is best seen as providing a framework for a 'guessing game.' The
game is

> trying to put a present value on contingent future events ... forecasting or
> making estimates as to the effect of things on the future ... establishing
> appropriate assumptions ... You like to think that it becomes a prediction,
> but it isn't really that ... We rarely set assumptions for a client without
> making them aware of the effect of varying those assumptions ... The clas-
> sic story ... talks about the actuary looking at the back window to set
> assumptions, but I think far and away the predominant view is today you
> look out the front window and make the assumptions. The back window
> may be a guide, but you're really looking at the future as to what you're
> going to get. Because the past isn't necessarily going to repeat itself ... You
> know you're going to be wrong from the start ... You want to be least
> wrong.

This view of actuarialism as futurology was shared by a range of
insurance executives we interviewed. The person in charge of insur-

ance and corporate risks for a large transportation company said that he had studied actuarial science extensively, but on the job his judgments about risk and responsibility were situationally based and future oriented:

> You're talking to someone who has taken some great courses on scientific methods of risk management. One of them was the Wharton School in Pennsylvania, another one was in Denver University. It was mathematical quantification of things. Great stuff. I suppose it would be really good for accountants because at the end of the day you could produce all of these rhetorical statements that would verify what you probably already knew when you started the exercise. I don't use too much in the way of mathematical equations to come to the conclusions that I do. It's usually based on working knowledge, insight into the business, and a sense of where it's going.

We interviewed a retired chief actuary for a large property and casualty insurance company. He described actuarial work in pricing insurance policies as 'God knows what to determine ... what they will eventually cost, a very difficult science ... It is judgment, it is experience, it is feel, touch.' He said that these subjective elements of actuarial work are necessary because formal quantitative analyses are perpetually subject to changes in law, company operations, political environments, and market conditions that have not been or cannot be taken into quantitative account. Actuaries have to continually 'adjust the embedded trends they see. This is the most difficult part. It is not an exact science, and because of society, because of the law, because insurance company operations are constantly shifting around, the actuaries have to be alert to make sure they can work out the answers.'

Insurance policy pricing is often contingent on political environments. For example, politics are omnipresent in the pricing of vehicle insurance. In jurisdictions with a private market, political influences on pricing and rating criteria are a major part of what provincial regulators deal with. In jurisdictions where there is a state-run vehicle insurance system, the politics are explicit and often featured in news stories. For example, a government seeking re-election will freeze premiums for political reasons, leaving it to their provincial vehicle insurance corporation to handle the financial fallout internally even if it builds towards a loss ratio security crisis. An actuary experienced in vehicle underwriting offered the example of whether there should be a higher premium for drivers who reside in the province's largest city because drivers there account for a disproportionate share of the claims costs. Actuarial calculations may indicate that these drivers should pay a 25 per cent higher premium than drivers elsewhere in the province, but the political calculus may prohibit any increase, and would certainly prohibit a one-shot increase. 'The art of the future is knowing how much to bring into the present. For example, how much of the change do you want to make in one year? You're going to load up the big city in one year, that's a political mistake.'

Politics often excludes actuarial criteria that create a more profitable risk pool. For example, unlike some state jurisdictions in the United States, Canadian provincial regulators exclude 'lifestyle' ratings, such as credit ratings, for vehicle insurance. This exclusion forces insurance company actuaries to remove factors that would make them more financially responsible on behalf of their company. As one vehicle insurance actuary expressed it in interview, lifestyle rating is 'the best management technique, which you're not allowed to use ... for determining good risk ... The person with a mortgage in the suburbs, with a garage, with a family, paying his bills, good credit record ... is your best auto insurance risk, is a person who has a sense of responsibility.' As we shall see in chapter 7, such formal exclusions do not prevent lifestyle criteria from entering underwriting decisions. They simply reinforce the fact that regulators focus on formal, objective actuarial criteria, thereby perpetuating the 'myth of the actuary' (Glenn 2000), while missing the reality that underwriting is based on assessments of moral character.

The politics of insurance product reform and legislative change can alter market conditions. These alterations must be taken into account by actuaries as agents of corporate governance. In a provincial jurisdiction we studied, the property and casualty insurance industry successfully lobbied for new vehicle insurance legislation. The new legislation contributed to the intensification of competition and a soft market, with greater insurance availability at lower premiums. This situation was compounded by a soft reinsurance market, making reinsurance less expensive, which in turn encouraged further price reduction risk taking by companies competing for market share. Moreover, new policy features were allowed under the legislation, features which actuaries were inexperienced with and could only speculate on. The CEO of a company operating in this environment outlined the actuarial complexities involved. He said that his company joined others in trying to sell more vehicle insurance because the new legislation, designed by the industry itself, *seemed* to allow for more actuarial precision:

> Anytime you can get a better handle on what you think your exposure is, you can try to price it better *in theory*, you want to sell more of it ... [But there was] an exponential effect where, in their rush to sell it, they [competitors] forced the price down, perhaps lower than it should be at this point in time, which tends to happen ... [There is] consumer switching ... likely a premium deficiency, if you will, in the market ... This is a very immature product and we haven't really seen how the costs are going to work just yet. There's a degree of conservatism that should be there in our reserving and should be there in our pricing that just isn't there at the moment ... Reinsurance markets are soft at the moment so we're able to buy reinsurance cheaper than we likely should. That's helped our enthusiasm and moved price down. Whereas in the early 1980s we had an interest rate phenomenon that was meaning we weren't accessing the [premium] money to invest, in the mid-1990s we had an equity market explosion ... That's going to come to an end again and much of the dynamic that actually sat there in the mid-1980s that got us into this mess in the first place [leading to the legislative reform] has the potential to some extent to repeat itself strangely enough in the late 1990s ... [It is a] take-all-comers environment ... very premature and so everybody is guessing.

This CEO discussed how the actuary's interpretive practice is related to both the corporate governance arrangements of the specific company and to local market conditions. Actuaries negotiate political economy within corporate governance criteria they help to establish and local market competitive forces they try to control:

> [In pricing the product] there are clearly places where we don't have enough data for that [pricing] to be credible. You have to then use industry data, but you have to interpret it. Where the science becomes a bit of an art is the actuary/product manager type being able to interpret your potential versus that industry past ... We don't blindly follow the numbers. There has to be judgment added to it ... [which] depends very greatly on the company and the people ... Many of the property and casualty companies don't even have [staff] actuaries ... We structured some of our field operations in such a way that we were trying to understand what our competitors are doing and whatever information we can get out

of the field it is then brought to bear. So it may well be that the right [actuarial] answer in territory 1 is a 10 per cent increase, but if the market is not there we can't take it. So the actuary is being asked to tell us on the basis of their science, if you will, what we should be doing. The field is being asked to tell us what they'd like to see us do in context. We then have a very small group of people that come at it from different disciplines ... [sometimes including] myself ... sit down and make our calls. There's an experience that's additive, tempers one to the other. If you know particular products are unprofitable, you may skew yourself more to the actuarial side because you wouldn't want to be writing more of that stuff. But, if it's thought to be otherwise, you may go closer to the market ... Markets evolve, and particularly as you get customers switching to where they are here in this province, it really causes the actuary a lot of headache and it makes it a lot more necessary to just use some judgment, part of which is tempered by markets.

The temper of competitive markets turns actuarial precision into actuarial speculation. As new policy terms are introduced and new features creep, a company cannot afford to stay out of the game for fear of customer switching. Customer switching leads to loss of premium revenues for investment. Lack of investment revenue creates pressure for premium increases, making the product even more unattractive. Customer switching also leads to adverse selection problems, as only higher risks stay in the pool. Higher risks bear higher claims costs, which also create pressure for premium increases, making the product even more unattractive. The primary way to combat customer switching is to offer the same new policy terms and features as competitors. However, this borrowing from competitors often means that actuaries and other company officials have little knowledge about how to price or manage what they have borrowed. An experienced underwriter for a large general insurance company made this point in interview:

It is amazing how many insurers fall by the wayside. Because many insurers ... have some compelling need to expand their operation into some new area without doing their homework. It's very easy today to take someone's insurance policy, photocopy it and make it available ... Nothing to prevent anybody from doing that. But these companies will not have the slightest understanding of what the intent is of the company that offers that contract ... If somebody is going to buy purely on price, more often than not they will buy a bogus product.

The political economy pressures on actuaries, and the interpretive latitude they have in negotiating political economy, mean that they themselves must be subject to regulation. While actuaries are an official cornerstone of corporate governance structures, these structures are also designed to govern them.

We have already made the point that insurance company actuaries primarily function as management executives who do little hands-on actuarial calculation. Therefore, regulation does not focus on their expertise in actuarial science, but rather on the ways in which they exercise their judgments. It is not their precision in prediction that is at issue, because no one can expect them to be very precise. Rather, it is the assumptions on which they operate, and the future scenarios they sketch based on those assumptions, that are regulated.

A senior executive of an institute of actuaries said in interview that regulation of actuaries focuses on the assumptions they use in setting standards and articulating rules related to product design and pricing. In making their assumptions clear, actuaries must not make a forecast 'sound like it is a prediction. It is not a prediction, it is an estimation based on certain assumptions.' It is also important to explore a range of assumptions in the process of justifying which ones will be used in actual products. 'You can start varying the assumptions and seeing what effects those things have, and that's where frequently the values are. It is not so much the absolute number as it is the variations in those numbers as you get out there.' Therefore, his institute focuses on regulating members whose assumptions are unduly aggressive, or who have missed something material in their assumptions.

Stories of insurance company failures indicate that regulation by and of actuaries is loose. For example, McQueen's (1996) account of the Confederation Life failure chronicles repeated laxity in actuarial audits and in the company's response to actuarial advice. Company decentralization meant that different actuarial methods were used across various units. There was no overall coordination and, if some figures were out a few percentage points, no questions were asked because a 'close enough is good enough' sensibility prevailed. When the company was known to be in financial difficulty, it used the same firm that had been its regular auditor for years. This firm 'had been part of the process by which Confed had so badly lost its way, and had approved all that had gone before' (ibid.: 135). Very late in the process leading to collapse, rating agencies still gave the company high ratings. For example, Standard and Poors' rating of AA indicated 'excellent financial security. Capacity to meet policyholder obligations is strong under a variety of economic and underwriting conditions' (ibid.: 140). A different firm of actuarial consultants was eventually hired, and they decided that the company had reached the point where it would become insolvent and therefore should stop selling certain lines of insurance. In their opinion, continued sales would be in violation of the Insurance Companies Act. Their letter of opinion was ignored and sales continued (ibid.: 185). The federal Superintendent of Financial Institutions indicated that the laxity evidenced in the Confederation Life case was generalizable. '"Auditors have been slow to accept really rigorous accounting ... This is getting better – but only when we write new rules ... there is, in regulatory and government circles in which I work, a high degree of skepticism about the capacity and independence of auditors"' (ibid.: 267). Such scepticism has accelerated with continuing scandals in various industries, such as the one involving the failure of Enron and its relationship with Anderson Consultants in the United States.

In his statement above, the Superintendent of Financial Institutions suggests that the elaboration of new rules will lead to better actuarial practice. But as we have seen, actuarial practice entails making interpretive judgments in the context of corporate culture and the political economy of competitive markets. These discretionary judgments lead to a course of action that differs from what has been standardized and articulated in rules:

> The preferred bureaucratic and legal way of dealing with these issues is the promulgation of rules. As is the case with scientific laws, art and judgment are required to connect those rules or laws to the actual phenomenon of experiment, observation, or economic life. But whereas scientists generally benefit from the order that this shared culture makes possible, economic actors strive perpetually to undermine it. Hence the presuppositions of accounting rules must themselves be codified and published, and so on until the whole Malthusian cascade presses up against the supply of paper and patience. (Porter 1995: 97)

The quantitative protocols, standards, and rules speak to the public character of how actuaries are to participate in corporate governance. Publicly, these technologies make actuarial work seem like painting by numbers. The numbers speak for themselves. Privately, the discretionary practice of actuarial work – sketching financial futures with varying assumptions that help to negotiate political economy – makes it more akin to postmodern painting. The numbers never speak for themselves. Actuaries look into the future with a kaleidoscope, not a telescope.

Insuring Corporate Governance

A multinational company that specializes in insuring corporate governance produced a marketing brochure entitled *Risk Management Solutions for Insurance Companies*. Far from suggesting that insurance companies have the actuarial precision to take the risk out of their operations, this brochure paints a cloudy picture of a future that insurers should worry about. Such portraits of impending gloom if not doom are commonplace in the marketing of any insurance product, and the marketing of insurance to insurers is no different.

The cover of the brochure is illustrated with a tall, stark office building reaching skywards. There is blue sky above, but there are also clouds. The clouds reflect in the windows of the office building, suggesting there may be stormy days ahead for the insurance company headquartered in it.

While the brochure's cover portrays the negative logic of the need for risk management, the text opens with a statement that makes it clear that risk has a positive side. The corporate risk manager for an insurance company that insures with this carrier offers a testimonial. The testimonial declares that his insurance company takes risks and therefore itself requires an insurance carrier with multiple lines available, good claims handling, and expertise in loss prevention.

Following the testimonial is a description of the carrier's wide range of products for insurance companies. For example, expertise is offered on how to manage solvency risks. Reference is made to the fact that insurance companies are venturing into new financial products and services beyond their traditional lines, and therefore face new risks of loss. Much like the state regulator helping to assess the subjective aspects of corporate culture and governance, the company offers 'customized solutions' that are supposed to 'enable insurance companies to control, finance or transfer risk in order to provide balance sheet protection.' One of the most significant considerations in this regard is whether the insurance company should retain some risks itself rather than pay inflated premiums to other insurance companies for protection.

The brochure lists a wide range of products related to moral risks posed by insurance company employees. For example, the errors and omissions package covers risks that arise in 'claims handling, loss control, financial advice, asset management, and life and securities product sales.' There are specific coverages available for fraud and other employee crimes, and for computer crimes regarding anything that is 'proprietary or a service bureau's computer systems, electronic funds transfer systems (EFTS) or customer electronic communications.' Insurers are also invited to insure against their own wrongdoing in employment practices, as well as various areas of general and fiduciary liability.

The errors and omissions insurance policies taken out by insurance companies play an important role in governing their underwriting and claims practices. For example, insurance companies with such policies are required by their carriers to develop training programs and procedures manuals to effect errors and omissions loss prevention. We interviewed a specialist in this field who said that there is perpetual effort to train agents on how to communicate with their clients, on the need to take 'ass covering' notes of conversations with clients, and on standards in office operations. A claims specialist for a vehicle insurance company said that some of the standard features on the application for insurance form were driven by the errors and omissions insurance policies held by the company's network of sales agents. For example, the client's signature was required on specific sections of the application, indicating that she had read the section and by implication understood and agreed with the coverage requested.

Increasingly, state regulators, appreciating how the insurance industry can govern itself in this way, require company employees or agents to have errors and omissions insurance. A life insurance executive we interviewed said that repeated misselling scandals in that industry have led some regulators to require errors and omissions coverage on agents and brokers. She observed that many insurance companies would still prefer to self-insure or gamble on their own agents to be honest. However, she continued, 'I'm surprised that insurance companies aren't requiring it, because in the absence of the agent being insured the courts are sure to go after the principal, being the insurance company ... [But it is] not driven by the insurance companies, however, its driven by regulation.'

Another source of regulation in this regard is industry associations. For example, the Registered Insurance Brokers of Ontario requires a member brokerage firm to have an errors and omissions policy to cover each employee, as well as a fidelity bond to cover theft by employees. The combined pressure from state regulators and industry associations means that the vast majority of insurance sales employees are so covered. For example, in 1997, 98 per cent of LUAC member agents were covered by errors and omissions insurance policies, up from 87 per cent in 1993.

As we document in chapter 6, the life insurance industry in particular is rife with morally risky behaviour by sales agents. In many contexts, misselling has been the norm. Moreover, misselling has been structurally fostered at the company level, for example, through commission structures designed to induce sales managers and agents to sell particular products to consumers that are more expensive but less advantageous than alternative products.

Clarke (1999: 115–16, 133–5) records that after a series of life insurance and pension misselling scandals in the United Kingdom, the brokers association FIMBRA had difficulty obtaining professional indemnity insurance for members. Many insurance carriers were reluctant to provide coverage because agents had proven themselves to be too morally risky. Professional indemnity insurers 'warned that cover might not be renewed ... or that higher premiums and excesses and exclusions regarding personal pensions [selling] might be insisted upon' (ibid.: 133). The Personal Investments Authority (PIA) as state regulator engaged a brokerage firm to develop new coverage for agents, but twenty-four out of twenty-eight underwriters approached rejected the proposal. FIMBRA proposed coverage for members through an exclusive brokerage arrangement. However, four different brokers' associations rejected this proposal, arguing that most of their members already had adequate coverage and that the premiums for the proposed scheme were excessive. They also argued that the excessive premiums were a result of the greater moral risks posed by the newer and smaller brokerage firms compared to the established and more reputable firms. They felt that it was unfair to ask the better risks to subsidize the poorer risks. They preferred a system that unpooled risks so that those who proved more upright would not be providing a safety net for those who might be led into temptation. The state regulator accepted an unpooling system in which agents were forced into the professional indemnity insurance market and 'if they failed to obtain cover they faced the deauthorization by the PIA' (ibid.: 135).

Various interviewees told us that life insurance agents are high moral risks and therefore difficult to insure. Difficulties extend beyond the endemic misselling that makes errors and omissions coverage risky. Disability insurance coverage for life insurance agents is also risky because of the commission-based structure of their employment. Facing a highly competitive sales environment in which failure to produce means no commission income and the threat of losing their jobs, life agents are prone to seek refuge in disability insurance claims. A senior underwriter for a life and health insurance company stopped writing disability policies for life insurance agents. 'If they've got disability insurance they are one of the worst risks ... They know how the insurance works ... whether its abuse, whether they know how to get around the system ... I would not take disability insurance on an agent. They're self-employed, don't forget ... and you tend to find that if somebody hasn't got employment income, they start to find soft tissue problems and stuff like that ... A lot of the claims that I know that we had from agents were a result of stress or back injuries, soft tissue injuries.'

We interviewed an insurance brokerage executive whose firm specialized in underwriting errors and omissions coverage for insurance brokers and agents. She said that brokers and agents are high moral risks in need of constant training about their responsibilities. One sign of the problem is the fact that, like insured persons in general, brokers and agents do not read their errors and omissions insurance policies. They simply assume that their insurance is adequate, and when a professional liability problem arises they expect their insurer to cover for them:

> [At training seminars] we always will ask ... 'How many of you in the room have read your professional liability policy?' You have a room of fifty people, maybe one or two people put their hand up! 'So you guys are ... saying your clients should be responsible for being familiar with [the policy], yet you as professionals haven't read yours. If you haven't done it, why would you expect your clients to do it?' ... [The broker's sensibility is] reading an insurance policy, at the best of times, has got to be at the bottom of my list of things that I want to do ... 'I've got what I need, I'm relying on someone else ... I've chosen the limits, I've chosen the deductibles, I know the insurers will get insured and that's it.'

This interviewee stressed that errors and omissions coverage is essential for the proper governance of insurance brokerages and agencies. She underscored this belief by pointing out that her own firm had errors and omissions coverage: a company that specializes in errors and omissions insurance for brokers and agents must manage its own professional liability risks through this form of insurance. She also pointed out that it is very rare for brokers and agents to self-insure for errors and omissions. 'And frankly if I had somebody say that to me, I don't know if I'd want to insure them ... It's not very professional, not very well versed, not very knowledgeable. They make bold, stupid statements like that and probably say other stupid things.'

Given the high moral risks posed in the insurance sales relationship, errors and omissions insurance is underwritten stringently. There are detailed investigations of agency operations which lead to risk segmentation and unpooling. We interviewed a partner in a small-town insurance agency who paid about $45,000 premium annually for a million dollars of errors and omissions coverage. He said that the errors and omissions insurance application process included a twenty-five-page questionnaire, reports from bankers, financial statements, loss ratio statistics, and reports from insurance companies whose products are sold through the brokerage. 'If you are a new client to an errors and omissions insurer without a track record, or with a checkered track record, they'll actually come in and do interviews with your employees and look through your ... customer files. And see what kind of rates you take when you answer a telephone call from a customer, what your paper trail is like when a customer asks for an increase or a change in coverage. Things like if a guy asks for a certain coverage, do you get him to sign something?'

Large insurance companies with their own networks of exclusive agencies also govern through errors and omissions insurance coverage on those agencies. We interviewed the head of agency operations for one such insurance company. He said that the owner/manager of each agency has compulsory errors and omissions coverage supplied through an outside carrier determined by the company. This arrangement allows the company to control the terms and conditions of coverage and thereby to govern agents. Coverage becomes at once a vehicle for structuring the moral responsibility of agents and financing the moral risk they pose:

> Any mistakes that their staff make are theirs. Like they're responsible. So there's a little more pressure on that. Society has changed, and there have been court rulings elevating the duty of care that is expected of agents ...

Big class actions against insurance companies for inappropriate sales practices, ripping off clients ... I negotiate the contract and I administer it so all the agents buy it from me. So I talk to them about potential claims, I talk to them about how to submit their premiums ... [which] are reflected by the size of their portfolio. The larger the portfolio, the higher the deductible, so they have some 'skin' in the claims. You have a $5 million book of business, you could afford a $5,000 deductible. If they have a few losses or potential losses of a similar nature, the underwriter from that company would call and say, 'What's happening with this agent? ... Better go check her out ... office procedures ... how do we prevent this from occurring?' ... Our agents are afraid of it because they think that the rates are going to go up. They don't want to report claims, but they need to.

We interviewed several agency owners/managers with this insurance company. They confirmed that they were 'afraid' of how they were being governed through errors and omissions insurance. One owner/manager said that, in spite of the extra expense involved, he had hired two very experienced and knowledgeable staff agents 'because errors and omissions claims can destroy.' He said that he thought about errors and omissions problems daily, and that this led him to review constantly the coverage of each client 'just in case there is a scenario where we forgot to sell, say, collision ... homeowners insured to value ... Errors and omissions must be avoided at all costs, and if that means making a little less, fine.'

We also attended a regional sales meeting of owners/managers for this company, at which there was considerable discussion about errors and omissions problems. The district manager said a representative of the errors and omissions carrier was going to visit each agency office and also hold a general meeting. He urged everyone present to attend this meeting, and to prepare beforehand. 'I would encourage you to look at your policies, think about who is covered and everything else like that. It's a very complex issue, errors and omissions insurance ... It's a totally optional meeting, [but] just don't ever have any errors and omissions questions [for me] because I won't be able to answer them.'

Errors and omissions insurers also govern the claims process. The small town agency partner we interviewed said that while potential errors and omissions claims were frequent, over a fourteen-year period he had only five claims reach the point of pre-trial discovery. Once a complaint is made by a policyholder that might lead to an errors and omissions claim, the entire process is strictly governed by the errors and omissions insurer. 'You have a full obligation of disclosure ... And if you don't, they have every right to deny coverage and will ... The right to ask for complete cooperation, opening your books and records and getting your people in to give depositions and all the rest of that ... The insurer becomes subrogated to your rights.' This interviewee also described the delicate negotiations involved in such cases. The aggrieved policy-holder must be cooled out, but the insurer cannot just make nuisance payments that will encourage future frivolous complaints. 'You don't necessarily want to steamroller them and end up in court, or just make a big splash out of it because you've got to live in the same community with them. You also don't want a company that is going to roll over and play dead and start shelling out every time somebody whines.'

An executive for a brokerage specializing in errors and omissions coverage for insurance brokers and agents concurred. He said that the main errors and omissions insurance company he dealt with special-ized in helping brokers and agents to 'maintain image in small markets ... If you're one of two brokers in a small town, word gets out that you've done something negative, it's not a good thing ... There may be clear-cut situations where the broker has erred, and rather than bring it to the attention of all the parties concerned, the errors and omissions insurer will go in and act as the primary insurer would have, and settle the claim. The client may or may not be aware that there was ever a problem with coverage.'

This interviewee also noted that errors and omissions policies are structured to encourage early and discreet settlement, if indeed a set-tlement is called for. For example, if the insurer decides on a settlement figure and the agent does not agree to it, the agent is responsible for any court-ordered settlement plus costs above that initial figure.

State regulatory agencies, industry associations, actuaries, and insurance on insurance company employees and agents combine to foster a system of self-governance. This system is effective to a degree, but the recurrent misselling scandals in marketing insurance products suggest that moral risks are endemic. New governance mechanisms may redistribute and manage those risks better, but the system, like a sponge, tends to soak consumers and quickly return to its original form. We now turn to specific analyses of market misconduct to under-stand why insurers themselves pose the moral risks they denounce and attempt to prevent in their clients.

6. Market Misconduct

While injury may be done in two ways, either by force or by fraud, fraud is like the sly little vixen, force like the lion; both are wholly foreign to man, but fraud is the more despicable. Of all injustice, none is more grave than that of people who, when they are most false, conduct their affairs as if they were good men.

Cicero, *On Duties*

People of the same trade seldom get together, even for merriment and diversion, but the conversation ends in a conspiracy against the public, or in some contrivance to raise prices.

Adam Smith, *The Wealth of Nations* (1776)

There are two fools in every market; one asks too little, one asks too much.

Russian Proverb

There is widespread and systemic market misconduct in the insurance sales process: insurers use deceptive sales practices and rely upon consumer ignorance in order to sell insurance products that are more profitable but do not suit the consumer's needs. Such practices are especially pervasive in the life insurance industry, and our analysis in this chapter consequently focuses on this industry in particular. We initially examine manipulative sales practices that disadvantage the consumer. We then explain these practices in terms of the structure and culture of the insurance industry. Finally, we consider the various governance mechanisms through which the industry tries to manage the misconduct generated by its own structure and culture. We argue that many of these mechanisms accentuate the aggressive sales culture and do not address the structural basis of market misconduct.

Market Misconduct

Market misconduct in the sale of insurance is widespread and subject to much public discussion. There have been recurrent public scandals regarding what the industry euphemistically calls 'misselling,' but which actually involves institutionally endorsed manipulation, deception, and fraud. The United Kingdom in particular has experienced a number of scandals involving the deceptive selling of life insurance and pension products (Clarke 1999). In North America, the use of misleading illustrations about returns on life insurance investment products has been a salient issue, reflected for example, in class action lawsuits regarding 'vanishing premium' policies. But there are many other routine practices through which insurance agents pose moral risks to consumers.

One way to manipulate the market is to control the context in which insurance sales are made to the point where it is too difficult for the consumer to go elsewhere. This approach, referred to by industry insiders as 'negative marketing,' allows the insurer to offer a combination of inflated premiums and inferior products by lessening competition. This situation occurs, for example, in the sale of mortgage insurance through financial institutions that are also providing the mortgage. The financial institution makes it too cumbersome and onerous to obtain mortgage insurance elsewhere, thereby allowing it to in effect charge an extra premium for ease of process.

There is also tied selling across different insurance products. General insurance companies and agents work to have a client insure several lines with them. In this effort, they pressure a client who is seeking one line, for example a vehicle policy, to also take out another line, for example, a home policy. There are usually inducements for doing so, for example a discounted premium or more favourable contract conditions on the additional line. Discounts in one line or feature may be made up for by increased pricing in other lines and features. This type of tied selling is illegal in many jurisdictions, but practised routinely and openly. The CEO of a property and casualty insurance company said in interview that his company was operating in a highly competitive vehicle insurance market. One response to the competition was tied selling arrangements, offering certain discounts on home insurance for the client who buys vehicle insurance. '[This is] a very aggressive marketplace where people are chasing business ... [The result is] a different emphasis on group selling, tied selling if you will, which is supposed to be illegal. But it's amazing when it results in a lower price the politicians look sideways, so do the bureaucrats.'

In their exuberance for increasing the company's premium income and their own commission income, insurance agents may overinsure clients. For example, 'negative option marketing' involves the addition of unrelated insurance coverage to a basic policy at an additional cost to the policyholder. Thus a home policy may have travel coverage added without knowledge of the policyholder. Also referred to as automatic add-on or positive billing, this practice is not positive for the policyholder because she has not been advised of the itemized cost or details of the extra coverage, and of course has not authorized it.

Insurance agents can inflate the insured value of an asset beyond its actual market value. There is a long history of overinsurance in the selling of property insurance, especially fire insurance (Heimer 1985: 51ff., 78ff.). Agents sell above asset value in order to obtain higher premiums and commissions, and the company then discredits the asset value in the event of a claimed loss.

We interviewed a senior official of an insurance brokers' association who said, 'A lot of frauds I have come across, it was the company people showing the agents how to do it.' He related the story of a company that routinely underwrites disability insurance for a group of professionals at 40 per cent of their gross income when the legal limit is 40 per cent of net income, which is about one-half of the gross. In the event of a claim the 'policy is absolutely, totally worthless ... They go to collect, one of the first questions an insurance company asks is ... your income tax return ... 'You are overinsured. And not only that, but you are misrepresented on your application' ... I see it ... time and time again with the same company ... If you routinely insure people for benefits they can't collect, it is win, win, win, win ... It is the best business you could possibly write.'

In an effort to enhance sales prospects, an agent may misrepresent the security of the insurance product, including the insurance companies that are underwriting it. In one jurisdiction we studied, an agent sold insurance that promised to pay the full replacement cost of a vehicle if it was destroyed in an accident or stolen and not returned. Facing heavy competition from the major vehicle insurance company in the market, he claimed that he held a Lloyd's of London contract to underwrite his policies in this field. He had no such contract, a fact that was not discovered for over a year when someone finally decided to verify the supposed arrangements with Lloyd's.

Insurance agents may also misrepresent the type of product that they are selling. We interviewed an investigator for a management consulting firm who had previously worked in the special investigation unit of a major life insurance company. This interviewee said that in his experience it was common for life insurance agents to sell college education plans as if they were savings plans, when in fact they are life insurance policies whose accumulated premiums can be used for the college education of the policyholder's children.

This last case points to one dimension of the widespread and thorny problem of agents misrepresenting the investment value of life insurance products. One approach is to tell the client that the premium contributions will eventually be 'returned' through the investment value of the life insurance policy, so that the life insurance is in effect at no cost. The client is not fully informed about the 'time value' of money, in other words how her money might be personally invested to obtain much higher rates of return. Indeed, it is the insurance company that takes the client's premium contributions and invests them for its own profit, while hoping to leave the client with the belief that she too has obtained a good deal by having the premiums eventually paid back.

At an insurance company's sales meeting we observed, the district manager instructed his sales managers and agents on how to sell a life insurance policy designed to have investment value and to avoid some estate taxes. He emphasized that clients are often impressed by a policy that returns enough to in effect pay for itself, and added that such clients overlook the fact that if they invested the same amount themselves in higher yielding and equally safe financial products they would be much better off. He used the example of a farmer's son, who, the district manager said, is likely to be ignorant of the time value of money he will spend on insurance premiums. 'About 30 per cent of the policies being sold now are starting to have return of premium on them. People just love that concept, I'm not sure why. The farming son, he's probably going to put out $300,000 to $400,000 over the life of the policy. If they can get that money back, the way a farmer thinks, they don't worry about the time value of the money or anything like that. If they can get their principal back they're more than happy.'

The district manager followed this 'pitch' to his agents with details on how they could manipulate a new universal life insurance policy to make similar offers to prospective clients. Over time, money from the accumulating cash value of a policy could be used to 'refund premiums.' The district manager told the assembled sales managers and agents, 'I'll put my market conduct and compliance hat on and say you really can't say it doesn't cost anything ... Even the way you've said it you would have got a yellow flag from a compliance officer.' At this point several agents in the room laughed, then pointed to the researcher's tape recorder and exclaimed, 'You turn that off!' More laughter ensued. Those present knew that from a regulatory viewpoint, this was no laughing matter. For example, life insurance illustration guidelines developed by the CLHIA in collaboration with state regulators explicitly prohibit such practices:

> Any summation of cash flows must take into account assumed interest to ensure a fair representation of actual costs to a client, at a reasonable rate. For example, it would be inappropriate to compare ... total cost of insurance over 'xx' years divided by the face amount without taking into consideration the time value of money ... Some examples of representative actions that would be considered violations of the Guidelines include ... using values from an illustration to show the client net cost values. For example, telling a client that after twenty years a policy has 'cost you nothing' because the policy withdrawals equal the premiums paid. (CLHIA 1997a: 29, 34)

An illustration is defined as 'any communication to a current or prospective client that shows numbers or graphs of future policy premiums and/or values, or features that depend on them, for an individual life insurance policy' (ibid.: 6). The problem with illustrations is that they are necessarily based upon speculative assumptions about interest rates, returns on various investment possibilities, and the practices through which insurance companies design and fund their life insurance products. Illustrations can only visualize future scenarios, and problems become fully evident only in retrospect.

The life insurance industry readily concedes that its illustrations only imagine the future. As in social scientific efforts at modelling and prediction, a limited number of factors have to be selected for analysis. The CLHIA guidelines on illustrations instruct the agent, since 'you cannot predict the future, the list [of relevant factors] should be presented as representative, not exhaustive' (ibid.: 18). The agent is to make a 'confident projection' of what the returns might be, based on reasonable assumptions. An article in the Life Underwriters Association of Canada *Forum* for May 1996, entitled 'Sales Illustrations: A Reasonable Approach,' makes it clear that 'reasonableness' is itself probabilistic and speculative. For example, 'for an illustration to be "reasonable" there should be a 50/50 chance of the actual results being higher or lower over the time frame of the presentation.' Of course no one can know in advance whether there is a 50/50 chance, or any other level of probability that might be conjured.

Industry guidelines do not require the illustration of possible future negative returns, although there is plenty of experience with negative outcomes (CLHIA 1997a: 22). More typically insurers offer illustrations that are overconfident and unreasonable, especially in retrospect. This was certainly the case in the various misselling scandals that transpired in the 1980s. Companies offered life insurance policies that assumed historically high interest rates would continue in the long term. One widely sold product offered 'vanishing premiums': a policy that required substantial premium payments over the initial years, but that would be fully paid up early on so that the policy would be in force for the remainder of the policyholder's life without the policyholder having to pay additional premiums. When interests rates declined sharply, the companies increased the period for collecting premiums. Policyholders who baulked at these unexpected extended payments found that the premiums were nevertheless deducted from the accumulated value of their policy. For example, the lead plaintiff in a class action suit involving approximately 400,000 Sun Life Canada policyholders said that 'without notification, the offset date projections were unilaterally altered by the insurer. In my case, from the originally illustrated twelve years to an astounding additional forty-three years.'

We interviewed an industry association official who said sales documents frequently indicated that agents went out of their way to project a rosy future for the person who bought into the vanishing premiums concept. Violation of industry guidelines regarding illustrations was routine. 'Some of these illustrations are coming out of the woodwork with happy faces drawn on them, arrows and comments and so on, that probably wouldn't meet the spirit of the guidelines, or even the words of the guidelines.'

We interviewed a vanishing premiums policyholder who had become active in seeking redress for himself and for other victims. His trusted life insurance agent in a small community had approached him with the new vanishing premiums feature. 'He went to my father's funeral. He went to our wedding. Why wouldn't I trust him? We babysat his kids. I thought, "Oh, that's nice of him, he's giving us something good here. He's doing what I need."' The agent recommended that the existing life insurance policies on the interviewee and his wife and son should be cashed in and used towards new vanishing premiums policies. Moreover, the new vanishing premiums policy allowed the interviewee's daughter to be insured without health checks. This was seen as a particular advantage because the daughter had previously been refused a life insurance policy by the same insurance company due to a permanent health condition. Illustrations at the point of sale indicated that the policies would be paid up in eight years. However, the offset dates were subsequently extended for several decades so that he would have to pay full premiums to the age of ninety! He estimated that after eight years he had sunk $35,000 into the policies, money which could have been invested for substantial personal returns rather than giving it to the insurance company to invest for its profitable returns.

> [He] sits and controls with these figures and he's telling you with this rosy glow that this company is taking all the risks. [He's] not talking about volatility, not talking about if the dividends go down, not even alluding to that ... 'You don't see any more premiums being paid out after eight years, do you?' That's how he's selling it to you ... Used all our emotions ... 'Well, now I can get you insurance for your daughter. When she was six they refused, but I told you I'd come back ... I've got the Cadillac of policies ... But the beauty is, we'll cash in your old policies and that will pay for the first couple of years of high premiums ... But you only pay for a set number of years and then it's paid up. You never have to pay again.' Never have to pay again! ... [But he did not mention] interest rates, or any of the rest of it, or that they could not predict accurately or properly.

The interviewee said that he did try to question some aspects of the policy at the point of sale. For example, he interpreted the contract to mean that the death benefit lump sum payment could decrease depending upon the long-term investment return on the policy. The agent lied, saying the death benefit level was guaranteed. At the time 'I didn't know he lied, OK, because I could only trust him ... I thought, OK, I must be misreading this.' The interviewee said that he asked for copies of the illustrations that had been used, but only received them four months after the sale had been made. It was only at this time that the required disclaimer sheet was also included explaining how the policy value could fluctuate and affect the offset date. He said that he knew clients of another company who were never given disclaimer sheets.

In retrospect, the interviewee had the creeping feeling that even the basic terms of the policy were unreasonable. For example, he calculated that while he signed for a rate of $7.74 per $1,000 coverage on his son's policy, he could have bought term life insurance at a rate of $1.87 per $1,000 coverage. Moreover, the replacement arrangement regarding his son's previous policy made the new policy even more expensive. Paid-up additions using the previous policy dividends brought the total to $94.90 per $1,000 coverage! 'I didn't sign a policy allowing them to do that with my dividends, did I? The rate that I signed for was $7.74, not $94.90 per $1,000. Is *that* not fraud? They increased the cost of paid-up additions, each year, without me even knowing it and realizing it. Cheating people. It was a scam.'

The recent development of more complex 'universal' life insurance products with myriad investment options has compounded the illustrations problem. These products are subject to 'feature creep': features are added to make a product seem potentially more lucrative in relation to long-term investment returns, without emphasizing that the risks lie with the policyholder and that the company is covering its own risks through several interrelated pricing and investment mechanisms. In an article entitled 'Illustrations: New Generation of Life Insurance Products Demands Full Disclosure,' the PPI Financial Group (1997) observes: 'As more companies jump on the new Universal Life bandwagon, concerns are also growing over aggressive pricing practices and feasibility of guaranteed long-term bonuses. There are mounting concerns too about the level and the thoroughness of the disclosure provided with sales illustrations of these and other new products – particularly some buyers and their agents may not know or appreciate how many factors can affect the long-term performance of these products.' This article also describes 'illustration warfare' in which computer software systems are developed to illustrate cosy returns over time without offering details on policies and how they are priced.

An article entitled 'Life Insurance Illustrations' (*Insurance Planning* 4(4), 1997) points out that illustrations typically ignore or downplay the following aspects of how insurance companies cover their own risks in universal life underwriting, while heightening the risk to policyholders.

First, policyholders are offered 'investment bonuses' if they continue to pay into the policies over specified time periods. What remains hidden is the fact that these bonuses are funded by lower basic interest rates on the policy compared to, for example, those available through bank investment certificates. The spread is often substantial enough that even after the 'bonus,' the overall return is less than what could be obtained from a simple bank certificate.

Second, there are various mortality and lapse rate assumptions built into these products, with mechanisms for companies to cover their risks if their assumptions prove wrong. For example, if the insurer's mortality experience is worse than expected, it can reduce the interest rate credited to the accumulated fund to cover the difference. Thus, while there may be a guaranteed level cost of insurance, this means little because the insurance company simply funds the policy through decreasing investment returns as necessary. Policy lapse rates are even more volatile, and are dealt with in the same way. Companies making aggressive assumptions with respect to investment yields and lapse rates will offer lower level cost of insurance guarantees and thus initially illustrate better policy values. However, unfavourable experience in mortality and/or lapses is met with increases in the spread on the investment component of in force policies to cover losses.

Third, some companies maintain 'minimum transfer thresholds' before funds can be transferred to higher yielding investments. In some instances, large balances must be kept in daily interest accounts, with only funds in excess of the specified amount being transferable to higher-yielding investments. 'For example, a relatively low-funded UL policy with a relatively high minimum transfer threshold would have earned 2.5 percent in the daily interest account in 1996. If this client had been able to transfer these funds into an equity-based interest option, the policy's fund value could have earned in excess of 20 percent. Obviously, comparing these two product illustrations at the same interest rate would be unfair' (ibid.).

Fourth, various policy charges and management fees are often not accounted for in illustrations. A portion of the funds invested are withdrawn by the company, usually monthly, to cover policy charges. In some products, the level of withdrawal increases with investment returns, but this is not illustrated or otherwise made explicit in the sales process.

These dimensions of universal life products mean that 'the probability that a UL policy's long-term performance will be identical to the values shown on its illustration is negligible. Policy illustrations are therefore best suited for their primary purpose of demonstrating a product's features, and not as a tool to compare the values of different products' (ibid.).

The PPI Financial Group analysis of universal life illustrations underscores the irony that, after all of the vanishing premium policy scandals, class action suits, and extraordinary payments in compensation, the life insurance industry is offering even more misleading illustrations:

> The significant spread between market yields and the policy's minimum guaranteed rates is downplayed and the variety of factors which may force the company to adjust (i.e. reduce) rates in the future is rarely mentioned. With the complexity and confusion surrounding long-term bonuses, 'guaranteed' cost of insurance and expense charges, and the fluctuations affecting basic interest rate guarantees, the potential for misleading illustrations of the UL level COI [cost of insurance] product is perhaps greater than ever before. This is highly ironic, coming as it does during a time when the insurance industry is under severe attack for alleged abusive marketing practices involving illustrations of the older versions of UL and participating policies. (PPI Financial Group 1997)

Life insurance agents systematically try to sell inappropriate products to prospective policyholders. The most common form of this market misconduct is selling whole life or universal life policies when the person is better off with a term life policy. As discussed in the next section, agents and their sales managers are structurally compelled to sell the more expensive and risky whole life and universal life products through better commission rates on those products. Everyday training and practice also reinforce that clients should be told to put more money into their participating policies to ensure that they do not end up with what is in effect an expensive version of term insurance or, worse still, nothing at all. For example, a manual for agents in a life insurance company we studied included an insert entitled, 'For a Few Dollars More.' This insert reminded agents that 'in many instances only a few dollars more per month will make a drastic difference in policy performance. UL is an expensive form of "term" insurance which many policyholders may have chosen unintentionally by selecting the minimum premium.' A later entry in the agents' manual repeats the lesson. 'Don't forget, this is still a Life policy and works better with more cash in the policy than not. Err on the side of conservatism! It is a much better surprise to tell your client he has actually more cash in the policy than originally projected, rather than having to advise the client his policy may lapse soon if he doesn't pay more pre-

mium. The point has to be hammered home with all possible policyholders.'

Life insurance selling is a continuous process. Companies introduce
new products and features not only to attract new business, but also to
persuade existing policyholders to change their coverage. An example
of persuading existing policyholders is provided in the previously
discussed case of the interviewee who cashed in his family's existing
policies and used the proceeds to fund the initial premiums on new vanishing premium policies. His trusted agent told him that the new policies were much better for his needs and convinced him that they could
be funded initially through the cash value on the existing policies.

Converting existing clients to new life insurance policies is a routine
part of the business. It has also been routine to sell new products that
are less advantageous than the products they replace. This practice is
referred to as 'twisting' or 'churning,' and it has been institutionalized
since the inception of life insurance (Zelizer 1979: 139).

Replacement policies almost always entail some immediate loss for
the policyholder. There are administrative charges for the new acquisition. Premiums may be increased as a result of the policyholder's
increased age and changing health conditions. The options available in
the new policy for waiver of premium, income, or settlement may be
less beneficial. Some previously guaranteed insurability clauses may
be altered or removed. Paid-up policy values may be reduced. Policy
loan levels may also be reduced or eliminated. The very availability of
policy cash values may be affected. There may also be effects on the tax
status of the policyholder and/or the life insured. Always in question
is whether these interrelated complexities of possible loss are fully
explained to the client in the context of trying to make a lucrative sale.
Some agents may not be capable of fully explaining these complexities
because they themselves do not understand them.

We interviewed an investigator about his experiences as a former
special investigation unit officer for a life insurance company. He said
that churning was routine. 'When they'd come up with a new product,
if you went through the files of the company you could see a whole
bunch of churning.' He said a typical scenario involved a young family
that was being churned into a universal life product that had higher
premiums and less coverage than what it replaced. He also said that
agents frequently churned clients by telling them another agent had
missold them an inappropriate policy in the past! This was sometimes
accompanied by illustrations indicating the poor performance of the

existing policy over time, compared to the anticipated performance of the new product the agent was trying to sell. The client would end up agreeing. "'I was misrepresented. I was sold this dog here ten years ago and I could have earned this [much more].'" The agent would reply, "'Well, I'm sorry but this was explained and it's clear what you bought, and for your circumstances at the time we're not accepting any responsibility. [But we'll take] all our money out, because I'm going to move it to so and so and they're a better company and I can trust them more.'"

This interviewee said that various creative schemes were developed to relieve innocent policyholders of their money. In one scheme, agents of the insurance company set up a charitable remainder trust and had a designated agent serve as the trustee. The approach was to have existing whole life policyholders cash in their policies and contribute the proceeds to the charitable trust, thereby receiving tax relief. A designated charity was to receive a lump sum on the policyholder's death, while investments in mutual funds were supposed to make the new life insurance policy self-funding. This was not a product of the insurance company itself. However, the president of the company and other senior company officials knew about the practice at least two years prior to the interviewee's investigation of it. Policyholders believed it was a company product and bought it because they trusted the company and its agents, they believed that they could do good through an eventual charitable donation, and because they believed in the promise of both tax relief and a policy that would be self-funding. They were ignorant of the fact that the principal transferred from the cash value of their whole life policies was no longer theirs:

> The clients, everybody I interviewed believed that it was one of the company's products ... 'It was so and so and I've known them for years and yeah, he's the office manager there. It was one of your companies' ... So the company is responsible, legally and financially, for all of this mess ... So you've got these people saying, 'Well I want to be where I was five years ago. I want my policy back with interest. And I want the cash value back ... [Tax lawyers advised me that] the charitable remainder trusts are recommended for people who have $600,000 in assets and more. Well, these [clients] are a bunch of guys like me. He's got a job and a house and a bunch of kids ... a lot of working class people. So now you get into ... the suitability of who bought it. Out of the one office there were about 250 people who sold this stuff.

Insurance companies also face more straightforward fraud and theft by their sales agents. The same interviewee said that there were cases of 'straight theft' in his company. For example, a client would make out the cheque for an annuity to the agent personally and the agent would keep the funds. An investigator for a state market conduct regulator said, 'One of our big types of business ... [is] the agent who sells a policy and "forgets" to remit the premiums to the insurance company. That's a fairly common endeavour.' An investigator for a management consulting company said that a 'popular' fraud among life insurance agents is to 'employ shells or confederates to take out policies, so that they can get their up-front commission, and then cancel it ... All the insurance companies know it, but it still goes on constantly.'

The urge to close a sale can also lead to forgery. An internal investigation by a major insurance company in the United Kingdom revealed a range of such offences, including 'forged customer signatures and falsified direct-debit mandates' (*Sunday Times* Money Section, 30 May 1999, p. 1). A former special investigation unit officer for a life insurance company said in interview that forgeries may simply be expedient. For example, the company he worked for paid agents twenty-five dollars to process forms with changed underwriting conditions on a policy. Many agents found it more convenient to forge a customer's signature rather than to take the time to meet with her to explain the changed conditions and obtain the required signature. When he reported this practice, the initial reaction of management and the legal department was to do nothing, arguing that these were not official policy documents. 'I said, "You have fraudulent signatures in your corporate records and you're a friggin' insurance company! That alone should cause some concern."' The head of one of the company's regional operations was subject to investigation. He was eventually dismissed, but with a severance package, after it was discovered that, among other things, he had condoned illegal signatures on insurance documents and submitted false expense accounts.

The Structure and Culture of Market Misconduct

Life insurance companies often respond to market misconduct scandals by denying responsibility. In public statements as well as internal communications, they sometimes use a 'rotten apple' theory to blame individual agents as unethical and irresponsible. They also use a 'blaming the victim' approach, in which consumers are said to be unfairly attacking insurers for what are actually their own poor choices.

We interviewed a former life insurance agent who said that he had sold many vanishing premium policies that turned out to be very disadvantageous to his clients. He said that at the time these products came on the market both he and the company felt they were reasonable value. However, it was when interest rates moved dramatically lower that the company engaged in wrongdoing. It tried to fund the problems through further premiums and charges to policyholders, and then blame agents for their shoddy work at the point of sale and policyholders for their failure to appreciate what they were buying:

> There are people now who dealt with me when I first started, and I didn't do a good job for them because I didn't know what I was doing ... I've got insurance policies that are probably out there that I'm not real proud of today, but I can tell you the day I sold them I was real proud of them ... I don't know that the insurance companies did anything wrong at first. They certainly did things wrong when they noticed that interest rates were going the wrong way. So I would think that probably five years before this [vanishing premiums scandal] started there was a problem and everybody knew about it except maybe the consumer ... I don't feel sorry for the company, they deserve everything they're going to get in these losses.

Life insurance company internal documents we examined promoted the view that it is not the structure and culture of company operations that yield market misconduct, but rather bad agents and disgruntled consumers. For example, a marketing manual for agents that provided guidelines on advertising and various print communications in the sales process stated that 'in all companies there are a number of producers whose questionable priorities hurt the image of everyone. It is these "bad apples" who have instigated the involvement of the government in regulating insurance market conduct.' This manual also warned agents to beware of consumers who second-guess their own product choices and then transfer blame onto agents and companies in the form of legal actions. After listing several large judgments against life insurance companies, and the threat of more to come, the manual states, 'Consumers are being sold more complex products to cover their life insurance needs and they rely on their insurance agent to act in their best interests and give them the best advice. This opens the door for claims made by disgruntled customers who are unhappy with their choices and are looking to blame their agent for poor advice or poor service practices.'

Some regulators also attribute market misconduct to the inherent make-up of people rather than to the structure and culture of the insurance industry. In the wake of massive life insurance and pension marketing misconduct in the United Kingdom, the chair of the Savings and Investment Board regulatory agency declared that structural change through regulatory mechanisms would not resolve the problems. 'We want to avoid over-regulation and too great an emphasis on prescription in all areas of financial services. Some hazards and dangers will always be there. Human nature will not change. People will still commit fraud.'

In spite of various efforts to blame the victimized consumer and the individual agent, it is widely recognized within the industry that market misconduct is institutionalized. It results from both the structural conditions of the life insurance sales process and the occupational culture that has become established in the context of those conditions.

One structural condition that favours market misconduct is the fact that insurance products are based on assumptions about the future that are difficult to calculate and assess. Assessments of the insured risk are typically based on limited information and are therefore subject to situational moral assessments and speculation (see chapter 7). As we have seen, companies develop a very complex system of charges, investment risk spreading, policy lapses, and policy conversion incentives in order to manage their financial risks. Even so, they are often wrong because these forms of financial risk management are likewise speculatively based on limited knowledge and uncertainty (Ericson and Doyle, forthcoming: chap. 2).

These product conditions make it difficult for the market to function. Insurers have difficulty pricing their products and in knowing where they stand in relation to competing companies. Consumers have difficulty knowing what it is they are buying and, as we have seen, even knowing how much they are actually paying. It is therefore almost impossible for them to shop comparatively. As Posner (1973: 8–9) observes, misconduct in the marketing of any product is more likely when the performance of the product is highly risky or uncertain, and when it is extremely difficult to assess the quality of products offered by an individual supplier or among competitors.

In the life insurance industry, these product problems are compounded by the aforementioned expansion of universal life insurance, with its 'feature creep' regarding investment options and special coverages. In the United States, 82 per cent of all individual life insurance policies in 1980 were whole life policies, while the remaining 18 per cent were term policies. By 1994, only 48 per cent were whole life and 14 per cent term policies, while 22 per cent were universal, 3 per cent variable, and 13 per cent variable universal (Insurance Advisory Board 1995: 21ff.). The introduction of more complex products in the past two decades has left many agents in a confused state as to what is actually being sold. When befuddled by the abstract system of insurance, agents focus narrowly and instrumentally on their own niche in the insurance relationship and how they can gain from it. It is their job to persuade sales prospects to believe in a future scenario that includes their particular life insurance products. Thus one company's training manual for life insurance agents instructed them to sell its 'future security planning system' by working on the prospect's perception of why life insurance must be a part of their secure future. The manual's philosophy is straightforward and pragmatic: 'since a person's perception is that person's reality, the perceptions are true.'

The insurance company structures reality for its agents and consumers through interrelated strategies. First, it establishes contractual relations with consumers that are enabling for the company and facilitate some forms of market misconduct. Second, it has peculiar contractual relations with its agents that are conducive to systematic misconduct. Recruitment and training are not designed to build a professional cadre of career agents, but rather to lubricate the revolving door of short-term employees who will sell to their social networks and then leave when their networks are exhausted. Remuneration is based almost exclusively on commissions, creating a strong incentive to market aggressively and to sell the high commission product rather than the right product for the consumer's needs. Third, it fosters an organizational and occupational culture that further promotes aggressive selling and systematic misconduct.

Contracts are the most important means through which consumers are protected from systematic misconduct by companies and their sales agents. Ideally, contracts create a community of fate between buyers and sellers by making clear mutual obligations and benefits (Heimer 1985: 231). Contracts vary widely across different industries and the products and services they sell. Insurance is peculiar because what is being sold is the contract itself, and with it the terms and conditions for payment if specified losses occur.

In structuring the insurance contract, insurance companies can protect themselves to the point where they seriously disadvantage the consumer. Market misconduct is embedded in the insurance contract itself. This point was made by a senior official in an insurance brokers' association. He said in interview that with life insurance contracts, 'the first truism is they give you everything on the first page, but they take it away on the subsequent pages. As corny as it sounds, the more subsequent pages there are, the less you are getting.' During the interview he pulled out a standard contract from a major life insurance company and analysed it as a contract to missell. He prefaced his analysis by saying 'the property and casualty business is more above the board, the sleaze I see in the life industry is pretty terrifying ... I'm talking widespread ... organized, deliberate.'

The interviewee pointed to clauses in fine print with legalistic phrasing, indicating that for some types of accidents there will only be a return of accumulated premiums rather than payment of a full death benefit. He said that the contract consists of the policy, the application, and the medical report. The policyholder signs the application and medical report permission forms but does not receive copies. This is a serious disadvantage because the policyholder has answered detailed questions on these forms that qualify him for the life insurance, but is left with no record if any of his answers are subsequently disputed in a claim. 'Did you ever get a contract back that didn't include the pages you signed? ... If the applicant doesn't get a copy of his contract to read, to correct it, he is being screwed. He is being set up, so that heads the company wins, tails the consumer loses.' He noted that the consumer has ten days from signing the contract to change his mind and obtain a refund. However, this option is not written into the policy but is on a separate piece of paper given to the policyholder. He said that the company's agents informed him, '"We are supposed to give it to the consumer as a separate document, but our manager says if the deal is shaky don't give it to them."' The interviewee underscored his points by making a comparison to a car rental contract:

Do you think they could have rented the car without having you sign the contract and show you the clause where you signed your collision coverage? Life insurance, they do it all the time, and that is a hell of a lot more significant than renting a car. But suppose you took that rental car back and said, 'OK, I'm done. The car is in perfect condition.' He said, 'Fine, there is a double charge for washing it, $100 charge for lube and testing of it.' You said, 'What? You never told me that!' He said, 'I don't have to tell you that!' You said, 'But it is not in the contract.' He said, 'Yeah, we don't have to.' How would you feel? That's what they do in life insurance.

Here the interviewee is underscoring the fact that life insurance companies in his jurisdiction were not required to disclose features of the particular insurance policy that affect the policy's value over time. He said that a proper sales prospectus would declare, 'This is not guaranteed. This is highly speculative. This is risk.' In contrast, a new guideline proposed by the industry association states, 'Some elements are guaranteed. The policy will govern.' He then pointed out that again the policy contract is the problem. '[The new guideline says] "You can pull out in the first ten years, but some charges *may* apply." *May* apply? I've got news for you. Read the policy. It says it *does* apply. It doesn't say, "*Caution*, if you pull out in the first ten years you'll lose 50 per cent of your investment." *That* would be disclosure. *This* [the guideline] is a sales tool. What the industry is trying to do is con the government into accepting this in lieu of real disclosure ... What it is is a bunch of sales bullshit.'

The contract also offers protective devices in relation to unscrupulous agents the company knows it employs. For example, the insurance application analysed by this interviewee contained the following statement: 'Information given by the applicant on life to be insured is not notice to [the company] unless contained in the written application. A representative is not authorized to place [the company] under any risk or obligation.' Whatever sales talk that might have passed between the agent and the insured is not binding contract talk. The underwriting information relevant to the contract is limited to what is contained in the written application, a copy of which is not routinely made available to the applicant.

The process for recruiting, training, and using life insurance agents also helps to structure market misconduct. The fact that life insurance sales is a tainted occupation is evident from an industry association guidebook to recruitment that recommends the use of 'blind advertisements' to recruit agents. Blind advertisements do not specify what the job is. The recruitment guidebook cautions that an advertisement that mentions insurance sales is likely to turn people away rather than facilitate recruitment. There can be few occupations where recruitment begins by disguising what the job really entails. However, as we shall see, deception is so institutionalized in the business that it is inevitably used in advertising for new sales agents.

We interviewed a career life insurance sales person who was initially recruited through a blind advertisement. He said that when he arrived for the initial interview he was surprised to learn that the advertiser was a well-known multinational life insurance company and that he was actually being recruited to sell life insurance. There was little to the interview except encouragement that he take the test for becoming a registered sales agent. He needed a job and therefore took the test, but failed it. The recruitment manager said that this meant he could not be hired by this company, but he then referred him to another major company's recruitment office, saying that company would not care about the failed test. The recruiter for the second company said, '"Don't worry about it. That's not important. We don't believe in that anyway."' Their 'test' was to have him recruit ten sales prospects and go out with a manager to sell to these prospects. Successful, he was then asked to develop a list of three hundred prospects.

An insurance market conduct regulator said that in his jurisdiction the test to become a licensed agent was not stringent, and that the test was all that was required to set up practice. The cover page of the test booklet informed prospective examinees of an instructional guidebook that should be read before taking the test. If the person answers the multiple choice questions correctly, she has only to pay a small fee to be in business. 'Gerry X can go in, and if he can pass the exam, if he's got $140, and if he can find a sponsor – the latter two aren't that hard – he can be licensed tomorrow. And he can be out there representing himself as an insurance agent, a financial planner, a consultant, whatever you want to call yourself. And all I've done is read a study material that is this thick, and all of a sudden giving you advice on insurance.'

A career life insurance agent said that companies are not concerned about the lack of rigour in recruitment and training because they intend to exploit the recruit's network of sales prospects and then cut him loose if he fails to expand or capitalize on this network:

> This business has been famous for its revolving door syndrome ... the fault of the insurance companies. To me what has happened is that it's the old expression, if you throw enough shit on the wall something is going to stick ... Managers were at the time required to recruit so many people a year, and to me that was a false economy ... 'Here you are, now three months, see you, you're on your own.' Move on to the next one, which was typically what happened in this industry. It's left a lot of bad taste in a lot of people's mouths, so you get these agents that don't know any-

thing, offset on their friends and family, and then the company forgets about him.

A senior executive of a life insurance brokers' association elaborated in interview on what he termed the 'sleaze factor' in agent recruitment. Recruitment is not based on the recruit, but on the prospect list the recruit can come up with among his family and friends:

> If you can come up with a hundred names, you get hired. And they tell you they are training you up for a career in life insurance, which is a lie ... The training is pretty mickey mouse ... the system wouldn't work if it actually required training ... They send out a so-called trainer or unit manager with this new career person, and they call on all those people on that list. And the purpose of that is ostensibly to train him on how to sell insurance. The con is, the purpose is to simply sell insurance ... When you get through the list, they say, 'OK Fred, you are on your own, go to it.' And at that point they stop paying him ... his draw. He flounders ... they cut him loose and then they have to bring somebody else in, so it is a revolving door ... When you call Aunt Martha, and explain to Aunt Martha that she should surely put some kiddie policies on the nephews, she might think it is a great idea and do it because you are there. Or she might think it is a dumb idea, but after all, you are her nephew, she better do something. So she would buy a little one just to make everyone go away ... That revenue will go to that manager for the rest of his life, not you. And now he has got an introduction to call back on that person in a couple of years and do a selling job. And it is honed to a science ... That's standard operating procedure for some companies.

While sales agents are to prospect for new clients among family and friends, managers are to prospect for new agents in their social networks. Managers' prospecting is rewarded with a fee or bonus for each new agent recruit, placing onus on quantity over quality. A market conduct regulator we interviewed complained that in his jurisdiction, 80 per cent of life insurance agents leave the occupation within the first year. He attributed this very high turnover rate to the way in which the sales system operates in general, but also to specific practices in agent recruitment:

> Some companies pay big bonuses to their managers for the number of bodies they have sitting in chairs at certain times. December, I get a lot of

calls from managers, particularly from career companies, saying 'I've got six applications here, I need these approved before the 25th of this year. It means up to $40,000 bonuses for me and my managers, based on numbers of people in seats.' Personally, I think that's a dumb way to pay people, but I think what you get is, whether or not you pass the exam, you get in there because the manager is focusing on one thing, not who is good for the job, but who can I get licensed.

A former life insurance agent we interviewed referred to such managerial practices as the 'churning' of agents. He said that companies structure this churning not only by offering managers recruitment bonuses and fees for acquiring agents, but also by rewarding them further for maintaining the book of policyholders initially signed up by agents.

There are employment-screening technologies to aid the agent selection process. Such devices are often not used at all, while in other cases their results are ignored if the prospective agent meets the bottom line of producing an attractive list of new sales prospects. Nonetheless, these devices offer insight into what moral qualities seem desirable in the life insurance sales recruit.

An industry-wide agent selection manual we examined offered a wide range of selection tools and tips. For example, it described a tool called 'Culture Fit,' designed to match a candidate to a field sales office in terms of the clientele and their market niche. In selling managers on this tool, the manual uses the exemplar of Dennis Rodman, a notorious professional basketball player who has been in trouble with various teams, the National Basketball Association, and legal authorities. The manual notes that while Rodman was a 'disruptive force' with the San Antonio Spurs, he fit much better with the Chicago Bulls and helped them to be winners. This material was published before Rodman experienced troubles with the Chicago Bulls and was traded away by them as well.

The manual offers other indications that it is good to recruit among the morally risky and fit them into the sales machine. For example, it recommends that entrepreneurial risk takers with a gambling spirit and disregard for the rules be recruited through their answers to the following questions: 'What would you rather have – a 20 per cent guaranteed pay increase or a chance to test an idea you have that risks 10 per cent of your pay for the chance to make 40 per cent or more?' 'Do you ever exceed authority or break the rules at work or in school?

Give me an example.' The manual concludes with a summary of its main tips on recruitment, beginning with the statement, 'All rules, including this one, are meant to be broken.'

Little formal training is provided after the life insurance agent is recruited. As one former life insurance agent stated pithily in interview, any training offered is 'indoctrination, not education.' This point was underscored in a training manual produced by an industry association: 'There is only one way to develop any skill – consistent, regular practice, under controlled conditions, with accurate feedback. You do not develop skills by reading! Study will improve your education, but only practice will develop your skills.'

An experienced life insurance agent we interviewed said that he was recruited by a large company that had a training facility at its headquarters office. Called 'the new man school,' the two-week instructional period for new recruits consisted almost entirely of learning scripts to make sales. A district manager for another company, responsible for agent selection and training, said in interview that the instructional booklet and test required by state regulators to become a licensed agent teaches 'everything that the government thinks you need to know, but of course it is totally useless. So forget everything you learned in that, and regulation stuff.' Emphasizing that the successful agent has to be 'self-directed' and 'self-managed,' he said, 'What you really need to do is almost literally live with these people ... and give them all the habits of making regular phone calls.' The company's training guide likewise instructed managers that 'coaching is an all-the-time activity.' The manual recommended that a periodic 'effort agreement' be made between the manager and agent, and that 'non-validating agents' (i.e., unsuccessful agents) be returned to the new agent induction process because 'the most common cause of failure is a lack of disciplined activity.'

Most market conduct regulators now require formal training credits on a continuing basis for licensed life insurance agents. However, a great deal of the instruction simply consists of people in the industry giving promotional talks on new products and features. No selling opportunity is missed, even at industry seminars and luncheon meetings that are supposed to provide broader knowledge of proper market conduct.

Several of our interviewees had begun their careers in life insurance sales, but quickly moved to other occupations in the insurance industry after discovering the market misconduct that was expected of them. An interviewee who moved into claims processing in the property and casualty insurance industry talked at length about his distaste for the life insurance sales process:

> It was one of those advertisements in the paper, and it looked great and I got sucked in. I was young, just out of university, and a pretty slick manager that got me going and wanted me to go out and hit my friends up to buy policies ... And first they really pushed that: if you believe in the product you should sell it to your family members, your friends because they need it, everybody needs this product because it is very important ... But then after that they'll encourage you to go door-to-door and then referrals ... So you'd meet somebody and the key is, even if you didn't close the sale, to try and get three or four names so that you can continue on, going on after those people ... I guess I'm too trusting for that business ... If I had a couple in front of me with small kids and they've got a fairly hefty mortgage, I would have difficulty trying to tell them that look, they need this product of $60,000 whole life insurance, and you're paying a premium of $120 per month, when they were just barely getting by, while they could pick up term life insurance for $30 or $40 bucks a month with coverage of $200,000 that would cover off their mortgage, have some money put aside for the kids and the family. And my commission on that would have been ... $150 for a sell of the term insurance, while on the whole life product I would have $600 or $700 bucks if I signed somebody up. And that's where I had the difficulty, where I would usually push the term life and then I'd go back to see my manager ... [who] would be pushing as much of the commission stuff that I could [get] because ... the manager that was directly above me, and the office manager, would get a cut of my commission.

Most agents are churned out of the business once they have churned their own family, friends, and extended social networks. One indication that such turnover is institutionalized in the industry is an industry association manual on agent recruitment and training that says an exemplary retention of agents record would be 70 per cent after one year, 35 per cent after two years, 24 per cent after three years, and 20 per cent after four years. The manual refers to these rates as 'survival experience'! In practice the rates of agent attrition are even higher. Clarke (1999: 95–6) cites LIMRA figures indicating that to maintain a direct sales force of 5,000, a company needs to recruit 2,750 annually: 1,400 will survive to year two, 563 to year three, and 307 to year four.

We interviewed a market conduct regulator who said that he issued between 1,500 and 1,800 new life insurance agent licences annually. Among these, 80 per cent would not be practising within two years, and most would have ended their involvement in the business within six months. One multinational life insurance company we studied experienced enormous agent turnover. A company executive told a brokers' conference that we attended, 'This year we're targeting to recruit 150 new, inexperienced producers. That's down from 450 last year. The reason that is down is that we recruited 450 new producers last year and had a net growth in our sales force of under 10! [laughter and exclamations from the audience].' An official of the same company lamented in interview, 'For every agent who sits down with somebody and doesn't do a very good job, there is somebody who does.'

The commission system has structured market misconduct for two centuries. In early nineteenth-century England, commissions were characterized by Charles Babbage (1826: 141) as bribery. As such, he said, they 'ought either to be immediately abolished, or else publicly acknowledged.' Babbage reasoned as follows: 'Let us now suppose the consumer, doubtful of his judgment, employs an agent of his own; it will never be contended that an individual or a body of men can, with any semblance either of justice or integrity, offer to those agents a premium to buy at their particular establishments the article they are instructed to purchase. If such a principle is once admitted, those who sell the worst goods will both find it necessary, and be able, to offer the highest premium for a breach of trust in the consumer's agent. Yet this is precisely the conduct of almost all the assurance companies' (ibid.)

Zelizer (1979) documents similar scathing criticism of insurance sales commissions in nineteenth-century America. An 1877 book entitled *Church of the Holy Commissions* offered 'a searing indictment on the commission system of agency compensation' (ibid: 7). As we have seen, the commission system remains central even after its acknowledged contribution to the market misconduct scandals of recent years (Clarke 1999: 76, 97).

The life insurance industry continues to rely on commission-based selling because their product is not consumer-driven. Life insurance is expensive, addresses remote future possibilities that people prefer not to dwell upon, and does not have the commodity appeal of material goods. Therefore it must be sold proactively and aggressively, and it is assumed that agents and their managers will be more proactive and aggressive if they are rewarded handsomely for an actual sale. Commissions at the point of sale can be in excess of 100 per cent of initial premiums, loaded up front. This creates an enormous incentive to make bigger sales, even if those sales entail too much insurance or inappropriate products. As one market conduct regulator told us, it can even create an incentive to pay the client's premium, because the agent will still receive a commission in excess of 100 per cent.

Managers also work exclusively on commissions. This gives them an incentive to actively recruit, pressure, monitor, and replace their sales force in the perpetual struggle to meet targets. In some career agent systems, branch managers and even marketing executives are compensated solely on overwrite commissions. In the words of a brokers' association executive we interviewed, this creates the sensibility that it 'doesn't matter how good the business is, doesn't matter how it is got, as long as it comes in they get paid.' A former SIU officer for a life insurance company said in interview that managers in his company sometimes became so greedy that they sold directly. To appear to be following company rules, they listed direct sales in the name of company agents, but collected all of the commission themselves. The new prospect commission structure was 100 per cent of premium for the agent, plus 50 per cent for the manager, plus 50 per cent for the office manager. Since this practice was against company rules, its exercise meant that the company was being defrauded and the insurance contract was in the name of a sales person to whom the client had never spoken. Our interviewee said that the company president nevertheless condoned the practice, which he termed 'working the contract,' because he saw it as one way of placating managers who were always pestering him for more commission returns. The SIU officer brought the practice to the attention of a marketing department executive. However, this was to no avail; he 'simply doesn't want to hear this stuff, period ... because "Once I know, I have to deal with it" ... which is very expensive financially, and reputation-wise.'

In addition to structuring commissions so that agents sell more expensive investment policies instead of term policies, life insurance companies offer commission incentives to agents to churn existing policyholders into more expensive replacement policies. Commissions for replacement policies are sometimes higher than commissions for new client policies. Such commission-based churning was a significant component of the life insurance and pension scandals in the United Kingdom (*The Economist*, 29 October 1994: 95; *Sunday Telegraph*, 18 December 1993; Clarke 1999). We interviewed a former in-house life insurance agent who later established his own insurance brokerage. He estimated that companies depend on replacement policies for about half of their new premium revenue, 'so it's not replacements to better the situation. It's internal replacements, companies that are reworking the book of business.' He also pointed out that particular campaigns to encourage replacements can be related to broader financing needs within a company or the wider industry. For example, he described a situation in which companies wanted 'to change their internal rate of return on their reserves that they have. So one of their only ways of doing that was to replace their old contracts out to get new contracts in there, so they could change some of the structure with the reserves that they had to keep in there.'

Churning existing clients into more complicated and potentially less prudent life insurance contracts is compounded by the development of universal and variable policies and associated feature creep. We interviewed the CEO of a major general insurance company that sold its life insurance company in the early 1990s. He said that this decision was taken because it became 'too costly' to do business. By this he meant that life insurance was not only a highly competitive business with insufficient financial returns, but also one which was characterized by unsavoury sales practices:

> It got to the point where there were so many life insurance companies pushing life insurance products to people that there was an over-saturation of opportunity and not a sufficient market to buy ... Well the business started to entice, if you want to use that word, sales agents to sell more business, and of course they're paid commission. So then they began to start changing products, and a huge product evolution took place from 1980 through until 1990 ... There were so many products, new products that came out. It was absolutely, utterly impossible for the consumer to know what they were buying. And with the enticement of companies, commission-wise, to get business, [agents] were going in and replacing existing business with new business. And that began a churning process.

Similar processes were evident in the United Kingdom over the same period. Clarke (1999: 49–50) cites the former CEO of the industry regulatory organization LAUTRO regarding his experiences as a regulator in the early 1990s:

> [It is] a market where complex products, often designed to exaggerate

their obscurity, are sold to consumers whose reliance on financial advisers is reinforced by infinite variations open to producers to differentiate their products from those of their competitors. Reliance on the advice of financial advisers means that the choice of product is effectively made by the latter. In the unregulated environment therefore, commission was the main determinant of choice by financial advisers, whether independent or tied ... In the special and some ways unique field of packaged financial services, where consumers are technically ignorant and susceptible to reliance on trust, commission presents special and damaging hazards. The public discussion in the mid 1980s was about whether such damage should be prevented by the direct control of commission or by market forces through disclosure. Those urging the latter won, the consumer lost. (Jebens 1997: 25–6, 34)

At the same time as more and more features creep into products, rendering them impossible for consumers to understand, more and more incentive features creep into the system of agent compensation to encourage agents to push the new products further. High-flying agents are put into the equivalent of frequent flyer programs, with regular, gold, and platinum status depending on sales performance. The higher the tier the higher the rewards to the agent, in terms of both financial compensation and discretion to handle clients differentially for even greater rewards. Greater discretion can include things like 'relationship pricing,' whereby top agents have some flexibility in setting life insurance premium rates for preferred customers who also buy other lines of insurance and financial products from them (Insurance Advisory Board 1995: 202). We interviewed a marketing executive for a life insurance company who described incentives to brokers beyond the commission structure. 'Works just like a frequent flyers program ... These points can be accumulated, and allow the agent or broker to attend a company conference in an exotic location. We just got back from Ireland. Or it could be used to purchase business equipment and merchandise or educational credits or studies ... Sometimes we run some short-term incentives within that overall program, where when we're launching a new product or something we may, say, double your points for the next three months on sales of this type of product.'

The fact that the commission structure also structures market misconduct is especially evident in situations where a company decides to put its life insurance sales staff on salary rather than commission. We interviewed a senior executive of a firm that specialized in employee benefit group plan sales and claims management. The company also sold individual life insurance policies to selected clients who were involved in group sales. The company had adopted a slogan indicating they were 'people you can trust.' Asked to explain this slogan, the executive gave the example that the salesperson who sold these individual policies to key group insurance clients was paid a salary with no commission. Scrapping the commission in this case removed the moral risk of encouraging the salesperson to sell the wrong product to these favoured clients, whose goodwill was needed for the group business:

> This guy is not motivated to sell the wrong product. He's motivated to service that need and find out what it is ... When we hired him and set him up that way, we had him tested by [a major life insurance company's recruiting system, and that company's recruiter] called me and said, 'You don't want to hire that guy because you know he's not going to be motivated.' I said, 'That's perfect, that's exactly what I'm looking for!' He said, 'You're going to lose money.' I couldn't afford to have my individual guy selling the president of the hospital a whole life policy which turns out to be the wrong product, and it's too expensive, and it's a good one because the guy makes 50 per cent commission the first year. If the president needs coverage we should be buying him term with one of the top five companies and here's why and at what price ... The trust concept, we embodied and embraced that.

The structure of market misconduct articulates with a sales culture that reinforces it. In addition to the commissions and bonuses that provide the incentive for aggressive sales practices, agents face a constant barrage of motivational messages aimed at augmenting their production. Motivational booklets and training guides published by industry associations, company manuals and meetings, conventions for top producers, and everyday monitoring by managers in the work environment are all designed to make the agent rationalize rejection and sell more. The trick of the trade is to blend money and egos to the point where they are inseparable (Oakes 1990a, 1990b).

An industry association booklet entitled *The Magic of Life Insurance* is designed to provide new agents with pointers that will motivate them to sell more efficiently. It begins with a preface that refers to the systematic market misconduct that has plagued the industry. '[D]uring the past decade, life insurance sales have steadily declined. At the same time, the public's approval rating of life insurance producers has dropped dramatically – from 80 per cent in the 1960s to just over 40 per cent today. There are many reasons for this decline, but undeniably one side effect. Too many producers have opted for the easier-to-sell investment-income vehicles and have failed to address the need for immediate protection in the event of a prospect's sudden loss of life.'

This message may not initially appear as a source of inspiration for the neophyte agent! However, its purpose becomes manifest in the context of what follows. It blames 'producers' (i.e., agents) for the past misfortunes of the industry, as if they were not subject to the structuring of their work environment that makes misconduct inevitable. It thereby sets up the premise of the booklet: that agents are responsible for the future fortunes of the industry, their company, their office, and themselves. If they follow the simple lessons of the booklet, they will do their part to turn the industry around.

As it turns out, many of the lessons in this booklet reinforce the culture of misconduct. For example, it stresses that 'Agents need to assume and work with the belief that everyone is underinsured.' It then goes on to declare that 'Life insurance will always be a pressure sale.' A preference is stated for 'benign pressure' in which 'the prospect is told the story of life insurance so skillfully, so orderly, so convincingly that he or she is led to *self-pressure*. And that's where the pressure belongs.' This statement is followed by 145 'life insurance power phrases' that can be used to put the pressure where it belongs. For example,

- 'The only thing worse than a home without a parent is a parent without a home.'
- 'You say, "Come back in September" Whom should I ask for if you're not here in September?'
- '"Insurance poor" applies now and it can apply when you're on your death bed; however, the meaning can change completely.'
- 'If you had a machine that turned out money, you'd insure it, wouldn't you? Well, as far as your family is concerned, you are such a machine!'
- 'Will Rogers said, "I'm not as much interested in the return *on* my money as I am in the return *of* my money."'
- 'The greatest killer of mankind is financial worry. This plan will eliminate that worry for you.'
- 'To answer a prospect who claims that his or her $10,000 policy will provide a lot of "dough," you might say: "That is a lot of dough,"

and spell "dough" on a piece of paper. Then say, "The 'd' stands for doctor; the 'u' stands for undertaker; the 'g' is for general expenses, and the 'h' is for hospital." When the prospect inquires about what the 'o' stands for, you can answer, "That, my friend, stands for the magnificent sum on which your spouse and children will have to live."'

- 'You're betting that you'll outlive your family, and your family is the stakes.'
- 'Where else can a person purchase peace of mind, dignity, respect, confidence, and happiness all in the same package?'
- 'If you had a garage sale today, what would go? If you die tomorrow, what would go next week?'

These 'power phrases' are enacted by convincing the sales force that they are agents of risk and morality. Far from acknowledging that they pose moral risks to consumers, agents should be morally righteous, confident that they are doing good deeds. This sensibility leads some agents to attribute quasi-religious overtones to their work (Oakes 1990a, 1990b). One agent we studied described his calling as 'saving souls.' In a booklet published by an industry association, a section entitled 'Motivating the Prospect to Act' states that

> Because people tend to procrastinate buying life insurance more than any other product, agents must be able to persuade and to help prospects take immediate action. People tend to regard themselves as immortal, and often neglect to take care of 'things' from which they derive no immediate benefit. Life insurance, being intangible and with proceeds payable at death, is frequently regarded as such a 'thing.' Where a proposed insurance program answers a prospect's needs, the agent is *morally justified* in motivating the prospect to take immediate action – assuming that the prospect has the ability to pay and is able to qualify medically. On this basis, the prospect may be motivated by discussing the potential financial hardship his or her survivors are likely to endure in the event of a prospect's premature death.

The sales culture not only fosters emotional pressure tactics to induce people to buy what they may not understand or need, it is also tolerant of the market misconduct that results. In their thirst for premium revenue, insurance companies are tolerant of sales misconduct for the same reason that they are tolerant of some claims fraud (see chapter 9): it is part of their loss ratio calculus. The sensibility underlying this calculus was discussed by an interviewee who had worked in a life insurance company's SIU. 'Let's face it, I mean every company looks at it, "How much is it costing us to live with this problem as opposed to the cost to fix it?" So as long as the cost to fix it is in excess, we're not going to be concerned about it ... You always have to appreciate the business side of it: I know they're not here to do me a favour today, they're here to make money.' This interviewee attributed the market misconduct in his company to 'the mood set and the philosophy of a commissioned sales force.' He said that the company sponsored 'extravagant award things every year. And I kept asking, "Why are you continuing this? It causes people to cheat and lie."'

In this culture of money and egos, one instructional manual, *The 21st Century Agent*, suggests that a cure for market misconduct is to become a well-heeled agent selling to wealthy clients. Unlike their less fortunate counterparts, such agents will transcend the financial incentive for unethical practices and market misconduct. The manual observes that life insurance agents are often 'hypocrites simply because they themselves are poor managers of money. They try to sell strategies of wealth creation when they have accumulated little wealth themselves. This creates two negative psychological conditions in the agent. One, a lack of integrity that inevitably comes from not practicing what one preaches. This lack of integrity will betray itself in sales situations with prospects and clients who are good money managers. Two, a state of anxiety about every sales situation, where the agent's own financial pressures take precedence over the client's best interests.'

Again the agent is to blame. He lacks 'integrity' because he has not become wealthy like the clients to whom he aspires to sell. He tries to compensate by taking advantage of clients who deserve better. Structure and culture are erased from the picture.

The Governance of Market Misconduct

State regulators, industry associations, and individual companies respond to market misconduct through four governance mechanisms. First, they elaborate rules of market conduct in efforts to shape compliance normatively. Second, they try to professionalize agents through improved selection and training and a redefinition of the agent's relation to consumers. Third, various surveillance technologies are used to both guide the conduct of sales agents and monitor their practices.

Fourth, alternative sales distribution systems are developed to cut out the agent as intermediary, or to change the employment relationship in ways that give the company more control. While these mechanisms govern market misconduct, they do not fundamentally change the institutional structure and occupational culture on which it is based.

State and industry association market conduct regulators are almost entirely reactive to public complaints. They respond to complaints by reiterating the rules of conduct and urging future compliance. Flagrant and systematic violations are investigated further, but typically in conjunction with industry associations using their powers of moral suasion rather than legal sanction. This approach is similar to compliance law enforcement in other fields (Hawkins 1984; Ericson, Baranek, and Chan 1989: 264–5). Some reasons for using a compliance model were outlined by a state market conduct regulator we interviewed:

> We simply do not have the resources to go out and check every insurance agency and whatever in the province about their market conduct ... Every company has to have some sort of complaint process system. Well, we don't have the resources to even go and review three hundred complaints processing systems and determine their adequacy because different companies are different, and different clientele, and we couldn't possibly. What happens, of course, is that we get a company that has an abnormal amount of complaints, then we become a little proactive with that company ... [We] put this out through [the industry association], then people say this is some sort of industry standard, and it's easier for me to challenge somebody by not living up to a standard that the industry itself has developed ... It gives some credibility that the industry has the standard ... So that gives me all the 'legal' authority I need ... The industry itself can be its best ally.

Except when major scandals erupt, market misconduct complaints by consumers are rare. We interviewed an official with a life insurance regulatory council. This agency was responsible for regulating the approximately 21,000 life insurance agents licensed in the jurisdiction concerned. The official said that his office received about four hundred complaints each year, but that 'the majority of these probably come from within the industry. Again, half our consumers don't even know they've got a problem, and it usually takes another agent who looks something up and says, "Well, they shouldn't have been handled in this way, you should go to Council, or I'll go for you."'

Larger jurisdictions with more substantial state regulatory operations do have some capacity for market conduct audits. However, such audits are only conducted on a tiny fraction of companies annually. They too are instituted as a reaction to complaint patterns, rather than being proactive, random, or systematic. State regulators also audit industry regulatory bodies that are sanctioned by the state. An official of a brokers' association subject to an annual audit described the arrangement as 'more like a management deal, they make a couple of suggestions about this and that. They don't come in to determine whether we've passed any tests, although of course financial information is audited.'

Many interviewees believed that the life and health insurance industry is subject to much less market conduct regulation than the property and casualty industry. This difference is related in part to the much greater level of claims disputes in the property and casualty industry, especially regarding automobile insurance. An executive with a life insurance brokers' association pointed out that in one jurisdiction he operated in, there was not even an official code of conduct for life agents. 'Now how would *you* regulate 25,000 agents if you don't have a set of rules talking about what they can and cannot do?' He felt that one reason for limp regulation was the political clout of insurance companies, both on the level of agents as powerful lobbyists with their local elected representatives, and on the level of insurance companies as powerful forces in the political economy. He said that CEOs of large companies call provincial ministers of finance directly to negotiate their political economic interests. 'When you buy one hundred million dollars worth of provincial bonds in a pot, you can talk to anybody you want.' He also observed that life agent regulation is typically in the hands of the industry itself, in the form of industry-appointed councils sanctioned by the state. 'In the prairie provinces, the regulator is a council and LUAC and CLHIA appoint the directors ... Sure makes it a lot easier when the lobbyist becomes the regulator!' This point was underscored by an official for a life agents' council:

> Like doctors or lawyers or accountants, you can bring five insurance agents in here and give them a scenario and get five different answers. None of them are wrong. It's more interpretation, particularly on the life side when you get into investments and everything else as to your future. There are different philosophies ... Council will generally not go behind a transaction to see what was broken unless it was something very obvious

[After giving the 'obvious' example of a case in which an agent sold a $900,000 whole life policy to a fifty-five-year-old woman with $15,000 annual income and no dependents]. As long as the consumer had clearly indicated what they wanted, and that the decision of the recommendation of the agent is consistent with the need, Council just says, 'Look, that's not our area of responsibility,' and don't get involved with it.

The former head of an insurance brokers' association said in interview that the regulatory model used in that association is one of 'enlightened self-interest.' He stated that 'the people in the business are best qualified to regulate the business' because they operate with 'responsiveness,' 'knowledge' and 'professional pride.' This was also the view taken by state market conduct regulators we interviewed. For example, one state regulatory agency had recently implemented an insurance ombudsman system to address consumer complaints. While an ombudsman's office was established in the agency's headquarters, its main function was to coordinate a system in which each insurance company was required to operate its own ombudsman and complaint process. The objective was to reduce the number of complaints handled by the regulatory agency, diverting them to the company level except in serious cases of last resort. An official in the agency's ombudsman's office, who was himself an experienced insurance industry insider, said in interview, 'The industry is very interested in doing this because, after all, it's a step forward toward self-regulation if they deal with their own complaints ... In an ideal world I would put myself out of business.'

An examination of how formal complaints are handled by market conduct regulatory bodies reveals that even in the rare case that a complaint reaches them, the primary response is to seek improved compliance from the agent rather than to punish and exclude that agent. For example, a life insurance council we studied was responsible for 19,000 licensed agents. In one twelve-month period, it received 260 complaints against licensed agents. Only 105 (40 per cent) of these complaints were assigned for investigation, and only thirty-three (13 per cent) were brought before the council for a disciplinary hearing. The disciplinary hearings resulted in eleven cases being dismissed with no disciplinary action. Among the twenty-two agents subject to disciplinary action, six were reprimanded, six had conditions placed on their licences, three had their licence suspended, and one was fined. Six dispositions are unknown.

The more serious market misconduct offences that result in disciplinary action tend to involve misappropriation of funds and serious underwriting errors (e.g., failure to inspect and document the risk as required; failure to include necessary and important insurance coverage). A scrutiny of information bulletins issued by regulators on such cases reveals that even serious infractions are not severely sanctioned. For example, in one regulatory agency we studied, an agent's licence was suspended for two years, rather than revoked entirely, after he had 'whited out and changed the birth date on an application for insurance, signed a policyholder's name to a change of beneficiary form, and applied dividends to be paid on account of a policy without the informed consent of the policyholder.' On appeal the suspension was reduced to eighteen months on 'the view that the Superintendent and Advisory Board had used the agent's denial of responsibility as an aggravating factor in assessing the penalty.'

Information bulletins published by regulators that report disciplinary decisions serve as shaming devices regarding the agents involved. Publicity about misconduct can be the greatest form of punishment and may effectively end the agent's career. However, with an eye towards creative agents who seize any opportunity for market advantage, some regulatory agencies explicitly prohibit agents from using such reports of market misconduct to competitively disadvantage their colleagues. Thus a regulatory agency's information bulletins contained the following: 'WARNING: The use of any information in this Bulletin to discredit another licensee or any other person is not permitted and may result in disciplinary action against a licensee using the information in such a manner.' One life agents' association we studied broadened this specific gag order through a defamation section in its code of ethics. An official with this association said in interview that this section was meant to deal with 'an individual [who] has defamed the institution of life insurance, or has defamed another company, or defamed the company's product, or its sales representative.'

In the context of scandals resulting from systematic market misconduct, some agents resist efforts to keep them quiet. As we have already seen, companies faced with allegations of misconduct try to blame agents as responsible individuals. Agents respond by blaming companies for creating the structure and culture of market misconduct. We interviewed a former SIU officer for a life insurance company who discovered a wide range of misconduct, including aggressive churning, manipulation of the commission system, and forged signatures on documents. When he pressed the company to take action, their labour lawyers intervened and advised that the company was unwise to proceed against agents because they would counter with unfair labour practice and unfair dismissal suits against the company.

There have been whistleblower lawsuits in the United States 'filed by agents who allege they were terminated by life insurers following investigations or allegations of churning. Many terminated agents allege that churning practices were consistent with the company's desires' (Blasingame and Smeljanick 1997). Similar lawsuits were launched in the United Kingdom following the life insurance and pension misconduct scandals there. For example, a company previously identified by the Financial Services Authority as displaying a 'cultural disposition against compliance' was sued by a former agent who claimed 'managers told staff to sell pension top-ups schemes and 10-year savings plans to meet branch targets, whether or not they were appropriate' (*Sunday Times*, 30 May 1999, Money Section, p. 1). He also claimed that agents were threatened with dismissal if they did not meet targets.

We interviewed an employment practices and errors and omissions underwriter. He identified life insurance companies as among the worst risks regarding employment practices, and indeed a type of business that many employment practices insurers would not underwrite. In his opinion, the vanishing premium scandals could be covered under an errors and omissions policy as a business loss, but life insurance companies also faced potential employment practices liability suits from agents on the argument that they were structurally induced to participate in market misconduct. In his opinion, if agents were 'buying into the corporate program, and it's a blatant lie or fraudulent or something like that, then you're not going to see it under an employment practices [insurance policy] because the employment practices [policy] is named perils ... [But if somebody] blew the whistle on the whole practice [of misselling] and then you fired their ass, you could get something that way.'

In response to the vanishing premiums scandals and other systematic market misconduct, life insurance industry associations have devised a number of additional rule systems, for example, guidelines on illustrations and codes of ethics. Clarke (1999: 52) argues that in the United Kingdom 'attempts to pin matters down merely stimulated further ingenuity, the net consequences of which were the development of a competitive culture of consumer deceit.' In Canada, a panel of consumer advocates and insurance industry experts – albeit convened by a major bank with a direct sales insurance company – pointed out that reforms need to be more substantial. More substantial reforms would include a requirement to disclose insurance commissions – for example, the enormous difference between term and whole life or universal life commissions – to consumers. This document also advocates a consumer bill of rights emphasizing informed choice, placing an onus on companies to meet their promises by imposing substantial penalties for failure to do so.

One useful reform might be a guide produced by state regulators that compares products across different life insurance companies. A guide of this type pertaining to vehicle insurance was published by the state regulator in a jurisdiction we studied. The main justification for this guide was the fact that vehicle insurance is a mandatory purchase and therefore there is an additional onus on the state to ensure that the consumer is informed and can comparison shop. When we asked a regulator why a similar guide is not published comparing life insurance company rates, she reasoned, 'It doesn't make sense for a government agency to provide a service for free which an agent or broker or company is receiving a payment for ... We would in essence be putting ourselves in competition with the service that's already being provided to the public.'

Industry associations have developed codes of ethics, ostensibly to regulate market misconduct. These codes articulate the moral risks posed by insurance sales agents and the companies they represent and proclaim that good practice consists of minimizing these risks. However, many of the clauses in such codes are simply declarations against a form of market misconduct that everyone in the industry knows is systematic and routine. For example, one code begins, 'Priority of Client(s) Interests ... The commission to be obtained from making the sale should have absolutely no bearing upon the life underwriter's advice to the client(s) or prospective purchaser(s).' This statement points to what everyone in the industry recognizes as a fundamental problem – the fact that commission-based sales do have a substantial bearing on advice to clients and prospective purchasers – and declares that it should not happen. In condemning a basic structural condition of market misconduct, but not actually changing that condition, codes of ethics can be seen as primarily directed at legitimization and as yet another marketing tool.

Instructional material and company manuals remind agents that ethical conduct is an effective sales tool. For example, an industry association booklet for agents is entitled, *Selling Ethically: How Do I Benefit?* One company manual states, 'it is seen to be an effective marketing tool for a company and its agents to be able to indicate that they are in compliance with the law.' Ethical conduct is especially recommended in the new relationship-selling model that is designed to persuade more prosperous clients to upgrade their life policies and other financial products as they accumulate wealth over the life course.

Agents are also reminded that overly aggressive misconduct can have negative financial ramifications for the company. For example, a life company's policy manual for agents warns them against the unauthorized churning of replacement policies because it might pose a financial risk to the company that would affect everyone's interests. 'An internal replacement will only occur when the policyholder has completed comparative information on the benefits, features and financials of both the existing policy and the proposed policy. Our intent is not to discourage the well-informed policyholder from making a change. It is to control the negative financial impact that a substantial volume of internal replacements would have on the life company.'

When market conduct is governed through rules and regulations, the focus is on an individual buyer/seller relationship and the credo is caveat emptor. We interviewed a brokers' association executive who was highly critical of the life insurance sales structure and practices. However, when asked about structural reforms that would better serve the consumer, he quickly invoked the buyer/seller model and caveat emptor. 'I'm a crusader for brokers' interests ... it is the consumers' responsibility to take care of themselves.' He said that the reforms to insurance contract provisions that he was recommending were 'to make damn sure the consumer is responsible for what happens. Because if he isn't responsible, he'll blame us.' This view of the consumer was also prevalent among regulators we interviewed. For example, a life insurance market conduct regulator said the insurance purchaser should be seen as being in the same position as the buyer of any other product:

> You want to go into a store to buy a shirt, fine, then don't go back to the store to complain when you find out two days later that the same shirt was half price ... The same is with insurance. I mean you have to choose the way you shop around, or at least understand the agent or broker

you're dealing with as to how many markets they have access to, and does that meet your needs. And it *will* change. I mean the same company, the same product may cost you different prices at two different agencies based on a number of different factors, and the companies may underwrite it differently based on the brokerage.

This view of the buyer/seller relationship fails to address how the buyer can possibly be aware that the price of the insurance product is highly variable. As we have seen, feature creep in life insurance investment products means that prices vary enormously by the specific options selected. As the interviewee above indicates, the same insurance product is also priced differently depending on the company's compensation and other arrangements with its agents and brokers. While price variation is also common in clothes sales – for example, the identical quality of blue jeans is priced differently for different niche markets by simply changing the brand identification label and the chain stores where it is sold – in the case of insurance it is virtually impossible for the consumer to be sufficiently informed and thus wary enough to make the purchase of the best product at the best price.

An alternative model is the professional/client relationship, which shifts responsibility for moral risks in the direction of the agent. This model suggests that an insurance company's agents are experts offering sound advice. It has expanded with the blending of life insurance into other financial products and services, especially with respect to wealthy clients. However, since the qualifications to be a financial expert in most jurisdictions are minimal, the problem of incompetent advice can pose as great a risk as plain dishonesty (Clarke 1999: 150). Moreover, as long as agent compensation is tied to commission incentives, professional sound advice will always be compromised. This point was underscored by an insurance underwriter and product developer for a multinational company:

> The people selling the product are perhaps motivated more by commissions than they are by what the job of an insurance professional should be ... counsel and guidance and helping people secure their future. And so there's that little bit of enigma to it ... it's a bit of a ... grab, that they don't provide service, that they're not truly bringing value ... You've got intermediaries saying, 'We're professional and we bring value,' but by the same token, by the way that they make their living and the way they're remunerated, it goes against how they can be truly professional when

they're not getting remunerated for their guidance, they're only getting remunerated when they sell you something.

There is little in the agent selection and training process to indicate that agents are being professionalized to a level that matches the marketing of their services as professional experts. An industry survey of life insurance sales agents in Canada posed several questions about selection and training (Life Insurance Marketing Research Association 1997: 31). Those surveyed were asked to respond to specific statements on a five-point scale: strongly agree/agree/unsure/disagree/strongly disagree. In answer to the statement, 'The company does a good job selecting sales managers or general agents,' 69 per cent responded in the negative or unsure. In answer to the statement, 'The company does a good job developing sales managers or general agents,' 70 per cent responded in the negative or unsure. In answer to the statement, 'The company does a good job preparing individuals for sales management positions,' 78 per cent responded in the negative or unsure.

We previously cited an executive with a life insurance brokers' association who explained that 'the system wouldn't work if it actually required training.' By this he meant that the agent herself is constituted as a commissioned seller in a buyer/seller relationship, not as a well-trained professional in a client/professional relationship. The commissioned seller is paid handsomely for sales made, and nothing for sound advice per se. She herself is churned out of the system as soon as she has exhausted her prospects for premium revenue.

Insurance companies also use surveillance technologies to govern the practices of sales agents. Surveillance is conducted through various databases that profile agents' careers and how they sell products; computer formats that control the information that agents present to sales prospects; ongoing monitoring of sales practices in controlled settings such as call centres; routine audits; and random undercover 'mystery shopping' inspections to audit sales practices.

In some jurisdictions, in particular in the United States, databases have been established by state and industry association regulators regarding the licensing status, educational credits, and disciplinary record of insurance sales agents. There are also various databases that compare agents' specific underwriting practices to those of other agents. For example, an insurance information services company we studied runs a premium advisory system that independently rates a property for comparison with the rate quoted by an underwriting agent. An interviewee employed by this information services company explained that it allows the insurance company subscriber to search 'our database for our experience and bills the rate for them right there, which they can use as an internal auditing method, but also forces the underwriter to apply some sort of methodology as to why they're coming up with a premium, as opposed to the broker feels that the account is under attack and we need this amount.' He also indicated how the rate established by his own company can be used by the subscriber as a standard against which underwriting discretion can be granted. 'Everybody has a level of responsibility, and perhaps a senior underwriter can deviate by 20 per cent, perhaps a supervisor can deviate by 40 per cent without getting a higher sign-off, maybe a commercial lines manager can deviate by 80 per cent and the regional vice-president can write it for nothing ... "You deviated 65 per cent, why did you do that? Who did you sign off with?"'

Agents are also governed through computer-based sales illustration packages. These packages control the information that agents are able to present to sales prospects and record what has been presented. For example, life insurance companies now script the sale of more complex investment-related products by using such computer-based packages. One package we studied constantly changes the products and features presented, and additional questions to ask the prospect, according to the ongoing information the prospect provides to the agent about herself. It also includes compliance standards in the information presented and assumptions made. For example, insurance limits are preset and not editable. Compliance-related information pages appear on the agent's computer screen if she does not access them herself. The agent is unable to access fields that would allow her to change assumptions about the investment returns on the product.

An agent's manual on this package summarizes its benefits. First, it is a format of control that provides 'a structured method of determining client needs.' Second, it provides a database on the agent's interaction with the prospect. Third, it prompts the agent about cross-selling opportunities for other lines of insurance and monitors whether these opportunities have been addressed by the agent. Fourth, this use of technology suggests professionalism, even if professionalism is otherwise absent in training or standards. 'It communicates to your clients that you are a professional provider of financial services and that you are focused on discovering and understanding your client's needs.' Fifth, it 'covers' the agent, creating a record of market conduct compliance by means of the compliance features built into the system regarding insurance limits, illustrations, and assumptions.

The surveillance of insurance agents through communication technologies is intensified in call centre sales operations. In a call centre we studied, sales agents were monitored continuously with respect to their underwriting practices, customer service, and productivity record. A manager said in interview,

> It's *very* regimented. There are all sorts of reports that are generated from our system to say when does the agent log-in, when do they log-off, when did they go for lunch, when did they come back, how many calls did they take, how long did the calls take, how much time did they spend processing the call ... I've got it scheduled to go in and record three calls per agent per day. And it stores the data, and the coaches come in usually six hours every week ... and pull up the voice clips from the agents in their team and the scores that we have, about eight different surveys that we use. We typically use a standard generic one that talks to customer service, etiquette, sales acumen, service, underwriting knowledge and so on. And we score it. Then we bring the agent in to listen to their call as well. They score it and then we match scores ... 90 per cent of the time they will score themselves less than or worse than we would have ... This is done twice a week.

The twice-weekly scoring of the agent, and the agent's self-scoring, was referred to as a 'call observation tour.' The tour protocol included a fifty-point inspection checklist on a recorded call covering everything from avoiding the use of insurance jargon to speaking with 'a smile in their voice' and making 'at least two attempts to bind the business in the call.'

The call centre was divided into twelve teams, each with twenty sales agent members and a coach. Weekly data on the individual agent's sales record, time in handling calls, and so on – as well as team data regarding the same – were publicly displayed in each team's office area. The statistics for the sales team and individual agents were as detailed as baseball statistics, and the pressure to perform must surely be comparable to that experienced by baseball players, albeit at much lower salary levels.

Insurance sales agents are monitored in other ways as well. In life insurance sales a follow-up survey of a purchaser is made in the weeks following a sale to ensure that she continues to appreciate what she has bought. Such surveys, governed by regulatory agencies, may be supplemented with a company's own customer satisfaction survey that addresses agents' conduct. A life insurance company we studied also maintained a consumer complaint registry, with quarterly review of agents subject to complaint. It also had a registry of replacement sales, including a 'quarterly report on different forms of churning activity with dividends to pay premium, early conversion, lapse/surrender followed by new issue, loan on old policy to pay premium on new policy.'

Insurance companies also conduct undercover surveillance of their sales agents through 'mystery shopping.' An undercover investigator poses as a customer and records the transaction for possible market misconduct or other problems. This type of surveillance is usually contracted to specialized companies. We interviewed an investigator who worked for a prominent management consultant firm. He described how his unit 'puts together undercover operations where we will pose as unwitting buyers of policies, and check on the suspected agents. This is not random virtue testing, we don't run out and just check any agent. But if you have a suspicion – someone who's selling a wrong service, or just selling to old people, and where they're cashing in on their term insurance – we'll put people out, video their room, and do what has to be done to see if this person is giving your clients the straight goods.'

An insurance company we studied used regular 'random virtue testing' to monitor the operations of its sales offices and agents. A marketing executive of this company said in interview that the focus was not so much on market misconduct, but rather on the 'professional' appearance of the office, the knowledge and helpfulness displayed by the agent, and the agent's efforts at cross-selling. The mystery shopping rating form used in this process had sixty-five items for the investigator to check. Ten items addressed 'branch appearance,' for example, whether the branch was tidy and whether posters and brochures were displayed properly. Six items concerned 'initial in-branch reception,' for example, waiting time and being greeted politely. Fourteen items constituted a 'needs assessment–auto insurance,' and a further ten items constituted a 'needs assessment–home insurance.' These items focused on how well the agent explained different coverages, how she tried to close the sale, and whether she tried to cross-sell other lines of insurance. Twenty items addressed the 'professionalism of the representatives,' dealing with everything from interpersonal skills such as 'eye contact' to whether there were interruptions and whether questions were handled competently. Five items were listed under 'final comments,' asking the investigator to assess whether the agent was someone from whom the customer would purchase various lines of insurance, and to make any suggestions for improvement of service.

In the United Kingdom, mystery shopping of insurance sales agents has been undertaken by a number of organizations beyond insurance companies. In response to life insurance and pension misconduct scandals, magazine and television investigative reporters, consumer associations, and state regulators all adopted mystery shopping as a way of documenting the systematic nature of market misconduct (Clarke 1999: 79, 99, 135–6).

The development of surveillance technologies to govern market conduct is linked to broader changes to the ways in which insurance is sold. New distribution systems for insurance products entail new ways of governing market misconduct.

The most significant new distribution system is direct selling. Banks and retail conglomerates have promoted their reputations and brand identification to attract insurance customers. Through advertising and cross-selling with other products and services, these organizations have prospects contact call centres or local retail outlets to purchase insurance. The advice offered is minimal, making it evident that this is a straightforward buyer/seller relationship. The seller is a call centre operative, subject to all of the workplace surveillance systems described earlier. The purchase of insurance is made comparable to buying baseball tickets over the telephone with a ticket agency.

The new direct sellers have 'positive brand equity,' in contrast to the 'negative brand equity' of many large insurance companies that are effectively anonymous or, worse, have been involved in serious market misconduct (Insurance Advisory Board 1997b: 31). The new sellers often refer to the involvement of their insurance company competitors in market misconduct scandals as part of their effort to attract customers (*Daily Telegraph*, 15 March 1997). They also distance themselves from traditional insurance company distribution methods through 'non-industry recruiting – All staff members recruited from outside insurance industry in order to avoid tainting of new outlet "culture" with attitudes, beliefs inherent in traditional distribution system' (Insurance Advisory Board 1995: 246).

In some instances established insurance companies are involved in new direct selling operations, but remain in the background in terms of the marketing effort. They establish 'branch access partnerships' whereby they '"rent" well-known, trusted brands in order to increase customer presence *dramatically'* (Insurance Advisory Board 1997b: 109). The objective is to embed insurance product marketing in the partner's existing retail environment, for example, supermarkets, department stores, bank statement mailings, utilities billing, and so on. These 'batched sale agreements' are like 'fishing in a stocked pond ... [a] calculated intertwining of marketing effort with partner's role in (often) routine customer transactions' (ibid.: 112–13). Said to be 'high touch, transactional' relationships, the ideal is that the insurance 'manufacturer customizes product offering to meet specific needs of partner's customers, gaining additional distribution outlet while expanded product range improves downstream partner's customer loyalty, incremental share of wallet of core business' (ibid.: 109).

An additional twist on partnership arrangements involves the new distributors partnering with each other and going after additional brand access arrangements. For example, the Bank of Scotland initially partnered with the Sainsbury food retail chain in the United Kingdom to establish the Sainsbury Bank, including insurance sales along with various bank services options. This enterprise then sought a joint venture with the Pat Robertson televangical ministry in the United States. The hope was to capitalize on the Pat Robertson list of followers in recruiting customers, believing that his 'clout with born-again Christians might produce millions of customers overnight for a phone bank based in the United States' (*International Herald Tribune*, 2 June 1999). In this case, there was a miscalculation. A strong negative reaction to the deal ensued in Scotland, with many of the leading institutional clients of the Bank of Scotland – including trade unions, universities, churches, and government bodies – threatening to withdraw their business on the grounds that they did not want to be associated with the religious dogma of the Robertson organization.

Direct selling of insurance exemplifies the new political economy of information services and marketing. The high cost of establishing the information technology infrastructure and databases limits the market to larger corporations. However, once the service is created there is a relatively low cost to extending the market, for example, through partnership arrangements. The result is 'a powerful tendency toward centralization and monopoly on an international basis. Thus, competitive forces in many information markets are likely to be rather weak' (Melody 1994: 261).

Direct selling is also connected to the market segmentation and unpooling that now characterizes the insurance industry. A newsletter for the insurance industry produced by an international management consultant firm included a section entitled 'the Majority of Customers are Not Profitable.' The problem was introduced as follows: '60 percent of average insurance revenue comes from the top 10 to 20 percent of brokers/agents. The bottom 60 percent – the majority – contribute only 15 percent ... 80 percent of the profits come from the top 10 to 20 percent of brokers/agents and, by extrapolation customers, when a traditional advisory distribution system is used. The bottom 50 percent of customers actually cost the company 10 percent of its profits!'

As we have seen, the problem for insurance companies is that in traditional, commission-based sales, agents are motivated to sell to relatively unprofitable prospects because their success depends on new sales. The solution is to get rid of unprofitable agents in these contexts by devising 'alternative distribution systems, especially for the 50 per cent of customers who are unprofitable in the advisor distribution model. The major objective is to adopt a service approach that matches effort/expense to the value generated for the effort/expense.' The poorer the prospect, the less the advice, substituting a direct sale in a buyer/seller relationship based on brand identification. The wealthier the prospect the more the advice: a personal sale in a client/professional relationship based on expert knowledge.

Clearly, direct selling entails a changed employment relationship and therefore a moral risk environment for sales agents. Agents who pose the financial risk of not bolstering profits sufficiently are to be cut out. More agents are to be employed in the heavily surveilled workplace of direct sales operations.

A marketing analysis for the industry includes a section entitled 'New World Order: Governance in the Collaborative Business System' (Insurance Advisory Board 1997b: 137). It proclaims that the 'first discipline' of the successful insurance operation will be 'relentless pursuit of efficiency; simply put, pure plays – either entrepreneurial firms without deep pockets or spin-offs of large organizations wise to the inefficiencies of proprietary value claims – constantly identifying collaborative opportunities to outsource suboptimal activities, profit from internal expertise, maximize performance of business system overall ... Winners Using Every Trick in the Book.' The 'second discipline' is the 'ethic of eternal reinvention': 'With one eye on the market and the other on themselves, future winners entrepreneurial, adoptive and built for speed.' The 'corporate culture' is to have an 'entrepreneurial bent, embrace of principled risk driven into organization by way of training, compensation, leadership.' This is to be furthered through 'structures designed to formalize "network" posture, social contracts built on compensated "impermanence" facilitate superior organization flexibility ... [e.g.] Liberal use of contingent workforce, part-time staff.'

We attended a conference for insurance brokers at which there was much discussion concerning new sales relationships and how they were being governed. A reinsurance company representative spoke to the conference about the 'new world order' of insurance business governance, and of the need to 'get with the times.' He used the example of a life insurance company based in the United States that is a 'virtual company,' with only fourteen employees who outsource all functions and services. He contrasted this to the 'control mentality' of traditional insurance companies: 'People feel they control things better when the people are working for them. And that's going to be cutting against the desire to be quicker, turn on a dime, that sort of thinking.'

Another new distribution arrangement is also changing the structure and culture of insurance sales and shifting responsibility for moral risks posed by agents. Instead of employing a captive or career sales force, some insurance companies have developed a franchise-like agency arrangement. An agent operates the agency as a small business, but under the name of the insurance company and subject to its governance system.

We studied a general insurance company that had implemented this type of agency arrangement. The person in charge of managing the new agencies said in interview that the system was designed to downsize both the sales force and headquarters management staff and to engineer greater business efficiencies:

> We were turning our agents over a lot and replacing them. And that's very expensive to bring them in, train them, you just get them up to speed, they're gone. So that was one of the issues. Really bad for the client: 'You just sold me this policy, where'd he go?' Not a good image ... [We needed to give the agent] more skin in what they were doing. So we terminate them from the organization and we contract [some] of them back. So now we've established a business relationship. Very different from an employee relationship that we've had in the past ... We pay them a higher commission rate to do that. They are *responsible* for the client service in their agencies ... Employees focus on work, these contracted individuals are focusing on results. Like what's the bottom line? ... 'I can run

my operations cheaper than you guys ever could.' And they can cut corners ... [If they don't] we reserve the right to put another agent in there [on thirty days' notice, which is] cleaner than the old system. The old system, because of the laws in protecting employees, you're entitled to so much pay and all that. And the new contract doesn't say that ... We want a little more of a risk taker ... [with the old system] it was very safe where it was, if they didn't make a sale today, well, 'So what?' Whereas these guys, they'll make sales. So what if they have no money!

This manager of agency operations said that in the short period in which the new system had been in operation, five agency operators had already been terminated, including two who had been using unacceptable sales practices. He stressed that the ability to terminate miscreants summarily, combined with effective control over who is operating the agencies in the first place, is another distinct advantage of this new distribution arrangement. Most new agency operators were former company managers or successful sales staff, and therefore already well known and trusted. Persons contracted from outside the company were invariably new to the insurance business. 'We did not want to recruit people from other insurance companies because they get some bad habits, we wanted people that hadn't been in the business.' When asked about the 'bad habits' he was referring to, he said, 'twisting or replacement ... you really have to guard against that in the insurance industry ... That's an easy way to sell but you're ripping off the clients. ... people don't understand the insurance products well enough.'

This interviewee made it clear that the agency arrangement was structured to favour the company's interests by downloading more responsibility for risk to the agent operator while increasing governance of him. This structuring began with the contract. In establishing the new system, a few prospective agency operators sought legal advice on the contract. '"My lawyer says this is kind of one-sided ... blah, blah, blah."' The company's response was "Hey, here's the contract. So you either have our contract or you don't" ... So we haven't changed our contracts ... and they stopped asking now because we're *not* changing the contract. It *is* one-sided because we're giving you this business. It is in our favour.'

The company used a number of mechanisms to shift responsibility onto its agency operators and to embed its liberal risk regime in their operations. The contract required agents to buy their own errors and omissions insurance. Moreover, they were required to buy it only through the interviewee as the agency system manager. 'I negotiate the contract and I administer it so all the agents buy it from me.' This stipulation allowed him to govern the agency operators through errors and omissions insurance contract obligations. More generally, having agency operators buy their own errors and omissions insurance was a means by which 'any mistakes that their staff make, are theirs. Like they're responsible ... Society has changed, and there have been court rulings elevating the duty of care that is expected of agents ... big class actions against insurance companies for inappropriate sales practices, ripping off clients.'

A second mechanism for responsibilizing agents into the company's new liberal risk regime was a linking of agents' commissions to both their claims losses and to their cross-selling of life insurance with property insurance. A poor claims loss record could result in a loss of commission up to 2 per cent, while good life insurance cross-selling could enhance commissions by a few percentage points.

An agency operator said in interview that the company kept adding hidden expenses without warning. The parallel with what insurance companies do with life insurance contract expenses passed on to the policyholder was not lost on her. 'So what was projected to be your income and what will end up being your income is not the same.' The compulsory selling of life insurance in what was primarily a vehicle and home insurance context was also seen as troublesome. Another agency operator said in interview that the company was structuring the agency relationship strongly in the direction of life insurance sales, but this was having a very negative effect on his relationship with vehicle and home insurance clients:

> I *have* to rather that wanting to ... [If I'm not selling life insurance] that's basically going to defeat myself in this business and in this company ... [But] we don't want to be seen as those wishy-washy, backroom [life insurance sales people], where we're just sitting around laughing about peoples' estates and property. We want to be seen as professionals because we care about the people that walk in the door ... *I* don't see life insurance as a way to boost income. I see it more as a way to let it go because I see some people, when you ask them too much, they just don't want to talk anymore.

A third mechanism for responsibilizing agents was a very formal and rigid system for auditing agency operators. There was an internal self-audit manual and reporting protocol to address everything from compliance practices and errors and omissions checks to office appearance and the 'professionalism' of staff. The company also hired a firm to conduct mystery shopping surveillance visits to each agency office on a regular basis.

Agency operators also felt both disciplined and disadvantaged by the fact that the company was running other sales distribution systems that competed directly with this new agency system. For example, the company partnered with a bank to open a direct sales call centre that sold many of the same products at lower premiums. When agency operators complained that this was direct competition, the company responded with an estimate that it was only taking away about 5 per cent of their business. An agency operator we interviewed felt that this estimate did not include potential new customers who no longer bother to visit an agency office 'and there's not a way they can calculate that.' He reasoned that if someone could get lower rates by going direct, 'wouldn't you? I would!' Other agency operators informed us that they were also aggrieved by a company group insurance initiative with a large client. This initiative allowed the company to sell optional life insurance to group members at a heavily discounted rate, again undercutting agency operators.

Another sign that the company's liberal risk regime was lean and mean was the fact that it required agent operators to pay for employment benefits that had previously been part of the company benefit package under the former career agent system. We attended a regional meeting of agency operators at which an employee group benefits expert spoke. She said that the company was trying to keep the cost of the benefits package low, like a 'stripped-down Chevy.' One of the agency operators complained that he and his colleagues would like to regain a number of the benefits included in the in-house benefits package. The group benefits representative responded, 'We can provide anything the agents want, but the agents have to be able to pay for it ... The established agents ... where they've got a huge book of business and a lot of income, they can absorb a lot of the cost. But a new agent, trying to build up a book of business, every $100 a month out there for benefits is a real drain on the bottom line.' She then advised cost-conscious agency operators to list their new employees as contract employees for the first three months of their employment. This tactic would save the agency operators the benefits premiums for this period, and also give them time to screen their new employees' health before approving them for the disability insurance package.

Agency operators saw the combination of efforts by the company to change their employment relationship as contradicting its advertised claim to be committed to community values and collective responsibility. The company's manager in charge of agency operations became choked as he related the same view:

> We're not nearly as family as we once were. Like the whole thing is changing. I think the economy is driving that. Like you're only as good as you were yesterday ... The downsizing, making people do more with less, I think all of that is putting more pressure on to have to produce, produce, produce ... There isn't such a thing as coasting ... Maybe fifteen years ago, we *never* terminated people. You had to be real bad to get terminated out of here ... It's unsettling, because what happens if you have a bad year? ... Or, a brand new boss and they don't like you? It's not the safe environment that we once had ... The new agency relationship will take everything a little further.

These new arrangements for governing the conduct of insurance agents place even more pressure on agents to generate premium revenue. As such they compound the structural and cultural basis of market misconduct. The recipe for market misconduct – commissioned-based retailing of complex products in an aggressive sales culture – is intensified in new distribution channels such as call centres and agency operations.

We now turn to an examination of how the insured are governed. Because moral risks are reactive at all levels of the insurance relationship, our analysis in Part II of risks posed by insurers and how they are governed ramifies into our analysis in Part III of risks posed by the insured and how they are governed. In efforts to select and rate policyholders, involve them in loss prevention, and limit their claims, insurers are forced to look in the hall of mirrors of their own moral risk attributes.

Part III

GOVERNING THE INSURED

7. Prospects as Suspects

There is nothing makes a man suspect much, more than to know little.
Francis Bacon, 'Of Suspicion' (1625)

Suspicion is a thing very few people can entertain without letting the hypothesis turn, in their minds, into fact.
David Cort, Social Astonishments (1963)

He who is too much afraid of being duped has lost the power of being magnanimous.
Henri Frédéric Amiel, Journal (1868)

Prospecting and Suspecting

Underwriters approach insurance applicants with suspicion. They assume all applicants bear moral risks that must be considered in the decision to insure and in the calculus of rating criteria to include in the insurance contract. As a result, applicants are required to report intimate details that lead to their placement in a category of suspicion that appears insurable. This approach 'in effect promotes suspicion to the dignified scientific rank of a calculus of probabilities. To be suspected, it is no longer necessary to manifest symptoms of dangerousness or abnormality, it is enough to display whatever characteristics specialists responsible for the definition of preventive policy have constituted as risk factors ... This hyperrationalism is at the same time a thorough-going pragmatism in that it pretends to eradicate risk as though one were pulling weeds' (Castel 1991: 288).

A training manual for agents in an insurance company we studied had a unit entitled 'Prospecting' and a subsection unit entitled 'Suspects.' Neophyte agents were warned that 'The world is full of prospects ... We can't tell you which are immediate and which are deferred prospects until we get some qualifying information ... Until that information is developed, any name we have should be called a *suspect*.' The manual describes the four-step process of turning the suspect into a bona fide prospect. First, the suspect must be motivated to buy insurance: 'make them aware of the need and to want to do something about it now.' Second, the agent must ascertain the suspect's ability to pay, not only immediately but 'on a continuing basis.' This determination is related to motivation since 'sometimes it's simply a matter of setting priorities on the demands for money and dealing with the important ones first.' Third, the suspect must be investigated for moral risks and qualified as acceptable to the company. The person should be 'not an obstacle, but rather an opportunity to build a profitable clientele. Be proactive and selective in your prospecting activity.' Fourth, the suspect must fit with the agent's 'natural target market' with respect to 'economies, social, geographic, education and age to name some.' The agent is told that if motivation, ability to pay, acceptable moral risks, and target market criteria are not there, the suspect should stand accused and be denied further consideration. Wasting time on a suspect can 'clutter up your files and cause a false sense of security. Be ruthless in getting rid of them.'

Instructional manuals for agents provide them with criteria for being suspicious. These criteria are used not only for decisions on inclusion and exclusion but also to rate the worthiness of suspects. Here worthiness refers to both the suspect's moral standing and the net worth of her assets. These twin moral and material aspects of worth determine her value as an insurance consumer. For example, an industry association's booklet on proven ways to cultivate suspects and turn them into prospects stated,

> Family history, education, career goals, family goals, buying habits, etc., can tell you a lot about your clients. Not only do you need to know their needs, but their fears, dreams, intentions, and attitudes. At first, this information will help you to determine their dominant buying motives; however, if you keep the appropriate records, it will also help you to determine their future needs and concerns. Equally important, though, is that in the process you learn more about your clients, develop a rapport with them, and earn a higher level of trust. Use probing questions ... And

listen carefully – it's important to be aware of nonverbal clues. Once you establish a database of key information on a client, you can customize your marketing and communications efforts to reflect individual needs. Through the speed and efficiency of your computer, you can target your client at appropriate times with the appropriate information ... It's important that you do not waste your efforts on those people with whom you can't seem to make a connection.

These instructional materials indicate that there is a direct relationship among market segmentation, unpooling risk, and redlining the undesirable. In insurance underwriting, knowledge of risk for marketing is entwined with knowledge of risk for the determination of insurance pools and their respective rates and contract conditions. Target marketing and segmentation are aimed at placing the individual in the insurance equivalent of a gated community, sharing risks only with those who are similarly situated.

We interviewed an underwriting manager for a multinational insurance company that targeted wealthier clients. He said that, like personal products manufacturers, insurance companies must keep developing new products and market niches in order to cream off the most profitable populations:

> Johnson and Johnson said ... over 50 per cent of their revenues come from products that they didn't even have four years ago ... [My job is to] seek out the best risks in any given class, be that a target class or something that we're looking to develop, investigate those risks for their suitability in terms of what price would be required to make them an acceptable risk ... We have expressed to [brokers] time and again and built up over time, what our likes and dislikes are from an underwriting standpoint. We've also shown them what our abilities are in loss control and claims and we work with them to say, 'Do your risks fit?' If so, let's pursue it aggressively ... Let's cut override deals, let's cut incentive commission deals, let's target a class of business together, let's make an exclusive wording.

The targeting and preferred terms of insurance can be highly specific. A former head underwriter with a large insurance company said that it is typical for an underwriter to look at his available capital and then select a specific type of insurance risk and population to 'invest' in. He said, for example, the underwriter might target Jewish businesses. He then 'frames his products, the things he is trying to get out of his capital he has got to play with, and then he instructs his branches across the country to go looking for those things and gives them a book of rules and underwriting criteria to work with as they select those risks from all over the place.'

In some areas of underwriting, such as personal lines, it is not a simple matter of pursuing a single target population with a single type of insurance. Rather, there is an effort to mix population risks across different lines of insurance. Thus a general insurance company's manual for agents directs them to 'Consider the distribution of individual risks among the various lines and respective classifications within a certain line ... Consider the *desirability* of the client's entire account. The supporting business should be better than average in its own classification if it is going to justify the acceptance of a risk that is slightly below the level of normal acceptability. Premium volume alone is not sufficient to measure supporting business.'

This example indicates that risk taking also comes into play. A property lines underwriter said in interview, 'Underwriters are able to look at all the bad things about a risk and yet not be paralyzed by that fear, but rather say, "Yes, this is one that I basically want to roll the dice on."' An insurance company manual for agents underwriting home insurance also warned agents not to become paralysed by their suspicions. While agents are responsible for making the right gambles, there is a need for risk taking in the context of loss ratio security assessment:

> In competitive markets, we are constantly being selected against ... It may be necessary to tighten standards as a result of poor experience, or if results are good, it may be time to loosen some ... There are those who consider underwriting to be a negative function: a process of declining or cancelling risks not meeting the criteria established by underwriting. In actuality, underwriting is a positive, forward-looking approach to writing insurance. It is through the application of ability, knowledge, experience and courage that risks can be selected properly and produce a profit for the insurer by keeping loss ratios and expenses at an acceptable level.

In what follows, we analyse how personal line insurers of homes and automobiles underwrite in such terms. We consider in each case the criteria used to market segment and unpool risks, resulting in either redlining (exclusion) or placing risks within the range of substandard, standard, and superstandard categories. We also examine the means through which knowledge of risks is ascertained, including both surveillance technologies and the efforts of agents undertaking inspections in the field.

Home Insurance Moral Risks and Unpooling

A home insurance company we studied issued a manual to agents listing nineteen 'risks not written.' The risks identified pertained to the condition of the property, the location of the property, ownership-occupancy-supervision patterns, moral qualities of the insured, and the insurance record of the insured.

Condition of property exclusions addressed the basic mechanical systems of homes, including dangerous heating systems, underground fuel storage tanks, and the absence of electricity or full inside plumbing. The presence of these physical risks can be read as a sign of moral risk, that the owner has not taken proper care to ensure the safety and maintenance of the property.

The manual called for explicit redlining of properties in undesirable locations. Klein (1997: 43) defines redlining 'as unfair discrimination (i.e. discrimination that is not based on differences in cost or risk) against a particular geographic area.' The manual identified certain inner city areas, small towns in some parts of the country, and mobile home parks in a particular town as being redlined. For example, the mobile home parks were described as 'closed due to exceeded underwriting limit' and as 'closed due to undesirable underwriting features.' The manual justified this redlining by stating, 'In areas identified as unacceptable, experience has taught us that losses are to be expected ... Insurance is designed to provide coverage for the unexpected.'

This company also expected losses under certain patterns of ownership, occupancy, and supervision, and redlined accordingly. Rooming houses in British Columbia were redlined entirely, while elsewhere in the country they were seen as possibly acceptable if owner occupied with a limited number of rooms to rent. The manual described rooming houses as 'a less attractive risk because they offer cheaper accommodations and have a higher turnover rate.' This company-legislated exclusion of the poor could not be more explicit. Among other things, the redlining of British Columbia excluded underwriting in much of the downtown eastside of Vancouver, which is one of Canada's poorest and most troubled areas (Haggerty, Huey, and Ericson 2003).

Other ownership-occupancy-supervision exclusions were similarly directed at defining what a home is and what is suitable for home insurance. Dwellings with more than three families residing in them were excluded. The prospect was required to insure her principal residence with the company before a second property could be considered for insurance. A prospect owning more than three rental dwellings, or three rental units within a single dwelling, was excluded from the home insurance program, although of course there were commercial insurance possibilities in such cases. There was also a specific exclusion related to supervision of activity in the home. On the assumption that babysitters are less responsible than parents, there was an exclusion of homes with a swimming pool where the family also used babysitters.

An unfavourable moral risk assessment of the prospect was also grounds for not accepting a home insurance application (see also Glenn 2000). A blanket statement informed agents that they could exclude any risk which, based on their judgment, contained such adverse conditions that it would be an improper subject for insurance. 'This refers to both the physical risk and the moral characteristics of the insured. Agents who have lived in an area for a number of years will usually know certain persons or risks in their area which would present an increased chance of loss, e.g. a risk the agent knows or suspects is a "hangout" for a local youth gang or for individuals engaging in illegal activities.' However, the moral risks involved did not have to be so dramatic. As Mary Douglas (1992) and Ian Hacking (2003) have taught us about the selection of risk and danger, literal as well as figurative dirt can spur risk aversion. Thus the manual identifies household dirt as a danger sign and grounds for denying the insurance application:

> Pride of ownership is an important factor in underwriting a home risk ... Poor housekeeping presents a physical hazard that is a greater risk than we wish to have on our book of business ... Homes lacking repair or painting, yards filled with rusty automobiles, childrens' toys on sidewalks and stairways, etc. present physical, moral and liability hazards to an insurance company. Poorly kept or poorly maintained premises may indicate a lack of responsibility on the potential client's part ... Obvious damage to furniture, carpets and other personal property can also indicate a moral or liability hazard ... [It] may be difficult to determine the difference between existing and new damage.

A final set of risks not written pertained to the insurance record of the applicant as suspect. The manual specifies a preference for some-one who has never made a home insurance claim. If there is a claims record, then the offender must show signs of rehabilitation – for exam-ple, taking better care of the property and not making more claims – in order to remove her suspect status:

> Our target market is 'claims-free' business. Therefore, as a company we do not want to accept business that has prior claims history in the past three years. We will accept a risk with a claim provided that there is not an indication of further claims and the risk is otherwise acceptable. Previ-ous losses may indicate that the applicant is overly claims conscious, care-less, or perhaps, lives in an area susceptible to certain types of losses ... The underwriter must be satisfied that the circumstances surrounding all previous losses do not include unacceptable physical or moral hazards.

The agent is offered detail on how to identify a troublesome suspect. A key sign is someone whose insurance 'has been cancelled, declined, surcharged, renewed with restrictions or refused to be renewed by an insurer ... Often, the pattern set with the insurer who cancelled the risk will continue. These clients do not present a quality risk to us.' A related consideration is whether the suspect's insurance has been can-celled in the past for non-payment of premiums. If this has occurred more than once in the past three years it 'may indicate financial insta-bility and may be a moral hazard ... [costing us] ... administrative fees and added exposure for the time on risk without receiving a premium.' Anyone convicted of insurance fraud of any type, or who has had a home insurance policy cancelled in the past three years because of 'material misrepresentation' is also to be excluded. An uncooperative attitude – demonstrated through an unwillingness to provide informa-tion requested about previous insurance coverage – is also grounds for exclusion.

This home insurer had similar guidelines for its own policyholders seeking renewal of their policy. Renewals were to be denied for a poor claims history, defined as more than three claims in the previous three years, or even one or two claims depending on the circumstances. Renewals were also to be refused if the person had made a fraudulent claim or engaged in any act of 'mis-representation' or 'non-disclosure.' Uncooperativeness during the period of being insured was also grounds for exclusion. Uncooperativeness was defined as 'where any insured has refused to cooperate in the proper writing or maintenance of the insurance coverage or in the settlement of a claim.' Blanket exclusion for anything else was covered by the statement that the agent can deny 'Any risk where there is an increased exposure due to deterioration in either the premises or the moral risk.' The agent was also told that if any of his clients became too morally suspect during the term of the policy, immediate cancellation should be considered. 'Note: if any of the above conditions exist, consideration should be given to cancelling the policy mid-term.'

In another manual agents were advised that when writing to clients to cancel or not renew their policies, the company's letterhead containing a slogan that included the word 'trust' should not be used. 'In most situations it is best to use the letterhead which includes the ... Trust positioning line in the blue bar at the bottom. In situations such as cancelling someone's insurance you may wish to use the basic letterhead without this feature.'

The vetting of morally suspect applicants by this company did not rest entirely with agents. If the suspect and her property bore specified risks, agents were required to turn the application over to the company's underwriting department for further consideration. Homes assessed at more than $400,000 had to be referred to the underwriting department, as did homes with more than two registered mortgages or that were used for commercial activity. Ownership was a key concern, with referral required if ownership was other than personal or for multiple ownership outside of a family. Homes that posed exceptional fire risks – log homes, those with irregular heating and electrical systems, and those built with unconventional materials – were also subject to referral. Family pets were a prompt for referral if deemed by the agent to be 'unusual or vicious,' for example 'pit bull dogs, boa constrictor snakes, black widow spiders or exotic birds.' Vacant homes also bore special consideration, because they could take on objectionable features: 'Dirt and dust will settle, transients may move in, vermin may build nests, vandalism may be prevalent, and fire reporting will most certainly be delayed. The moral hazard may increase if the vacancy is caused by an inability to sell or rent the house. A vacant house could be an enticement to children.'

If a decision is taken to underwrite home insurance – to convert the suspect into a prospect – the next step is to structure the insurance policy so that the undesirable risks regarding the person and property are excluded or addressed through special provisions. The moral risks for vacant properties are illustrative. Since insurers require property owners to be the primary policing agents for property (see chapter 8; also O'Malley 1991, Ericson and Haggerty 1997), vacant property is especially risky: the self-policing mechanism is absent. As a result, if a vacant property is underwritten there are a number of exclusions of coverage as well as requirements to engage someone else for the policing task. Thus the property insurance company in question only permitted a basic, standard rating for a principal residence temporarily vacant. It also stipulated

- [the client must establish that] the dwelling will be under the care of a competent person; during the heating season a competent person [will enter] the dwelling daily to ensure that heating is being maintained *or* the water supply is shut off and the systems drained; the windows and doors are securely closed and locked; all rubbish is removed from the dwelling.
- loss or damage caused by water escape or rupture, vandalism and malicious acts and glass breakage is not covered.

Regular home insurance policies similarly include special clauses to address losses that are difficult to police. 'Mysterious disappearance' of property is one example: the policyholder loses a valuable item and the loss is not attributable to theft or a fraudulent claim. The company dealt with this morally risky area under a special package, carrying additional premium, advising agents to 'be cautious to whom we sell this coverage.'

A related type of loss is accidental breakage. The company made a moral distinction between the accidental breakage of useful items compared to those they deemed decorative or frivolous. Accidental breakage of useful items was covered under the standard policy, but nonutilitarian items were only covered by a rider to the policy with an additional premium. 'Accidental breakage of china, glassware, etc., whether dropped, knocked over, or broken while being cleaned, is not covered. The intent is to exclude decorative items which do not have a specific purpose to the dwelling (example: Royal Doulton figurine). A glass chandelier provides light for the dining room and therefore has a purpose to the dwelling.'

Deductibles provide an especially ingenious way of eliminating coverage and recouping the cost of coverage. For example, the company established a minimum $1,000 theft deductible for prospects with no previous insurance or no insurance within the previous twelve months

TABLE 7.1
Home insurance deductible and premium surcharge/discount levels

Deductible ($)	Premium surcharge/discount (%)
200	+20
500	none
1,000	−10
1,500	−15
2,000	−17
2,500	−20
3,000	−23
5,000	−30

and for tenants who live on the ground floor or basement suites of apartment buildings, or who share units with people who are not related to or in common-law relationship with them. Since the poor are especially vulnerable to theft, and most of the victimization they suffer falls under the $1,000 cut-off point, this structuring of deductibles is especially regressive against the poor.

In general, the discount or surcharge for the level of deductible chosen is designed to ensure that the policyholder who suffers a relatively minor loss pays for it through the premium structure anyway, and therefore could just as easily self-insure against such losses. For example, the company offered the surcharge and discount structure reproduced in table 7.1. The greater the deductible the greater the assumed self-policing vigilance over small losses. In this case, the cost of opting for the lowest deductible is so prohibitive that anyone who chooses it is signalling that she is a moral risk and will pay for that fact through excessive premiums.

Slater (1997: 42) observes that price in general is not a reflection of value per se, but 'a social compromise between the agendas of wants followed by each private individual. It is an aggregation or averaging of individual decisions rather than a social entity in its own right.' However, this definition fails to take into account how product marketers fix prices. In the insurance industry, the fixing of prices is uniquely difficult because the cost of the product itself is not known before selling it. A best guess is made, complicated by surcharges and discounts for the minutiae of assumed moral risks.

Home insurance pricing creates a class structure based on market segmentation and moral risks. The insurance company in question had a wide range of price levels, broadly divided into standard, superstandard, and substandard. The standard market was described in interview by a district sales manager as 'married with children, $45,000 income and up by area. Because I'm sure you can appreciate there are areas we'd rather not do business in [laughs], like the downtown eastside and some of those areas that are ... lower effect.' He added that the standard market segment reduced his district's 2,000,000 people to 200,000 targeted by the company. The company further signified its preferences by suggesting to agents that they send letters to people in this category stating, 'Based on my personal observation, your home appears very well-kept and is just the type we like to insure.'

The company also had a superstandard or 'preferred class.' According to the company manual, 'The rates for preferred are much lower than that of the standard class.' The agent was warned that upward mobility must be earned, therefore the preferred rate should not be given to a new prospect just to provide that prospect with a break on the premium and thereby secure her business. 'You must always ask yourself if it is fair to other customers who pay the proper rates (sometimes higher) whether or not they [new customers] should get a break in their premium. Sometimes we treat new customers better than customers who have been with us for years and have had no claims.'

Another home insurer we studied targeted superstandard prospects exclusively. Its target market started with properties valued at $400,000. When approached by suspects with property below this level, the company employed a number of elements to make their product uncompetitive. These elements included higher premiums, higher deductibles, insured rather than replacement value, and on-site inspections where every fault was found to justify the other elements. A senior executive of the company explained in interview, 'We're the rich peoples' insurance company ... [Standard market companies] inhouse does not support them betting $2 million on a home. They just don't have that capacity. We do ... [The] other market is just [the] $100,000 home ... We won't accept it, so it's an easy differentiation.'

An underwriter for this company said in interview that one marketing approach was to target wealthy commercial insurance clients and cross-sell home insurance to them. Corporate executives with the power to place lucrative commercial insurance with the insurer were also sought for their worthiness as personal lines clients. 'No offence to different levels in the company, but if the mail person also had their personal lines with us, are we going to be interested in keeping that? No. And is that going to be the best deal for that person? No, because that's not our target.' Another underwriter for the same company observed in interview that the executive client's good experience with home insurance helps to sell the commercial lines. Home insurance claims handling becomes a marketing feature not only for home insurance but also for various types of executive protection and commercial insurance. 'Let's say we just paid a claim ... on the personal lines. You have a nice homeowner loss, carpet got ruined for a few thousand bucks, and you still have our personal expertise. Well most [executive] clients haven't had a directors and officers loss, but they'll feel pretty comfortable that carpet got cleaned really well. And that's the same mentality that we bring throughout all of our claims transactions. And those fundamentals are our target market per se.'

This interviewee continued with an example of a house fire claim that involved a $10 million loss to the building and contents, and another $6 million loss for the policyholder's living expenses caused by the disruption. The fire was started by real candles burning on a Christmas tree, which ignited the tree itself. It is worthwhile to speculate on how such a moral risk would have been addressed by a claims department dealing with a standard or substandard market client. In the present case, the underwriter seemed delighted that he could use this extraordinary claim to market to his superpreferred clientele. 'We've got to keep this guy in the lifestyle he was accustomed to. Front page like every newspaper in the country ... The loss was handled in a most professional and forthright manner, and now today we have like twenty-three of the top twenty-five homes, in terms of value, in the province. These are the people we want and we paid a big loss on one of them. So we can use that as fearmongering.'

At the opposite end of the spectrum are substandard pools, or what some companies refer to as essential insurance. One company's manual for agents declared that poor and marginal suspects high on moral risks may still be acceptable if they appear profitable:

Essential Insurance is designed to meet the needs of potential clients who are unable to purchase insurance to protect their home and belongings. Some of the reasons for this are:

- number of claims
- unusual physical or liability exposure
- location of risk
- cancelled or refused renewal by their insurer

- declined or surcharged by their insurer
- does not meet our risk selection guidelines

Essential Insurance is just that – a *reduced coverage* policy designed to insure those people experiencing difficulties in obtaining necessary protection against large losses. This product addresses the fact that, from an underwriting perspective, there is a premium that we should be willing to accept for almost every risk. For almost every risk there is a coverage and a price that will make the business profitable to us, and at the same time, provide a much needed service to the customer.

Elsewhere the manual instructs agents on what substandard suspects might be converted to prospects. Cross-selling opportunities are one key indicator. Essential insurance 'allows us to offer insurance to desirable clients who may live in an undesirable area. For example, you may have a potential client who lives in the downtown core of a major city, but who also would bring their auto to us and who needs life insurance. The key is to sell Essential Insurance to people who we would like to have as clients because of the other opportunities they offer, either now or in the future.'

Essential insurance is written as a named perils policy, meaning that any given peril can be added, removed, or altered as the individual case is addressed. Any changes can also be accompanied by adjustments to premiums and deductibles. For example, if the agent feels that vandalism is more likely than usual, the vandalism peril can be removed from the policy, or it can be retained but with a higher premium and/or deductible. Remarkably, agents were instructed to sell this peril-by-peril assessment as a positive feature of individual consumer choice. A brochure on essential insurance told prospects that 'with the addition of special endorsements, your basic coverage can be personalized for your individual needs.'

Standard policy features thus become expensive options – ranging from 30 to 70 per cent higher – in the essential insurance policy. Theft coverage was only available as a separate, expensive endorsement to the policy, at the discretion of underwriters. The deductible minimum was set high at $1,000, and the range extended to $10,000.

In the middle of describing these dimensions of essential insurance to agents, the manual asserts in bold-face type: '**Agents are advised to avoid clients who present a moral hazard.**' However, it was otherwise equivocal in this regard. Essential insurance is insurance *for* moral risks, structured to profit from the suspect's disadvantaged position in the insurance-rating hierarchy. Thus another segment of the manual lists especially unfavourable elements that may render the suspect ineligible even for essential insurance, but then states that discretion may still be exercised:

> Although Essential Insurance can be used for most clients who are having difficulty obtaining insurance there are still a few circumstances that may make a risk unacceptable.
>
> • insurance has been cancelled more than once in the past three years because of non-payment ...
> • the applicant has been convicted of fraud
> • the applicant, within the last three years, has a home insurance policy cancelled as a result of material misrepresentation
>
> However, even in these cases, there may be extenuating circumstances which the underwriter feels make the risk acceptable.

The most significant indicator of moral risk was a history of claims recidivism. This company used postal codes to identify all local areas of Canada on a five-point scale of unpooling as follows:

> • superstandard – preferred target market – low claims frequency and low loss ratio.
> • standard – current market – average claims frequency with low to average loss ratio.
> • substandard – high claims frequency with low to average loss ratio (high theft/burglary).
> • substandard – high claims frequency with high loss ratio, includes areas with two to three years very poor experience.
> • redline – identified unacceptable areas where we do not want to be competitive.

The spiral downward to substandard status and redlining was tied to claims frequency and its impact on loss ratios. As suspects spiralled downward through being claims offenders, they were surcharged for their morally risky behaviour of failing to take proper preventive action. The manual stated, 'All claims are surchargeable, whether preventable or non-preventable.' For new customers transferring their insurance from another company, one claim in the past three years was to be surcharged 5 per cent with a $500 minimum deductible. Two claims in the previous three years were normally grounds for not accepting the insurance application. For renewal of the company's existing policyholders the penalty structure was as follows:

Claims History	Surcharge
1 past 3 years	5 per cent + $500 minimum deductible 'unless eligible for claims forgiveness. Remove claims free discount if applicable.'
2 past 3 years	25 per cent + $500 minimum deductible
3 past 3 years	30 per cent + $500 minimum deductible 'underwriter may choose not to stay on risk'
Theft claim	Discretion to use theft deductible endorsement which increases on the theft peril only.
Specified perils package	Not offered following second specified perils package claim.

Note: Policies will be reviewed by underwriting after every claim. Higher deductible or other underwriting action may be warranted.

Agents were told in the manual that this penalty structure induced the insured into 'sharing a greater interest in their potential losses.' Clear evidence of how a claim can affect their premium and contract provisions provides the insured with an incentive to reduce the frequency of claims and the company can 'retain good clients.'

Agents were also instructed that the selection and rating process is shot through with discretion. Their job is to treat an applicant for insurance as a suspect and figure out whether she should be converted into a prospect. The underwriting department's job is then to rate the applicant in whatever way seems profitable and justifiable. Another manual of the company reminded agents, 'Don't forget. The determination of risk eligibility will not dictate the way a risk is rated. In their rating of policies, companies may forgive certain claims, not surcharge ... or allow insureds to pay back losses. You should remember that the exercise of determining a risk's eligibility is separate and distinct from rating practices.' Another manual elaborated on the underwriter's discretion:

Depending on the length of time insured, other business, experience on the risk and the types of claims, we could cancel after one claim if the circumstances were such that it is a situation we do not see improving ... A long-term client living in a poor part of town might be given different consideration as a client living in a newer part of town who has only just recently written a policy with us. Each case is judged on its own merits and demerits ... Only after all other avenues have been explored should we consider cancellation. The other types of underwriting action include: restricting coverages; increasing deductibles; surcharges; or exclusions.

The discretionary assessment of moral risk and unpooling that results can be blatantly unfair and discriminatory (Squires 1997). One way in which Canadian-based insurance companies negotiate the legal regulation of their unfair moral risk and market segmentation practices is to create subsidiaries that sell only to the identified segment. This practice was explained by a university-based actuarial scientist we interviewed. He said that in order to offer 'a different price for superselect policyholders' a company will 'run their superselect through one of their subsidiaries, a different company.' This avoids state regulatory control of equitable pricing. He identified one company that in fact ran four companies for its four different layers of unpooling and associated pricing. He said that any mixing of the books of business across these companies would be 'breaking the law.' When the prospects have been pre-screened by the company – for example, because they are part of a professional association group – the company may even cut out the agent in order to save the commission fees and increase capacity to offer lower prices and better contract terms to the select. For example, 'they want to offer lower prices to an association business by doing it through direct mailing, but they don't want to tell their agents we're undercutting your ability to sell and get your 12 per cent commission because we're going to go to the professional engineers ... and give them 10 per cent off if they direct write ... They do it through their [subsidiary] ... and they don't even tell the agents that has ever happened.'

Home Insurance Surveillance Systems

Insurance company manuals evidence the formal structure of moral risk evaluation and unpooling. These manuals articulate not only the rules of inclusion and exclusion but also the discretionary latitude of underwriters to speculate on moral risks that might prove profitable. In order to make discretionary judgments – to decide when the rules should be construed as constraining or enabling – the underwriter requires detailed knowledge of moral risk. This knowledge is available through computer-based information systems that track the insurance records of properties and those who insure them. Knowledge is also gleaned through inspections of properties of insureds by agents in the field.

Individual companies are increasingly less likely to undertake their own home inspections or direct field investigation of an applicant. Instead, moral risk assessment is centralizing into data systems operated by information service companies that supply the insurance industry. In Canada, there is an information system company that provides most of the home insurance industry with basic data on insured properties and persons. There are also various brokerages that do inspections and provide data services, especially for the few large insurers that do not participate in the above-mentioned information company's system, and for superstandard and large commercial account cases. An underwriter who used brokerage services in this way said in interview that it is no longer feasible to send his own staff on inspections: 'with the way costs are nowadays you can't afford to do that on everyone. So we have to take a little bit on trust ... dealing with the right broker. So that's crucial, and even within brokerage houses there's certain people I deal with and certain people I won't. There's a principle in insurance you may have heard that everyone operates on good faith, and it's not practised by everyone frankly. There's always someone trying to work an angle and get a better deal.'

The information system company referred to above has established considerable trust in its abstract system and is used by all but a handful of home insurers. It offers an online information service to insurers about homes and home insurance policyholders. It also offers geographic information system mapping by postal code of the insurance claims made on properties. According to one company document, 'over 90 percent of all habitational insurance claims filed in most Canadian regions' are included in this mapping. A company official we interviewed said,

> we have a map book that we can provide that basically outlines some major cities, by postal code colour-coded – red-bad, green-good – with regard to the different perils that are insured against: flood, water damage, windstorm, hail, burglary ... Claims data with compusearch, map it onto a postal code map of the city, we have visual indication of what's happening where with regard to what peril ... Some of them are now tak-

ing it one step further and using it as a marketing tool ... where do we want to try and grow our business? ... [You can figuratively] walk up and down the street and see the types of claims that are happening around you ... You may want to 'run' the apartment building and if they've got 150 water claims then obviously the piping is bad.

A linked database incorporates any on-site inspections that have been done on the subject property. In keeping with the market segmentation practices of the insurers it serves, the company offers bronze, silver, gold, and platinum inspection reports. Bronze is for the substandard market, silver and gold for standard homes with moderate replacement values, and platinum service is reserved for 'carriage trade' homes. The platinum assessment includes not only 'a detailed description of liability exposures, with diagram and photographs,' but also 'uses the Marshall and Swift high-value computer program to determine a "brick-by-brick" full replacement-cost reconstruction estimate. Updated quarterly and using details gathered by highly qualified field representatives, the program provides information on material costs, wage rates, contractor profit and architectural fees and integrates unique variables such as location, crew size, trades specialization and acquisition of materials.'

Another linked database tracks the home insurance career of the applicant. In the words of a company official we interviewed, if the applicant 'moved from Newfoundland to Halifax to Montreal to Toronto to Vancouver, you would see where all the claims are happening.' We attended an agents' meeting of a company that used this system. Agents were informed about an instructional session on how to use the system and told when use was mandatory. Written materials distributed at the meeting said this database 'provides access to historical person and property claims information for all regions of Canada. Each time a new policy is written or a reinstatement past 90 days post-renewal, a system query must be performed to scan for previous losses ... [This] eliminates the need for letters from prior carriers; identifies undeclared losses, estimated at up to 20 per cent of new applications; [provides an] effective fraud fighting tool; and, identifies poor risks and areas before they become part of the agency book of business.'

The database on insured persons links to a database of the Insurance Crime Prevention Bureau of Canada (ICPBC). If the applicant has a record of fraudulent claims, or is under investigation by ICPBC, a flashing screen flags this suspect status for the agent making the query.

Reciprocity with ICPBC includes their access to the information services company's database.

The database on insured persons also links with credit information systems. Credit bureaus have become global authentication intermediaries, informing their clients in an instant whether the consuming suspect before them is a palatable risk. The company therefore linked with a major credit information broker to provide, in the words of a promotional document, 'state-of-the-art on-line credit information on consumers across Canada.' The document established the need for access to this database by stating, 'A study done by a major U.S. insurer showed a strong relationship between poor credit status and unfavourable loss experience – especially when the poor status is a recent development. The average loss ratio for homeowners with a current poor credit rating was 127.5, compared to a loss ratio of 61.1 for homeowners with a good credit rating.' The document proceeded to list the many features of the credit database beyond the consumption trail of the surveilled suspect:

- Computer-to-computer link-up with credit-grantors' computers.
- Single access for both spouses' files.
- Free fraud alert messages on all applicable credit files.

Credit Warning Messages
- The mismatch of the input address and the address on file, indicating that a potential fraud is occurring on a specific application
- Invalid social insurance numbers
- Heavy inquiry activity, a strong barometer of fraud or credit overloading by a customer applying for credit in many places

Credit Fraud Predator
This enhancement provides a security check against thousands of addresses, social insurance numbers and phone numbers that are known to be fictitious or to have been used previously in fraudulent activity. It also signals the use of addresses verified as being vacant lots and the use of social insurance numbers of deceased persons.

- Off-line and on-line scoring systems to identify applicants most likely to become seriously delinquent or bankrupt

Delinquency/Bankruptcy Predator Score
Measures an individual's susceptibility to delinquency and personal

bankruptcy. This score can review all or selected accounts, pre-screen applicants or identify low-risk accounts not previously contacted. This score is programmed directly into the supplier's credit reporting system. This on-line feature means that any credit report can automatically include a score as a gauge of an applicant's likelihood to become seriously delinquent or bankrupt.

A company official we interviewed said that this credit-rating feature was sold to insurers as a means to evaluate moral risk, segment markets, and redline.

There's moral risk and there's physical risk. Moral risk is how do people manage things? What's their financial health? ... [Our credit database] is more of individual financial health ... that goes with our claims tracking system, as well as with an overall score for that [residential] area ... An obvious credit-claims-area score is walk down Powell Street or Cordova [in downtown eastside Vancouver] as opposed to walking through Shaunessy [an established Vancouver area of multimillion dollar homes]. If you were an underwriter, where would you see it, put your risk? It's just a financial, actuarial way of measuring it.

Market conduct regulators in Canadian provinces explicitly prohibit credit-based lifestyle rating of home insurance. A good reason for this prohibition is the fact that credit history as an underwriting guideline frequently has 'no justification or actuarial support' (Powers 1997: 137–8). Nevertheless, as our data indicate, insurers routinely use credit data as a central component of market segmentation. A university-based actuarial expert we interviewed said that lifestyle ratings are pervasive in spite of provincial regulations. There are 'sophisticated databases and I know companies now that have different prices as a function of postal code to the sixth entry, ethnicity, lifestyle, agency location, etcetera.'

A home insurance company we studied employed two marketing analysts. Their primary task was to supply underwriters with fine-grained analyses of insured populations and properties through data-matching across a number of linked datasets. A marketing manager for the company said in interview,

We want agencies to have more well-defined sales territories, and we want them to focus more within those geographic boundaries. And as part of our work to establish those boundaries we have licensed GIS [geographic information systems] which allow us to map, physically map our customers. Really anything with a postal code, so it could be our policies ... claim frequencies, severity, different customers by line ... single-line versus multi-line ... a picture of our clients and where they are on the ground. And then have Statistics Canada information that we can also map ... at the enumeration area level ... a sense within a particular area how many dwellings, what kind of families, what kind of incomes, those kind of things, so we get an understanding of the marketplace ... And then we license a segmentation system ... which combines information from Revenue Canada, Statistics Canada, Print Measurement Bureau and so on, and builds market segments based on these. So you have segments like 'mortgage in suburbia' and 'downtown blues' and things like that. So they're named to reflect the people who live in these neighbourhoods. And it's based on the premise that birds of a feather flock together, neighbourhoods are often times made up of very similar people ... And we also code our own customers with that same code so that if agents are interested in mortgage and suburbia market, we can tell them how many we actually have of that particular market segment and whether in fact there's any more opportunity to continue to market to people who look that way. And we can also look at the performance of those different market segments in terms of claims frequency, severity, and whether in fact they're a profitable segment to the market ... [There is also] a psychographic component in it because it looks at peoples' behaviours as well. It looks at their vehicle purchase behaviour, their family make-up, their media usage, their different product usages, and so on ... The 'mortgage in suburbia' ... index very high on all the mini-van kind of things ... [we purchase the] total vehicles in operation database ... broken down by year and vehicle class ... to the point of knowing how many Mustangs are on a particular street ... [We also buy Statistics Canada census data directly] to build our own life stage segments which we can then bring back in and map ... age and family status and number of kids and those kinds of things.

These integrated 'dataveillance' systems simultaneously identify target markets, screen applicants, and grade for standard, superstandard, and substandard ratings. We interviewed an official of an information service company that was working on standardization of applications for insurance. He said that direct marketers have influenced the information system development because of their need to screen people instantly over the telephone or Internet. '[They're] using good database modelling stuff to make sure that they're getting the cream of the market, they don't take everybody who phones in. They find out within fifteen seconds whether or not they really want you, based on things like your telephone number and your address. Obviously they've got databases of where prior claims have existed, high crime areas and so forth.'

Communications to existing customers also vary by their profit potential. For example, the above-mentioned marketing manager for a home insurance company said that he used a 'client data system' for differential communications to market segments. A company document advised agents that this system was designed for 'generating life-time clients with a lot of value ... [It] can help you keep a database of information about your customers by keeping specific personal client information so that you can personalize your phone calls or letters. It can also be used to track the commission revenue they generate for your agency and the expenses incurred by clients (especially your time) leading to an "account profitability."'

Previous researchers argue that insurers have difficulty measuring both moral risk and the effects of their efforts to govern through moral risk assessments (e.g., Baker 1996; Powers 1997; Knight 1997; Glenn 2000). They further contend that insurers' judgments of moral risk are not based on formal, technical criteria as much as 'rules of thumb' and an 'I know it when I see it' sensibility (Baker 1996: 256). In contrast, we have documented that moral risk criteria are embedded in dataveillance systems that screen and rate the insured. Furthermore, the agent is required to maintain vigilance in the field to feed the dataveillance system with continuous details about moral risk. Face-to-face evaluation and computer-based technologies interface.

In this context, the field agent is not simply a free-floating moral governor with unfettered discretion. Rather, she is equipped with close-ended forms and computer-based formats for her surveillance tasks. The underwriting rules are embedded in the moral classifications of these forms and formats, and the agent is thereby compelled to think and act accordingly.

Agents may be systematically penalized for a poor loss ratio on their book of home insurance properties. In one company we studied, sales commissions varied from 12 to 18 per cent depending on the quality of the book's loss ratio. A company manager said in interview that this 'quality bonus' structure was entirely 'driven by the claims performance of your book ... you've managed the risk better ... the company can make more money so you can as well.' He said that some effort was made to compensate agents constrained by working in agencies located in poorer areas, but also disincentives to keep them from underwriting too much 'bad' business. Agents with 'a chunk of "downtown blues" business are given other territories to offset this. [A condition] might include instruction that if there is enough "downtown blues" business already, if you're going to do flyers, if you're going to do any sort of direct contact, just don't do it down there. If you're going to go fishing, let's go fishing up here where maybe you don't have as much business or in fact the fish are bigger.'

We interviewed a former insurance agency operator who referred to such practices as 'frontline underwriting.' He said that vigilance at the frontline was crucial for his agency's bottom line. 'If there was something on the books somewhere which meant that Joe Blow was a bad actor, we could care less about how he felt about it. We just didn't want anything to do with him. We *guarded* our loss ratio very, very carefully because having a good loss ratio over the book of business is what enables you to negotiate favourable rates and to go to new insurers and sign them up if you need them.'

This interviewee said that he regularly conducted home inspections as part of frontline underwriting. These inspections allowed him to spot physical risks and moral risks as signs of each other. '[I'd look for] potential liability hazards ... ditches or big vicious dogs ... you name it ... general tidiness. If there's fourteen wrecked cars in the front yard – I'm not saying people can't collect wrecked cars, but it's often indicative of people whose housekeeping may not be good and it's a value judgment.' Home inspections also provided an opportunity to read the overall moral character of the suspect applicant. Sometimes an applicant was rejected because he had a 'gut feeling' that the person was simply 'bad luck.' Anything in the applicant's insurance background that would suggest trouble, even a single claim, was at times 'sufficient all in itself' to deny insurance. There was a particular concern to weed out those suspected of being 'claims conscious,' which he defined as people who, 'when something bad happens they don't think of getting grandma out of the hospital, they think of getting grandma a lawyer.' A willingness to assume higher deductible levels was taken as a sign that the applicant was willing to share the risk and not claims conscious.

This interviewee employed a creative strategy for extending his knowledge network about moral risks. He and his partner in the insurance agency joined the local volunteer fire department. He said that this position gave them visibility and prestige in the community and thereby served as a marketing tool. At the same time they worked with the fire marshall, which not only gave them inside information about investigations but also knowledge of fire prevention that could be marketed to customers as a special expertise. Last and by no means least, this arrangement gave them 'no small amount of credibility with our insurers, especially when my partner became fire chief.'

A parallel strategy was to connect with the local police and security equipment firms through membership in Neighbourhood Watch. This strategy gave them knowledge of 'questionable clientele,' as well as crime prevention knowledge that added weight to their efforts to persuade customers to buy upgraded locks, home alarm systems, and so on. With respect to both fire and crime risks, he said 'questionable clientele' were simply rejected. 'You heard about it because you were tight with the police there and the fire department ... Premium doesn't matter ... Next to $300 in premiums, if you have one loss you're going to wipe out twenty years' worth of that $300.' He reiterated that this frontline vigilance was driven by insurers' monitoring of loss ratios in the agency's books. He expressed this pressure figuratively by saying that insurers are always looking for 'pig iron under water' – a situation in which there is no risk of fire – and, by the way, 'make sure your policy excludes rust.'

Other insurance agency operators we interviewed gave similar accounts of the centrality of moral risk judgments to their loss ratio security. An interviewee who operated an agency under exclusive contract with one general insurance company said that moral risk assessment of the applicant's personal habits and lifestyle was his key to frontline underwriting.

The moral risk is everything here ... Moral risk is the person, and the well-being ... the person thinks of in insurance. Some people say, 'Oh, I'll buy insurance because eventually I can use it.' No, we don't want you using it. We want you respecting the fact that you have put it in place to provide comfort and peace of mind ... People who just treat life as one day at a time, and possibly no future goal, and sitting there throwing things around in their house – or for that matter even themselves, excessive drinking – they can all lead to a bad moral risk which will eventually lead to a loss ... If you see someone who has moved every month, once a month, they definitely don't really care. They can just pick up and leave anytime. I want to make sure the person can't pick up and leave ... As soon as I see roommates ... one person can steal off the other and then claim theft ... [Under previous ownership of this agency, ten years ago, with homosexuals] no one would even touch their insurance package ... it was complete prejudice ... [Now] they have to explain everything to us because we don't want to know later on if they're common law man and man. That's just the way it is. We have to know that so we can insure it, insure the risk. And they're fine. The risk, their houses are clean, and you know we have to take photos etcetera.

Automobile Insurance Moral Risks and Unpooling

Private sector automobile insurance is also governed through systems of moral risk assessment that result in systematic unpooling. In this section, we explore the ways in which such systems operated in Ontario at the time of our research. According to the *Financial Post* (6 June 1997), 'One-third of all insurance dollars in Canada are spent to buy car insurance in Ontario.'

Since automobile insurance was mandatory, it was an 'all comers' marketplace in which the insurance industry was required to insure all legally qualified drivers. This requirement was addressed through three different types of risk pooling. First, there was an inferior substandard pool called the Facility Association. All applicants without previous auto insurance, as well as applicants with a poor record of claims or other moral risks, were placed through the Facility Association. Some insurance companies were designated as 'servicing carriers' on behalf of the Facility Association, meaning they issued and serviced policies but loss ratios were distributed across the participating companies. Second, there was a substandard pool referred to as the grey pool. This pool included drivers who scored poorly on selected risk criteria, but who nevertheless were deemed better risks than those in the Facility Association. All insurance companies had the option of placing selected drivers in this pool. If they did so all premiums collected from the policies went into a special pool from which claims were paid. Third, each company operated its own standard pool, which some referred to as their preferred pool. Typically the preferred pool had gradations of preference which moved some policyholders into superstandard categories.

All drivers were screened on the basis of a formal risk points system. Points were assigned on the basis of the person's insurance record, including at-fault accident claims, convictions for various driving offences or insurance-related crimes, material misrepresentation of claims, fraudulent claims, and cancellation of policies for non-payment of premiums. Someone with four or more risk points was deemed eligible for the Facility Association pool, while those with one to three points could be assigned to the grey pool. An applicant with no insurance record because she was a new driver was highly suspect and therefore immediately assigned to the Facility Association. An applicant who refused to disclose full information about her past auto insurance record was also a candidate for the Facility Association. Insurers who participated in this pool were able to charge much higher premiums than for standard pool customers, and it was potentially profitable to insure these risks.

An inspection of one insurance company's manual for rating automobile insurance applicants reveals more fine-grained criteria for deselecting them to the Facility Association. As specified in table 7.2, this company excluded applicants with particular records of at-fault accidents, criminal or traffic convictions and suspensions, failure to meet insurance obligations, and vehicle types and uses. At-fault accident criteria hold the insured person responsible for previous claims arising from accidents she imputedly caused. Conviction criteria apply to Criminal Code convictions in general, Criminal Code convictions involving the use of an automobile, and convictions under the Highway Traffic Act of the province. Much of the basis for exclusion concerns the person's failure to meet insurance obligations, including a record of material misrepresentation, fraud, non-payment of premiums, not providing required information to underwrite or settle a claim, not signing or following the conditions of required documents, and not providing information about previous insurance. Vehicles known to be hazardous because they are modified ('hot rod'), no longer serviceable by manufacturers' parts, kept in a foreign jurisdiction, or driven in auto sport contexts are also grounds for exclusion.

While the Facility Association was a high risk pool with very high premiums, agents were instructed in a company manual not to mention this fact to deselected applicants. Rather, 'When explaining to a client that they are being insured under Facility Association, be positive: an alternative insurance plan rather than a "high risk" plan; policies are renewed annually to see if they qualify for "preferred rates"; clients deal directly with the company and get the benefit of our claims services and network of offices.' Agents were also told that regardless of the formal risk points system, standardized across the industry through the pro-

TABLE 7.2
Criteria for Assignment to the Facility Association

Accidents
- Two or more at fault accidents in the past 5 years
- One at fault accident in the past 3 years if the principal operator has had less than 3 years' driving experience in Canada

Convictions and Suspensions
- One or more Criminal Code convictions in the past 3 years
- Any driver who has sustained a criminal conviction involving the use of an automobile in the past 3 years
- One or more major traffic convictions in the past 3 years
- Four or more minor traffic convictions in the past 3 years
- Two minor traffic convictions in the past 3 years and one at fault accident in the past 5 years
- The principal operator has had his or her licence suspended one or more times (either admin or demerit) for 14 days or longer in the past 3 years and has had less than 3 years' driving experience in Canada

Failure to Meet Insurance Obligations
- One or more policy cancellations for material misrepresentation in the past 3 years
- One or more convictions for auto insurance fraud in the past 10 years
- Three or more policy cancellations for non-payment of premium in the past 3 years
- Two policy cancellations for non-payment of premium in the past 3 years and two minor traffic convictions
- Two policy cancellations for non-payment of premium in the past 3 years and one at-fault accident in the past 5 years
- The applicant or any operator fails to provide required information at time of writing the insurance coverage or in the proper settlement of a claim
- The applicant or listed driver refuses to sign an OPCF, the terms of which have been agreed upon as a condition of the insurer accepting the risk
- Proof is provided that the vehicle is being operated by a driver who has been excluded with an OPCF 28A
- Failure to provide previous insurer information (name of insurer, policy number and expiry date)

Vehicles and Uses
- The vehicle is garaged more than 6 months (school-term basis) in the United States
- Vehicles for which parts are no longer available or manufactured
- Vehicles used for racing, speed tests, timing, or rallying
- 'Hot rod' type vehicles

Source: An insurance company's auto rate manual

vincial regulator, there was always room for discretion based on the company underwriters' intuitive wish to gamble. 'If the risk qualifies for the facility, it may still be written in the regular market (the company's preferred book) ... rather than in the residual market.'

The company also had formal grey pool selection criteria. A checklist in the agent's manual identified the following as grounds for grey pooling: a principal driver is under the age of twenty-five or licensed less than three years; the insured resides in specified high risk areas of cities; the insured operates the vehicle regularly outside of Canada; the insured opts for an income replacement benefit of $1,000 or a medical rehabilitation and attendant care benefit; indexation; and any moral risk explained by the agent. The manual then elaborated on some moral risks the agent might be attentive to which 'would not generate a definite pool assignment but should be considered in the overall assessment of the risk.' 'A claims conscious attitude' might be signified by previous comprehensive insurance claims, or by 'accident benefit claims (regardless of fault).' 'An attitude of indifference to laws' might be signified by 'license suspension in excess of 14 days.' The applicant's health condition might also be taken into account, for example, a person who is seventy-five years of age or older may give added meaning to the term 'grey pool' because 'with age, health deteriorates and may cause slower reflexes, lack of co-ordination and poor eyesight.' The value of the vehicle insured was also a consideration. Vehicles valued at more than $60,000 were said to 'reflect a variety of increased risks, e.g. many are specialty vehicles which may be target for theft.'

These indicators reveal the arbitrariness of the pooling process. Class-based arbitrariness can be detected in case examples in the agent's manual regarding how to exercise discretion in pool assignment. One case presented was that of 'a doctor [who] insures a 1994 Ford with full coverage. He has had one accident benefit claim (incurred a broken leg while a passenger in a vehicle involved in an accident), one comprehensive claim for a windshield repair and two traffic violations which are more than a year and half old. The doctor has been insured with us for 10 years and has three lines of business [insurance with us]. Each risk must be assessed on its own merits. With the information presented in this example, it is likely that you would not pool this risk.' The next case juxtaposed to this one was that of a man 'Single, age 26 and owns a 1977 Chevrolet Chevelle. He had modified this vehicle to include a powerful motor and oversized tires. The windows are all tinted a deep black. He has no appraisal for the vehicle. He has had one comprehensive claim within the past six months for attempted theft of his vehicle. This risk does not meet the selection criteria, however when assessing all the information this risk would be an example of one we may pool.'

For many insurers, deselection into the grey and Facility Association pools was not intended to eliminate unwanted suspects. Rather, it was a means of justifying higher premiums and more stringent contract conditions for those deemed inferior. The provincial regulator allowed different rating, pricing, contract, and risk distribution criteria for each pool in order to attract insurers willing to deal with substandard risks. All pools were potentially lucrative, although different insurers specialized in different pools depending on the market niches they hoped to profit from.

One profitable niche market involved the further segmentation of the high risk suspects in the Facility Association. As described in interview by a provincial government regulator, several companies 'skim off the risks that nobody else wants but are better than the average Facility risk.' A case study of one company that facilitated this market segment illustrates how a substandard insurance market is organized for profit. Through special underwriting expertise, policing of claims, and financial arrangements, this company was able to profit substantially from automobile market unpooling.

The first element was taking advantage of the auto insurance market unpooling practices fostered by the largest companies. The largest companies creamed off the preferred standard and superstandard insured by offering them attractive premium rates and contract features. This left the prospect of some reasonable substandard risks being assigned to the Facility Association, which itself could be creamed by substandard market specialist companies. The president of one substandard market company is quoted in a newspaper article as saying 'the trick of the non-standard trade ... is to take on "reformers," namely high risk drivers likely to improve their driving habits. If we hit these people in the pocket book, we get their attention.' The company had specialists who knew how to cream the least worst risks from the Facility pool, for example, requiring some driving experience to eliminate the most risky neophyte drivers.

The second element was lack of competition from the largest and most profitable automobile insurers. Most other companies did not care about specializing in this small market segment and therefore did not develop the requisite underwriting expertise. The relative lack of competition in the segment, combined with expert knowledge in underwriting, set some of the basic conditions for lucrative returns.

A third element was cooperation from the provincial regulator in allowing much steeper premiums for this risky population. Facility Association risks involved a filing of rates to the regulator that was separate from the filing for standard risks. This separate filing allowed substandard market companies to circumvent fairness criteria that would be invoked if they tried to underwrite in terms of the standard market. A company official explained that

> if you file rates for a standard type of risk, you can't file a rate for a non-standard risk. Because you have to set the rate levels that are going to be fair for all types of drivers. So where a company is, say, identifying the better risk, and they set a rate for example for liability insurance at say $800, they don't want to insure the bad risk because they can't get enough money for it [because of the fairness criteria]. So our base rate might be $1,500 and we only insure the bad ones. They're the only ones who come to us because of the higher rates. So as such, with the higher rate base, we can get the kind of premium we need.

A fourth and related element was a special surcharge structure for substandard risks on top of the already enhanced premium base rates. Surcharges were permitted on a number of driver attributes such as accident and conviction record, as well as for vehicle attributes such as expensive cars.

A fifth component was a premium pricing strategy that made the product attractive to those prospects the company wished to include, and unattractive to those suspects it wished to exclude. Prospects were offered rates more attractive than those offered by other insurers under Facility Association arrangements. On the other hand, suspects were discouraged through pricing that was higher than that available through the Facility Association. A company official explained, 'In that way we end up with a better experience than Facility and our rates are lower.' She said that even though other companies contribute to the Facility Association, they do not object to these creaming practices because they in turn have advantages in creaming the better risks in the standard market pool.

A sixth component was a premium pricing strategy with an eye to making profits while meeting regulatory requirements with respect to investments. Given the lure of high premium pricing allowed by the provincial regulator, the company was willing to use discretionary latitude in betting on the morally risky. As one company official expressed it, 'We say that almost any risk can be written, at a price ... It's rare that we refuse a risk ... My attitude is a good risk is one who pays enough premium.' The high premiums were also fostered by a regulatory requirement that the company had to stay within the capital reserve limit of underwriting premiums at 275 per cent of capital. This prevented the company from entering into more speculative capital investments, and meant that it was a rare example of an insurance company that makes its profits from its premium pricing largely independent of investment performance. As Baker (1996: 252) observes, 'Insuring people thought more likely to be careless (or even arsonists or thieves) may, in effect, load the dice, but that simply changes the odds, not the fact that the dice will produce profitable results over the long run. All that is required to keep the game afloat is the collection of a higher premium for the morally hazardous.'

Seventh, the company also profited from a scheme through which their clients could debt finance their premium payments. Because the premiums were so high, averaging about $3,000 a year, and the segment population was relatively poor, most had to debt finance their premiums. Regulators allowed the company to surcharge 3 per cent of premium for this privilege, as well as regular interest and collection of two months' premium up front. The balance of payments was spread out over ten months through a pre-authorized payment on the insured's bank account. This resulted in a finance charge equivalent to about 8 per cent, which was well above the market at the time. Indeed, this financing arrangement was the most lucrative component of the company's operations. For each $100 in capital the company was able to generate $275 in gross premium from which was derived $21 in premium financing charges, $17 in underwriting profits, and $7 in investment returns. In other words, annual earnings were about $45 on each $100 of capital invested. A company official we interviewed agreed that this profiting from unpooling was regressive against the poor to the point where a substantial proportion of clients could not afford it. 'The premiums are much higher than average, and in many cases the lower earners, they do have problems ... About 40 per cent of our policies are cancelled at one time during a twelve-month period for non-payment of premium.' He added that many of these cancelled policyholders join the ranks of uninsured drivers in the province, estimated at 10 to 15 per cent of all drivers.

An eighth element was structuring of administrative costs that covered expenses. For example, the high rate of policy cancellations was very expensive to administer, but these costs were also handled through the extraordinary premium rates. A company official we interviewed said that the situation was straightforward. 'The administration costs are higher in this class than in the standard business. Yet, on the other hand, looking at it realistically, because the premium level is so much higher there's less paper per $1,000 premium you might say.'

The ninth component was a distribution system through brokers that gave them incentives to turn the better Facility Association suspects into prospects. Brokers were willing to promote the product because the premium rates were better and their own commissions were higher compared to other Facility Association insurers.

A tenth component was reinsurance arrangements that covered each loss in excess of $200,000. This spreading of the risk was also paid for by the insured through higher premiums.

The eleventh element was a reform of key personal injury claims benefits that were available under previous legislation. Company executives joined others in the industry to bring about this reform as an important means of controlling their claims costs. A company official explained in interview that under the previous legislation,

> people who were unemployed at the time of an accident could collect benefits from the first day. And there was no relationship between what they had lost and what they were getting. The whole concept of insurance is to replace what is lost. If the unemployed person that had an accident, or so-called accident – they weren't losing anything because they kept on collecting the welfare, or unemployment insurance, it didn't change their life at all. And because the government required us to make payment within ten days, as soon as we received an application for funds – and we didn't have an opportunity to check it out properly and there were no controls on it – we found that 40 per cent of people who were on benefits from us, the weekly benefits, were unemployed at the time of the accident. What does that tell you? When you have a [general population] unemployed rate of about 10 per cent, yet 40 per cent of your claimants were unemployed at the time of the accident, you can assume that 75 per cent of them were fraudulent claims ... [With the new legislation there is a] twenty-six–week waiting period for the unemployed person before they could collect benefits ... [this] made an enormous difference in the number of claims we had.

The twelfth component for governing the profitability of this market segment was contracting with a private policing firm whose investigators were former public police officers. An insurance company official said in interview that experienced police investigators are much better than adjusters in cultivating informants, interrogating suspects, and acquiring evidence of fraudulent claims. Moreover, they have established relations with the public police that are useful in facilitating investigations and cracking down through criminal prosecutions:

> There's a firm of licensed private investigators that have offices here in our building and they're all ex-police officers ... And when we have injuries and I think they were injuries resulting from very minor accidents, we usually send them out rather than an adjuster. Because we find that if you send an adjuster out, the adjuster will have the tendency to phone the person and say, 'I'll be at your house at seven o'clock at night,' and the person is ready for them. If I send out a private investigator without an appointment, you'll find they'll go and knock on the door, 'Hello, is John Smith in?'
> 'No, he isn't.'
> 'I'm here from the insurance company. He'd like to get his car fixed.'
> 'Oh yeah, he's at work. He's just down the street.'
> So they'll go and catch him at work and then say to the person, 'Well, I guess you realize that it is fraud to put in a claim for injuries when you're actually working, and for loss of income, and obviously you haven't [stopped working]. I suppose you want to withdraw your claim?' When people realize they've been caught on the spot then they'll usually withdraw these fraudulent claims ... The police department is very anxious to have them work with them, prepare a case, and they know they're going to do it with proper evidence and so on so that charges can be laid ... Many companies will just refuse a loss and turn down a claim and do nothing more, we believe in having the person charged with fraud. So our people, realizing the police departments don't have the funding, will actually prepare the case for them, give them all the evidence and everything, and then they just lay the charges and get the credit for it.

This prosecution and punishment approach to fraudulent claims is the thirteenth element for profiting from this suspect population. As the interviewee indicates, and as we document extensively in chapter 9, most insurance companies handle fraud internally and almost never prosecute. But in the inferior substandard pool of insured drivers, there is a perceived need for a law enforcement crackdown as an individual deterrent. Just as high premiums are seen as a deterrent because 'we hit these people in the pocket book, we get their attention,' so prosecution of fraudulent claims is justified as a deterrent that is good for business.

A fourteenth and related element was the policing of professionals who serviced personal injury claims. The interviewee suggested that the general deterrent effect of prosecuting fraudulent claims was not on the public at large, most of whom would not be aware of such prosecutions. Rather, it was felt among the legal community, who were less willing to take on litigation of a questionable claim against this particular company. '[Our prosecution policy is] common knowledge among lawyers rather than the public at large. And when these same people go to a lawyer for a phony injury claim, the lawyer's going to be very reluctant to handle it when it's our company's claim.' There was also direct policing of law firms. 'We encouraged a group of companies, eleven other companies to join us in an action against one law firm that had some law clerks there that were handling fraudulent claims. The clerks were charged and convicted of fraud.'

This company was a highly profitable enterprise. At the time of our data collection, the company's return on equity over a seven-year period averaged over 20 per cent annually, whereas the industry average was slightly under 10 per cent. A company executive pointed out that in the standard pool market, insurers have to cut rates substantially in order to be competitive. In the substandard market this was not necessary: the objective was not growth for the sake of growth, or to become the largest company, but simply bottom-line profit in a niche market.

During an interview with an executive of a consumers' organization, we learned that other industry insiders profited from this company. This interviewee had a long record of advocacy on behalf of insurance consumers. However, in the middle of the research interview he suddenly asked the researcher whether he had bought shares in the insurance company analysed in this case study. When the researcher replied that he had not, the interviewee said with considerable emotion, 'Oh, that is too bad. I'm sorry. I wish everybody I knew had bought it ... I bought them at $10 when they first came on the market ... In no time flat they went up and up and up. And I thought it was so silly of me just to buy 100 shares so I bought a few more, like 200 more, and went up to 17 and to 19 and to 24 and I was buying all the way along. Got to

24 and it split. Well it just took off after that. It got up to 35 and it split again!'

The provincial regulator had a policy and procedures manual on rates and classifications that declared: 'The rate regulation system should encourage competitive and fair prices. Fairness applies to both the insurer and the consumer. Fairness requires that the industry as a whole should earn a reasonable return and that consumers should not pay *excessive* rates ... [B]ecause insurance is mandatory, rates should not result in the industry earning *excessive* returns ... [T]here must be a causal relationship between the classification variable and loss propensity.'

Our case study reveals that the system does not 'encourage competitive and fair prices' to those deselected into this substandard pool. The insurer earned excessive returns and the insured paid excessive rates. Loss ratio security was tightly managed through mechanisms that ensured this morally risky population posed an exceptionally low financial risk for the insurance company. Indeed, the premiums and means of financing them were so high, and the policing of claims so tight, that more than one-third of all clients defaulted on their policies over the course of a year and thereby joined the ranks of the insurance poor.

The provincial government stepped in to address the problem of the uninsured through its Motor Vehicle Accident Claims Fund. A government official familiar with this operation said that it was funded by a one-dollar levy on each Ontario driver's licence issued, and by effort to recover losses caused by the uninsured driver. He said the loss recovery effort resulted in only 22 per cent recovery of what the fund paid out in losses caused by uninsured drivers. Recovery was limited because the uninsured are also among the poorest members of the population. The reason why they are uninsured in the first place is because unpooling makes it impossible for them to afford insurance:

It's the lower socioeconomic element that you're trying to say, 'Drive with insurance!' If their premiums are two, three, four thousand dollars a year, they can't afford it ... In the more serious losses, I mean this almost becomes like a penalty for life because a lot of these people are from a poorer socioeconomic background ... A general labourer making $1,500 a month, I mean we'll take $100 a month from him for the rest of his life so that he can save his licence if he wishes to operate a vehicle. It'll never pay back the $200,000 or $250,000 debt that he may have incurred as a result of not operating the vehicle with insurance. It's a penalty ... Fifty years' worth of case files teaches us there will always be uninsured and uniden- tified drivers on the highways no matter how stiff you make the fines and no matter how many police officers you put on the road ... [The] cost of full enforcement far outweighs the cost of administering the fund.

As this official indicates, the fund was not set up to address the structural problem that poor people with risk points cannot afford auto insurance. Instead, it provided a punishment structure when they offended and a means of compensation for their victims. Moreover, this official made it clear that victims were compensated begrudgingly. Moral risks always loom. There was a fear that if the availability of compensation in accidents with uninsured drivers became widely known, victims would flood the system with questionable claims. Therefore, the fund worked hard to make its benefits unknown. The official said that publicizing the fund

would attract frivolous claims and it would increase our exposure overall ... If you need us you'll find us ... The social work departments [of hospi- tals] are aware of us, but only because it's more like they go out and pull in the information. We're not pushing it out ... People contact us, we'll provide them with information about how the program operates ... If we were to advertise in a full-fledged way, provide brochures ... we'd proba- bly double our claims within a couple of years ... The whole approach pre- supposes that you know what you're looking for ... You might not know that accident benefits are available to victims of car accidents. I mean how many times are people involved in car accidents in their lives?

This official said that the fund was administered by the government in order to circumvent moral risks that would arise if it was adminis- tered by the auto insurance industry. For example, if the industry administered uninsured driver claims through the Facility Association, it would pose the moral risk of shifting expensive claims it should handle through regular channels into Fund claims. A management consulting firm was engaged

to look at possible alternatives including having the Facility Association take over the responsibilities of the fund and divy it up amongst the insurance companies, the idea being that companies could absorb this kind of loss, and surely they could. I mean it's a big premium market and this is a drop in a bucket expenditure for them. Of course the whole thing is that it's got to be set up in such a way that the claims don't become the subject of manipulation or something like that. Because the second you put $2 million on the table – and you have some industry-directed board, Facility Association, whatever the entity might be – if those executives are also sitting on the board of various insurance companies, or are officials of those companies, you may end up with situations ... 'If we let the Fund pay the claim then we don't take the $2 million hit,' and for a small insurance company this might be significant ... You don't want this to become a little profit engine ... because it could be if you have free rein to set the tariff or whatever you want.

With so many specialized market segments within the broader substandard pool, there were many unique approaches to niche marketing. For example, we learned of brokers from a particular ethnic background who sold exclusively to new immigrants from their own background, using only one insurance company and an inflated Facility Association rate.

In the higher echelons of market segmentation there were various marketing ploys to cream the best risks. An auto insurance industry research specialist told us that a recent study found that special driver education training courses make no difference in crash rates. Nevertheless, insurers promote premium discounts for having taken such courses. In actuality, this was a creaming strategy and form of socioeconomic lifestyle rating because 'people who can afford to pay thousands of dollars for training their kids, they're good customers ... classist, it's economic, it's a market loss leader if you like.' A member of Parliament in a province with a private automobile insurance market took on unpooling issues as a political interest. She observed in interview that preferred customer cherry picking is sometimes based on what other insurance coverage is available to the client in the event of a serious personal injury accident. For example, the employees of large corporations with generous sickness, accident, and disability insurance plans are a superstandard target for auto insurers because such employees have substantially lower personal injury claims costs on their auto policies. She said that seniors into their seventies are also a low risk market and ripe for cherry picking. Some brokerages in the province advertised to the fifty-five-plus market exclusively. If someone younger responded to the advertisements, they were offered undiscounted rates and the suggestion that they might find better rates elsewhere.

Automobile Insurance Surveillance Systems

Various information systems are used to gauge the risks of drivers and their vehicles. Private information system companies supply information on a driver's insurance claims record as well as on aspects of the person's driving record. For example, in a jurisdiction where demerit points for driving infractions are assigned by the government's motor vehicle licensing branch, insurance information system providers supply their clients with demerit point data. Even if a court or other government body decides that these points were awarded inappropriately, they sometimes stay on the record. An executive with a consumers' association concerned with auto insurance practices said in interview that this record can be used as a bargaining chip with clients in negotiating insurance coverage. 'They won't change anything on those records unless the insurance companies instruct them to. So if the insurance company says, "We'll give a break but we're not taking it off the record,"' that is their way of keeping you with them. Because if you leave and go somewhere else, you are not going to get the break because they are going to look at the record.'

Vehicles are embedded in a number of information systems. In North America the Vehicle Information System (V.I.N.) is a key tracing device for automobile manufacturers, insurers, vehicle registration authorities, licensing authorities, and police (Ericson and Haggerty 1997). Some jurisdictions, such as Ontario in 1996, introduced formal inspections of vehicles as part of underwriting the insurance of them. According to a manual for agents in an automobile insurance company we studied,

Section 232.1 of the Automobile Insurance Rate Stability Act, 1996 requires auto insurers in Ontario to inspect all passenger vehicles before issuing insurance policies. The inspection program offers insurers significant opportunity to reduce insurance fraud, by creating barriers to:

- insuring non-existent or phantom vehicles with the intent of submitting an insurance claim for theft of vehicle (paper cars).
- insuring a previously damaged vehicle and collecting the market value of a similar vehicle in good condition.
- submitting a claim for collision or vandalism loss for damage which occurred prior to obtaining insurance.
- import and export frauds.

... The inspection program is expected to provide at least a 4:1 return on cost, reducing fraud costs in Ontario by at least $20.1 million per year.

The manual proceeds to offer agents extraordinary detailed instructions on how to conduct the vehicle inspection. The inspection includes a check of the V.I.N. and of the car's make, model, and year. A checklist and narrative description of unrepaired damage, as well as modifications and custom additions to the vehicle, including stereo and cellular phone upgrades and anti-theft devices, is required. The checklist for physical condition of the vehicle includes twenty-four items for inspection. The odometer reading is to be recorded. Three different Polaroid camera photographs of the vehicle are to be taken except if it is new (under 12,000 kilometres on the odometer), old (ten or more years), or a vehicle insured by a client whom the agent has known for at least five years. A photograph is to be taken of 'the federal compliance label on the vehicle door, showing the V.I.N. (If the label on the door is missing or damaged, a photo must be taken of the place where it should be).' Two angled shots were to display all sides of the vehicle, for example front and right side, and back and left side. The manual offered agents several pages of tips on how to take the best photographs.

The agents as inspectors pose a moral risk because they may collude with the insured in defrauding the company. Consequently there is a need to inspect the inspectors. 'To minimize fraud within the inspection system, the company will maintain a control system, such as the use of sequentially numbered inspection reports. In addition, the insurer should establish a method of quality control over completed reports to verify the accuracy, completeness and inspector's signature.'

The manual makes it clear that the vehicle inspection system is useful for governance purposes beyond the control of fraud. While justified in the name of fraud control, data are collected that enhance the broader underwriting and claims databases of the company and industry. 'Because insurers may choose to use inspection information for other statistical purposes, it is important to ensure that all data is accurately recorded ... The inspection process can also aid accurate underwriting and rating on a policy (km/year, for example can be checked). In addition, inspection reports and photographs are useful in the settlement of subsequent claims on the vehicle, particularly if the inspection indicates prior damage, or the vehicle is a total loss or unrecovered theft.'

This legislated and tightly formatted system for data collection is designed to limit the field agent's discretion in underwriting. Nevertheless, there is always room for discretion. For example, the manual directs that 'For vehicles with liability only, if the client does not come in for the usual [inspection], the policy must be referred to underwriting. Underwriting will consider retaining the risk and placing in grey pool or cancelling on renewal.'

As we learned in the case of home insurance underwriting, field agents are encouraged to use field inspection opportunities to size up the moral character of the insured. Another auto insurance manual for agents in the same company states plainly, 'Agents working in the field are in the best position to know or observe any undesirable characteristics of the clients as operators of the vehicle. The company relies on field staff to communicate all such information to the underwriting centre.' The primary manual includes a section entitled 'moral risks,' which states simply, 'You cannot measure the potential impact of a risk if the exposure is based on a person's attitude, dishonesty and/or carelessness. Moral risks will in the long run have a negative effect on underwriting results.'

On the other hand, as we have also learned from our analyses of home insurance underwriting, discretion is encouraged because insurers find it difficult to turn away premium dollars. In spite of the formal rationality embedded in inspection forms and computer-based information systems, companies make it clear to their agents that profitable underwriting depends on their intuitive eye for who might be a good bet in spite of a poor rating on formal criteria. Thus, the same manual that provided such tightly governed guidelines on how agents should conduct vehicle inspections – and how they should use other information systems on vehicles as well as the applicant's driving and insurance records – nevertheless told agents that 'the heart of underwriting' is discretion to underwrite the morally risky even if guidelines are not met:

Depending on the degree of variance from the guidelines, special action may be taken to classify a specific risk ... [This requires] creative thinking – how to modify a risk to make it acceptable rather than just declining ... that 'certain feeling' you develop which says that something is not right and more than routine investigation and action seem necessary ... The purpose of gathering information is to narrow the gap between the information available and the unattainable ideal of having complete knowledge. What underwriting analysis is all about can be defined as sensing and finding the unseen, the unspoken, the unwritten elements of risk. You need to look beyond the obvious, as the face value may not be enough ... knowing when to make a decision and how much information to gather are key elements in good decision-making. This becomes the fun part of decision-making because you are taking a reasonable risk or an educated guess.

The aim in looking beyond the obvious to find the true value of an auto insurance suspect is not primarily outright rejection. Rather, it is to turn the suspect into a prospect for whom a profitable risk rating and premium level can be found. This approach is made possible by the large number of moral risk market segments available. Contrary to Glenn (2000: 801) – who argues that 'even motivation for profit will not induce companies to create new rating categories if they operate on the belief that the current ones are designed to restrict moral hazards' – insurers create a hierarchy of moral risk market segmentation for profit.

From the consumer's perspective, the market segmentation practices we have documented in this chapter operate to collective disadvantage. A leading actuarial scientist observed in interview,

> The whole ideal of insurance works on the pooling of risk ... Those categories of the collective were very broad even fifteen years ago ... You'd have to have a couple of claims in a short period of time to see your premium change very much. Now it is going with the philosophy of the rest of society that you are responsible ... The whole concept of a pure accident is almost disappearing. There is no pure accident anymore. If you have a claim, you are partially at fault. And you need to change risk categories ... [This is a] move to more and more slicing and individualization, and more and more passing the responsibility back to the claimant. If it goes too far, people will say that this isn't insurance any more ... As soon as I have a claim, my premium goes up. So over the next six years I pay the claim. Well heck, I can run my bank account to do that.

As this actuarial scientist stresses, unpooling practices are intended to make the insured responsible within the moral risk market segment to which she is assigned. In the next two chapters, we document how this responsibilization pervades insurers' regimes for loss prevention and claims processing. The insured's status as a suspect is continuous.

Insured persons are suspected of not doing enough to prevent losses that are costly to insurers. And, when losses occur, insureds are treated as offenders, people who have not done enough to prevent the losses on behalf of the insurer. Their offending is penalized through higher premiums and more stringent contract conditions, playing back on the processes we have identified in this chapter.

8. Agents of Prevention

*Not being able to govern events, I govern myself and apply myself to them, if they will
not apply themselves to me.*

Montaigne, 'Of Presumption' (1580–8)

*Uncertainty and expectation are the joys of life. Security is an insipid thing, and the
overtaking and possessing of a wish, discovers the folly of the chase.*

William Congreve, *Love for Love* (1695)

*Security depends not so much upon how much you have, as upon how much you can
do without.*

J.W. Krutch, 'If You Don't Mind Me Saying So' (1967)

The insurance system requires each insured to govern her own risky
environment and secure it against loss. Ideally, if each insured is reflexive about risks and makes rational choices to minimize them, there will
be security for all. This security will materialize not only in a safer
environment, but also in a better loss ratio for the insurer and lower
premiums for the insured.

We again focus on automobile insurance and property insurance.
Automobile insurance addresses a broad spectrum of risks and fields
of insurance: catastrophe, property damage, crime, personal injury,
disability, and wider aspects of health and well-being. It is also at the
core of political struggles between individual autonomy and social
constraint. Home and commercial insurance address risks related to
the core institution of property and how it can be protected. People
work hard to chase both prized possessions and security technologies
that protect these possessions.

Automobile Accident Prevention

As we have seen, scientific and technical knowledge required for actuarial precision is limited and equivocal. It is therefore difficult to make the economic logic of underwriting insurance fit squarely with the scientific and technical logics of what might be the risks at stake. The usual response is to underwrite the risks regardless and then try to control the risk environment through the preventive activity of the insured. The more loss ratios deteriorate, the greater the pressure for preventive measures. Ironically, insured persons may be disciplined as agents of prevention because underwriters have been undisciplined in their risk taking.

Insurers are active participants in automobile accident prevention. In Canada, private automobile insurers mobilize accident prevention through their industry association. In the United States, while there are also industry association initiatives, a given major company such as State Farm is as large as the entire Canadian industry and therefore has the capacity to develop prevention initiatives on its own. Canadian industry association efforts include some funding of safety research and the promotion of safety. Considerable effort is also devoted to legislative reforms. For example, in Ontario reforms to increase penalties for driving without insurance, to introduce graduated licensing, and to require that automobiles be inspected before they are insured, were all heavily backed by the industry association. As an industry association official told us in interview, pressuring for these reforms was important because 'loss prevention has a dramatic effect on the bottom line of the product and it also has a dramatic effect on the image of the industry, both of which are a concern to us, the trade association. So we find ourselves partaking, participating, partnering in a host of loss prevention initiatives.'

State-run automobile insurers institutionalize prevention programs as part of their government's responsibility for the health and well-being of citizens. For example, in 1995, the Insurance Corporation of British Columbia (ICBC) spent $35 million on road and traffic safety programs. A 1996 management consultant's report to this insurer commented that 'it has become a major international player in crash-injury prevention, far out of proportion to its size and far more than almost any other insurer in North America. Typically, private insurers only undertake similar initiatives acting together in industry associations, whereas a monopoly public insurer has a far greater self-interest, mandate, and ability to prevent losses.' The same report opened with a letter from the consultants which indicated that, in spite of this massive effort,

> vehicle insurance in [this province] has experienced rapid and sustained increases in costs over at least a 10 year period ... [T]he current system is broken ... A new course includes fundamental changes to the insurance product itself, the way it is delivered and administered, the relationship [the insurer] has with its customers and stakeholders, and the way safety and driver attitudes are aligned with a safe roads policy ... [Solutions include] comprehensive cost avoidance programs which focus on the causes of motor vehicle accidents – driver attitude and behaviour and other environmental factors – [which] must be permanently altered to do their part in both reducing current costs and closing the gap between inflation and claims trends.

The report urged three approaches for aligning drivers to road risks: road safety engineering, 'tough safety publicity,' and a law enforcement crackdown. These approaches were taken up by the insurer and referred to as 'The Three Es: engineering, education and enforcement.' An official said in interview that the three elements formed a mandate to change 'the culture and environment of road use' which would in turn meet the mission statement goal 'to help take the risk out of road transportation.'

This consultant's report and related documents produced by the insurer were replete with statements that prevention is essential to loss ratio security. For example, a table in another document identified seven areas of 'investment' in prevention: impaired driver road check enforcement; impaired driver administrative driving prohibition and impounding of vehicle for driving while prohibited; impaired driver clinical assessments; speed corridor enforcement; photo radar speed enforcement; road traffic engineering improvement; and auto crime prevention. The cost of investment in each area was given, totalling $272 million, followed by expected 'net returns,' estimated at $746 million. The same document identified 'three core business processes' for loss ratio improvement. First, 'prevention of crashes and auto crime: road user behaviour, road design, vehicle design, auto crime and fraud prevention, influencing transportation planning, driver licensing.' Second, 'selling loss protection products and services: new product development, liability protection, personal injury protection, vehicle damage protection, vehicle licensing.' Third, 'facilitating recovery from loss: claims handling, personal injury rehabilitation, vehicle repair, focus on wellness and best outcomes.'

This emphasis on harm reduction as a business enterprise was linked to individual driver responsibility for risks on the road. A key manoeuvre in the political language of responsibility was to erase the word 'accident' and substitute 'crash.' 'Accident' connotes unpredictability and lack of motivation, while 'crash' connotes a cause and intentionality. Where there is a cause and intentionality there can also be an attribution of responsibility.

The use of 'crash' rather than 'accident' is well established in the airlines business. There it relates to the need to attribute responsibility for both preventive safety efforts and the settlement of huge insurance claims costs among multiple parties. 'Crash' has entered more recently into the political language of automobile accidents, but the intention of attributing responsibility for prevention and claims settlement is the same. More specifically, the intention in the automobile arena is to make the driver responsible for accident prevention and accidents that occur, as these relate to insurance business operations.

We interviewed an official of a vehicle insurer who said that 'accident' had become a censored word in any public discourse. 'Officially we're not allowed to use the word "accident." When we're talking to the public, we have to say "crash" ... [This is] an attempt to get away from this idea that accident was just a poor chance event, that in fact it has a very definite cause.' A colleague in the road safety division of the same company embraced 'crash' as the better term because it relates to the empirical reality. She claimed unequivocally that only 3 per cent of accidents do not involve driver responsibility: 'It should be "crash" as opposed to an 'accident' ... If you're talking to the public about the problem and trying to get them to take some ownership, then it speaks more specifically to the event as it should be described, as opposed to something that was beyond their control in every case, an accident, couldn't help it ... If you can get everybody to slow down and everybody to stop drinking and everybody to buckle up, you'd have a substantial reduction in the crash incidence.'

The 1995 annual report of ICBC was entitled *Signalling Change*. The opening message from the president immediately signalled the change in question. 'Crashes do have causes, and we would rather prevent them than pay for them. We're not the police and we're not a driving school, but as insurer for all ... motorists, we have a responsibility to

Table 8: 1
Approximate estimations of how crash problems and auto crimes
contribute proportionately to each claim dollar

Crash problems and auto crime	Percentage of $2.238 billion
Speed and dangerous driving	27
Impaired driving	16
Fraud	15
Vehicle design/operation	6
Auto crime	6
Road design/operation	6
Driver inexperience	6
Driving while prohibited	1
Other factors	10
Other claims	3

invest in prevention and to reward good driving ... We're becoming a loss prevention company rather than 'just' an insurance company ... We have changed from fixing up broken lives, broken bodies and broken vehicles to getting right to the causes and stopping claims before they happen.'

An ICBC five-year plan for loss prevention, drafted in 1997, declared that 'the overwhelming factor in crashes is driver behaviour, which is implicated in one form or another in about 91 percent of crashes.' This declaration was accompanied by data estimating 'how crash problems and auto crime contribute proportionately to each claim dollar' (table 8.1). These data, expressed with the authoritative certainty that insurers seem compelled to muster, clearly pave the way for a focus on individual drivers as the locus of responsibility and governance. Drivers are taking too many risks, and therefore are justifiably targets of education and enforcement. Of a total $2.238 billion claims paid, 27 per cent are attributed to speeders and dangerous drivers, 16 per cent to impaired drivers, 6 per cent to inexperienced drivers, and 1 per cent to drivers previously prohibited from driving. Fraud against the insurance company accounts for another 15 per cent, and theft from and of vehicles for 6 per cent. Vehicle design is not treated separately but paired as 'vehicle design/operation' (10 per cent), leaving the implication that even when there are design faults the operator still bears some responsibility for how she handled those faults. Similarly, road design is not treated as an independent deterministic factor, but as 'road design/operation' (6 per cent). Again, the implication is that while the road engineering may be faulty, so is the driver who fails to take it into account in her rational calculus of driving.

The declaration of driver responsibility was also represented schematically (figure 8.1). Drivers are said to account for 91 per cent of all crashes, either because of their own poor conduct (61 per cent), or because they failed to calculate road risks they should have been aware of (25 per cent). Thus, in only 9 per cent of cases can it be said that the word 'accident' may be more appropriate because there is no driver responsibility: vehicle only (3 per cent), road only (2 per cent), or vehicle and road in combination (4 per cent).

These are moral statistics. Accidents, or rather crashes, don't just happen. Drivers make crashes happen. Drivers can therefore be made responsible for preventing them through education about risks to be avoided and taken. Drivers can also be made liable for crashes in the settlement of insurance claims because they should have been aware of the risks. The crash is an indication that the individual's risk calculus went wrong and requires remedy through a reconfiguration of engineering, education, and enforcement. Ideally, the sciences of vehicle, road, and social engineering, as applied to actuarial science, will pave the way for a risk-less environment. When the seemingly irrational is made rational – when 'facts most arbitrary in appearances will come to present, after more attentive observation, qualities of consistency and regularity that are symptomatic of their objectivity' (Durkheim 1964: 28) – then what first appear as accidents can be understood as not accidents at all, but only crashes. Drivers can be made culpable not because of motivation and will per se, but because they are held accountable for being aware of crash risks and the consequences of miscalculating them. This has become 'the dominant theme in the cultural organization of accident reality' (Gusfield 1981: 41).

This responsibilization of knowledge of risk plays off broader social movements. For example, the victims' movement – exemplified by organizations such as Mothers Against Drunk Driving (MADD) – also declares unequivocally that individuals who harm others are culpable regardless of their ignorance, miscalculations, or mistakes. Ironically, this dominant cultural sensibility also contains a strong blaming the victim component. People who are simply not reflexive enough about the risks because of ignorance or an error in judgment are to bear the brunt of engineering, education, and enforcement. As we discovered in chapter 7, everyone is a suspect. In the realm of prevention, individu-

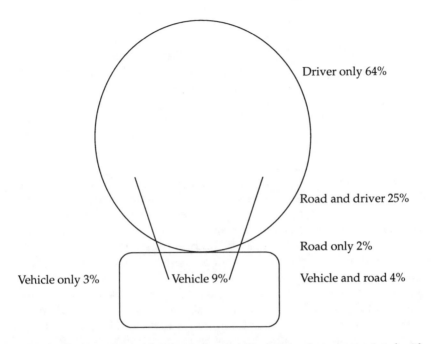

Driver only 64%

Road and driver 25%

Road only 2%

Vehicle only 3%   Vehicle 9%   Vehicle and road 4%

Figure 8.1   Proportional levels of association of major factors associated with crashes: vehicle, road, and driver crash interactions

als are suspected of not applying themselves sufficiently to the risk environment, and they become targets for remedial action even when they have done nothing else wrong. Just about everything is reduced to 'personal failure, the inability of individuals to negotiate an all-encompassing risk environment, in which the accident should not happen' (Green 1997: 154).

'Crash' is meant to impel everyone – insured drivers and insurance company engineers, educators, and enforcers – towards preventive action. A Canadian organization called SMARTRISK, which is backed by insurers as well as other private corporate and government sponsors, devotes itself to making people smart about driving risks. An interviewee involved with this organization declared the word 'accident' a scourge because it leads to denial of responsibility and therefore inaction. Drawing the analogy of how belief in knowledge of health risks leads to effective preventive action, he said that catastrophic crashes can be prevented through similar figurative language as a motivator of action. Traffic injury and death are not treated seriously enough 'because we call them accidents, which is a word defined as an unavoidable act of fate, that's the attitude we all have. We know that if people think something is fate, then the most sophisticated way to cope with that is denial.' He observed that if six children die in an auto accident, there is denial. In contrast, if six children die of meningitis, it becomes ' a national story, national outpouring of resources ... belief it's preventable and we go into a vulnerability mode where everybody wants to vaccinate.'

The figurative language of statistical figures (see e.g. table 8.1, figure 8.1) and tropes (e.g., 'crash') helps to constitute a public culture of political action that also governs individual practices. However, in the control culture of actual practices a different reality appears. In the workaday world of accident prevention through engineering, education, and enforcement, there is less faith in causal claims and attributions of responsibility. A traffic accident research analyst – employed by the insurer that produced the figures on driver responsibility and banned the word 'crash' from its official vocabulary - said in interview that 'accident' is the better word because 'there's a substantial element of traffic crashes that are uncertain, things that can't be predicted no matter how many variables you have in the equation.'

Insurers are pragmatic. In the practical world of dealing with prevention efforts and settling claims, the meaning of an accident is made to vary according to whom the insurance operative wants to hold responsible. For example, we studied a private sector insurance company that had a unit specializing in accidental death and dismemberment insurance. An employee of this unit said in interview that the company defined something as accidental if it was pragmatic to do so in sustaining a profitable insurance relationship. For example, group plan insured who died from auto accidents attributed to their being impaired still had claims paid:

> That's a debated one in the industry, but the industry generally pays because we deal with a lot of unions. And the employers and the unions tend to be tough and they say, 'Well, the problem is they left a beneficiary, the spouse, who's got children, and that's not their fault.' And our argument has been ... this is wrong, he shouldn't have been drinking and driving, it's illegal ... [But ultimately] the accident still happened, so it's there. Our feeling is that if it's an accident we pay ... An accident is an accident ... We use the statistics [i.e., actuarial costing] ... We price our product to

include all accidents, whether it's their fault or not ... [If we did otherwise] the rates would be a lot cheaper, but we'd be in litigation, we'd never get our money, recover our money. It just wouldn't work. I can just imagine trying to sue somebody for $200,000 who was making $20,000 a year ... we'd be in litigation forever.

Another contradiction between the emphasis on individual driver responsibility and the pragmatism of insurers concerns the introduction of partial fault or no-fault features in what are ostensibly at-fault systems. In the jurisdiction that provided the graphic figures on driver responsibility for crashes (table 8.1, figure 8.1), there was a very powerful lobby to keep the insurance liability system as an at-fault system. The spearhead of this lobby was the Trial Lawyers Association, but it had scores of allies in the victims' movement – for example, MAAD, the Brain Injury Association, the Coalition of Persons with Disabilities, and community crime prevention organizations – and in coalitions of business enterprises such as local chambers of commerce. These professional, business, and community interest groups campaigned actively for an insurance liability system based on individual driver responsibility, and sometimes combined their resources to bring in high-profile advocates such as Ralph Nader.

The insurer clearly had an affinity with this powerful ideology of individual responsibility for the purposes of its crash prevention campaign. However, at the same time the insurer introduced various no-fault and partial fault policies to meet its pragmatic goal of governing claims costs. For example, in order to govern fraudulent soft tissue injury claims it developed a policy of 'no crash, no cash.' This policy meant that if there was no evident material damage in a reported crash, there could be no personal injury claim arising from the crash. Another internal policy placed a cap on the amount paid for soft tissue injuries, forcing the accident victim to suffer inadequate compensation and/or seek shared claims costs with other disability insurers. Such policies limit the insurer's responsibility for the drivers it is trying to responsibilize. The bottom line is the moral utilitarianism of compensation arrangements more than the moral determination of individual responsibility. The question is how compensation can be justified in the particular case, and how it might be absorbed by the automobile insurer or shared with other disability insurers with deep pockets.

In some cases, responsibility is attributed in a strict liability manner simply because it is the easiest way to turn ambiguous accidents into unambiguous crashes. For example, when one vehicle runs into another from behind, the driver in the rear is held responsible regardless of the actual risk (mis)calculations of both drivers that led to the accident. In other cases, adjusters have discretion to deal with ambiguous accidents by assigning partial fault to each driver. Thus an adjuster for the insurance company we studied said that he agreed entirely with his company's approach to responsibilizing drivers because it is necessary to help settle claims. '*You* are responsible for getting behind that wheel ... There's never no one at fault ... I can't go and blame God for putting snow on the ground, or putting black ice on the ground ... I have no problem telling people the point they are at fault for an accident because of the snow or the ice.' However, he then described a variety of ambiguous situations in which it was necessary to blame more than one party and assign partial fault to each. For example, there can be ambiguity over when a red light turned green when vehicles are involved in an accident at an intersection. If there is no supporting material damage or third-party witness evidence, the solution is to go '50–50' because 'no matter how much you trust your claimant, the other adjuster trusts their claimant. And we can't hold no one at fault, because someone is at fault here ... You really trust that person, but then a lot of people know how to sell stories too, so maybe you just told me a story.'

Another adjuster for the same company said in interview that pragmatic assignment of responsibility can sometimes work in the interests of the injured party whose compensation runs short. This is a socializing feature of having a state insurer providing insurance coverage to both drivers in an accident. For example, an accident victim with catastrophic injuries may find that the responsible driver's insurance coverage limit runs out and she is left with inadequate compensation. One solution is to declare the otherwise not responsible party to be partially at fault, so she can then claim compensation on her own insurance as well.

Engineering

While crackdowns on responsible driving are used to control loss ratios, a little room is left for attributions of responsibility to road conditions and vehicle design. As indicated in table 8.1 and figure 8.1, most of these attributions are still combined with the responsibility of drivers: drivers should be aware of the conditions of roads and their vehicles and take precautions accordingly. Only in a tiny fraction of cases may crashes be deemed accidents, in the sense that their cause is attributable to forces external to driver control: vehicle condition (3 per cent), road condition (2 per cent), or some combination of the two (4 per cent).

Road conditions that arise from poor traffic safety engineering are typically the responsibility of government, managed through provincial ministries of transportation and municipal transportation infrastructure programs. However, in provinces with state automobile insurance systems, insurance corporation dollars are sometimes used to engineer safer roads. This was the case in ICBC. Although there was a provincial Ministry of Highways, its road improvement for traffic safety efforts were sometimes supplemented by ICBC. We interviewed a senior road safety executive who gave the example of using insurance corporation money to add left-turn lanes on a city corridor street. She said that neither the Ministry of Highways nor municipal government were willing to fund this traffic flow and safety improvement at the time. The insurer decided to fund it because 'we get returns of 22-to-1' on the dollars invested. By this she meant that there were accident reduction savings to the insurer – with spillover cost savings to the courts, hospitals, and other components of the social infrastructure – that justified this measure as a good business investment.

Both public and private sector auto insurers govern the manufacture of safe vehicles. Until the 1990s, the standard for whether a vehicle was safer was simply the cost of the car, using the manufacturer's suggested retail price! A CLEAR vehicle rating system now assesses the crashability, damagibility, and theft vulnerability of each type of manufactured vehicle, as well as the protection of individuals in them. The owner of a model that rates poorly is subject to higher insurance premiums and more unfavourable insurance contract conditions. The possibility of a resultant negative impact on sales of the model is intended to encourage manufacturers to improve safety features. The supporting system is the Vehicle Information Centre of Canada, which is funded by the entire auto insurance industry on the basis of a levy in relation to market share, and by a certification fee paid by auto and safety product manufacturers. This system constitutes a normal population of automobiles in Canada, as if they are autonomous from drivers, road conditions, and other contaminating influences on accident rates and insurance risk.

Publicity is another vehicle of governance. One pamphlet for consumers ranks cars and their respective insurance costs. Another pamphlet publicizes vehicles that do not meet the standard for vehicle theft deterrrent systems, while a third publishes theft rates reported to the police.

The availability of safety devices engineered into vehicles does not mean that they will be used, or used properly. In order to govern the safe practices of drivers and their passengers, a provincial government auto insurer we studied developed an inspection and education program. For example, it sent inspectors to locations where vehicles queue for extended periods, in order to check on how headrests were positioned on car seats and to advise accordingly. Pamphlets on headrest safety were distributed, and the program was reinforced by spot radio advertisements addressing the same issue. Subsequent research assessed whether this social engineering inspection and education campaign led to better use of headrests.

Education

The headrest safety example illustrates how educational efforts combine with safety engineering improvements and surveillance to make the insured operate as an agent of prevention. Everyone is treated as a responsible driver who nevertheless can make bad decisions because she fails to assess all of the risks and/or engages in too much risk taking. This approach to prevention is exemplified by a slogan used by a researcher for a provincial government auto insurer: 'It's not bad drivers, it's bad driving.' He evidenced his statement by referring to an internal study of high-risk drivers, which found that they had similar personal attributes to a matched group of Rhodes Scholars. While they are aware and bright, they need to be educated on their responsibilities.

This is the approach of the SMARTRISK Foundation. Similar to the harm minimization approach to illegal drug taking (O'Malley 1999), smart risk involves awareness of risks, helping people to evaluate risks for themselves, and choosing a course of action that minimizes risk to self and others. An interviewee involved with SMARTRISK programs explained that, similar to campaigns for fitness or environmental improvement, the strategy is,

> Accept right as our very premise that life is about taking risks, that for the most part risk taking is fun, that risk is how we grow and develop and challenge ourselves. But the good news is there's this thing called smart

risk. And probably the worst thing about not taking smart risk is that you may never get to take risk again ... We believe that people are as motivated or perhaps more motivated by seeking pleasure and the ability to do things as they are at the abhorrence of pain and consequences. And traditionally safety has been framed as, 'Here's the consequences, you'd better change your behaviour.' And we're trying to frame it more as, 'Here is the opportunity to take risk and wouldn't it be great to take lots of it?' Risk is what life is about ... [Gives the example of a person deciding whether to dive off a bridge]. People will say that is high risk, but our take would be that if you're a great swimmer, you know how deep the water is, and you're jumping off feet first, then the risk is completely different than if I don't know how to swim, I'm jumping off head first, I don't know how deep the water is, and I'm doing it because my friends are teasing me.

This organization took the view that risk taking, especially among youth, is not based on rational assessment of detailed scientific evidence. Rather, in the electronic media environment of celebrity, brand images, and sound bites, smartness about risk is sparked by how one's risky actions are perceived in popular culture. Brand-identity marketing approaches are necessary

because risk is a fairly scientific concept and we don't live in a particularly scientific-rich culture. People put as much weight in astrology as they do in astronomy. We live in a world where people are bombarded with the risk of the day ... Most behaviour isn't cognitive ... You manage risk appropriately not necessarily because you know you are, but because it's the thing to do ... It's cool, because you want to be seen and perceived as somebody that's really great at managing risk, not so much because you want to avoid getting hurt ... Most kids aren't putting on a $180 pair of Nikes because they want to prevent inversion injuries to their feet or for some logical reason. They do it because they're marketed in a way that makes you want to wear them, because you believe that you're going to be better than you've ever been before in your life ... We're not huge advocates of legislation. I'd rather see young people put on bike helmets because they've been marketed as a fashion statement and they think they're good for them.

This organization mobilized various celebrities in the risk-taking business to help market smart risk among the impressionable. For example, the Canadian military acrobatic flying team 'Snowbirds' was used as a SMARTRISK ambassador. 'They appear to take very high risk, but because they've got the right training and the right gear and the right attitude they can do it again and again and again.' Professional race car drivers were used in a driving skills program cosponsored by an auto manufacturer.

As positive as smart-risk marketing tries to be, it is impossible to escape the negative logic and fear that looms behind risk-taking decisions that went wrong. As the interviewee above said, 'the worst thing about not taking smart risk is that you may never get to take risk again.' Playing on the effects of electronic media and popular culture, the organization produced a video called HEROES that was shown in school visits. The video featured teen music, dance, and body images, except the teens portrayed were partying in spinal cord units and using wheelchairs. The video viewing was followed by live presentations, the first from young auto accident survivors who, according to the interviewee, emphasize 'that these aren't accidents, that they're predictable and preventable. They talk about the things that change, the real taken-for-granted things like bowel function, bladder function, sexual function, really all the things that have to do with body image. We then bring out a young person from the community that we're visiting who has learned a script, and talks to the audience not about what you can't do but what you can do ... It's *your* life. You're in control. All we can do is give you the choices and leave the decision up to you.'

Crash prevention education is embedded in everyday life as both a spectacle and a moral lesson. While dramatization frames the issue in assumed universal standards and moral order, it also makes clear what individual risk management practices are to follow.

A visit to the local shopping mall or fairground may result in confrontation with 'The Convincer.' Attended by local police but paid for by a private insurance company, 'The Convincer' is a mechanical device that demonstrates why seatbelts should be worn while driving. In the words of a marketing manager for the sponsoring insurance company, 'You ramp it up ten feet or so and it slides down and wacks into this wall and you're wearing your seatbelt and you get a sense of in fact why you might want to wear your seatbelt.'

Purchases made at a local liquor store in British Columbia at Christmas time may be packaged in a special bag. The bag is an ordinary brown paper one, but it is adorned with an original crayon drawing that conveys an anti-drunk driving message. The artists are school children who have been educated on their responsibility to prevent drinking and driving. In this instance, the children have been mobilized in turn to educate adults on their responsibilities. Sponsored by the provincial government auto insurer, this program is aimed at the hearts as well as the heads of drivers and future drivers by mobilizing support of the school system and liquor distributors as agents of responsibility.

There is also a smart risk approach to education about the prevention of impaired driving. For example, ICBC distributed a 'Parties with a Punch' brochure that was part of a broader 'Road Sense' education program. The brochure explains how to prepare party food that will help regulate effects of alcohol consumption, and how to pace the serving of food and drinks. Included are seven recipes for non-alcoholic drinks called 'mocktails.' The minutiae of instructions governing self and others includes, for example,

> Serve high protein munchies. Alcohol works really fast on an empty stomach, so put out food as soon as your friends show up. Foods like chicken wings, cheese, and guacamole are best. *Avoid salty things.* They feed a thirst. If food is running low, order in. And keep them eating! Who cares about diets? This is a party! Food keeps people happy and it lessens the need to drink ... *An ounce of prevention* ... Most people over estimate the volume of an ounce. Keep a one ounce glass at the bar and make using it a house rule ... Strategically place pitchers or jugs [of water] next to your food at the bar ... *Get the party out of the kitchen* ... Plan some things for your guests to do so they don't have to rely on liquor to loosen up.

Road Sense campaigns use advertising formats to make drivers feel better about their participation in risk-less driving. These formats rely on dramatic visuals and shocking numbers more than sophisticated risk analyses. It is hoped that such dramatization will stir emotions that prompt people to drive more safely. As a senior executive involved in one such advertising campaign stated in interview, 'These things take multiple generations, smoking, the fitness thing. Safe driving used to be seen as fairly trivial, now it is seen as an economic and social problem, like the environmental issue.'

A provincial government auto insurer developed a road safety index similar to a weather index. Various real-time driving conditions – for example, weather conditions and time of day, seasonal traffic flows – were related to accident risk data to derive the index number. The index was broadcast in the same way that various weather indices are reported on television and radio spot news. The program was quickly scrapped because it made people all too aware of the limits of quantitative analyses and of a simple index for addressing the complex multicausality of individual crash risk. An insurance corporation official said in interview that radio announcers had started to make fun of the index. One announcer used a sound clip of a wheel of fortune before announcing the index figure in a derisive manner:

> We'd say the index is extremely high in the afternoon on Friday, it's an 8, it's November and it's dark. And they'd say 'This is nonsense!' ... As the weather got really bad, people said, 'What, it's gone down? If any day is a 10, today has got to be a 10. This is absolute nonsense!' Well, what happens is people moderate their driving when the weather is severe, and they stay off the road and crash rates actually go down. So that's the truth, but their perception didn't fit with it. So I mean the whole idea just became a public relations disaster. I mean we made the national news when we brought it out, and everybody thought what a fantastic idea. And then it just fell over because it didn't fit with public perception.

A more workable approach to road sensibility formation is to compare crash risks as a social problem to other social problems, such as crime. For example, advertisements inform people that they are twice as likely to experience a motor vehicle property loss than to be burgled, and much more likely to die or be seriously injured in a car crash than to suffer the same consequence through violent crime.

Road sensibilities are believed to be stirred even more when shocking crash statistics are blended with shocking visualizations of the horrible results of risk taking gone wrong. For example, in its 1995 *Annual Report*, ICBC reproduced one of its advertisements that included a sequence of photographs of a car–bicycle crash and anguished parents looking on, with data on crashes and their causes appearing at the bottom. The *Annual Report* explains how both numbers and visuals can merge in appeals to drive more safely: 'The numbers tell only half the story. Even the appalling crash data below cannot communicate the shock, numbness, grief and pain felt when a loved one is injured or killed in a vehicle crash. In addition to all the other Road Sense activities, ICBC has invested in an ongoing series of hard-hitting ads to remind us all of the very human and personal costs of poor driving behaviours.'

Many of the advertisements in this campaign dispensed with graphic numbers, relying instead on pictures, sometimes with brief captions, to have people visualize their responsibilities as agents of prevention. An interviewee involved in marketing one Road Sense campaign referred to a television advertisement that pictured a mother's frantic call to her husband, voiced over a video of teenagers destroying the family minivan. The minivan is the icon of the middle Canadian nuclear family, symbolizing good values, stability, conservativism, and preferred insurance risks. But in this advertisement the family has failed to govern their risk environment by ensuring that high risks, such as teenage novice drivers, were under proper control.

Some advertisements in the campaign used reality television formats (Doyle 2003) to bring home the consequences of bad driving. For example, medical response and morgue scenes were depicted with actual paramedics, health service professionals, coroners, morgues, and slabs. One television ad featured a high school student re-enacting how her sister died in a car crash. There were visits by high school classes to insurance claims centres, which included a viewing of badly crashed vehicles on display. One such display we observed was of a Porsche that had been totally destroyed by a young driver who crashed at excessive speed. The message was that high performance vehicles driven by people with high performance identities can yield catastrophic consequences. An insurance corporation strategist involved in this fear mongering among young people said in interview,

> We've got to get them more afraid when they get in their cars because they're just taking too much for granted when they're driving in certain conditions ... To me, one of the huge areas is this whole notion of popular culture and consumer culture - if you read the instructions on the promotion of alcohol, they read like the creative direction for the promotion of vehicles! A one-to-one relationship with your social prowess, your sexual prowess, I mean it is just alarming ... [High risk young drivers are not deviants but] naïve consumers of a culture that promotes speed at every single turn ... *Dukes of Hazzard*, movies like *Speed, Speed Vision* on cable TV, commercials, children's programming, cartoons, and their toys – you name it! ... For every ounce of prevention there's a pound of recreation.

ICBC developed anti-car culture advertisements similar to the format used in counter-consumer culture magazines such as *AD Busters* (see Klein 2000). These advertisements were developed through extensive interviews and focus groups with youths addressing their perceptions of vehicles and identities. There was a parallel effort to target peer influences on young drivers, for example, the girlfriends of high-risk male teens, to have them encourage slower performance on the road if not in other matters.

The consumer culture of youths was also engaged in advertisements promoting safety technologies. For example, ICBC sponsored advertisements that promoted the wearing of helmets while cycling. These advertisements featured an Olympic mountain-biking medallist adorned in the latest cycle fashion gear as depicted in commercial magazine advertisements. There was intertextuality with these fashion advertisements: the helmet was depicted as part of being fashionable, supported by a caption, 'Are you in the right gear?'

In a provincial government automobile insurance operation we studied, researchers tracked the effects of a smart-risk advertising campaign. For example, there were surveys regarding name recognition of the campaign, and acceptance of particular advertisements and the law enforcement crackdowns associated with them. While there was considerable evidence of campaign awareness and acceptance, an additional research effort to measure the effects of the campaign yielded disappointing results. A researcher said that, for example, the anti-speeding part of the campaign had results that were 'dismal! ... Speeds dropping by about maybe 1.2 per cent ... We look at changes in attitudes and changes in behaviours and changes in the bottom line, which is the claims picture ... and none of it has really changed that much.'

The inability to demonstrate a relation between smart risk discourse and drivers' practice led some to conclude that the campaign had another agenda. We interviewed an actuary who referred to the campaign as 'public affairs traffic safety ... a lot of money being spent is more look good than do good.' Another interviewee, representing a consulting firm that worked regularly with vehicle insurers, described the campaign as a 'teflon' approach that would not influence long-term driver socialization or reduce claims costs.

Interviewees saw smart risk campaigns as a politically expedient move with political economic motivations. Law and order campaigns in the name of public safety are a long-established means of mobilizing political consensus. An interviewee employed by a crash injury research organization that had a provincial government auto insurance corporation as a client said that their smart risk campaigns were more a performance of public authority than an effective tool of harm minimization. 'Sometimes they have to address issues that are perception, not reality ... [for example, the belief that] people who run red lights are a real problem. Well, there may be no empirical evidence that people who run red lights are causing crashes, but the public is annoyed. It's like the difference between running a campaign to make kids street proofed against the tall, dark stranger when in fact, don't worry about the tall, dark stranger, it is somebody in your family.'

A loss ratio security consultant to vehicle insurers across North America said, 'Prevention was never an altruistic thing to help you survive ... [It's] politically expedient ... [they] can't crank up premiums, so they really had no other choice ... than to go into the prevention field.' An interviewee employed by a vehicle insurer to help create a smart risk prevention campaign said that each creative suggestion for an advertisement, brochure, or other measure had to be vetted for its cost-saving potential. He felt that this vetting was a clear indication the insurer was moving away from its social mandate: 'Every one of the issues that we bring forward in the company that we're going to spend money on enforcement-wise, or advertising wise, goes before a committee of people that look at it from an actuarial point of view, and we have to substantiate what we're doing from a cost point of view ... We've made it into an enterprise, a business enterprise, as opposed to a small, nice-to-have socially good enterprise ... It's the first time I've seen the company actually get behind going after reducing deaths, injuries, and costs the way it has, and I'm certain that's because it ties specifically to saving money.'

Enforcement

Advertising campaigns are embedded in law enforcement crackdowns in the hope of achieving some short-term crash reduction and loss ratio improvement. Behaviour modification of insured persons is the goal, and advertising becomes part of the enforcement strategy. Road Sense means both a 'sensing' of the road via surveillance mechanisms such as photo surveillance cameras, intersection traffic light surveillance cameras, and police checkpoints, and the resultant 'sensibility' of the driver aware of the risk of getting caught for infractions. Thus the enforcement efforts are also educational and feed into the advertising, just as the advertising paves the way for enforcement. An interviewee involved in these campaigns stated, 'You make your enforcement very high profile so you increase your apprehension ... So the advertising is there to support the enforcement activities, but it's also to create the context and create the kinds of support that you get in a community that you're going to do that kind of enforcement. And so our advertising has really been around creating a context, giving public support, then introducing more enforcement.'

A report of a management consultant to a provincial government auto insurance corporation included a section entitled 'Support for Enhanced Enforcement.' This report declares with authoritative certainty, 'It is now well known that changes in criminal or other illegal behaviour (e.g. speeding) depend on the perceived risk of apprehension, and that enforcement must reach a "critical mass" in order to establish that perception ... Present levels of traffic and auto crime enforcement fall short of this objective and are frequently reduced, as they are not a police priority when in competition with other "more serious" crimes against individuals.'

In spite of considerable research evidence that the police are not as busy as imagined (Ericson 1982, 1993; Ericson and Haggerty 1997), they manage to create the perception that they are doing more important things than what the particular constituency wants them to do. In the present case, the lack of police attention to driver performance enforcement – in spite of the fact that crashes cause much more injury, death, and property destruction than crime – was used to justify insurance corporation dollars being spent on buying public police time for speed and impaired driving crackdowns.

The management consultant's report proceeded to justify the funding of public police in cost effectiveness terms. For example, reference was made to an earlier five-month pilot project in which the insurance corporation gave the police $2.4 million to expand impaired driving checkpoint inspections. The project 'involved the purchase of police overtime for ten independent municipal police forces ... and use of media advertising. This pilot resulted in a 10–20 per cent reduction in impaired driving crashes (as measured by claims data), and $5.3 million net savings; a 1:3 cost/benefit ratio ... The long-term solution, like that for speeding enforcement, may be a dedicated police force funded by the insurance corporation.'

The insurance corporation subsequently implemented a longer-term program to fund public policing, referred to by one corporation executive as 'leveraged enforcement personnel.' In doing so, it was participating in the trend towards public police/private sector partnerships and cost recovery efforts (Ericson and Haggerty 1997; Loader 1999). From the viewpoint of the provincial government insurance corporation, the enforcement pay-off can be justified as a public good even if the primary motivation is to save money. Thus an interviewee involved in an enforcement crackdown said that the insurance corporation had a 'moral duty to invest in loss prevention ... beyond profit and loss.' If the state is unable to fund enough police through other mechanisms, then the auto insurance corporation can contribute and thereby steer policing in its desired direction. 'I guess it is the greater good argument. Is it not good use of money, no matter whether it comes from us, or from government, whether it comes from taxation or from your insurance policy, does it matter?'

This interviewee also pointed out that corporation-funded police road checkpoint inspections served 'secondary' criminal law enforcement purposes such as recovering stolen property, detecting drugs and weapons, and serving outstanding warrants. This is a reversal of the argument that the police 'govern through crime' (Simon 1997). Here the police govern through driver performance inspections, one offshoot of which can be occasional detection of criminal contraband or wanted criminals.

The insurance corporation also ventured into partnerships with other state and private sector organizations to fund private policing initiatives. These efforts were largely directed at the prevention and enforcement of auto crime. An auto crime funding advisory committee gave money to business improvement associations to fund private security operatives who targeted auto theft hot spots (Huey, Haggerty, and Ericson forthcoming). There were also stolen auto recovery policing partnerships with Canada Customs, Ports Canada, traffic by-law enforcement units, and crime watch groups. Technologies, such as surveillance vans and licence plate scanners, were also part of the contribution to policing.

Enforcement crackdowns include calls for legislative change. A management consultant's report to a provincial government auto insurer advocated a number of legal enhancements for the policing of driving while impaired. First, a legislative change to allow roadside testing for drugs other than alcohol was advocated. Second, administrative solutions for immediate punishment were developed to circumvent the cumbersome aspects of due process in criminal procedure. Third, behavioural change of convicted impaired drivers was to be effected through an ignition interlock breath-testing instrument fitted into the offender's vehicle. The cost of the technology was to be borne by the offender. Behaviour change was also to be enhanced through clinical risk assessment and rehabilitation programs for impaired drivers. Again, due process for the offender was to be eroded in favour of system rights to calibrate her risks and treat her accordingly.

Legislative changes were advocated in other areas. As the provincial government's auto insurance corporation was to merge with its motor vehicles branch, there was a desire to enhance the capacity to collect outstanding insurance and driving infraction-related debts from recalcitrant drivers. The recommendation was to 'Ensure that all premiums, subrogation and claims recoveries, judgments and traffic fines are defined in such a way as to be cause for the insurance corporation to use all collection remedies presently available for premium debt.'

Graduated driver licensing was another legislative change advocated by auto insurers in the name of making insured persons agents of prevention. In the Ontario private insurance auto market, the insurance industry invested heavily in lobbying for a system that includes three levels towards a full driver's licence. In stage one, for example, the novice driver must be accompanied by a passenger with a minimum of four years' driving experience, and this passenger-as-agent-of-prevention must not be impaired above the 0.5 per cent blood alcohol level. Moreover, the level one driver cannot drive between midnight and five in the morning. The restrictions lessen with each level, as do the insurance premiums.

Graduated licensing is a system for more stringent regulation of new drivers, in other words, the young and new immigrants. As exemplified in an internal document of a provincial government auto insurer, it is justified on the view that responsibility must be actively *demonstrated* over time by the insured as agent of prevention. Only with a gradual record of risk-less behaviour can the driver be rewarded with a full licence and lower insurance premiums. 'Individual drivers must demonstrate to society that they can be *trusted* with this responsibility before receiving a driver's license. To keep a license over time, a driver must retain this *trust*.'

Here the onus is placed squarely on the individual driver to demonstrate trust by building a risk-less record. In contrast the insurer, in conjunction with the motor vehicle licensing and regulatory authority, is to act with distrust until the insured can prove her responsibility. For example, the same report advocates a change in driver licence testing procedures to include 'attitudes and motivations – concern for safety and the willingness to exercise responsible driving behaviour.' In addition, the road test should serve 'as a diagnostic and educational tool, with more emphasis on identifying specific deficiencies and prescribing corrective training required before re-testing is permitted.'

An interviewee involved in the development of these enforcement approaches said that consideration was also being given to creating incentives not to drive. The best predictor of crash risk in the province was the experience of the driver: 20 per cent of new drivers were involved in a crash in the first two years after being licensed, compared to 8.3 per cent of remaining drivers. While new drivers could be nurtured as agents of prevention through graduated licensing, high insurance premiums, and unfavourable insurance contract conditions, they could also be encouraged not to drive at all. The idea was for a 'passport for young people other than a driver's license, so that they were encouraged to use alternate transportation. And maybe they get "frequent flyer" points and they would get rewards with it ... go to a movie. And it was an I.D. that could get them into places, and maybe even get them reductions on taxis if they'd been drinking. There's lots of things you could do if you think about what we're involved in is taking the risk out of road transportation.'

Another thing that is done by auto insurers to make driving risk-less is the mobilization of 'community' as an agency of prevention. A provincial government auto insurer we studied had an internal document that advocated the cultivation of 'road sense communities' in which 'stakeholders are brought together to collectively develop and implement road safety initiatives.' One such initiative was 'speed watch' groups of volunteers with speed reader boards, organized through the insurer's regional offices. This was supported by efforts to 'publish community crash results intended to promote community ownership and motivation. *Community Speed Watch* groups will be expanded to include all major communities and will broaden their mandate to include unobtrusive evaluation of speeds and a more proactive reporting of results to their communities.' Such community empowerment is also fostered by private auto insurance companies. A major company in the United States distributed radar guns to community groups so that they could deter risky driving among their neighbours.

As we learned in chapter 7, the auto insurance contract is an instrument of enforcement. The failure of a driver to be smart in her risk taking can result in changes to premiums and contract conditions that make her pocketbook smart. This smart-money exacted as penalty is in turn designed to make her smarter in her driving behaviour.

Ironically, auto insurers participate in smart risk campaigns that declare they are taking as much risk as possible out of driving, but they must also leave some risk in the insurance contract as an incentive to drive carefully. This point was made by a smart risk campaign specialist we interviewed. 'We're trying to take the risk out of transportation ... [but] one could argue that you want to do just the opposite. You want to put a lot of risk in there because if you take the risk out, if you cover people totally, they have no incentive to drive carefully.' This interviewee observed that there are two extremes in this regard. At one extreme is a no-fault system with full coverage, which may make people less smart and less responsible about their driving behaviour. At the other extreme is a system of no compulsory insurance, which was the situation in Canada until the 1970s. People driving without insurance suffer lasting financial consequences from an accident and therefore have a great deal at stake in being smart about their risk taking.

Some insurance contract provisions simply exclude at-fault drivers. For example, a provincial government auto insurer we studied compensated personal injury differently between 'at-fault drivers' and 'innocent victims.' At-fault drivers were insured for medical, rehabilitation, and restricted wage loss benefits, but not 'non-financial' loss benefits such as pain and suffering, which were available to their victims. Moreover, in contrast to their victims, at-fault drivers were required to have optional coverage at extra premiums to receive compensation for certain types of financial losses, such as additional wage-loss benefits (past and future wages) and future health care. In a document justifying this differential coverage, the insurer stated simply that at-fault drivers 'still must suffer the consequences of their actions.' The same insurer also introduced a $250 'Crash Responsibility Charge' for those in an at-fault accident.

This insurer mounted a contract-based crackdown on drivers who were especially irresponsible. While its smart risk campaign emphasized that the cause of high crash rates and excessive insurance claims was *driving* habits, in general, it also singled out a dangerous class of *drivers* in need of a more severe contract punishment structure. An internal document that mapped a five-year prevention strategy said that

a sense of urgency exists concerning the need to address that small group of drivers who habitually engage in risky driving behaviours such as drinking and driving, speeding, running red lights and driving danger-ously. These 'habitually dangerous drivers' also are the most likely to avoid normal consequences of their driving behaviour by not paying fines, driving while prohibited, and engaging in fraud to elude other legal or financial retribution ... Our intent is to explore ways to positively influ-ence driver behaviour by setting insurance rates in accordance with a per-son's driving record and past crash experience, by aggressively collecting unpaid fines and by vigorously pursuing outstanding debts using all civil remedies available. The insurance corporation is also exploring the con-cept of reducing insurance benefits to habitually dangerous drivers if they are deemed to be at-fault in a crash ... [This] right pricing ... will encour-age motorists to drive safely.

This insurer used another contract-based enforcement mechanism to foster risk-less driving environments. Based on the fact that the great-est risk is simply driving itself – the more kilometres driven, the higher the risk – one strong rating criterion is how much the insured's vehicle is driven annually. This criterion was addressed through preferred rates to those who declare that they will use their vehicle primarily for 'pleasure' and not drive it to work on a regular basis. An interviewee who was involved in proposing escalating premiums by actual mea-sured distance driven said that such a scheme would have the effect of curtailing nonutilitarian driving by high-risk inexperienced young drivers. 'Would you hand your keys to your twenty-five-year-old, or your twenty-two-year-old, who is going to, just for the fun of it, on Fri-day night, drive to a distant town and back, if you know that was going to put you over that edge and you're going to have to pay a whole lot more premium next year because your kilometres are going to be more?'

Enforcement of preventive efforts through contract conditions is entwined with the market segmentation practices analysed in chapter 6. In contrast to the crackdown on dangerous drivers described above, a private auto insurer we studied creamed the market of people who epitomize 'family, safety and security,' to join its family of low claims policyholders. A vice-president said in interview that he and his col-leagues were 'working feverishly to brand the company ... Family, Safety and Security. Safe driving programs, auto theft combatting ... discounts to customers who are not claims-related customers ... to be part of the company family, that's the concept ... It's these added values that we're looking for.'

Home and Commercial Property Accident Prevention

The 'added values' of the insured as agents of prevention are also a feature of home and commercial property loss prevention. Through engineering, education, and enforcement, the insurer mobilizes the insured to prevent property losses that will harm both of them.

In some respects fire, theft, vandalism, breakage, fraud, and other property losses are conceived as accidents for insurance purposes. They are contingencies that can be subject to insurance risk assessment and priced accordingly so as not to disrupt the otherwise normal transactions of property relations. As such, they are normal accidents that arise in the course of everyday commercial activity. In the case of crime, the accidents occur because of the imperfections of market relations and the surveillance systems that govern them. Indeed, the surveillance systems are sometimes purposely kept imperfect so as not to disrupt the smooth flow of market relations, where such disruption could be more costly than a tolerable level of crime.

On another level, as in auto accident prevention work, property losses are treated as if they are not accidents at all. Responsible parties are singled out for blame not just after the fact, but also for failures to prevent property losses. Just as all auto accidents are treated as crashes, so all property accidents are treated as losses for which someone should be held responsible. While property losses can be absorbed by the proper calibration of loss ratios in insurance systems, those ratios can be improved by making the insured more responsible for prevention.

There are also different contexts for making commercial and personal property insurance compulsory compared to auto insurance. Compulsory property insurance is not driven by the state in the public interest, but by private lenders such as those that invest in commercial ventures or provide mortgages. Absent these compulsory aspects, self-insurance of property is common. Moreover, because of the institution of private property and the privacy associated with it, it is usually more difficult to establish adequate surveillance of preventive security measures for commercial and personal property compared to automobiles.

In our analysis of home insurance in chapter 7, we showed how market segments are created in relation to preventive security capacity. People living in risky environments may be redlined, or subject to high deductibles and expensive purchases of preventive security technology in order to qualify. At the lowest ends of insurance unpooling, prospects have to sell themselves by undertaking loss prevention plans (Knight 1997: 228–31). Some cannot afford the luxury of personal property insurance and absorb whatever losses they suffer.

In the commercial insurance market, the capacity of insurers to enforce preventive security measures depends on market conditions. In the 'hard' insurance market in Canada in the 1980s, insurers raised premiums and tightened contract conditions, including preventive security requirements. The extraordinary premiums and loss prevention expectations had an increasing impact on the capacity of business enterprise to invest and expand. As a result, large corporations developed various self-insurance and internal preventive security arrangements. For example, 'finite risks' – losses that are largely known over time – were self-funded to keep costs down and benefit from tax write-offs of the losses. 'Concentric risks' – unexpected large losses – were covered by setting aside reserves that also allowed investment opportunities and had tax benefits. A 'blended risks' strategy combined these other methods with traditional insurance, but with high retention levels.

A corporate risk manager whose organization took this blended risks route in the late 1980s said, 'buying insurance ... [is] just pouring money out of the window, and if we can arrange self-insurance and prevent the losses from occurring, minimize the losses if they do occur, then that's really what risk management is all about. And we only buy insurance ... to cover catastrophic risk ... We self-insure to $250,000 [for each incident] ... [In the past] ten years, we've never had a loss which has approached that.' This interviewee added that even for catastrophic losses, the insurance coverage was arranged through a reciprocal insurance agreement set up by his organization and several others in the same business. In the event of a catastrophe, this reciprocal insurance entity retains $2.5 million, at which point reinsurers come in at various layers up to $650 million.

A corporate risk manager for another firm described his role as 'asking those "what if" questions, and looking, and coming back to what is the threshold of pain for the particular company you're working for, financially.' He said that after some 'horrendous losses' in the past three years, his firm faced such unfavourable insurance conditions that it decided to self-insure more risks through its own captive insurance company. 'The reality is, you can hit insurers with a couple of losses, and they just blink. But after you've hammered them, they start getting pretty testy and pushy, retention levels up and rising premiums ...

[even though] they've had premiums for 14 years without it ... [Now] any benefit of loss reduction goes straight back in our own pocket ... the reward potential is huge.'

The increased financial risk involved in self-insurance leads to a greater focus on loss prevention. The corporate risk manager for a railway company that had recently changed from traditional to self-insurance arrangements gave examples of more stringent internal systems for loss prevention at two extremes. In an effort to mitigate disaster as trains pass through rugged mountains, 'We fly helicopters in and we control the avalanches. There's risks, we've been hit, so you take the preventive action that's available with the technology to do it.' At the other extreme, the smallest details of preventive safety are made the responsibility of individual workers. The interviewee described his approach when he visited a remote field operation building and discovered a discharged fire extinguisher that had not been replenished. 'Everybody has got to be a risk manager today ... [A worker said] "You're from head office, why aren't you going to do something?" I said, "Let me give you a fact here. The fact is if this place burns down because that fire extinguisher didn't work, it's not me that's going to be out in the cold. It'll be you. So I suggest that you make it your problem."'

In the soft commercial insurance markets of the 1990s, many insurers, already suffering from the loss of business to self-insurance operations, loosened their loss prevention requirements in order to attract business. We interviewed a commercial underwriter for a multinational insurance company who said that if a prospective or existing client fails to take a loss prevention measure on a critical matter, the company might 'get off the risk.' However, 'it's pretty much that competitive right now where somebody will always take everything out there. If it's that bad a risk, there's probably some decent [premium] money in it.' This trend was confirmed by a corporate risk manager with extensive experience in both the hard insurance market of the 1980s and the soft market of the 1990s. In the hard market there were 'frequent inspections ... [insurers would] insist that certain areas which they deemed to be risky became better protected. In the absence of doing that they would consider getting off the risk, or more likely, and my experience was ... they would increase the premium until ... it was more than a recommendation, it was a mandate instruction in order to retain them as an insurer for the risk ... [In contrast] in a soft market you can get away with murder and they want your business anyway.'

Engineering

In soft market underwriting conditions, insurers work with their commercial clients in more of a compliance relationship to improve the loss prevention environment. We interviewed a loss prevention technical service specialist for a multinational commercial insurer. He had a team of loss control engineers who inspected commercial properties at the underwriting stage and made recommendations for improvement. He said, 'We may underwrite it without them complying with the recommendations ... We work with underwriting all the time and the broker to try and help get the client motivated to comply with the recommendations.'

This interviewee described the underwriting of a commercial firm that had an inadequate sprinkler system. A new system would cost $350,000, and the approach taken was to have a new system installed over several years to spread the cost. If a complete new system were demanded at the outset as a condition of underwriting, the client could easily have found another insurer and a profitable insurance relationship would have been lost. Moreover, the insurance broker involved also had an important relationship to both the client and the insurer which may have been lost if the client was pressed too far on loss prevention details. The interviewee used this case to illustrate that an inadequate preventive security situation may still be underwritten 'because it makes good business sense to write it because we're trying to grow with this broker. Or, this is one insurance plan in twenty, the other nineteen are spotless and it's potentially $10 million or whatever, $12 million in premiums and I'm willing to take one bad one to write the other nineteen good ones.'

The multinational insurance company that employed this interviewee had 380 engineering and loss control specialists in its technical services division. A brochure describing the services offered by this unit said its purpose is to 'help customers think about the unexpected.' Among over a dozen specialties offered in this regard were general liability, products liability, crime, business interruption, workers' compensation, and machinery and equipment. One specialty was 'behaviour-based loss control evaluations [and] training for your supervisors and managers in behaviour-modification techniques to encourage actions that reduce loss.' Media damage control specialists were available to deal with organizational failure to control damage. The brochure offered an example of how one of the insurer's media damage control specialists was able to address a problem of air pollution that was making workers ill. Attributing the problem to a faulty air conditioner, the company was able to save worker medical examination costs of $100,000 and quickly restore production. No mention was made of the fact that such media engineering can also save the insurer substantial liability claims costs.

The loss control expertise of private insurers is used by state regulatory bodies that have downsized their own inspectorates. For example, in Ontario and Quebec the safety inspection and certification of certain boiler machinery has been shifted from government inspectors to insurance company inspectors. The insurance company inspectors act with the authority of government inspectors, including the authority to close a plant if its boiler machinery is deemed too risky. The cost of inspection is incorporated into insurance premiums.

Private insurers also provide inspectorates that govern some of the state's properties (Scott 2002). These private sector inspections of the state are not only directed at safety conditions in buildings and workplaces, but also government-owned leisure facilities such as parks, sports grounds, and playgrounds with peculiar liability risks. A more complex private insurance-state relationship exists regarding fire loss prevention. In many Canadian jurisdictions, a small proportion of fire insurance premiums (about 3 per cent) is transferred by private insurers to help fund municipal government firefighting systems. As part of this arrangement, private insurers inspect the municipal firefighting systems to ensure that they are efficient when called upon. The inspection process involves numerous organizations, including for example the Fire Underwriters Survey that inspects municipal firefighting equipment, water supply, staffing, and training; the Canadian Standards Association and Underwriters Laboratories of Canada that test equipment, alarm systems, and building components; and commercial inspection companies such as the Insurers' Advisory Organization, which also has a school of loss control technology with courses available to fire department personnel.

The insurance industry collaborates with the state in other loss prevention initiatives. In Canada, one of the largest sources of catastrophic loss for insurers is flash hailstorms. After heavy losses in the 1990s, the insurance industry and government collaborated in a loss prevention program that involved having airplanes drop silver iodide in storm clouds to make the resulting hail smaller and therefore less damaging. Aware of their own risk taking in this risk reduction effort, the organizations involved formed a separate corporation called the Alberta Severe Weather Management Society. This move provided corporate limited liability as a way of protecting against liability claims that might ensue if the experiment went badly wrong and was blamed for further damage.

Loss prevention inspectors and experts we interviewed emphasized that their mandate was to reduce moral risks through technical solutions. While human beings are always suspect and often untrustworthy, technical systems are a source of greater confidence and trust. A technical services manager for a multinational insurance company explained in interview, 'I don't like – and insurance companies traditionally don't like – relying on the human element. If I have a choice between a trained fire brigade, or an adequate sprinkler system with a reliable water supply, I'll take the sprinklers any day ... If I have an adequately engineered system ... dump in fifty gallons a minute over a twenty-foot high group-A plastics [pipeline] ... I'll take that over, "Well I have a guy, I have good housekeeping, and I have good management attitude, and these guys do self-inspections."'

This interviewee also addressed the substantial difference in reliance on technical systems across different fields of loss prevention. Fire loss prevention is more reliant on technical systems, and on what he described as 'twenty volumes of standards.' Crime loss prevention is more limited. It is based much more on the client's accumulated loss experience and self-reporting of preventive efforts. He said the underwriter just decides 'I feel good about it ... You just go out and look at it and see what you need. And then you have to weigh the exposure and the cost and try to sell a customer on the fact that they need to spend the money to avoid the loss.' We accompanied this interviewee on an inspection of an existing policyholder's property. He advised that the company should buy some large concrete planters to position in front of the plate glass entrance to the office area to prevent someone from driving a vehicle into the glass in a smash-and-grab theft operation, and that the company install an anti-prying plate into the front entrance door to protect against crow-bar entry.

Education

The limits of technical solutions, and of human beings who interact with them, lead insurers to participate in broader education campaigns aimed at turning insureds into better agents of prevention. Furthermore, inspections are expensive, and it is impossible to have insurance inspectors make frequent visits to properties to better secure compliance with safety standards. Thus, various steps are taken to socialize the insured into acting as their own inspectorate and agents of prevention, including prevention of moral risks to which they or other human beings are susceptible.

Private insurance companies incorporate lessons in prevention into their marketing campaigns and underwriting processes. A home insurance company we studied is illustrative. A customer who visits one of the company's storefront agency offices is confronted with a rack containing dozens of brochures devoted to the minutiae of personal and property safety. Brochure titles include, for example, 'Keep Home Fires Burning Safely,' 'Fraud Coalition,' 'Protect Your Home, Vehicle, Family Safety Guide,' 'Safe Conduct,' 'Kill Switch,' 'Your Guide to Poisonous Plants,' and 'A Better Way to Record Your Personal Property.'

The brochure on the recording of personal property is a model of governing the insured to be an agent of prevention. The cover of the brochure pictures a woman in an elegant kitchen, smiling at her young daughter who is looking up at her while hiding something behind her back. The image here is not only the company's market niche of well-off nuclear families, but also the need for family members to visualize whatever might have hidden implications for loss.

Inside the brochure there is a format for recording a household property inventory. Property items commonly found in each area of the house are listed, with columns to record the current value, replacement value, and serial number of each item. There is also a space for recording the total value for each room or area. The brochure is punctuated with reminders about the value of keeping such detailed records. For example, there are pictures and captions on valuable items such as silver and jewellery and the need to have a proper record of them. A video camera is displayed with the caption, 'If a picture is worth a thousand words, a videotape of your property is worth millions.' There is an additional encouragement to use this surveillance mechanism. 'As well, you should consider videotaping your home, room by room. This, and the completed form, will give you a true picture of your property. Keep the inventory and the videotape in a safe place, away from your home. A safety deposit box is ideal.' The brochure is designed to make the policyholder simultaneously aware of the necessity of loss prevention, appropriate insurance coverage, and a detailed record to reduce suspicion of exaggerated claims. The brochure declares, 'It is far better to be prepared, even if it's just for that added peace of mind.' But with such attention to detail, the precautionary mind can never be at rest.

This insurance company also promoted reflexivity about loss prevention, the value of its products, and self-inspection through distribution of a safety card game. While this card game was designed for children, it was seen as something that insurance-consuming parents would play with their children. A company official we interviewed said that the game was distributed as both an educational device and a sales tool, and noted that while children do not buy insurance 'parents do ... If we make the kids safer, then who knows, you might end up with less claims down the road. However, we did make sure our logo was on all of the cards. I mean, if they're going to flash them at home, we might as well let the name flash in front of the parents ... I'll give you one of these, you can stick it in some little kid's [Christmas] stocking.' Another company official informed us that this card game was a great marketing success. Over 600 insurance company staff 'volunteered' their time outside of normal work hours to distribute 175,000 copies. 'We had our staff go into the schools and play the game with the kids and the teachers ... [I]t's seen as volunteerism and being part of the school system and the community ... There's the visibility that we're after.'

The company also sought marketing visibility by co-sponsoring a community 'safety village' that was a popular attraction for primary school classes. Another insurance company was a major co-sponsor. The two insurance companies in turn engaged a large number of private corporate and state agency partners who contributed expertise and/or money to the enterprise. An insurance company interviewee who was involved in developing this enterprise said that it 'is very much the buzz word in governance now, is the whole concept of partnerships, which has been used as a euphemism for offloading ... It's a new way of business.' A colleague employed by the same insurance company in public and community relations said that the decision to invest about a million dollars in the project was based on the strategy of being 'seen as doing something with safety, that's community based, and education ... It's the *spirit* of the village that we really like because we've got the police there ... a volunteer board of community leaders ... they're there for the community. They're not there for the individual sponsors ... It's the spirit of volunteers and then just safety and education.'

The safety village is a small theme park on a rural highway accessible from three medium-size cities. It includes an entrance building with offices, and two classrooms dedicated to instruction about traffic, fire, and crime safety. Beyond the entrance building is the village itself, with a roadway in which children drive miniature electric cars and thereby experience signs and situations of traffic safety. There are also miniature buildings that represent what is typical in contemporary Canadian villages.

School buses full of children, their teachers, and parents approach an entrance dominated by signs of the two sponsoring insurance companies. Large signs of the insurers also adorn the classrooms, with one captioned, 'Educating Today for a Safe Tomorrow.' The insurers' logos and signs puncture every experience in the safety theme park. For example, they appear on the toy cars, including the caption 'Helping Children Play Safe'; on certificates given to children to recognize their 'graduation' from this academy of safety; and on the insurance preventive safety marketing brochures strategically placed for the parents attending, and for the children to take home to their parents.

'The Wall of Honour' in the foyer of the entrance building indicates that corporate sponsorships can be formed easily when an educational enterprise is conducted in the name of children and safety. The Wall of Honour lists dozens of private corporate, community, and government sponsors, from private security companies to McDonald's. The safety village itself neatly mimics the commercial reality of contemporary Canadian village life. Miniature buildings, standing on lots costing their sponsors $10,000 each, represent large fast-food corporations, clothes retailers, and drugstores, as well as the local homebuilders' association, the Royal Canadian Legion, the Humane Society, and so on. A telephone company provides a telephone booth, where children can practise '911' emergency calls prompted by a voice mail script. The local newspaper is represented by a newspaper box. A railway company offers a railway crossing to be experienced on the toy-car drive through town. A street is named after one of the models produced in the local car manufacturing plant.

Back in the classroom, children are given instructional materials sponsored by Canadian Tire Corporation. The police and firefighters who provide the classroom instruction are not supposed to endorse particular businesses directly. However, a firefighter does mention that the safety ladders he uses in a demonstration can be purchased at a large chain hardware store, informing us later that he always 'drops' the name of this corporation because it donated $90,000 to the enterprise. On their break from this implosion of commercialized knowledge of risk, children are treated to doughnuts provided by the large doughnut chain that also sponsors a building in the safety village. When they receive their insurance-company endorsed graduation certificate, the children are further rewarded with a local mini-golf centre pass and a McDonald's restaurant voucher.

Community volunteer organizations, public police, and firefighting agencies are also involved. The mega-organizations of community safety are represented by signs in the village theme park: Crime Stoppers, Neighbourhood Watch, and Block Parents. Local police and firefighters staff the classrooms to provide the safety lessons they used to offer through visits to schools. They are clearly the state's partners, albeit surrounded by dozens of private corporate sponsors who signify what our insurance company interviewee had pointed to: partnerships are a euphemism for offloading state involvement in safety and security and provide a new way of doing business.

The decentring of public police officers in this context is best symbolized by 'Officer Broker.' Officer Broker is a robot who patrols the safety village, complete with a mini-television screen that shows safety videos. This robocop is also sent on the road to shopping malls, where it further blends lessons on preventive security with risk-less mass consumption. At a construction cost of $30,000 to its insurance industry association sponsor, Officer Broker exemplifies the way in which private insurance companies have reconfigured themselves at the fulcrum of preventive security initiatives and market their products accordingly.

Insurance companies are able to broker with a large number of other corporate sponsors who sell security products that make insured subjects into agents of prevention. They are also able to broker with business enterprises that sell hamburgers, doughnuts, and clothes because they too derive promotional benefit from marketing (in)security, especially as it involves children and their families. As a school teacher mentioned to us during our visit to the safety village, the children return home imbued with this division of labour in risk and responsibility. They are keen to instruct their parents and siblings on risk prevention strategies that would not have been attended to or even thought about otherwise. They are equally keen to instruct on the best places to buy hamburgers, safety devices, and insurance.

Insurers penetrate the educational institutions in other ways. For example, the Insurance Bureau of Canada, representing the property and casualty industry, distributes educational packages to schools (Insurance Bureau of Canada 1996: 27). These packages are titled

'What Is Insurance?,' 'Choice Chance Control,' 'Risk and Street Cents: Teacher's Guide,' 'Risk Management for an Entrepreneurial Venture,' 'Risk: A Teacher's Guide,' and 'Scruples: A Teacher's Guide.' These materials provide lessons in preventive security, including the moral risks faced by the insurance industry and the responsibility of the insured to help minimize them. 'Scruples' in particular educates about insurance fraud and how the insured subject has an obligation to combat it.

State-controlled insurance corporations are also active in school-based preventive security instruction. In Canada, provincial government workers' compensation boards provide teachers with educational packages to instruct students on safety. In British Columbia, the Ministry of Education requires thirty hours' instruction on workplace safety as part of the compulsory career personal planning curriculum in high school. The Workers' Compensation Board not only provides instructional material to help teachers meet this requirement, but also teachers' packages for all school grades beginning with kindergarten. An insurance official involved in these programs said in interview that they aim to 'change the attitudes of kids before they even get into the workforce ... making it an expectation that it's a way of life, that it's not something that you do at work, it's something that you do all the time.' A colleague was asked why the training in preventive security started in primary school. She replied 'Obviously those grade 1 to 5, to 6 maybe even, they have no experience, no concept, no understanding of what work is. So we have used the concept of work, but have applied it to things like at school, at home, at play. Because when you're playing even, there's a bit of work involved when you have to clean up ... There's the thread right through to grade 12.'

A teacher's manual for grade 8 students is illustrative. Under the motto 'See it. Think it. Do it' – with obvious intertextual reference to contemporary Nike advertisements that declared, 'Just Do It' – the manual advised teachers that 'providing thinking frames that include hazard recognition, problem solving skills to evaluate the hazard and decision-making skills to eliminate or control the hazard will help to make safety a transferrable skill.'

The manual recommends that reflexivity about risks should be embedded in routines from the beginning of the school year. The best way to make students smart about risk is to organize a school safety week at the beginning of term 'when there is confusion and classes are still unsettled.' This week should focus on disaster planning (e.g., fire drills, earthquake drills), hazard recognition, accident and injury prevention, first aid, playground safety, safe travelling to and from school, personal safety, dealing with bullies, and conflict resolution. Lessons in smart risk can be enhanced by guest experts from police, fire, workers' compensation, and health agencies. They can be dramatized through a theatre sports show involving students and their parents: the audience suggests a risk, and teams act out scenarios for dealing with them on which they are evaluated competitively. A school safety song contest is also recommended, using international safety symbols (WHMIS) and a familiar tune by the pop group The Police. The song as policing, and policing of how the song is produced, is illustrated in the following recommendations.

The WHMIS Song – You're Watching Out for You
If you or a student can play guitar, strum the cords provided. This song goes to the tune of 'Every Breath You Take, [I'll Be Watching You]' Police hit (or 1997 'I'll Be Missing You' by Puff Daddy). Use song as a model for students to compose their own safety song. Give students the option of making a music video in which they perform the WHMIS song or their own composition ... The students must memorize their parts. They cannot read from notes or lyrics sheets 'on screen.' Cue cards held up behind the screen are okay, but they must not be visible to view ... Use a combination of self-evaluation, peer evaluation, and teacher evaluation. Some criteria to include in the evaluation of videos are: creativity, quality of production and editing, scientific accuracy, clarity of plot, entertainment value, participation and coordination of actors, and obvious effort.

With jingles of risk and responsibility running through their minds, students can be taught the more serious business of hazard recognition and response. Hazards are to be graded to give students a sense of seriousness and priority in risk analysis of their immediate environment. In the process, they will also learn their place in the division of risk response ability as it relates to responsibility:

A Hazard: This type of hazard requires immediate attention. Hazard can cause serious injury if not corrected immediately.

- Must be reported to the teacher, parent or employer to be eliminated immediately.
- Someone may need to be left at the spot while someone else goes for help, or a marker might be left to alert people to the danger.

Examples: a spill on the floor, jagged glass or metal protruding. On the school ground this could be an intruder alert, finding a condom or needle in the playground, since these things pose serious life-threatening hazards.

B Hazard: This hazard is not immediately dangerous but if left unattended, the situation would deteriorate and injury could occur. Correct as soon as possible.

• This type of hazard should be reported verbally and in writing to the teacher, parent, employer or the Safety Committee.

Examples: a loose bracket on a playground toy, sticking wheels on a trolley cart, or a loose handle on a carrying case.

C Hazard: General maintenance items that should be addressed but pose no immediate concern. Plan to correct at a future date.

• This type of hazard must be reported in written form to the teacher, Safety Committee, or employer, for future repair.

Examples: a creaking swing requiring oil, peeling paint that is allowing the wood to splinter, a broken fence, etc.

The division of labour in response ability and responsibility is to be taught through a number of formats. With given scenarios of hazard recognition and response, the student is to complete a 'Rights and Responsibilities Form' that addresses her responsibilities and those of the authorities involved at school (teachers), work (supervisors), and home (parents). In science classes, where risks may be high because of interaction with unfamiliar technologies, there should be a formal 'safety contract': 'The contract provides an opportunity for taking personal responsibility for safety in the classroom and can be used as an accountability tool.' Students should also be given lessons on how to govern the safe practices of their peers without being scorned as a smart risk alec.

Take Three! – 3 Seconds for Safety
It is always difficult when you see a co-worker or peer doing something unsafe, e.g. not using their personal protective equipment (goggles) or using an unsafe procedure to get the job done quicker. What do you say without coming across like a know it all or goodie two shoes? ... How can we communicate without either party feeling embarrassed or defensive? ... Without words? Yes! This is where the signal 'Take 3' [See it! Think it!

Do it!] comes in. Using the three middle fingers, you can get the person's attention and give the signal. For example: 'Hey Bud' ... and show the Take 3 signal.

The manual proceeds to describe how every conceivable form of risk taking in contexts outside of the school can be made risk-less. For example, ladder-use safety is taught through a video, a video viewing guide, a form for answering a quiz, and a ladder-safety form with three columns of risks to check.

Risks at home are governed assiduously. For example, it is recommended that 'student commitment to sewing safety' be reinforced through having students sign a detailed 'safety commitment form.' The form makes it evident that the neophyte sewer should be on the lookout for pins on the floor, scissors on the chair seat, an iron left on, pattern paper near the iron, sewing machine oil left out, and so on. Similarly, the kitchen is to be inspected with a special risk checklist, aided by video instructions:

> Using the Hazard sorting form, sort the potential kitchen hazards into the three hazard categories: physical (mechanical, falls), material/substances (fire, hot grease, toxic cleaning chemicals, poisoning) and exposure over time (poor lifting techniques).
>
> Design a 'safe kitchen,' money is no object. Remove as many potential hazards as possible. Be creative! With a partner, make up a verse for a kitchen safety 'Rap,' which highlights one or more kitchen safety rules. When it is complete perform it, at a safety week assembly, for another class, or a younger grade.

In all of their home inspection activities, students are instructed to involve their parents and make them keenly aware of their responsibilities. For example, under a heading, 'Homework Activity,' students are instructed, 'With your parents, complete a Hazard Evaluation from the information you collected on the Home Hazard Recognition form.'

A workers' compensation prevention operations official we interviewed said that just as the economics of insurance shifts between soft and hard markets, so do prevention efforts. While many of these efforts to introduce smart risk programs into the schools are 'soft' approaches, with the hope of long-term benefit, there are also 'hard' campaigns similar to those used by auto insurers in their law enforcement crackdowns. He mentioned an advertisement sponsored by his organization that depicted a worker who died in an accident and the person in the workplace who was responsible for the death. This form of social responsibility advertising was justified by another interviewee involved in the advertising campaign. She said that there is a need to spark 'moral outrage' about work accidents that parallels the crackdown on impaired driving:

> We would like people to cringe when they say, 'Oh, I can't find my safety glasses, oh well,' just like they cringe now when someone says they will have 'one for the road' ... You would like people to say, 'That's like fingernails on the chalkboard. Stop that. You've got to be safe. Stop now and you'll be safe ... [A forthcoming report is going to recommend] giving out fines directly to workers for violation of regulations ... individual responsibility ... You should have that in your arsenal, and they do in other jurisdictions, and I think it's the right thing. It just feels right and it's partly because I think the threat of penalty has made a difference in other fields of social legislation such as drunk driving.

In addition to the marketing of prevention through social responsibility advertising, this workers' compensation board regularly fed graphic data to the media to dramatize in their news stories. This strategy was in part adopted because of focus group research with teenagers who indicated that such statistics have greater impact than dramatic photographs or videos of work accidents.

A member of a research organization devoted to worker health and safety observed in interview that while prevention campaigns are ongoing and involve substantial expenditure, relatively little evaluation is made of their impact. 'Most of the effort that goes into prevention is training ... a lot of which has no clear and unequivocal relationship with injury outcomes. So there's a lot of hopeful and superstitious behaviour related to prevention without much good assessment that these things actually make a difference.' In part, evaluation is limited because the effects of either long-term socialization or fear-mongering through advertisements and graphic data are difficult to isolate and measure. In part, these campaigns are motivated by state-operated insurance corporations that have political and economic agendas beyond preventive effects. In practice, prevention is largely mobilized through the insurance contract provisions stipulated at the point of underwriting and their enforcement during the ongoing insurance relationship.

Enforcement

The preventive efforts of workers' compensation insurers pertain to property conditions, as these may pose personal injury liabilities. In jurisdictions where workers' compensation is dealt with largely through the private insurance industry, including many American states, insurance companies sell workers' compensation as part of their broader commercial insurance packages, and the relation between property and personal protection is entwined.

Workers' compensation insurance is designed to protect the employer from the costs of being sued by the injured worker, possibly to the point where a heavy damage award might jeopardize the business and cause suffering to other employees, and to provide defined benefits to the injured worker. It operates in a hypersensitive environment of moral risk and responsibility, including responsibility for prevention. A workers' compensation board prevention officer we interviewed said that each prevention communication developed was carefully vetted regarding sensitivities over moral risks and responsibilities. 'You have to be very careful how you phrase so you don't blame employees, or blame employers, or put them against each other ... Anything I write goes to a manager that's familiar with the industry ... through probably an officer ... the director of the whole division, every director, and vice-president ... They read it for political sensitivity more so than errors or facts.' He also noted that there are taboos on the nature of publicity that can be used to dramatize prevention crackdowns and seek compliance from particular systematic violators. For example, the claims history of a particular firm is not normally publicized, even if it is bad, because of privacy considerations, including the potential for injuring the firm's competitiveness.

The central mechanism for the enforcement of prevention is premium assessments paid by employers, rated according to loss experience. Additional financial penalties can be levied for poor preventive security arrangements detected through inspections, informant tips, or claims inquiries. A workers' compensation board executive observed in interview, 'At the end of the day, employers are driven by costs. If they're not interested in the premium incentives, or they're just prepared to pass the cost of the accidents onto their consumers, then you need the regulatory side.'

On the other hand, if the rating structure offers steep penalties for a worsening claims record or substantial rewards for safe conduct, there may be pressures within a given workplace to cover up unsafe facilities and practices and not report accidents.

Another enforcement mechanism is a deductible structure that makes the employer share in the cost of the claim. For example, the employer may be required to pay the first number of days of an injured worker's lost time. In some jurisdictions, such as Nova Scotia and New Brunswick, employees are similarly forced to have 'skin' in preventive safety by the inclusion of a deductible-like provision in the claims they make. They receive no compensation for the first number of lost work days, on the presumption that this will make them both more safe and less inclined to make frivolous claims. The contract stipulations also prohibit employers from paying employees to cover their losses over these days.

Workers' compensation officials we interviewed stressed the need to enforce prevention through mechanisms that ensure employees have 'skin' in their safety. The threat of direct personal loss is especially potent. A senior executive of a workers' compensation board spoke fondly of a large multinational corporation that manufactured

> explosives and [is] heavily into textiles and chemicals. A very dangerous organization ... to work in. In the very beginning, the way they dealt with prevention is they said, 'If you work for the plant, you have to live within the blast range of the plant that was making explosives.' This caused a number of people to work safely, knowing that their family was at risk ... 'Oh, you want to be a manager, well you have to live between [the plant and] where the workers live.' This did a lot to embed a culture of prevention within the organization. And they have a rate of accidents that is almost two orders of magnitude lower than what it is for the province [as a whole] ... That tells you what the extremes of possibilities are. They don't even make explosives anymore, but the attitude is still there embedded in the culture of the organization ... What we have to do is work on fostering that internal responsibility through changes in beliefs and attitudes in the workplace.

In other areas of commercial insurance, the enforcement of preventive security occurs largely in underwriting processes. In crime prevention, for example, underwriting agents may be required to inspect premises in detail for crime vulnerability and preventive security arrangements. In one insurance company we studied, the inspecting agent is required to give details on money to be insured and how it is protected. For example, the safe is to be rated by maker, certification through the underwriter's laboratory, thickness of steel, and locking devices. Burglar alarm systems are rated by the extensiveness of coverage and nature of response. Fidelity bonds for employee dishonesty require separate applications. The applicant must give up any other information about his insurance and retail business record required by the insurers. Finally, the agent offers an assessment of the state of the building and good housekeeping of the proprietor, as well as the proprietor's business standing in the community. These details are followed up with specific preventive security requirements built into the contract. For example, this insurance company had three basic grades of burglar alarms for retail business policyholders, depending on the crime risk rating of the type of business. Shops deemed especially vulnerable to property crime – for example, those dealing in cameras, pharmaceutical products, compact discs, and guns, as well as those with late night hours (e.g., convenience stores and video shops) – require the highest grade.

In a passage that resonates with academic analyses of how the policing of private property is based in insurance mechanisms much more than criminal law and the public police (O'Malley 1991; Ericson and Haggerty 1997), the Insurance Bureau of Canada observes,

> With rates of violent crime and other Criminal Code offences sharply higher in Canada over the last decade – and the public demanding action from police whose resources are severely constrained – there is reason to believe that low rates of clearance for property crimes could deteriorate further, leaving insurers more vulnerable to crime-related losses. The most promising solutions may be found within the insurance mechanism itself. Possible actions include: devising minimum standards for property loss prevention devices and their use; refusing coverage or levying premium surcharges where loss prevention is below the minimum standards, and offering premium discounts where loss prevention exceeds minimum standards.

These practices are now standard. For example, an insurance company we studied offered home policyholders a 10 per cent premium discount for any one of a burglar alarm, linked to a monitoring station, a fire alarm or a sprinkler system. It also offered discounts on the purchase of some of these systems, even though inducements for the sale of property insurance were technically prohibited by legislation. Such technicalities are routinely overlooked when it is in the interest of more technology for loss prevention. The company actively marketed these prevention features as part of its promotional campaigns to policyholders. One campaign involved a mail-out to 500,000 policyholders and cost $750,000. Included in the mail-out were a new 'plain language' insurance coverage booklet and a magazine with loss prevention ideas and promotion of security products.

Insurers are also preoccupied with another major field of loss prevention, namely, controlling claims by the insured for compensation. Fraudulent claims are known to be extensive because of the institutional arrangements, social relationships, and moral economies of insurance. In many contexts, fraud is treated as a routine part of doing business and tolerated to a considerable extent. External law enforcement remedies are extremely rare because they disrupt the smooth flow of insurance organization and business relationships. Instead, fraud is handled within the private justice system of the insurance industry and its peculiar focus on loss ratio security.

9. Claims of Fraud

Without some dissimulation no business can be carried on at all.
Lord Chesterfield, *Letters to His Son* (1749)

There are some frauds so well conducted that it would be stupidity not to be deceived by them.
Charles Colton, *Lacon* (1825)

Insurance Fraud

The insured are treated as moral risks in all facets of the insurance relationship. In chapter 7 we revealed that, at the point of underwriting, insurance prospects are treated as suspects and subject to investigations that place them into a particular market segment. In chapter 8, we explored the ways in which insurance makes the insured become agents of prevention, and as such always suspected of not doing enough to minimize risks on behalf of insurers. In this chapter, we turn our attention to the claims process.

When the insured make claims, they are always suspected of exaggerating their losses for personal gain. The nature and extent of insurance fraud by claimants, however, is difficult to specify. Efforts at specification exemplify what the social reaction perspective in criminology shows about crime in general (Ericson 1975, 1993; Ditton 1979). What is regarded as fraud depends on the particular context and set of practices within which a given insurance company investigates claims (Clarke 1990; Baker 1994). In particular, different loss ratio security requirements will lead different insurance companies to treat claims variously at face value, as exaggerated, or as false. Even when claims are judged exaggerated or false, insurers make 'nuisance payments.' Sometimes it is too costly to develop evidence to sustain a claim of fraud; in other instances the insurer wants to maintain its relationship with the policyholder and will try to recover the claimed loss by premium increases and changes to the insurance contract. Moreover, even when fraud is alleged, the case is nearly always handled by internal mechanisms rather then by seeking public remedies through civil or criminal law.

The 'dark figure' of insurance fraud is best described as a black box: no one can possibly know the true extent of fraudulent claims. What is known is a function of the governance processes through which the insurance system creates the phenomenon it seeks to control. The manufacture of insurance fraud was described by a senior official in an insurance fraud control organization we studied. 'The scary part is, as we continue to increase the fight, we continually uncover more and more fraud. So people say, "You are putting all these dollars in there, but the problem is increasing." You can't say something is fraudulent until you find it. There's been such a growth in "insurance fraud." It has probably always been there, it is just that more has been uncovered than ever before.'

A starting point for understanding claims of fraud is to regard any effort to maximize an insurance claim by deception as fraud. This is the position taken by the Canadian Coalition Against Insurance Fraud, an organization backed by insurance industry associations in Canada. For example, in a popular magazine article on insurance fraud, the then executive director of this organization, who was also vice-president of the Insurance Bureau of Canada, offered the following definition: 'It's any act or omission resulting in illicit collection of a property and casualty insurance benefit ... [It includes] fabricated claims, to inflation or padding of legitimate claims and false statements on applications.'

This comprehensive definition is typical of organizations that represent the need to crack down on insurance fraud in public culture. However, in the control culture of actually trying to govern fraud in the claims process, the definition loosens. One definition that appears in insurance company manuals for claims adjusters says that fraud occurs when the claimant misrepresents facts with the intention of having the insurer act on them. For example, one such manual declares, 'For fraud to exist there must be a falsification of fact, knowledge of the statement's falsity by the person making it, and intent by the insured that the insurer will act on it.' While this definition seems broad and encompassing, the manual immediately notes, 'Slight exaggeration in the amount of the claim itself will not constitute fraud (although this may represent a moral hazard from an underwriting perspective), however falsifying documents to support an exaggerated claim would constitute fraud.'

The distinction between exaggeration and fraud is typical. An auto claims adjuster, employed by another insurance company, said in interview that while 'everyone exaggerates,' fraud is clear-cut falsification of a document or material evidence. Her company offered a five-hour training session that tried to specify the fine line between exaggeration and fraud. Another interviewee, involved in organizing this training program, was asked how the line is drawn. He replied, 'If *you* could give us the answer to this, you'd be a hero.'

The answer is that insurance adjusters and special investigation unit (SIU) officers take a pragmatic approach. When asked in interview to define fraud, an insurance claims investigator employed by a multinational management consultant firm replied, 'You see we're not the cops, so it's easier. We pursue it when we're paid to pursue it, and that's it ... We're driven by our clients ... They're driven by fear and self-interest.' An SIU manager for an auto insurer said that this pragmatic approach to fraud has three elements. First, it must be determined that the claimant intended to deceive for personal gain. Second, the magnitude of the loss must be great enough to make further investigation worthwhile. Third, further investigation and enforcement must be both viable and efficient. If sufficient evidence is unlikely to be gleaned, or adequate enforcement mechanisms are not available, the determination of fraud dissipates.

The combination of intentionality, loss magnitude, and investigative pay-offs also leads to distinctions between 'soft core' abuse of the system and 'hard core' criminal fraud. We interviewed a consultant on surveillance systems to detect insurance fraud. He said an example of 'soft core' abuse in auto insurance claims is the claimant who has a minor neck injury that becomes a major injury, usually on the urgings of a lawyer. 'Hard core' abuse is an 'injury ring' that stages a fake auto accident followed by multiple claims from several 'injured' parties. Similarly, an SIU officer for a workers' compensation insurer distinguished between '20 per cent abuse' and '5 per cent criminal fraud' among all claims. He said 'abuse' is largely accounted for by 'malingering individuals ... off on claim a couple of extra weeks longer than necessary simply because they've gone back to the doctor and said, "I need a couple of extra weeks" ... We're in an injury system, not an adversarial system. On balance of probabilities, we give the nod to the claimant.' (For detailed analysis, see Ericson and Doyle, forthcoming: chapter 3.)

While the 'nod' may be given to claimants in routine cases, especially where their health and well-being is concerned, in extreme circumstances there can be exceptional latitude for claims settlements. The claims settlements in Florida after Hurricane Andrew are a case in point (Baker and McElrath 1997). Extreme circumstances led to pragmatism with disastrous consequences for insurers. The volume of claims and the fact that many companies were not prepared for such volume at one time left them exposed to fraud by claimants and construction suppliers. We interviewed a disaster planning specialist for an insurance company that had substantial Hurricane Andrew claims. He said that the company not only overcompensated claims, but also had cars, cellular telephones, computers, and other property damaged and stolen from the temporary field claims centres set up by the company. 'Fraud is always a component of everything ... Fraud costs us almost as much as catastrophes do, if not more.' Following the Hurricane Andrew experience, the company established a permanent disaster claims unit that included 'catastrophe teams running up and down the [Atlantic] coast' following potentially disastrous storms, at the ready to provide an immediate and hopefully efficient claims service that would reduce fraud and other crime.

In such extreme circumstances, as well as in more routine cases, fraud is viewed as opportunistic. It is based on the view that since one has been paying premiums for a long period – which have swelled the investment coffers of the insurer and been distributed to others in the pool who have suffered losses – a payback of extra magnitude is justified in the event of a claim. The assumed sensibility of the insured in this regard was articulated by an executive of a property and casualty industry association:

[A responsible policyholder is] an individual who understands the contract started in June of one year and ended in June of another and provides a peace of mind for that duration. If you didn't use it you get exactly what you paid for. A person who doesn't have a sense of that, after twenty years of paying for something you can't hold and you can't see, and you can't show your neighbours, is a person who is going to come into being an opportunistic fraudster. He will inflate the claim, cover the deductible. He will turn the Timex into a Rolex, he will do something to get his money back because he sees it still as his money. Not a sentiment he has for anything else he purchases.

Claims adjusters and SIU investigators we interviewed took the view that a policyholder is not satisfied with paying thousands of dollars in premiums every year for various insurances, and expecting only peace of mind in return. When the opportunity arises for extra benefit from an unexpected loss, 'everybody does it' (Gabor 1994). A special claims investigator for an auto insurer observed in interview, 'People pay into this fund every year a lot of money, and they see it being abused by others, and so when it's their turn it's like they've hit the lottery. And it's like my turn to get the money, and it won't hurt anybody, the insurer has got lots of money.' An SIU officer for a workers' compensation insurer said that his company conducted focus group research to better appreciate the sensibilities of claimants. 'We were amazed, *every* respondent, they knew somebody that was defrauding us. So it has just become accepted. And the hue and cry doesn't go out because it is not coming out of your tax fund, it comes out of your employer.'

The view that even the most respectable insured will commit insurance fraud opportunistically is supported by our interviews with claimants. For example, we interviewed a claimant who was middle-aged, married with children, a university graduate, the operator of a small business from her home, a practising Christian, and block captain for her local chapter of Neighbourhood Watch. The claim was made after a major winter storm in which most properties in her area suffered damage as well as lack of electricity for an extended period. The claim was for rental of an electrical generator that she told the insurance company that she had hired, but in fact she had borrowed it gratis from a neighbour.

When asked to explain her fraudulent act, the interviewee referred to her relationship to the insurance company, situational opportunity, and social justice. She had a longstanding relationship with the insurer, which had insured her farm property and been part of the community for generations. This brand loyalty was related to her economic relationship with the insurer. She had been paying premiums for a long period without any claims and, as block captain of Neighbourhood Watch, had been especially vigilant about security and loss prevention on the property and in the community. A situational opportunity arose to make the false claim because she knew from her neighbours the insurer was not requiring receipts for this type of claim. All of these elements combined in what she regarded as a moral relationship of social justice. She originally made a claim for an item on the grounds of her property that was worth twice as much as the claim for the generator, but that claim was denied because the loss in question was not covered by the insurance contract. This rejected claim created a discrepancy between the company's sales story of trust, its promise to be there when needed, and its denial that the item was covered by the contract. She felt that she deserved something – regardless of the contract, and even if compensation for the generator was only half of what it would have been for the other item – because, while the insurer was facing substantial claims for the storm, it had a deep enough pocket to provide some compensation for what had been suffered more generally in the storm. Her moral neutralization (Sykes and Matza 1957) of the fraud, and her sense of moral economy, were strengthened further by the fact that she had also used the generator to help some of her neighbours, thereby saving the insurer from having to reimburse them for rentals. In concluding the interview she related that in matters of insurance and risk, and in life and security more generally, God is her tutor. 'If there is something that I've got to do, He'll give me a hint, and otherwise I'll muddle through the best I can. And I think He's given me fairly good directions.'

The detection of fraud in everyday claims adjusting is routine. In a vehicle hit-and-run insurance claims centre we studied, out of an average of sixty-eight claims each day, five were judged fraudulent based on material damage assessment. These claims were denied on the spot. However, an additional thirteen claims were believed to be fraudulent but not investigated further because the company decided it was more expedient to pay the claim. Cases involving personal injuries and disabilities are even more ambiguous and difficult to assess (see Ericson and Doyle, forthcoming: chap. 3). Studies of bodily injury claims arising from vehicle accidents in Massachusetts (Weisberg and Derrig 1991, 1992) judged 32 per cent ($n = 597$) of one sample and 47 per cent ($n = 1,154$) of another sample to have involved dishonesty.

In public pronouncements, fraud, like everything else in the insurance business, is treated as a known and quantifiable entity. An ICBC document declared that in 1996, fraud cost that corporation $308 million, which represented 15 per cent of all claims costs. An anti-fraud specialist used this same figure during an interview, and then commented that it 'is probably being conservative, because where I grew up everybody tries to screw us.' The visualization of insurance fraud facts is exemplified in the following industry association document:

> The crime of insurance fraud is growing in Canada; its economic impact is exceeded only by that of tax evasion. Property and casualty insurers in Canada believe that at least 10 per cent to 15 per cent of household, automobile and commercial insurance claims are fraudulent – either completely fraudulent or inflated. That's about $1.3 billion a year in fraudulent claims that must be paid from the premiums of all policyholders ... [I]nsurance fraud has costly secondary consequences; staged 'accidents' and deliberately set fires, medical examinations required because of false personal-injury claims and, of course, the wasting of costly and all-too-scarce police resources.

The claim that insurance fraud is growing is not substantiated with a one-time figure of fraudulent claims and their costs. Such one-time figures are in any event made up. They are made up to create a dramatic sense of rampant 'social inflation' that justifies anti-fraud enforcement as well as higher premiums and more stringent contract conditions. That is, they legitimate more governance for other insurance industry purposes beyond the control of fraud per se. Industry insiders themselves admit that these visualizations of social inflation are themselves fraudulent claims. Thus, in an editorial entitled 'The Mismeasure of Fraud,' written by the editor of *Canadian Insurance* magazine, the following assessment is given:

> Although we have seen in countless media the estimate of fraud in Canadian property and casualty insurance – 10–15 per cent of claims or roughly $1.3 billion – few actually know where this measurement came from or, for that matter, how accurate it is. My exhaustive research has turned up only one reference to this number. A judgment in a 1992 New Jersey Supreme Court case stated that 'insurance fraud is a problem of massive proportions that currently results in substantial and unnecessary costs to the general public in the form of increased rates. *In fact, approximately ten to fifteen per cent of all insurance claims involve fraud.*' No one really knows how much these particular judges knew about insurance fraud, but the estimate lives on. Since the Canadian Coalition Against Insurance Fraud clearly borrowed the name from its U.S. counterpart

(Coalition Against Insurance Fraud), it is quite likely that this number was also extrapolated to fit the Canadian environment. (Harris 1998: 5)

The Presumption of Fraud

The official discourse on insurance fraud is mainly intended for general public audiences of insured persons. The hope is to turn them into agents of fraud prevention who will refrain from exaggeration themselves and serve as informants on other fraudsters. Insurance claims adjusters and investigators need no such urging. Their working assumption is that everyone commits fraud. They experience fraud on an everyday basis, knowing that it is a moral risk institutionalized in the insurance relationship.

The former chief actuary of a property and casualty insurance company said in interview that this presumption of fraud provides insurers with a convenient justification for an aggressive approach to claims management. It is 'financially the most expedient view of the claim. I will squeeze, extract, cajole. I'll do anything I can to keep the costs of claim down. And I'll squeeze the customer, *victim*, in the process.' Reaction by the customer to this blaming the victim approach was anticipated in the infrastructure of claims centres operated by this insurer. At each claims centre, there were surveillance cameras covering the entrance and front desk, and panic buttons in the adjusters' offices.

The same insurer had basic training programs to ensure that its adjusters operated with a presumption of guilt. Training included watching a video in which a fraudster 'spills his guts' about how the company is being defrauded. The hope was that this video would play on the emotions of adjusters, making them feel embarrassed at being duped. An SIU investigator for the company complained that in spite of their basic training and experience, some adjusters continue to see too much good in people. Some adjusters, especially at the outset, 'couldn't find fraud files if their life depended on it ... They want to believe and trust everybody.' This SIU officer believed that the best thing that can happen to correct this problem is for the adjuster to be 'burnt' by a major fraud. She will then be converted to routine distrust. 'You can give excellent customer service, and be suspicious at the same time.' Our observations of several claims adjusters working for this company confirmed that they were indeed well socialized into the presumption of fraud. One adjuster said that this sensibility is crucial to job performance, namely, minimizing claims, and that his greatest job satisfaction is fraud detection. 'I like denying those claims. I feel satisfied when I have caught you in a lie.'

Given this attitude, it is not surprising that claimants frequently complain that they are treated as suspects. At the height of traumatic victimization, they are blamed for not having prevented the loss in the first place, and for exaggerating their suffering. A claims analyst for an auto insurer we studied said that research conducted by his company revealed,

> The number one complaint people have with the claims process is that they're being treated as a criminal. That essentially they're not being given the benefit of the doubt and that they're presumed guilty, and it's up to them to prove their innocence ... You have claims adjusters that want to make sure that there's no fraud involved, so they ask a bunch of questions that really put people off. Especially after they've had a crash, they need some support mechanism, not being interrogated ... People don't trust us because they feel we don't trust them ... When we're doing some research around new products – when we ask people, 'What are you looking for in an insurance company?' – well, the number one thing is trust. They want to feel that we can deliver on the promise. Because people are not actually buying a product, they're buying security and they want to make sure that if something happens to them that in fact we'll be there for them. It's the gap between the expectations and the actual realities of what happens when you actually have a claim that sets off the negative reactions toward the corporation ... [Trust means] you're not going to treat them as the guilty party. That you're going to take more or less the face value of whatever their story is. That this preoccupation of fault is not going to be the issue ... that the insurance company is going to be there to help you, not to question you.

Service and suspicion are always in tension. The trick of the trade is to operate with the assumption of fraud without making claimants feel so guilty that it puts them off. An SIU manager for an auto insurer said that he taught adjusters to give everyone good claims service at the outset because it is also a good interrogation technique. 'We're good to our good customers, and we're good to our bad customers. And the more nice we are, the more information we get ... [If fraud is detected] then you don't need their trust, they're gone!' A consultant on fraud control, who worked with insurers across North America, concurred that adjusters should always be kind to liars. 'The thing to do is just smile and be friendly all the way through, and before you cut the cheque, do the extra investigation and then present them with what you have ... "I'm sorry, we cannot pay this because ..."'

Interrogation with a smile begins with the initial call to the insurance company claims centre. Claims call centre operations we studied were structured to induce the claimant to talk openly, when they are most upset and therefore least likely to manipulate their account. We interviewed the primary consultant for an auto insurer's new claims call centre operation. He said that a key strategy was to have call centre operators sympathize for about five minutes before proceeding to data collection. This strategy was not based on genuine empathy, but rather its pay-off for improvement of loss ratios. 'And I can show you that's worth 15 per cent difference in paying claims, in costs, and your satisfaction goes way up ... enormous money maker.'

A 'service quality supervisor' for a general insurance company made the same point. He said that the initial call is crucial for establishing the factual baseline from which to assess subsequent accounts and additional and altered claims. The first call 'is where you get the most accurate information, immediately after a loss.' The vice-president of claims for the same company underscored the need for the call centre operator to obtain a detailed account from the claimant before she has an opportunity to talk to friends and associates and learn how to pad the claim. 'You've got to find out that it was a Sony 29-inch TV. Twelve hours later, how many people has that person already talked to? The guy at work or the next door neighbour has already said, "Oh yeah, tell them you had a 32-inch TV."' She said that if a certain sized TV is claimed, the adjuster can go out and inspect or check the size of the dust ring, or double-check with the store where the set was purchased. Again the key is for the call centre operator to 'take that extra time, even if it is ten minutes, and get details at that point ... These people have been violated. They want to spill it out.'

A property and casualty industry association official we interviewed said that his organization's research indicated that insurance fraud is first and foremost a crime of opportunity committed by older, educated, and higher income populations. Nevertheless, just as there is inequality in moral risk attributions during underwriting and in preventive security efforts, so too the presumption of fraud operates unevenly across classes of insured populations. Market segmentation, unpooling, and redlining are all constituted in part through presumptions of fraud.

A clear illustration of segmentation and unpooling through the presumption of fraud was provided by a claims analyst. He said that his company devised a sophisticated 'moral cost analysis' based on an assessment of the ratio of claims awards to personal income. The intention was to measure the 'claims award basis relative to need or desire and relative to opportunity ... One hundred bucks isn't anything to me ... Why would I lie for $100 bucks? I get more gain off of the moral cost to me, in a sense it's just self-image ... A street person down there, one hundred bucks is a bunch more.' Those who have high moral cost considerations, in other words, the wealthy, are naturally better moral risks. Those without moral costs, in other words, the poor, are obviously not worth the risk.

Market segmentation in the presumption of fraud was also evident in claims operations we observed. For example, an auto insurer had designated claims centres. All claimants were required to have damaged vehicles inspected at these centres, and they could also be interviewed by bodily injury adjusters. Claims personnel acknowledged considerable variation across claims centres in terms of the presumption of fraud and how clients were treated.

A material damage estimator who had worked in different centres and was now based in one that had a wealthy catchment area said that customers were treated very differently in his present context. 'We deal with a lot of people in the legal community and this type of thing, and people know their rights ... You can't attempt to bamboozle someone, they're well educated and they're well read and if they don't know themselves they know somebody who does know. So it's better to be up-front, straight-through, and people appreciate it more.' He gave as one indication of preferred treatment the fact that this centre authorized a higher percentage of new rather than used replacement parts in repairing vehicles. 'We have a lower usage of used parts than I think in any other claims centres. Partly we have newer cars coming in here, but partly again it's the clientele.'

An interviewee involved in a special anti-fraud investigation unit compared this centre to two others that had more fraud because their catchments were 'lower income, more ethnic population, East Indian, Vietnamese, or Asians.' He said these populations were especially likely to commit insurance fraud where they have breached the insurance contract in the crash and 'they don't have the monetary capacity to replace that vehicle if they don't try to cheat the system. They do the same thing with welfare or employment insurance ... double dip.' A colleague who had just moved to one of these centres as a bodily injury adjuster concurred. He attributed high levels of fraud to the East Indian population in particular. He also remarked that an indicator of the suspect catchment population was the fact that the claims centre itself had recently been victimized, with the theft of computers and automobiles.

Claims adjusters for companies that targeted wealthy policyholders noted similar differentiation in treatment. One such adjuster talked about the adjustment of working for an upmarket company compared to a middle market general insurer. The policyholders he now faced were 'very high end consumers ... millionaires ... lot of stress handling these types of claims because they're not your average Joe on the street, they're very business oriented. They know how to negotiate. They know when they're getting screwed.' His company had an explicit policy of treating claimants generously in order to continue the relationship and premium cashflow.

Market segmentation, unpooling, and redlining in the presumption of fraud is accomplished in an environment of considerable discretion among adjusters and SIU investigators. These claims operatives are permitted to use their situational intuitive judgments about moral risks of fraud, and to adjust actual payments to what the claimant can be made to accept.

A subcultural term for a claimant who commits fraud is 'red.' 'Red' can be read as 'communist,' as someone who is a source of social inflation and thus antithetical to the proper functioning of the insurance system. To ferret out reds, company manuals and training programs identify myriad 'red flag' indicators. While a multifactorial analysis of red flags can be computer-assisted, it also requires the experienced and keen eye of the claims operative. As expressed by an antifraud claims investigator for an auto insurer, 'I've never had a claim that is the same. It is like a snowflake really. Never two flakes the same.'

The view that no two cases are the same suggests that many elements can be interpreted as red flags and used to justify further investigations for evidence of fraud. As Baker and McElrath (1997: 147) found, property claims adjusters 'rely on their experience and intuition to assess whether the claims fit their expectations.' Similar to journalists (Ericson, Baranek, and Chan 1987; Ericson 1998) and the police (Shearing and Ericson 1991), adjusters use figurative language and a vocabulary of precedents to tell stories about how they make their decisions, rather than explicit rules of thumb. One adjuster told Baker and McElrath (1997: 147), "'I look at the car they drive, the other things in the house, the way they carry themselves." Other social attributes mentioned were the character of the home or neighbourhood, employment status, business or professional background, immigrant status ... perceived wealth, and what another adjuster called, "life-style that indicates a basic honesty."'

Our observations, interviews, and scrutiny of adjusters' manuals revealed eight interrelated sources of fraud red flag indicators. First, the insurance record of the claimant is a key indicator. If the claimant has ever been deemed fraudulent in the past, or merely subject to a previous fraud investigation, the case is treated with extra suspicion. A history of repeated claims of the same type – for example, repeated thefts of car stereo systems, especially if they are upgraded 'after-market' systems beyond what the manufacturer provided at the point of sale – is a ground for additional attention. Simultaneous claims for different types of insurance is another red flag. For example, a bodily injury claim following an auto accident may be investigated if there are simultaneous workers' compensation claims. There is also scrutiny of whether the claim was made immediately after insurance coverage was purchased. For example, a claims tracking specialist for an auto insurer said that, in a one-year period, he found sixty-two cases in which policyholders added extra comprehensive and/or collision coverage and then made a claim on the same day.

Second, the employment, income, and credit records of the claimant are all read as suggestive of fraud. An unemployed person or someone on welfare is judged to have a greater incentive to seek returns on the premiums she has been paying over the years, or to create liabilities for others who are insured. An adjuster for a multinational property and casualty insurer said that he routinely engaged in such socioeconomic stereotyping because, often enough, it pays to do so. 'The person is on welfare, they're claiming they slipped and fell. There's no witnesses. It may not necessarily be fair, but you might have some prejudices that you might put some red flags on that claim right away, which, I guess, is fine.'

Difficulties during employment are also scrutinized, for example, whether an accident is reported close to a date for changing jobs, or just before lay-offs or a business closure. Some interviewees said that their claim trends increased significantly with government tightening of employment insurance. An individual's peculiar reasons for not liking a job are also taken into consideration. For example, an auto insurer we studied developed a new red flag indicator system for its bodily injury adjusters. This system included a specific question about the claimant's job satisfaction in an effort to ferret out malingerers before they are given the opportunity to obtain greater satisfaction from insurance fraud.

Credit record is a related fraud indicator. We attended an industrywide conference on insurance fraud at which a panel discussed the virtues of credit checks. One panelist described a datamatching system linking credit to claims records and observed, 'If somebody is responsible in the handling of credit, they are going to be responsible behind the wheel.' He then advised, 'That should be a red flag, when somebody won't give you an authorization for credit.' He further advised that claimants should be told that credit checks are part of good claims service because they help to expedite claims processing by weeding out the 15 to 20 per cent of claims that are fraudulent. Claimants should be told, "If you score bad we'll investigate it, but the odds should be in your favour." So it's really not just a fraud detection tool, it's a customer service tool.'

Third, race and ethnicity were used as indicators of fraud. These ascribed statuses cannot be used officially to identify fraudulent claims, but they are used unofficially. For example, we interviewed a claims tracking specialist for an auto insurer who said that he routinely tracked the race and ethnicity of personal injury claimants. He said he did so because personal injury claims vary significantly by race and ethnicity, and the data are therefore useful as 'hit probabilities' that make a potential fraud investigation worthwhile.

Claims adjusters we observed and interviewed regularly referred to race and ethnicity as key red flag indicators. A claims manager for a multinational property and casualty insurer said that his staff starts with the name on the file as an indicator of ethnicity. Ethnicity in turn signifies the claims culture the person participates in. '[We have] adjusters who will look at an insured and say, "that kind of person with that kind of name is likely to do this." I guess a lot of that is based on their experience.' An auto insurance adjuster referred to an area in which he worked and observed, 'East Indian clientele are always looking to scam you.' A full-time fraud investigator with the same company identified other groups as too 'claims conscious ... the Persian community ... the Vietnamese ... there is just a high incidence of fraud within these two groups ... their population is very small, but every time they walk through the door they seem to be claiming for the world. It doesn't make sense ... they hang around with other bad people.'

The tendency to identify successive waves of new immigrants as especially prone to fraud is commonplace. A claims adjuster for a multinational property and casualty insurer stated that

in the 1970s it was the Polish, in the 1980s it was the Chinese, and now in the 1990s it's Russians ... You have certain groups coming over to Canada in floods, and now it seems the way the rush is, there's a lot of Russian claimants coming over ... One of the people I used to work with, he said they actually have a claims adjuster who is East Indian ... He would tell all of the adjusters, 'Never believe a word that these East Indians say because it's our culture. It's acceptable to ... stretch the truth. So if they tell you one thing, investigate it.' Is that stereotyping? Well, no, it's probably just smart. Well at least now we know about it ... There are certain groups of individuals in Europe, or say Russia, or whatever, they see Canada as the country that 'they just give us all this money.'

Some interviewees who advanced such arguments recognized that overrepresentation of fraud in certain racial and ethnic groups was related to structural aspects of political economy. For example, an SIU officer for a workers' compensation insurer said that she had particular problems with immigrant workers in the farming and fishing industries. She said that 'a lot' of these workers

are illiterate, they don't speak English, documents come in where we are unsure about where the cheques are going, we're unsure about the validity of the medical reports that come in ... Generally a particular ethnic background ... people that are in their fifties, sixties, seventies, they're illiterate, there's a labour contractor overseeing them, has an ethnic connotation as well ... People are submitting claims ... and in some cases because they are expected to do so [by the labour contractor] ... When the mail strike was on, we set up a process by which we would deliver cheques at the front [desk] here ... We were amazed at the number of cheques that didn't get picked up ... Well any cheques that don't get picked up when there's a mail strike become a potential lead on what's going on. And you start to cross-match addresses, postal codes, names, areas, offices, that sort of thing, and you'd be amazed at the variables that jump up.

Fourth, there may be incongruities in stories that claimants tell about their loss. In some cases, an incongruity is based on technical evidence.

For example, an auto insurance claimant might report the theft of equipment from her vehicle, but the vehicle's wiring is not compatible with the equipment reported to have been stolen. Incongruity in a story is also assessed in terms of changing accounts, or accounts that are based on socially anomalous circumstances. Thus, a common instruction in the manuals of auto insurance claims adjusters is to be on the lookout for parents or grandparents trying to cover for recalcitrant young drivers. One manual flagged the fact that 'A middle-aged housewife or grandparents would not, as a rule, drive a sports vehicle or "muscle car."' An auto claims estimator we interviewed described his experience with such a case. 'A sporty little car brought in by a grandmotherish kind of person ... It was towed in and I asked the owner of the car, an older woman, to come in and just back it up for me because I wanted to see the front, we had it placed against the wall. And she couldn't get it in reverse. She'd never driven a standard car. So obviously it wasn't her car. We suspected that, but it sort of proved it. It was her grandson's, who owed us thousands and thousands and thousands and he had umpteen [demerit] points on his licence ... a transferred vehicle.'

Further investigations of the claimant's story may be initiated simply on the basis of there having been several occupants in the accident vehicle, with each making a claim. A claims tracking analyst for auto insurance companies said that one study he conducted showed that while only one in six cars have passengers, the majority of bodily injury claims involve multiple claimants. The interviewee described the practice of 'squatting,' whereby the driver will look for a fancy car, drive in front of it, slam on the brakes, get rear-ended, and thereby set up the at-fault claim.

Possible self-injury is also examined carefully in other types of accident insurance. We interviewed a specialist in accidental death and dismemberment insurance who talked at length about red flags surrounding where precisely a finger is cut off. She referred to a case in which a doctor who was deeply in debt severed his own finger in an effort to collect a large benefit. However, the cut was suspicious because it was 'too clean' and a fraud determination was made. 'It has to be cut right here. Not if it is cut just a little bit up here, that's not a finger loss. Now to a consumer, they say, "That's not good, I've lost my finger." But it has to be cut here, OK, so we always have an issue of where the finger is cut ... And so you really have to watch that carefully, there could be a lot of abuse to this.'

Fifth, the claimant's demeanour in encounters with adjusters is under scrutiny for signs of deception. An auto insurance adjuster expressed his preference for 'when people have eye contact, looking at me, body posture, sitting up straight ... When I ask questions, and they tell me right away, and they don't have to think about it ... or ask your buddy or whatever, was that true or not.'

Sixth, fraud is deemed more likely when the claimant immediately starts to focus on claims benefits and how to manage them. Adjusters refer to this focus as 'claims consciousness.' A bodily injury adjuster for an auto insurer said that he is immediately suspicious when the claimant states at the outset that she will be off work for a long time. 'I think that's a sign too, because nobody knows.' Someone who 'doctor shops' is also seen as a potential malingerer. 'This doctor probably told them to get back to work, so I'll go find somebody else, that happens a lot too.'

Seventh, too little or too much cooperation in the claims investigation are read as signs of deception. A claimant who is reticent to answer questions is suspect. Some auto insurance adjusters we interviewed said that they suspect claimants whose native language is not English, and whose English suddenly deteriorates and native language accentuates. On the other hand, claimants who seem too cooperative are suspected of being gleeful about apparent loss because they will receive cash or replacement goods.

Eighth, the claimant who is too legalistic is treated as fraudulent, at least in the sense of trying to extract more than she deserves from the claims process. A manager for a multinational property and casualty insurer observed, 'The type of person that is a fraudulent claimant, a lot of times are represented by counsel.' One of his adjusters told us that legalese is an immediate red flag. 'If they go to a lawyer, you've got somebody who's got dollar signs on their mind. Or they've been approached by a lawyer right away ... [which happens] all the time. There are a lot of lawyers out there and they're hungry for business.'

Surveillance

The investigation of insurance claims fraud is based on a number of linked surveillance mechanisms, including special investigation units, private investigators, informants, and data systems.

Special investigation units (SIUs) are the private police forces of insurance companies. They have expanded rapidly in the past fifteen years, as premium revenues have become less stable in highly competitive market conditions and the strategy has arisen to secure loss ratios by a crackdown on claims. We attended a conference of the National Insurance Crime Bureau (NICB) in the United States. Executives of that organization reported that in 1993, only 33 per cent of insurance companies had SIUs. By 1998, 80 per cent had SIUs. This sharp increase was in part related to the fact that some states began to legislatively mandate SIUs. In some jurisdictions, regulators required insurance companies to have an SIU capacity that accorded with the level of premiums they collected. One large company was identified as having 340 full-time fraud investigators in 1992. By 1998 the number had risen to 1,200, and the company was operating its own SIU training academy.

Canadian-based insurance companies have also expanded their SIUs over the same period, especially with respect to auto insurance fraud. The CEO of a general insurance company said in interview that auto insurance fraud - especially personal injury rings – was 'beyond control,' and that his company was following others in augmenting its SIU. He had just hired a former detective of a public police force to head up the effort. 'She's only been with us two months and already she's more than paid her salary.'

Provincial government auto insurers in Canada have also expanded their SIUs. One such organization we studied had grown to fifty investigators and six managers by the late 1990s, all of whom were former public police officers. It developed a number of subsidiary units, including one dedicated to bodily injury fraud, one dedicated to material damage fraud, and one that used a dataveillance system to identify suspects for special investigation. A bodily injury investigator and a material damage investigator were assigned to each of its decentralized claims centres to investigate fraudulent files identified by adjusters.

SIU officers are heavily dependent on adjusters to detect fraud initially, and to feed them relevant information. The manager of an auto insurer's SIU said in interview that 90 to 95 per cent of the unit's cases were based on referrals from claims adjusters. Similarly, the vice-president in charge of claims for a general insurance company said in interview that his company's recent effort to move from just 'processing claims' to a crackdown on fraud involved not only expansion of the SIU but also better training and auditing of adjusters as agents of surveillance. 'You don't even know fraud is happening if you are just "processing" claims ... SIU units are useless unless they are getting the leads from the front-end.'

Private investigation companies are also engaged to conduct surveillance for insurance fraud. One advantage of private investigators is their extensive networking with the public police. For example, a management consulting firm hired a dozen commercial crime specialists away from the public police, some of whom specialized in insurance fraud. One of these private investigators explained in interview how his company's police networking was valuable to insurers regarding auto fraud/theft rings:

> There are so many car thefts and it's very difficult to get the police to say that your car theft is more important than the next one. So a lot of times what will happen is the companies will engage us and we'll work as a liaison between the police and the insurance investigators and the car company and whoever else may be interested ... If the [insurance] investigator wants something done, say, with the Dallas police department, well he's got to find some contact. Whereas all we have to do is pick up the phone and call our Dallas office and either have someone from the Dallas police, or someone from the FBI or something working there, so we could get this thing done overnight.

Another advantage of private investigators is their connection with informants in the criminal underworld. The same interviewee had worked extensively in undercover investigations as a public police officer, and he brought his informant contacts as a saleable commodity to his private sector employer. 'I spent my entire adult life in the company of criminals and so I understand them.'

A third advantage is the fact that, compared to public police, private investigators working on behalf of insurance companies do not have to be concerned about much legal due process. An investigator for another management consulting company described the freedom of the private insurance investigator compared to the public police officer:

> When you are investigating as a police officer, you have to be concerned of other persons' rights under the Charter [Canadian Charter of Rights and Freedoms] ... When I'm a private investigator for an insurance corporation ... I'm saying, 'You're the policyholder, I'm the company. Either we talk or we don't settle. Your choice.' ... *I* have the right to remain silent and they certainly do not. *I* have the right not to pay them ... [If the claimant says] 'I want to see a lawyer,' *I* say, 'You're not going to see any lawyers.

You're going to talk to us this morning. This is our policy. You want any possibilities of being paid, let's talk.'

We interviewed a private investigator for another management consultant company who was likewise a former commercial crime detective with a public police force. He concurred that lack of due process is a central feature of what he sells to insurance company clients, compared to what he could do as a public police officer. 'Although you do have a lot of legal authority in the police, you also have your hands tied in a lot of respects ... When I go to interview someone, I don't have to caution them.' He said that his public police experience and networks gave him 'influence over the police' in making deals, because he could do things they could not, and therefore solve cases for them. He offered the example of an informant being involved in criminal activity, but protected from prosecution because of the information he was supplying on a car fraud/theft ring. 'He was a car thief and I didn't want to use the evidence against him at a later time, I was just trying to get the other guy ... [and] recover the cars. I made the argument with his lawyers ... [that] I'm not cautioning your client during this interview, therefore whatever he says is completely no use in a criminal court and can't be used against him ... that's the difference between the private police and the regular police.'

This interviewee underscored his point by describing a claims investigation of six containers that had been shipped to the Caribbean and allegedly destroyed by arson after their arrival. He immediately flew to the scene in the Caribbean, where he discovered that the containers were still in customs bond in a warehouse. He was able to interview a few people surreptitiously without legal niceties, and quickly confirmed that the claim was fraudulent. This instance of summary justice was complete when the insurance company immediately denied the claim.

It's very, very rare that clients want the police involved in things for whatever reasons. The problem with insurance fraud is that almost everybody does it ... The difference between us and the police ... they [the insurance company client] called here at 4:00 in the afternoon, 9:00 p.m. I was on the plane to the Caribbean Islands. No fooling around, assigned the case and you're gone ... If it's local police, it's not going to happen. If it's the Royal Canadian Mounted Police, it better be a big case. And they're not going to get on the plane and fly down because it's a big machine, the Mounted

Police, and they need permission. And also, foreign police officers don't go and do investigations in foreign countries without going through external affairs and embassies and that, because peoples' noses get out of line. But people like us, that's no big deal, we just go down.

This case example illustrates that relative inefficiency is one reason why the public police are not turned to more often. Another reason is the preference for private case settlement. Private settlement avoids unwanted publicity about the insurance company's own procedural propriety. Insurers manage their own system of summary justice in which they variously tolerate fraud or enforce through the insurance contract. The use of private investigators distances insurers somewhat from their relationship with the policyholder. If there are problems with a particular investigation, responsibility can be displaced to the investigator and his firm. The private investigation contract can also be cancelled.

We attended an insurance industry 'issues' conference organized by the multinational management consultant firm, KPMG. Several speakers gave testimony to public police inefficiency in insurance fraud investigations, and to the fact that the public police take a 'police yourself' view of this problem. A former RCMP commercial crime officer turned private investigator said that he learned this police view twenty years ago as a novice constable. He wanted to prosecute a case in which he discovered that a suspect had inflated a household burglary claim, but his sergeant told him to forget it because 'nobody cares about insurance fraud.' The former commissioner of the RCMP, now a commercial crime unit head for KPMG, gave testimony to the RCMP as a cumbersome, expensive, and outmoded bureaucracy. 'Imagine how that kind of structure has outlived its usefulness, for all intents and purposes, in business, where time and money really count. And you have to get to the bottom line as quickly as you can, because if you don't, your competitors are going to whip you.' He referred to a KPMG survey indicating that one-half of Canada's largest corporations were dissatisfied with the public police response to fraud. As a former police executive, he said that, for their part, the public police take the view that 'Royal Bank of Canada just declared a one billion dollar profit, they can afford to cover their losses.'

Private investigation firms function as informants to insurance companies. It is not always the case that the insurance company takes the initiative in suspecting fraud and then contracts with the private investigation firm. Private investigation firms produce their own knowledge of fraud as a commodity, and then sell it to insurers as useful to their loss ratio security. An investigator employed by a multinational management consulting firm said that his company specialized in selling the fraud commodity. 'We track criminals, guys who are pulling frauds. And let's say that one of these criminals is going to get in bed with [your insurance company] ... We would call you up and say, "Do you want to buy a report on him? We will tell you what he is all about." ... Because we have informants that tell us ... Sometimes we'll just give the information with the hope of getting an engagement at a later time ... If you're in business, a firm of our stature comes to you and says that, you pay attention! ... It's a real career limiter to let these kinds of things happen.'

To this point, we have discussed more elite private investigation operations with respect to insurance fraud. Another segment of the private investigation industry is populated by low-skilled, low-paid operatives who spend long hours trying to capture disability claimants on camera doing things that seem to belie their claim. For example, according to Lowther (1996), in 1995 ICBC used private investigators on 4,400 disability surveillance assignments, at a cost of $8 million. This custom accounted for the livelihood of about 80 per cent ($n = 600$) of registered private investigators in the province. We interviewed an SIU manager for an auto insurer who explained why photo surveillance was always contracted out to private investigators:

[It is] a market benefit to us in that the skills required to be a private investigator are quite a bit lower than to become an SIU officer and the marketplace is flooded with private investigators, so on a market basis their rates are quite competitive. Some of them are using a [fee system] ... if we can't get this guy on tape or whatever, there's no charge ... In a number of cases, we get two hours for one. They can bill us for ten hours, they'll put in twenty to try and get that ten because they're looking for repeat business. They know if they're not successful, the adjuster is just as likely to try another private investigator the next time, who perhaps has a better way of videotaping a subject.

Due process constraints are often absent in competitive environments of private investigation companies trying to secure more contracts. Reported cases of illegal entry to premises, collecting information extraneous to investigations, and collecting for other investigative purposes beyond detection of disability claims fraud have been commonplace (Lowther 1996). Guidelines developed by insurers for contracting with private investigators illustrate some of these concerns. For example, an auto insurer we studied had guidelines with respect to procedural propriety in investigations, including:

- Do not induce a person who is being investigated to engage in an activity in which that person would not otherwise be disposed to engage.
- Do not alarm claimants or anyone else, nor give them reasonable cause for apprehension for public safety and security.
- Surveillance is authorized only:
  - When conducted from a public vantage point
  - In circumstances where the person being investigated is not in a position where he or she would have a reasonable expectation of privacy.

A claims fraud specialist for this insurer said that the company had experienced problems with private investigators, which he attributed to low standards and poor ethics in that industry rather than competitive and sometimes ruthless contracting practices to save insurers money. 'The problem is that we don't want them investigating our claims when using practices that might end up getting us on the front page of the newspaper ... Now if there is any sort of behaviour that goes against what we've agreed to them in writing when they come aboard to work for us, we just terminate the relationship.' The company also required private investigators to consent to being continuously surveilled themselves. For example, each contracting private investigator had to sign a consent form giving the insurance company permission to check the investigator on databases, criminal record systems, and other data systems 'over which the company has custody or control or which the company has DIRECT authority to access ... I further authorize that any and all such searches and disclosures may be periodically made by the police and at the discretion of the insurance company for the purposes mentioned in the paragraph above.'

Insurance fraud investigators rely on informants to augment their surveillance web. A bodily injury adjuster for one insurance company we studied said that 14 per cent of his unit's caseload derived from informant tips. A brochure produced by the ICBC urges everyone to provide information about fraudsters in their midst. It assures that the informant is not an isolated individual, but rather among eighty callers each week to the corporation's tip line. It also assures that the effort pays off, as 10 per cent of tips result in either denial of a claim or recovery of some benefits already given.

Informant tip lines are not only a means for generating cases to investigate, but also a vehicle for the legitimation of the informant system. The insured population is called upon to protect the integrity of the risk pool. The appeal is to the common pool as commonwealth, ignoring the unpooling that often leads the insurance poor to fraud as a way of covering the steep premiums they have been paying. Thus the aforementioned brochure to recruit informants is titled, 'Fraudulent ICBC Claims Hit You in the Pocketbook.' It tells the prospective informant that anywhere from $160 million to $320 million in annual premiums are consumed by fraudulent claims. While there is no bounty for tracking down a fraudster, the prospective informant is told that the reward derives from the fact 'insurance fraud costs us and that costs you. If we can put a stop to this kind of fraud, we all win.'

Some insurers do not operate their own public tip lines, but rely on Crime Stoppers to generate cases (Carrière and Ericson 1989; Lippert 2002). A workers' compensation insurer we studied worked with Crime Stoppers and, according to an SIU officer we interviewed, received forty to fifty tips each month, some through Crime Stoppers, others provided directly to the SIU. The Canadian Coalition Against Insurance Fraud partnered with Crime Stoppers as part of its crackdown on insurance fraud. The campaign included informant recruitment posters that criminalize insurance fraud, although insurance fraud is very rarely prosecuted criminally. One poster has 'They Cheat You Pay' at the top, and 'Call Crime Stoppers and Stop Insurance Fraud' at the bottom, with a hand holding a telephone in the middle. The following appeal to the integrity of the risk pool is also made: 'When someone makes a false or exaggerated insurance claim, your insurance costs go up. Cheating on an insurance claim is fraud. And that's a crime. If someone you know is committing fraud on their home, car or business insurance policy, you can report it to Crime Stoppers. If your tip helps the police or your insurance company catch an insurance fraud, you may be eligible for a cash reward. And your call will remain completely anonymous. *Stop paying for a crime you didn't commit.*'

Another poster pictures an ominous bar and heavy doors to a penitentiary, with 'Slam the Door on Insurance Fraud' at the top and 'Insurance Fraud is a Crime Call Crime Stoppers' at the bottom. The message is not only that insurance fraud is a criminal offence, but also that imprisonment is the punishment. The appeal is to the punitive sensibilities of prospective informants, even though prison sentences for insurance fraud are extremely rare.

Informants are also cultivated by an insurance company's SIU. We interviewed a manager of an auto insurance company's SIU who said that, as former police officers, all of his investigators had 'informants that they've cultivated over the years in the police business.' In addition, there was a confidential source payment system to sponsor 'a few individuals that are especially active in trying to develop sources and information, or where it's a theft or a chop shop or items of that nature.'

Whether influenced by informant recruitment strategies, or simply gleeful that they can turn someone in as an act of good insurance company citizenship, some individuals become proactive insurance fraud investigators on their own initiative. An auto insurance SIU officer described a case in which such an informant came forward with unique evidence. The informant's hobby was to use a scanner to tap cell telephone conversations. While engaging in this vicarious pleasure, he overheard a woman conspiring to report falsely to an adjuster that she was employed by her uncle's firm. The informant taped this conversation and gave the tape to the insurance company. SIU officers waited until the woman signed all of the claims forms indicating her false employment status, then proceeded against her.

Informants are also produced during the course of an investigation, in much the same way that police detectives use threats, or promises of leniency, to induce co-suspects to inform on each other (Ericson 1993). An auto insurance SIU officer said in interview that this was a common method used in auto injury ring cases. For example, he described a case in which a woman involved in staging an accident eventually turned informant and revealed her co-conspirators' methods for faking the accident. A truck without occupants was pushed down a hill and into thick bushes. 'It cost us thousands of dollars to "rescue" these people. And to create their injuries, one guy got a rock and started hitting his girlfriend in the back, and her kidneys. These people got severe injuries from their own selves. One guy hit himself in his head until he detached the retina in his eye. And then he bit the girl's lip, and he bit it right through so she needed stitches.'

Claims service providers are another source of information routinely cultivated by both SIU officers and adjusters. Auto insurance claims operatives develop relations with police traffic accident investigators, tow truck drivers, ambulance crews, and body shop staff to have them watch for signs of fraud. An adjuster told us in interview that good relations turn these people into claims agents. For example, a body shop manager recently called to say, 'I towed it out of here because I wouldn't inflate the bill for him.'

Surveillance is also organized through computer-based data systems. Red flags of suspicious claimants are automated, forming a collage of shades from pink to ruby. We studied an automated claims investigation system developed by an auto insurer. The monitoring of the claimant begins at the instant that she telephones the claims centre to report her loss. Based on a 'graphical user interface,' the telephone claims centre, prompted by the caller's driver's licence number or vehicle licence number, immediately provides information about the claimant: whether she is insured, the type of coverage, previous claims, whether other parties have called the centre about the same accident, and whether a more intensive examination of the claim through an algorithm system is likely to save money. The telephone number of where the claimant is calling from is also recorded in case she becomes abusive. An adjuster based in the telephone claims centre explained how the system immediately identifies claimants who are more ruby than pink:

[It flags those] who have a poor history with us for payment of claims, for criminal activity, all kinds of different things. [SIU] can enter a 'hard match' on that individual file. They will flag that file ... When that particular customer calls us with a claim, and they offer their licence number ... the system will do a search automatically against that person in the customer database ... And what happens to that adjuster is they go 'enter' and 'enter' doesn't work because the system locks. It says this is a 'hard match,' this customer is not a desirable customer, please refer to a special investigations unit right away ... 'Soft matches' too, which is where the system won't lock up, but it'll show a flag and this agent can go and verify because it's matching against the names, so this is the John Smith that is in fact the bad person ... [It is all aimed] to save money on those ones that are fraudulent potentially.

We attended a conference for SIU investigators in the United States at which dataveillance companies made presentations on 'fraud recognition for the future.' A partnership was formed among three organizations: the National Insurance Crime Bureau provided data on prosecuted fraud cases, as well as a valid claim data pool for comparison; a credit information company provided credit data; and a third company offered modelling technology. The modelling technology company said that its models were used to review about half of all credit card transactions in the United States. It had been working with the credit data company for several years to develop use of credit bureau data by the insurance industry for both underwriting and claims processes.

A spokesperson for the credit data agency said that the partners were developing an online fraud score system, which he referred to as a 'fraudulent analysis machine.' He told the assembled SIU investigators that this system provides simultaneous access to insurance, credit, and other records on the claimant. It can use this information to predict a given individual's contribution to property and casualty loss ratio security. It can also streamline the case selection process for SIU investigators. Most cases typically rest in the claims department for an extended period before they are referred to the SIU, and in the interim they become cold cases from an investigative viewpoint. The new system promises to identify hot cases for instant referral. It also promises to weed out SIU referrals that lack substance, and that are based on subjective and discriminatory criteria. It further promises to select out both cases 'dumped' on the SIU by an adjuster who does not get along with the claimant and surveillance orders from adjusters that are unnecessary and may constitute harassment. To underscore this last point, the presenter related a story about an innocent claimant who was put under surveillance. After a period in which he was not found doing anything untoward, the investigator regressed to entrapment methods. The claimant complained to the police about being stalked, and still without relief, committed suicide. The presenter then peered into the black box of the fraud differentiation machine. 'Our system is broken down into 300-plus variables that look at delinquency, bankruptcy, inquiries, mortgage history etc. ... We may have forty variables just on mortgages. Have you ever been late? How many times over thirty days? How many times over sixty days? How many times over ninety days? Those are *behavioural*. That's why we're using those. They've been proven to be predictive in the insurance industry.'

The system segments insured populations into subgroups, with a percentage score for their fraud potential. For example, a particular sub-group may be identified as making fraudulent claims 80 per cent of the time. This fraud score is 'not based on biases, it's based on statistical backing and known outcomes.' The modelling company representative described the technology as follows:

> It comes out of the computer chess world ... Our guys were the world computer chess champions ... Computer chess is an enormous database ... of moves waiting to happen. Just like that big basement of data you have in your company. What you are trying to do is find the best pattern of play across the board, combination of moves, just like combination of things happening in a claim, to get a mate. And you're looking for subtle combinations ... They can be combinations of weak variables and strong variables: two pawns and a rook are going to wipe out a queen on the chess board, just like a couple of subtle things going on in the claim that you guys are able to look at and say, 'Aha, I've got it!' ... Half of our credit card transactions that happen every day in this country go through our model for fraud detection, real time. I mean when you swipe your card our fraud models are reviewing that transaction and making a decision ... What we are looking for are the spending patterns in that case. In the insurance data we're looking for the claims patterns.

In chapter 7, we analysed moral risk market segmentation practices for the selling of insurance. The modelling technology company representative made it clear that his device for the deselection of fraudulent claimants was based on a parallel consumer segmentation model. He compared the sorting of fraudulent claims to a study of yogurt consumption by the Nielson rating agency. 'Who is really eating yogurt? The people in the far end of the distribution, this is Pareto's law. Ninety per cent of your problem really exists with 10 per cent of your customers. So you're looking for the tails and they are just like fraud.' He added that the system can 'peel our data like an onion,' with each layer offering a subset. In the case of yogurt, it is heavier eaters who differ from the previous layer. In the case of fraudulent claimants, it is the increasingly fraudulent until one gets to the rotten core. To bring home his point he drew another market segmentation analogy: marketing models differentiate between how 'the ladies who are exercising get leotards, and the guys on the couch get ex-lax. So in this instance, we are going to find the very same things in your claims data.' He then discussed how data on consumption of myriad consumer products would be incorporated into the insurance product fraudulent analysis machine:

We swim in the big data pool ... Maybe consumer data about how much Cheese Whiz someone eats is indicative. Maybe their entertainment patterns are useful. What movies do they watch? ... We built a movie recommendation system. Go to a video store and it will tell you what movies to check out, based on your taste. You just rate a few movies and pretty quickly it will come back and say, 'You'd probably like to see Humphrey Bogart in *Casablanca*.' But that data is unbelievably predictive ... We can tell you what type of car somebody is going to drive, and what colour, with frightening accuracy ... So that is the sort of data that we in the future would like to drag into this process. And it is out there. There's data that gets sucked down on everybody. Every time you use your credit card, and the thing goes beep at the scanner, we've got something on you ... [Our credit data system offers a] drag them through the coals approach.

The other link in this datamatching system is NICB data on fraud convictions, called 'The Terminator.' This appellation drew obvious reference to the Arnold Schwarzenegger film of the same name, associating its mechanical nature, total power, and ability to achieve 'justice' without bother of due process.

Insurers use a variety of other dataveillance technologies to address particular types of fraud. A simple claims frequency analysis can reveal patterns for further investigation. For example, we interviewed a claims fraud data analyst for an auto insurer who said that he analysed claims by telephone numbers, used to call the claims centre. Multiple claims from the same telephone number are referred to the company's SIU. He also used cluster analyses to identify names, addresses, telephone numbers, and characteristics of multiple claimants involved in the same vehicle accident, with the intention of identifying suspected staged accidents and fraudulent bodily injury claims.

The same company operated a range of other datamatching systems on clients. Some of these systems were specific to particular sources of fraudulent claims. For example, there was a perceived problem with 'fixers' for new immigrants. In the words of a claims fraud data analyst, new immigrants often use a fixer who 'helps you with a job, helps you get your driver's licence, helps you with insurance and so on ... A variety of those things that are commonly done we regard as fraud.' The interviewee explained that the triggering information was data from the province's driver licensing system. The driver licensing system allowed translators to help new immigrants without facility in English to obtain a licence:

The average person taking a [first driving] test ... almost 60 per cent fail-ure rates on this test. There are translators [whose clients] have 98 per cent pass rates and take an average of seven minutes. I think they're cheating, I do not believe those numbers. We pull in the claims history on all those people. We're going to see if we see the same people on multiple sides of the accident. We're going to see if they're involved with the same sales broker selling insurance. We're going to exchange some of their names with other government service agencies ... Translators' names ... I get those, I get the licence, I find the accidents. I run these back, start looping back and doing patterns and start building networks. And then after we've got them, then we pull files, and I'd have, you know, a full room like this with files and spend a week reading. At the end of the week we'd know who's doing what. We know how it is being run, how it was being set up, then surveillance would go out ... This last year was the first time this company ever did that. They had one [detected case] about eight years ago. Now every couple of months a major group is getting busted.

We interviewed a fraudulent claims data analyst for a provincial government auto insurer who undertook 'vulnerability assessments.' He compared specific claims costs to those experienced by other insur-ers as a way of revealing outliers and therefore potential sources of sys-tematic fraud. He said that his corporation was 500 per cent above the industry average on auto glass expenditures, 1,000 per cent above on brain trauma claims, and the 'North American champion' in whiplash claims.

Tolerance

While the surveillance system scans incessantly for fraud, there is a great deal of tolerance even when fraud is detected. Fraud is tolerated in the context of four related considerations. First, it is often difficult to substantiate evidence of fraud that meets criminal or even civil law standards of proof. Second, because of the difficulty in developing suf-ficient legal evidence of fraud, and the cost in doing so, it is more effi-cient to make a 'nuisance payment' that closes the claims file. The indemnity principle is sacrificed to expedience. Moreover, the claim-ant's insurance contract can be altered after the claim to transfer more of the risk to her (through higher deductibles, lower limits, or exclu-sions), and premiums can be raised to recover the loss over time. Nui-sance payments are systematized in some contexts of auto insurance

claims. For example, body shops routinely report that what was designated as claimable damage is actually old damage, but the insurer
decides the cost of sending out an estimator to investigate further is
not worth it. Claimants who have their stolen vehicle returned frequently use the opportunity to repair old damage. A fraud investigator
for an auto insurer described this scenario, and how claimants are
dealt with when confronted with the fraud:

> Whenever someone gets a car stolen, at that point it is an opportunity for
> that person to get a lot of little things fixed on the car that were damaged
> already. And if we can't prove it was not damaged before, we give them
> the benefit of the doubt. So we grind our teeth, bite our tongue, and say
> OK we'll fix it. It is like a house insurance policy. You get broken into,
> your TV gets stolen, VCR gets stolen. Might as well claim the golf clubs at
> the same time because it is costing you $500 [deductible] anyway – golf
> clubs that you never had ... [When a claim is denied on suspicion of fraud]
> we sell it to them, we give them a way out ... If you tell us that you were
> involved with this, that you made a mistake, we will just leave it at that.
> We won't process your claim, but you just won't have a claim. We won't
> charge you with anything ... When we are busy we are trying to get clo-
> sures ... It is time management. Do I look, or don't I go? Nah, I'm too busy.
> I'll just sit on my butt and do another claim. Pay it.

This interviewee indicated that such an approach may be taken even
when the fraud is more substantial. He told the story of a young university student who was involved in a single-vehicle accident with his
motorcycle. Following the accident, he dumped the motorcycle into
water off of a local marina, then claimed that it had been stolen. Investigation of the recovered vehicle indicated that the ignition had not
been tampered with, and the claimant was brought in for SIU interrogation.

> [I said] 'You are a young kid, you are a college student ... you have a
> bright future ... you don't want to make a mistake that will affect your
> future. Based on what we have here, it appears your bike was not stolen.
> It was involved in an accident, it was dumped because it was involved in
> an accident. It was all smashed up.' And then at that point he just put his
> hand to his face and then he admitted to us, 'Yeah, I dumped it.' ... It says
> to us we really did our job at that point ... When you get evidence for
> criminal charges you have to be very careful ... Give them a Charter warn-

ing ... They get nervous, 'Why is he warning me about my rights?' Then he is not going to help me as much. And we work on information. And when we are busy, we are trying to get closures. If we didn't give him the warning ... some of it would get thrown out of court ... We need him to get the conviction, you know what I mean? ... And we could be spending $2,000 on defence counsel, and the judge says, 'Pay the claim.' Like this case, we achieved our same goal without doing that.

Third-party liability insurance is another field in which nuisance payments are common even when the stakes are higher. An accounts manager for a multinational insurer in this field said that he regularly made nuisance payments to fraudulent claimants in exchange for withdrawal of their claim. Some claimants are 'making a fraudulent claim and we pay them off a small amount to make them go away. Because if it goes to court or anything like that, it's going to cost us more anyway, we won't get our money back.' He offered the example of a claimant who said that he had choked on a toothpick in a box of cereal. The insurer did not view this claim as credible, but the claimant hired lawyers and persisted. The insurer then offered to pay the claimant's legal costs and other expenses to that point. If he refused this offer, the insurer threatened to bring a countersuit against the claimant's daughter, alleging that she had put the toothpick in the cereal box.

Third, in following the marketing trend of relationship management (see chapter 7), insurers may try to maintain good relations with policyholders even when they have been defrauded. Policyholders who have falsified their claim will nevertheless continue to provide premium revenue over time. They may also be customers in other lines of insurance that are especially valuable, leading the insurer to overlook a particular instance of a fraudulent claim. A former senior vice-president of a multinational insurance company said in interview that he preferred to hire in-house adjusters, rather than rely on independents, because they are more sensitive to relationship management when making their judgments about claims. He said that in-house adjusters are socialized into 'your culture, your philosophy,' where 'service is the name of the game.' They know how to minimize or deny a claim more diplomatically, including those that entail fraud. They also know when to pay claims to avoid conflict, always half-watching in terms of the future premium revenue the claimant represents.

There is substantial variation across market segments. A substandard market customer who pads a claim is less likely to be maintained as a policyholder than a superstandard customer. We studied a company that operated exclusively in the superstandard property and casualty market. Part of its marketing strategy was to offer a superior claims service, which included in-house adjusters with a demeanour of professionalism, and a 'no-hassle' replacement of expensive losses. A claims manager for this company said that this approach was possible because of high premiums and relationship management associated with the continued generation of those premiums. Taking claimants at face value not only justifies the higher face value of insurance policies, but hopefully a view among claimants that

> 'Maybe I don't need to over-inflate that claim, or maybe insurance companies aren't as bad as I thought they were.' And that's another way of combatting fraud. I mean obviously we don't intend to pay anything more than we have to, but there are sometimes [we do] ... When people discover that you're not going to nickel and dime them to death, they tend not to do it to you. But ultimately it comes down to the relationship, or the conversation between two individuals. How do you feel about the person you're talking to? ... I can't recall the last personal complaint call I got from anybody, but again it's us, we don't get complaints. I mean, where I used to work before, we used to get complaints because we wrote a lot of automobiles and that's where most of the complaints come from. I used to get a complaint a day, that was not abnormal. You're dealing with people screaming at you constantly. It kind of wears you down. This is a much nicer place to work. You don't get screamed at.

An additional aspect of fraud tolerance as part of relationship management is the possibility that an allegation might prove wrong. Given the equivocality of definitions of fraud and associated evidence problems, allegations of fraud may be deemed false or unfair.

Fourth, there are specific contexts with particular types of insurance that make too much policing of fraud intolerable for the smooth flow of social and economic relations. For example, workers' compensation insurers face sensitive labour and management issues that make them reticent to police fraud too heavily. An executive of a workers' compensation insurer made this point in interview. He said that while an auto insurer might be successful in initiating an enforcement crackdown on disability fraud through widespread publicity and advertising campaigns, he was restricted from doing so. 'Labour would consider it an affront to suggest that workers would be defrauding the system. They do not believe that moral hazard is a significant issue ... and that before you deal with that you should deal with [employers'] claims suppression, for instance.'

These four components of tolerance combine to institutionalize both fraud and nuisance payments in the insurance relationship. For insurers, the question becomes how much fraud is consistent with the smooth flow of business and the protection of loss ratio security.

The claims process involves the micro-negotiation of political economy and fiscal responsibility. The insurance claims adjuster sets up the negotiation by taking a minimalist position to limit the claims payment. This minimalist position is partly based on the knowledge that fraud is institutionalized in the relationship. The assumption is that first, the claimant presents an inflated claim knowing that the adjuster will try to minimalize it. Second, the claimant knows that if she persists to a reasonable degree, she may be offered a nuisance payment because the adjuster needs to close the file efficiently. Third, if she is reasonable in finessing her claim, the claimant may be able to garner extra compensation for her reasonableness.

The adjuster's starting position in claims settlement varies considerably by the field of insurance, the type of claim, and the market segment of the claimant. However, governed by loss ratio auditing, quotas, and penalties for exceeding specified claims levels, adjusters must try to draw the line for negotiation at minimal levels. A simple and routine example is the effort to limit auto rentals while a claimant's own auto is missing after a theft or is being repaired. In our observations, some adjusters would not inform policyholders of their entitlements in this regard, and if a claimant raised the matter they would try to argue that it was not a legitimate claim in the circumstances. We interviewed a claims service quality supervisor for a major auto insurance company who said that his adjusters were required to discourage auto rental claims even when they were legitimate under the contract terms. The policy was to limit such claims to situations where the damaged vehicle cannot be driven and there is no alternative transportation available. 'You don't jump at it ... If they say, "My wife picked me up in the other car," they probably don't need a rental.' Here the deception is on the part of the adjuster, on instructions from the company.

More is at stake in disability claims faced by vehicle, workers' compensation, employee benefit, and accidental death and dismemberment insurers. As we document more extensively elsewhere (Ericson and Doyle forthcoming: chap. 3), disability insurers engage in a range of fraud-limiting surveillance and work-hardening strategies. A former adjuster for an auto insurer said that his company's practice was to 'deny until they hire a lawyer. So there's no question they were entitled to these benefits, it's just deny them and hope they go away.' This ex-adjuster was now a personal injury lawyer, and he said his previous employment made him aware of the systematic practices through which insurers try to minimize claims. For example, he was working on a case in which a quadraplegic was denied a claim. A private insurer with whom she had an accidental death and dismemberment policy and the provincial government auto insurer both denied the claim on the grounds that her total disability was not caused by a car accident as she claimed. The lawyer was attempting to gain access to the private insurance company's records to show how they denied such claims systematically, using medical grounds concerning the ultimate cause of the disability.

Lawyers are sophisticated about fraud tolerance and the going tariff for a particular type of case. They can be a great nuisance to insurance claims departments, and a nuisance payment is the most expedient means of getting them off the case. An adjuster for a multinational property and casualty insurer explained the dynamics:

> The number of claims that can be proven to be fraud are minimal ... You're lucky maybe if you have two fraudulent claims in your whole lifetime ... [More common are] questionable claims ... nuisance claims ... a lawyer gets that claim and they understand how the industry operates and they understand that lawyers are expensive. So insurance companies generally, in certain smaller claims, have a vested interest in settling, just based on economics ... [Of course] if they want too much money and they're not willing to budge, you've got to decide, 'Do I deny the claim and go through court? Or do I pay up the bucks?' That happens all the time.

As we discuss in the next section on enforcement, disputes over insurance claims rarely reach the courts. Indeed, many law firms specialize in settling cases out of court. We interviewed a litigation manager for an auto insurance company who said that personal injury lawyers in her jurisdiction worked on contingency fees: 20 per cent if the case is settled before examination for discovery, 25 per cent after that, and 33 per cent if there is a trial. The company's 'Adjuster's Handling Guide' and 'Litigation Management Guide' provided adjusters with intelligence on trends in litigation and on law firms. Some law firms were known to make money through the volume of cases they handled and therefore settled quickly. The litigation manager said that some 'haven't been to court for years.' Equipped with such knowledge, the adjuster can lowball with confidence that it will be accepted. A bodily injury claims manager for the same company described his job as providing intelligence on 'legal shops,' just as material damage adjusters develop knowledge on body shops. 'Normally the adjusters in the field don't have the ability to read the lawyers ... I'll say, "OK, this lawyer, we'll go two hours before trial and then he'll settle."'

Claimants are discouraged from becoming plaintiffs. A liability claims specialist for a multinational insurer said in interview that about 50 per cent of the claims she handled involved lawyers for the claimant from the outset. Another 20 per cent of cases involved lawyers who were engaged by the claimant as the claims process developed. She said it was the policy of her company to try

> to get in touch with that claimant before they could talk to a lawyer, because you want to show them that someone is responding to their claim ... [If the claimants] indicate that they are going to see a lawyer, I will try to talk them out of that ... At our company at least, they don't teach us to try to screw the claimant, in other words, don't try and get out of it as cheap as possible ... I may sweeten the pot at a later date. But I'm only sweetening it, not necessarily because I think the claim is worth more, it's just that they've taken the position that they might go to a lawyer. And really, if you look at it, probably the nice claimants get less than the people who put up a fight. That's the way it works.

Enforcement

We have previously documented an enforcement crackdown on insurance fraud, beginning in the 1990s, fuelled by an exponential increase in SIU operations and 'dataveillance.' Many industry officials argue that this increased policing is simply a response to increased fraud, although they recognize that fraud itself is an artifact of how the industry defines fraud and organizes to address it. For example, we interviewed the former president of a multinational insurance company who attributed increased fraud to the moral economy of liberal risk regimes. People commit more insurance fraud in political economic conditions of downsizing, marginal employment, and unemployment. He also perceived a 'moral decline' in the Canadian population. He attributed this decline to the immigration of populations with different moral standards with respect to fraud, and to an individualistic culture in which moral neutralization of fraud against a large and distant corporate entity is easy to rationalize.

Beyond such structural and cultural possibilities, there are several changes within the insurance industry and its systems of governance that have fostered a fraud enforcement crackdown. A U.S. industry executive indicated to us that the contemporary boom in fraud policing has been driven by increased pressure on the companies to keep premiums down. In the past, increased claims costs could more easily be passed on to the consumer in higher premiums. The executive indicated, however, that new laws in California and other states which restrict premium increases forced the companies to take stronger anti-fraud measures instead to enhance their loss ratio security.

A Canadian provincial auto insurance company we studied which was operating under a government-mandated freeze in premium increases responded in a similar fashion. The freeze prompted a heavy crackdown on fraud as one method to contain costs, and this insurer, in keeping with other disability insurers facing similar problems, expanded its own SIU as well as policing functions performed by its adjusters. An interviewee who did fraudulent claims data analyses for this company said that the enforcement crackdown was devised because 'they were squeezed for money, so they wanted it. And it looked like ... a cost-free way. You don't have to raise premiums, you don't have to lower your service, you just get cash. And no one is going to stand up and say, "I'm in the fraud lobby," and lobby for keeping the money. So it looked good.'

This interviewee is addressing the politically sensitive environment in which provincial government auto insurers operate. However, private auto insurers also try to capitalize on law and order sensibilities. The main audience for fraud crackdowns is a public concerned that others may be ripping off the insurance system more than they are. The main technique in mobilizing public sentiments in this regard is a blend of moral outrage and moral suasion.

Moral outrage campaigns are based on dramatizations of the fraud problem in public media. The above-mentioned provincial government auto insurer launched a well-financed antifraud media campaign to accompany its enforcement crackdown. An interviewee involved in this campaign said that it paralleled other efforts by the insurer to combine preventive enforcement strategies with social advertising (see chapter 8). He drew parallels to the success of crackdowns on impaired driving, saying the hope was 'to move [fraud] a bit from an accepted approach to a public wrong.' Catchy slogans for fraud detection emerged, such as 'you lie, you cry.'

We attended a conference for SIU investigators in the United States at which two journalists talked about how insurance fraud could be dramatized to good effect on television. These journalists had extensive experience working with insurance companies, police, and the National Insurance Crime Bureau in televising fraud cases.

One journalist described his experiences with an investigative journalism show on which he had done insurance fraud pieces. He told his audience, 'We compete in a prime time atmosphere with shows like *NYPD Blue*, and it has got to be interesting or they are not going to want to do it.' He provided an example of journalists joining with local police and insurers to set up a sting operation regarding staged accidents. The journalist-insurer-police enforcement team staged accidents in order to expose lawyers and doctors who build any accident claim they can get their hands on. Here the team's deception was portrayed as noble in the fight against the deception of others. Viewers were in turn encouraged to carry a camera, pen, and paper in their vehicles. These instruments were to be used to record towing companies and other runners for personal injury lawyers who show up immediately at an accident scene to encourage the victims to work with them in building the insurance claim.

The journalists emphasized the value of surveillance footage in exposing insurance fraud (see generally Doyle 2003). One journalist remarked, 'What is going to drive the insurance fraud stories is getting the picture ... So we have a huge staff of people who are very good at it ... They'll spend months in a place getting the stuff that they need to get ... Some stories have TV written all over it. If there is surveillance tape that is compelling, it is a no brainer. If there is a device that enables you to get pictures that you weren't able to get before, or a new technique investigating an old problem [use it ... One company has] the greatest hits library of workers' compensation stuff ... it's picture driven.'

The journalists showed a video clip to illustrate workers' compensation greatest hits. Pointing out that more than a thousand police officers on Long Island were collecting more than $32 million a year on disability pensions, the clip showed surveillance footage of some of these pensioned officers in their new hobbies and careers: lifeguarding on a beach, professional wrestling, rodeo rough-riding, and hang-gliding. One journalist told the assembled SIU officers that this dramatic footage was an invaluable way of emphasizing two key points about insurance fraud. First, everyone is doing it, even police officers, therefore everyone should be watching out and reporting it. Second, he identified what he called the 'outrage factor': these fraudsters receive substantial tax-free disability payments and make additional money working elsewhere in tasks that are even more physically demanding than their former occupation.

In the previous section, we showed that a great deal of suspected fraud is tolerated because the cost of investigation to develop sufficient evidence is too great, both financially and in terms of maintaining an amicable insurance relationship. Adjusters may also turn a blind eye to confirmed frauds for reasons of expediency. When some enforcement is deemed necessary, it is, in the vast majority of cases, handled internally rather than pursued through civil or criminal legal procedures.

Another reason why insurance fraud enforcers use internal mechanisms is their understanding that the public police are structured to ensure that fraud cases are diverted from the criminal justice system (Ericson and Haggerty 1997). Furthermore, in some U.S. jurisdictions such as Florida, SIU investigators are restricted from actively encouraging the police to prosecute people who defraud insurance companies because prosecution is construed as a violation of 'bad faith' legislation. More generally, insurance officials concede that police simply view fraud as a private policing matter.

We interviewed a former police officer and now insurance fraud investigator for a private investigation company. He said that insurers view prosecution as of no moral consequence in terms of punishing the offender, but of great consequence in time and money. 'You'd never get [a genuinely punitive] sentence first of all for somebody who was a first-time offender on fraud cases, a $20,000 deal. You'd get a suspended sentence, conditional discharge ... There's more of a penalty [through internal means]. And why clog up the system with another case that will take years to solve, and by the end of it nobody is going to get a real penalty? He'll probably end up getting his money.'

This view was common even in relation to large-scale and systematic fraud. A representative of another fraud investigation organization said that insurance companies think only in terms of the bottom line, and it is difficult to show them that money is being saved through prosecution. He noted that proceedings can take years to resolve, and even if $3 million restitution is eventually ordered by the court 'the problem is you're never going to see the $3 million' because of investigation and legal fees.

Some insurance claims executives we interviewed said that their policy on enforcement was simple, they never prosecute. A claims executive for a life and health insurance company seemed taken aback when we asked her about prosecution of fraudulent claims. 'We *never* do that. The insurance industry as a whole does not do that ... We can waste a lot of time and that translates into higher premiums for other people. You can put in an invalid claim to us. If we recognize it's invalid we just write to you and say, "No, you're not totally disabled." Even if we discover that there's no validity at all ... a lie, we can't do anything other than deny your claim. And you can sue us. And we might pay the claim.'

This interviewee underscored her point by referring to an exception that proves the rule. Several years previously, the company joined with twenty-five other companies in pursuing a major case of systematic fraud. Nurses working in a variety of hospital and clinical settings had noticed very similar stories on insurance claims reports, and they notified their medical authorities. Investigators for the insurers determined participants in a fraud ring, including two doctors who were key players in manufacturing false claims. The insured were cut off from payments, and investigators turned over their evidence to prosecutors. However, no prosecutions ensued, and some individuals involved sued some of the insurers. Here efforts made towards prosecution were not only inefficient but counterproductive.

Automobile insurers routinely handle fraudulent material damage claims by simply denying them. The penalty lies in the fact that the claimant must pay for damages incurred in the reported accident. Additional penalties can include an insurance record as a fraudster, with implications for a downgrade in market segment and therefore higher premiums and less favourable contract conditions. These penalties are negotiable. For example, if the culprit is cooperative in the investigation the claim may simply be denied with no record of fraud being officially recorded.

We interviewed SIU investigators for an auto insurer who offered examples of claims denial as an effective form of summary justice. A claimant reported that his $50,000 sports car had been burnt beyond repair, which he attributed to arson by members of a motorcycle gang. The SIU investigator suspected from the outset that the claimant had burnt the car himself. During an interview with a friend of the claimant, who was offering an alibi, the SIU investigator told the friend to inform the claimant that he would be charged with criminal fraud if he did not withdraw his claim. The claim was withdrawn immediately and the claimant was $50,000 poorer.

In another case, a drunken youth destroyed his car in a single vehicle accident and then tried to absolve himself of responsibility to protect his insurance record. 'He got pissed, smashed up car, single vehicle. He lied to me. He said he only had one and one-half beers. That's a breach of your insurance coverage. He left the scene of an accident. That is another breach right there. He tried to get a friend of his to say he was the driver. He was digging himself a big hole here. The claim was worth about $15,000. Didn't pay him a penny. Denied it ... Doesn't even count as a fraudulent claim. It is just a breach of coverage.'

A case illustrating the investigative process involving 'red flags,' and a summary justice outcome without prosecution, was offered by one of the SIU investigators we interviewed. A reported stolen vehicle was not recovered after several weeks. Since 90 per cent of stolen vehicles in the jurisdiction were recovered, claims involving disappearance were usually subject to further investigation. The SIU officer was initially suspicious because the vehicle was manufactured with an anti-theft device. The claimant explained he had an extra ignition key under a rear seat floor mat, and the thief must have found the key to start the vehicle. An investigation of the claimant's finances revealed that he was overspent. 'His lease payments were about $650, his rent ... $400. The amount of money he was making on his job doesn't even cover the costs of his expenses, besides the nice clothing he was wearing, and cellular telephone and pager he has.' When asked where he was at the time of the theft, the claimant said he was visiting a distant Canadian city. He failed to produce travel documents to support this alibi.

The SIU investigators contacted officials at the nearest border crossing to the United States, where surveillance cameras photograph the licence plate of each vehicle crossing the border. This check revealed that the claimant's vehicle had crossed the border on the same day it was reported stolen. Independent of their own inquiries to this point,

SIU investigators were contacted by a private investigator in San Diego who specialized in recovery of stolen vehicles that enter Mexico from other parts of North America. This private investigator had identified the car in Mexico as a suspected stolen vehicle, and contacted the Canadian insurer in the hope of gaining a fee for assistance in its recovery.

The claimant was then confronted with the fact that the vehicle had been driven into the United States and eventually sold in Mexico. It was suggested that rather than visiting a distant Canadian city at the time, he himself had driven south, sold the vehicle, and then tried to double his return by making a fraudulent theft of vehicle claim. The claimant withdrew his claim. The SIU closed its case by recovering a few hundred dollars the claims department had paid for a replacement vehicle rented by the claimant. This money was to be collected by applying it as a debt against the claimant's driver's licence, which he had to pay at the time of licence renewal or be denied renewal. When asked if prosecution was ever considered in this case, the investigator replied, 'It's lots of paperwork to file charges to Crown for review ... They would turn it down because there are so many other things flooding the system already ... They wouldn't think about it, they'd just say, "See you later."'

Civil litigation is one route for addressing problems of systemic fraud by the insured and their professional case builders, as well as systemic efforts by insurers to control fraud. It is also used occasionally to punish a serious or recalcitrant fraud suspect and to recover losses from claims wrongly paid.

Civil proceedings allow an insurer to effect additional punishment of a fraudulent claimant and recover costs if there is a significant loss involved. They are usually easier than criminal proceedings because there is a lower standard of proof. In specified contexts, the insurer can also sue for money spent on administration and investigation, and for punitive damages.

We interviewed an SIU officer for a provincial government auto insurer that was cracking down on fraudulent claims. Referring to recent civil action successes in which the insurance company had been awarded $150,000 punitive damages in one case and $50,000 in another, he remarked, 'So they owe us for lying to us.' Commenting that 'a lot of these people don't have any money,' he said that a working group was considering how to step up collections including 'seizing homes, assets, drivers' licences, those kind of issues so that if they don't have the money, we're going to get it somehow.' The crackdown also involved liaison with local media to publicize big cases in the hope that potential fraudsters might say, 'Maybe we'll just go somewhere else to fraud ... the workers' compensation board.' The first twelve civil suits under the fraud crackdown initiative were publicized systematically in order to set the social deflationary tone of the campaign:

> We can't get them criminally sometimes ... so we 'advertised' that we're now taking these people civilly ... It's going to cost you, Mr. Claimant, for making a lie to us ... There was one ad there called, 'Blind Man Drives.' He came into us and said he was blind, then he left, went around the corner, and got into his car and drove! And we caught him seven times driving! That's fraud: pure, outright lie. A person who is blind is a serious, serious claim worth a lot of money ... We advertised it, then we did a customer service follow up ... to see how people felt. And the ratings went up 30 per cent ... in regards to positiveness, that we're doing something.

The same insurer also initiated some criminal prosecutions as part of the dramatization of its enforcement crackdown. These prosecutions included publicity as punishment for convicted fraudsters, and as a deterrent to others so inclined. A management consultant's report on how the company could control social inflation through fraud enforcement had recommended 'public exposure for individuals convicted of fraud, including newspaper advertisements showing their pictures and describing their crimes.' We interviewed a media relations specialist who was carrying through this recommendation. He said that the main focus of the publicity campaign was 'the more sophisticated, the organized, the fraud ring. That is much more effective in drawing attention to the whole issue of insurance fraud and the effect that it has on you and your premium.' Such cases give maximum benefit in the manufacture of public indignation. He cautioned that there must be careful selection of cases, and astute timing of news releases, because insurance fraud is tolerated as a normal crime. It is only the big, exceptional case that accords with media logic and therefore has a dramatic effect. 'We're not out there every week saying we've busted another fraud case, and yet another one ... If you put that message out often and too heavily I think you run the real risk of being seen as a hammer, I guess, and the organization which views every case as the potential fraud ... You could put out this message too often or too strongly and that's going to work against your efforts in achieving public support for the fight against crime.'

An SIU manager for an auto insurer said that he recommended prosecution when 'our *only* likelihood would be to win.' An SIU investigator for the same company concurred, saying 'if we're wrong, it's going to be everywhere ... very risky. So you have to be absolutely sure those are good cases to take. It goes through a very stringent committee to actually get it approved to sue civilly.' The process included having a case 'lawyered' prior to going to the committee. The committee included a senior company executive, a corporate lawyer, a regional manager of claims, and a litigation department lawyer. This committee in turn made its recommendation to a senior finance committee for final approval, indicating once again that decisions about fraud enforcement are assessed in the broader context of loss ratio security.

Although criminal law enforcement is rare, there are specific contexts in which it is used more actively to deter particular problems of insurance fraud. We studied a provincial government auto insurer that experienced a very high level of fraudulent hit and run claims. Insured who damage their own vehicle in an accident they cause report that the damage was at the hands of another driver who left the scene of the accident unidentified.

In an effort to better manage hit and run fraud, the insurer entered into a partnership with the city police department. The insurer had a large claims centre that was part of the same building as police headquarters and a police division. All hit and run claims in the area were processed through this centre by a special claims team. The team included dedicated material damage adjusters and examiners, as well as public police officers who specialized in hit and run investigations.

The location of the hit and run claims team in the same building as the police department was a strong sign that hit and run claims are police matters because they involve an allegation of a criminal offence. There would be dedicated police investigation from the outset. The corollary was that those contemplating a fraudulent hit and run claim would be subject to intensive police scrutiny.

To underscore this deterrent message regarding fraudulent claims, the insurer had a special hit and run line at its claims call centre. The caller was given a prompt if the claim involved a hit and run. The first communication on the hit and run line was a recorded message that informed the caller about the dedicated hit and run claims process and the involvement of the police. As described in interview by a claims analyst for the insurance company, 'When you call in there, there's a message that you now get designed to deter you from making fraudulent claims. It spells out basically all the horrible things that will happen to you if you are making a fraudulent claim ... There's been some fairly significant drops in fraudulent claims.' A colleague who was involved in recommending this system said that before its inception she had produced data on hit and run frauds, showing that they were 'way out of hand.' Since implementation of the message system, 'we got about 30 per cent hang-ups ... So that was a few million bucks we got [saved] right away, and customers loved it. And it started creating an impression we could do something.'

The special claims team approach was expanded to four different claims centres. We observed the operations of a team at one of these centres. The team included three dedicated adjusters and a police officer, as well as estimators as needed. An average of sixty-eight hit and run claims were processed daily. All cases were processed by the dedicated adjusters; the police officer only became involved in cases where the damage exceeded $500.

An adjuster we interviewed said that, as a very conservative estimate, 30 per cent (20/68) of hit and run claims each day were fraudulent. He stated this high proportion was 'a fact of life. I mean, taking regular claims, you face the same dilemma. You know this person is lying through their teeth.' However, three-quarters of these suspected fraudulent claims were not pursued as fraud because of a combination of evidence problems, the expense of further investigation in relation to the value of the claim, and a concern not to offend a claimant who may occasionally be innocent. The adjuster observed that in a typical case 'A lot of them say I don't know where or when it happened. I just discovered this damage while I was washing my car. And there is very little you can properly investigate.' He also expressed the concern that 'the odd claimant, if you've denied their claim, they'll go right to the top ... and it all trickles down ... People in head office or customer service will look at it and they'll say, "Is it worth the publicity?" ... It's our image and whether we're going to be in business five or ten years from now.' An examiner echoed these sentiments but also emphasized the need to give the claimant the benefit of the doubt because of evidence problems. 'If I can't prove it, I would be more troubled if I denied a claim and it was legitimate.'

Adjusters used various tactics to induce suspected fraudsters into dropping their claims. For example, many claimants report hit and run victimization when in fact they have damaged their own vehicles by scraping them up against buildings, trees, and other objects. According to an adjuster, when this scenario is involved, the tactic may be 'to advise them again that we're going to send the samples into the lab. If it comes back as non-vehicular the claim is denied in its entirety. In the meantime, I'll request they take an application for payment under the Insurance Motor Vehicle Act for hit and run, get it notarized, which is going to cost them twenty-four dollars, and once I receive it back I'll send in the samples. A lot of the time I'll never receive it back, they just disappear.'

On average, five of the sixty-eight claims each day were explicitly alleged to be fraudulent. An adjuster said this determination was evidenced on 'strictly the material damage issue. A lot of the estimating staff would love to make decisions based on what the claimant is telling them and whether we believe them or not, but it is more a damage issue.' Where material damage evidence justifies a determination of fraud, the insurance solution is to deny the claim and record the matter on the claims data system. The claim is 'denied in its entirety. We won't pay it as a collision claim, and won't as a hit and run claim. They're flagged under our hit and run warning system ... we put them on there for about three years. So any time they put forth another claim it's automatically flagged and it's investigated more thoroughly.' As a provincial government auto insurer, this adjuster could not cancel the policy following a fraudulent claim.

The police officer was left with the decision of whether to charge a claimant with hit and run because he was in fact the one who had left the scene of the accident and then fraudulently reported it. An adjuster commented, 'the only ones that are going to get charged with hit and run are the ones the police are going to investigate, and I guess that depends on the mood of the officer at the time.' The police were perceived as moody by insurance claims staff. For example, a difficult or undeferential claimant suspected of deception was sometimes ticketed for minor violations, such as having a headlight or tail light out of order.

There was considerable tension between insurance claims staff and police. The nub of the tension was the police framework of interrogating suspects with an eye towards criminal law enforcement, versus the insurance framework of questioning customers and tolerating fraud. An adjuster said of the police, 'They don't have competition and they don't care about customer service. We had one officer here on site who would call a claimant a liar to his face, then he would take him into a booth and browbeat him, someone who is making a false hit and run claim. That just rubbed the centre manager the wrong way ... We can't do that ... We're in the customer service business but the police just don't care ... [In one case the police told the claimant] "If you try and put forth a hit-and-run claim we'll charge you with criminal mischief." Well, we can't do that. We just deny.'

This tension nicely illustrates our point that the insurance system makes and governs fraud through its moral risk relationships and loss ratio calculus, which are usually antithetical to external law enforcement processes and solutions. In the more usual insurance-police relationship the police serve the information needs of the insurance system but otherwise leave the resolution of fraud to the internal relationships of that system (Ericson and Haggerty 1997). Each company manages its own policing apparatus to ensure that it can shape and distribute moral risks in ways that achieve loss ratio security.

Conclusions

Insurance is a core institution in governing modern societies. It has become increasingly significant because contemporary societies encourage a minimal state and governance based on local knowledge of risk.

As we argued in chapter 1, the state has three dimensions: it is a country with bounded territory, a nation with a population of citizens, and a sovereign authority with a political regime. The contemporary state is minimalized as it gives ground to, and partners with, private sector institutions on each of these dimensions. It becomes one institution among others, trying to act for the general interest according to principles of public service. In this process it not only shapes other institutions but is itself 'governmentalized' by them.

The state as country fragments into territories largely controlled by other institutions that include and exclude according to their own peculiar requirements. Private corporations, for example, enhance their territorial jurisdiction through disconnected capital, surveillance technologies, and private justice arrangements that protect their spaces and places for strategic action. The exercise of will and choice largely transpires within the criteria of private institutions the individual manages to access.

The state as nation fragments into populations largely constituted by other institutions that seek members in terms of consumption preferences and habits. Each private corporate institution forms its own populations and criteria of inclusion and exclusion, variously operating in conjunction with and beyond the population management strategies and technologies of the state. In this competitive consumption of consumers, an individual's consumption behaviour is under constant surveillance to authenticate her private corporate citizenship. Through market segmentation and risk pooling strategies, private corporations divide their citizenry into consuming populations who will choose to spend freely and take risks with them.

The state as sovereign authority fragments into the risk management regimes of private corporate institutions that make the consuming subject more responsible for her own choices, including risk taking and security provision. Because they provide knowledge for risk taking, these regimes are entwined with liberal conceptions of choice, freedom, and liberty. But choice is not freedom or liberty. Rather, choice is an instrument and objective in governing populations. An institution provides its participants with choice as agency: a capacity to act within the parameters set by the institution. Choice as agency is accompanied by the discourse of corporate and consumer rights, but always with the caveat that in liberal risk regimes rights are accompanied by responsibilities. Those who are not responsible are given no choice. They are simply excluded from further participation in the institution concerned.

Liberal risk regimes operate on six basic assumptions. First, a minimal state is possible because people have sufficient self-restraint, willingness to share, and capacity for self-governance to allow institutions beyond the state to provide social solidarity. Second, a 'free market' can provide security and prosperity by encouraging fragmented individuals and collectivities to participate in market relations that stimulate economic growth and address risk. Third, emphasis is placed on knowledge for risk taking as well as risk management. As participants in fast-moving and fluctuating markets, people must become knowledgeable risk takers who can adapt to changes in their lives. Fourth, the emphasis on being knowledgeable risk takers entails individual responsibility: each individual is to be her own political economy, an informed self-sufficient consumer of labour markets, personal security markets, and other consuming interests. Fifth, within a liberal risk regime of responsible risk taking, all differences, and the inequalities that result from them, are seen as a matter of choice. Conceived as choice, inequality is also seen as inevitable. Sixth, the state is itself posited as a risk that must be subject to vigilant monitoring and perpetual reform.

The fragmentation of the state as country, nation, and sovereign authority into the liberal risk regimes of private corporate institutions is exemplified in the operations of the insurance industry. We have argued throughout that insurance is *the* institution of governance beyond the state. It takes up ground left by the downsizing of the state and effects governance based on local knowledge of risk.

The insurance industry shares many of the goals of the state. In pooling risks, it provides security and solidarity among its populations, which in turn form moral communities. It is thus a moral technology of justice, addressing the realities of distributive justice, restorative justice, and individual and collective responsibilities. However, in the very process of pooling risks it also unpools them. It deselects bearers of moral risks who do not contribute to the integrity of the risk pool. In this respect it articulates the liberal risk regime's preference for individual choice and responsibility over collective well-being. It favours a rational choice model of justice and individualism over social justice and collectivism.

The insurance industry also employs the same methodologies as the state. First, it is embedded in law. The insurance contract is a kind of legal bond to the institutional territory, population, and sovereign authority of the insurance company, underwritten by state regulatory processes. Insurance also helps the law to assign liability for loss to the party most able to distribute the loss through insurance. Second, like the state, the insurance industry uses elaborate systems of surveillance and audit to govern at a distance. Third, those systems are built and used by professional experts charged with making practical decisions about who and what to insure, and on what terms. These experts are quintessential applied social scientists, moving from macro-analysis of global trends to the micro-detail found in actuarial tables. Fourth, the insurance industry develops its own policing apparatus to patrol its institutional boundaries, protect the well-being of its populations, and promote the authority of its liberal risk regime.

In using the methodologies of law, surveillance, expertise, and policing, the insurance industry is loosely coupled with the state. The industry actively invites the state to regulate selected aspects of its practices, such as how it invests its capital and how it markets its products and handles claims. The state in turn actively encourages the industry to underwrite risks. Insurance relieves the state of having to compensate losses and also provides employment, tax revenues, and capital that is invested in government bonds.

The state for its part collaborates with the insurance industry at the level of ideology. As part of its efforts to minimize itself, the state actively promotes individual responsibility for risk. This promotion begins with an attack on the welfare state, including the moral risks posed by state insurance arrangements and the malingering and dependency that result. The state limits its role to turning people into responsible risk takers and managers, offering at best a temporary safety net when things go wrong. It replaces welfare state social transfers with liberal state moral risk transfers. The individual is now responsible for controlling her risk environment through market-based security product consumption, including the purchase of insurance. This emphasis on individual responsibility means that risky events are treated as if they result from human motivation and intention, and actors who may become involved in risky events are then judged in terms of moral blameworthiness for failures to minimize harms. Insurance-driven systems of governance presume that all chance can be tamed and that all risks are moral.

While insurers desire hard evidence of risk to price their products, manage their populations, and process claims, the limits of knowledge pose continual problems. These limits are especially evident in trying to address the likelihood and effects of natural disasters such as earthquakes, or the epidemiology and treatment requirements for medical conundrums such as soft tissue injury. However, even areas in which actuarial precision seems possible are problematic. Fire insurance rates, as we noted, are based on limited statistical support; fires are rare and their causes multifaceted while building, protection technology, and management practices are in perpetual flux. The proliferation of investment-related life insurance products has resulted in actuaries not knowing how to price some of them, at times with serious financial consequences for both policyholders and the insurance companies concerned.

Faced with inadequate scientific and technical knowledge, insurers turn to knowledge of moral risk. The risks that are defined, produced, taken, and managed by the insurance industry always include moral assessment of the people and harms involved. First, insurance produces and responds to moral risks through its actuarial practices of classification and probability calculation. What is statistically normal provides an ethical norm of governance. In this respect all actions that are classified and calculated by insurance occur under a description of moral risk. Second, insurance risks are also moralized and subject to attributions of responsibility through the ways in which they are posed as dangers. Addressing a risk as danger inevitably entails moral evaluations concerning probable outcomes, their mitigation, and who is responsible for them. Third, in combination with the ways in which they are embedded in actuarial classifications and evaluations of danger, moral risks arise in the interactive dynamics of the insurance relationship. Here, moral risk refers to the ways in which an insurance relationship fosters behaviour by any party in the relationship that immorally increases risks to others.

Our conceptualization of moral risk is much broader than the term 'moral hazard' more commonly used by insurers and previous researchers. Typically, only the insured is seen as posing moral hazards. Yet we discovered that private insurance is socially organized to offer incentives to other parties in the insurance relationship to engage in risky behaviour with immoral consequences. Insurers themselves are often influenced in ways that encourage them to put others, including their policyholders, employees, competitors, and governments, at risk.

Moral risks are posed by the insured party if the cultural relationship is strained; for example, if the insurer is seen as distant and anonymous, or there are discrepancies between sales stories and claims stories that create a sense of bad faith; if there is a lot at stake in the economic relationship regarding premiums paid and benefits sought; if there is an opportunity created because of the inadequate selection of the insured population and/or inadequate policing of the claims process; and if the insured is able to morally neutralize her behaviour as just in the circumstances. Parallel factors are at work concerning moral risks posed by insurance companies and their employees: for example, if there is a cushion from the consequences of risk, very high economic stakes, low visibility and inadequate policing, and readily available justifications to morally neutralize their risky behaviour. Moral risk and regulation permeate the business of insurance and complicate the simplistic assumptions of liberal risk regimes that the best model for governance entails a minimal state, market fundamentalism, greater risk taking, strong individual responsibility, substantial inequalities, and treating the state as a greater risk than alternatives in civil society. In their decisions about loss ratio security, corporate governance, and market conduct, insurers pose risks to each other, their employees, policyholders and to the political economy.

Political economies are negotiated in complex relations among state legislators and regulators, insurance industry associations, and global and local insurance companies. The negotiation occurs in the course of underwriting, investment, reinsurance, compensation schemes, and competitive relations.

Insurance underwriting is based on probabilities and possibilities for taking risk, and is therefore surrounded by uncertainties. It is a form of gambling: a bet is wagered with the integrity of the risk pool of policyholders. One reason why the insurance product is unique is that the consumers are part of the product. The product is the consumers and their relationships in a risk pool. The consumer's prevention efforts and claims behaviour affect the nature of the product. New risks, unknown at the time of underwriting, inevitably arise because of the dynamics of human interaction within the risk pool.

Uncertainties are not limited to the behaviour of policyholders. Developments in science and technology, and their mediation through the tort liability legal environment, also lead to the discovery of new risks for which insurers are deemed liable even though they were unaware of them at the time of underwriting. We pointed to the example of environmental liability underwriting, which was initially conducted in the dark. Insurers wrote occurrence-based policies that meant they were responsible for a pollutant that was there but unknown at the time of underwriting.

Unknown or highly speculative financial risk exposure can also lead underwriters to pose serious moral risks for their companies and everyone else involved in their insurance relationships. Life insurance is infamous for wildly inaccurate guesses about mortality rates, the length of time policyholders remain in the risk pool, and investment return projections. Major miscalculations about persistency, and about long-term interest rates, have caused enormous liabilities that companies have only been able to handle by passing on the financial consequences to policyholders, seeking help from government, or selling off their business to competitors.

Insurers seek profits by securing their loss ratios to the point that there is a reasonable amount available for investment. While investment portfolios should be both prudent and profitable, the tendency is to gamble for better investment returns. Experience often proves wrong and what first appeared prudent can look irresponsible in retrospect. However, insurance companies are cushioned from their investment risks by corporate limited liability rules as well as compensation schemes that pay policyholders up to a certain limit in the event of a company's insolvency. These mechanisms are a source of moral risk to the extent that they reduce insurance company incentives to avoid more risky investments. In the extreme, insurance companies speculate wildly on investments, and run up huge deficits in financing them, knowing that the fallout will have limited negative impact on directors and officers.

Another context in which the political economy is negotiated is the business of reinsurance. The originating or primary insurer lays off his bet with other insurers in order to spread the financial risk. Reinsurance, as we demonstrated, is fraught with moral risk judgments and implications. Reinsurers treat their insurance company partners in the same way as they treat ordinary policyholders: with suspicion. Partners may be less attentive to loss ratio security if they are covered by reinsurance. One indication of systemic risk is the fact that primary insurers provide contingency reserves for reinsurance that is not recoverable. Recurrent scandals in which primary insurers and reinsurers blatantly deceive their partners about risk exposure, a practice known in the industry as 'passing the trash,' are another.

Insurers also address their solvency risks by giving policyholders compulsory insurance on their insurance. Compensation schemes are organized by the industry to provide policyholders with coverage up to a specified limit in the event that their insurer becomes insolvent. All member companies pay into the fund according to the level of premiums they underwrite, and they are collectively responsible to the policyholders of an insolvent company. These compensation schemes are supposed to make member companies more vigilant about governing the risks posed by each other's underwriting, investment, and reinsurance strategies. In the event of a failure by one of their members they would be required to pay significant compensation. However, the costs of this scheme are passed on to policyholders through an additional charge on premiums!

The insurance industry typifies the highly competitive environment fostered by liberal risk regimes. Solvency is an omnipresent issue, and mergers and acquisitions are commonplace. Competition as a threat to solvency is fuelled by six interconnected processes. First, there is over-capacity. Second, this over-capacity is compounded by the entry of the major banks and other financial institutions into insurance company ownership and cross-selling. Third, new information technologies and direct selling techniques are being used to substantially alter sales distribution systems. Fourth, parallel competitive environments are found in other branches of the financial services industry, for example, in the sale of mutual funds and other investment products that compete with life insurance. Fifth, all of these trends foster competitive development of increasingly specialized products for segmented markets. Sixth, there is also a trend towards self-insurance, especially among large corporate entities.

Insurers govern the problems posed by these competitive pressures through four interconnected mechanisms of corporate governance. These mechanisms include state regulation, industry associations, actuaries, and insurance on insurers' practices.

State and insurance industry regulators are part of each other's liberal risk regimes. The state governs corporate governance, and corporations in turn govern the state. The starting point for state regulation is the licensing system, which governs the qualifications and reputation of insurers allowed to participate in the market. The corporate licence embodied in the legal form of limited liability is also an enormous privilege, cushioning risks taken by directors and officers, and transferring risks to other parties such as stockholders, creditors, and policyholders. A primary focus of state regulation is public confidence in the insurance industry and the protection of policyholders. Thus regulators address reasonable underwriting, investment, reinsurance, and marketing practices that protect policyholders from 'undue loss.' The state's regulatory approach in this regard can be characterized as governing at a distance, trying to foster and improve the corporate governance mechanisms of insurance companies. State regulators are a valuable source of expertise, refereeing, and rationalization among members of a fiercely competitive industry. They also help to self-moralize the corporation as the cornerstone of self-governance. The subjective and ethical aspects of corporate governance are increasingly the focus of regulation, on the principle that if corporations are to take more liberal risks, their directors, officers, and agents must receive instruction about their moral responsibilities in doing so. A company's reputable corporate culture has itself become a 'good' that increases its value in the competitive environment of mergers and acquisitions.

Insurance companies not only invite state regulation they deem useful, they also participate in the governance of state governance. Insurance company executives sit on insurance legislation reform committees alongside regulators and legislators, and they usually take the lead in the direction and specifics of legislative change. State regulatory bodies are typically staffed by former insurance company employees, and by those who move interchangeably between industry and regulatory positions. Insurance industry associations and members are strong lobbyists with governments as well as active in local party politics.

Insurance industry associations are another powerful mechanism in corporate governance. They coordinate the activities of member companies through information and communication systems, and through regulatory functions that include standards, rules, rate setting, and sanctions. These industry association activities not only shape everyday practices, they also make evident the hierarchies and power relations among member companies. In practice, insurance industry associations are dominated by a handful of the most powerful companies. This dominance means that a handful of the largest industry players effectively shape government legislation, policy, and practice with respect to insurance. For their part, state regulators must figure out the distribution of power among companies that control the association, and then use that power to achieve the regulatory outcome at issue. The key industry association players in turn use state power to achieve the regulation they want, including the control of each other. Mutual control is always problematic because of competition among companies. Thus, while industry associations try to pool information resources that will serve the entire industry, companies are reluctant to participate fully because they fear relinquishing competitive advantage. Their culture of distrust in this regard has meant that they have much less substantial and efficient information pooling resources than those shared among the major banks. While insurance industry associations may effectively govern governments, they struggle to regulate their own members, who are constantly positioning for profits, mergers, and acquisitions.

Actuaries are another locus of corporate governance. The quantitative protocols, standards, and rules of actuarial science speak to the public character of how actuaries are supposed to participate in corporate governance. Publicly, these technologies make actuarial work seem like painting by numbers: the numbers speak for themselves. Privately, the discretionary practice of actuarial work – sketching financial futures with whatever assumptions will help in the negotiation of competitive advantage and political economies – renders it akin to postmodern painting: the numbers form a collage that begs creative interpretation. Actuaries give authority to the loose interpretation of data in the context of a company's culture and competitive environment. They negotiate political economies within corporate governance criteria they help to establish and local market competitive forces they try to control. As competitors introduce new policy features and terms, a company cannot afford to stay out of the game for fear of losing business and adversely affecting the risk pool among remaining policyholders. Competitive markets foster actuarial speculation rather than precision. Indeed, precisely because of this speculative environment, actuaries have increasing responsibilities to regulators, based not only in their formal knowledge of how to do things, such as capital adequacy testing, but also in their nose for corporate wrongdoing and capacity for whistleblowing.

The practices of insurance companies are also governed by other companies that insure them. Like any other responsible company, an insurer obtains directors and officers' liability insurance, errors and omissions insurance, insurance benefits packages for employees, and so on. Analysis of how insurers of insurers rate the moral risks posed by their clients is especially revealing of how the insurance industry governs. For example, there are significant liability exposures regarding investment practices, sales fraud, failing to provide needed or requested coverage in the contract, and claims mishandling. Some insurers find it difficult to obtain affordable liability insurance coverage of these morally risky fields and end up self-insuring. Similarly, some benefits packages are difficult to obtain on behalf of insurance company employees because of the nature of the employment. Insurers face the irony that the very structure of the employment relationships they create sometimes makes their employees exceptional moral risks for insurance coverage.

The marketing of insurance products bears moral risks that have proven especially difficult to govern. In particular, recurrent scandals in marketing life insurance products suggest that such risks are endemic to the way sales practices are structured. While new governance initiatives may redistribute and manage these risks better, the life insurance system, like a sponge, tends to soak consumers and quickly return to its original form. Our analysis of life insurance market misconduct illustrates that insurers pose the same moral risks that they denounce and try to suppress in the behaviour of their clients.

Backed by actuaries and other company managers who speculate on rosy futures, life insurance agents are inclined to misrepresent their products to clients. They push inappropriate policies and offer overconfident and unreasonable expectations about the investment value of policies. Longstanding problems in this regard are compounded by the recent introduction of complex, investment-related universal life policies. These policies, as we described, are subject to 'feature creep': features are added to make the product seem more lucrative in relation to long-term investment returns, without emphasizing that the risks lie with the policyholder and that the company is covering its own risks through several interrelated pricing and investment mechanisms. Existing policyholders are a particular target for these new features. They are encouraged to convert, even though the new policy may be less attractive financially than the former policy.

When the whistle is blown on life insurance sales misconduct, companies respond publicly by applying a rotten apple theory to agents and a blaming the victim approach to policyholders (caveat emptor). However, within the industry everyone knows that the issue is one of a rotting barrel rather than individual apples: agents are made morally risky by the structural conditions within which they (mis)sell. These structural conditions are fivefold. First, market misconduct is embedded in the insurance contract itself through myriad clauses and investment-related conditions that many agents, let alone their clients, fail to understand. Misconduct in the marketing of any product is more likely when the performance of the product is highly risky or uncertain, and when it is extremely difficult to assess the quality of products offered by an individual supplier among competitors. Second, market misconduct is fostered through recruitment, training, and use of life agents. New agents are recruited on the strength of their networks of family and friends, and once these personal affinity networks are exhausted, so is the job. Third, market misconduct is promoted through the incentive structure of commission-based selling. Agents are offered higher commissions for products that provide more lucrative returns for the company, and therefore push these products even though they may be less appropriate for the client than a cheaper and lower commission alternative. Fourth, the competitive market conditions leading to 'feature creep' are conducive to market misconduct. The complexity of product features makes the product more difficult to understand. Fifth, market misconduct is embedded in a sales culture that motivates and reinforces systematic (mis)selling. Agents face a constant barrage of motivational instruction aimed at convincing them that the selling of life insurance is a moral act rather than a moral risk.

Insurers and regulators govern market conduct, but not through mechanisms that fundamentally alter these basic structural and cultural realities. Governance mechanisms include state regulation, professionalization, surveillance, and the development of alternative distribution systems.

State market-conduct regulators, paid for by the industry, are almost entirely reactive to complaints. Most of the complaints originate with competitors in the industry rather than policyholders. The compliance model of enforcement means that formal proceedings are rare and punitive sanctions isolated. Codes of ethics have been encouraged by market conduct regulators in many jurisdictions; however, specific provisions – for example, that commissions should not influence sales practices – often merely condemn practices that everyone knows are structurally induced and systematic. In condemning basic structural conditions of market misconduct without attempting to change them, such codes are legitimization devices and a marketing tool.

Professionalization is another response to market misconduct. Since incompetent advice can pose as great a moral risk to the consumer as plain dishonesty, better training seems a sound approach. However, as long as agent compensation is tied to commission incentives, professional sound advice is always in danger of being compromised. In practice, the life insurance selling relationship is not one of professional/client, but rather of buyer/seller, and the credo is still caveat emptor.

A third and related response to market misconduct is more intensive surveillance of sales operations and agents – better surveillance is often portrayed as contributing to greater professionalism. Computer-based sales illustration packages build in state compliance regulations and otherwise compel the agent to structure the sales process in a format favoured by the company. They also record for review by managers how the sales case was actually illustrated. Many agency operations are subject to 'mystery shopping' by undercover surveillance operatives who check on their sales conduct, and when sales are organized through call centres every telephone transaction is recorded and potentially subject to review.

New distribution systems such as call centres offer the greatest potential for altering the structural and cultural basis of moral risks posed by insurance sales agents. The buyer/seller relationship is made explicit, and the sales process is recorded and therefore reviewable. Interpersonal selling is increasingly reserved for more wealthy consumers, where 'relationship management,' and a more professional approach, become important. However, always eager to increase market share through diversification of distribution channels, large companies run one sales distribution system (e.g., direct sales) that undercuts another (e.g., agency-based personal selling). This places even more pressure on those selling on commission in traditional agent-customer situations, and therefore may accentuate market misconduct.

As illustrated in these efforts to address market misconduct, systems for governing insurers and the insured overlap. At the point of underwriting, agents must ensure that all insurance prospects are treated as suspects until they are qualified according to company specifications. There is a direct relationship among insurance market segmentation, moral risk assessment, and exclusion of the undesirable. That is, knowledge of risk for the administration of marketing is entwined with knowledge of risk for the determination of rates and contract conditions. Target marketing and segmentation are intended to place the prospect-as-suspect into the insurance equivalent of gated communities, where she will share risks only with those who are similarly situated.

Home insurance underwriting provides an example. As we have seen, the home insurance applicant is subject to a series of interconnected moral readings regarding the condition of the property to be insured and its location. Some types of property and some locations are simply 'redlined' and not underwritten. The applicant herself is scrutinized on morally desirable criteria such as 'pride of ownership' and 'good housekeeping.' Demeanour in the application process, such as 'cooperative attitude' in the provision of information requested by the agent, is also relevant. The applicant's insurance record is called upon to establish her insurance claims history and how responsible she has been in preventing previous harms to her property and to the insurers' loss ratio.

Governance in liberal risk regimes involves obtaining data about populations with offensive deportment, then manipulating their conditions in order to change the laws of statistics they are compelled to obey. This actuarial liberalism is at the core of how insurers unpool their populations into different market segments. In the field of home insurance, national databases fed by cooperating insurers provide information about the claims history of the insurance applicant and the property to be insured. Links are made to credit information systems that function as authentication intermediaries, informing insurers in an instant whether the consuming suspect before them is a palatable risk. Data are also purchased from state taxation and statistical agencies on the demographics of consuming populations as these relate to market segmentation.

Agents' field judgments feed the data systems, as the interpersonal and technical dimensions of moral risk interface. The field agent engaged in 'frontline underwriting' is not a free-floating moral governor. Rather, she is equipped with closed-ended forms and computer-based formats for her surveillance tasks that embed underwriting rules and review her decisions. She is penalized through the structure of commissions for having a poor loss ratio, and rewarded with a 'quality bonus' for a good loss ratio.

Once the insurance applicant-as-suspect is turned into a viable prospect, market segmentation data are used to assign her to the appropriate risk pool. Superstandard pools are formed for wealthy clients, who are offered superior claims service for expensive insurance rates. Substandard pools for high-risk customers are made profitable through high deductibles, excluding some standard policy features, and making others expensive options. State regulation of unfair market segmentation practices is evaded by creating subsidiaries or specialized companies that sell only to identified segments.

Once insured, the policyholder is required to be an agent of prevention responsible for governing her own risky environment and securing it against loss. Ideally, if each insured subject is reflexive about risks and makes rational choices to minimize them, there will be security for everyone. This security will materialize in a safer environment plus the financial benefits of lower claims costs for the insurer and lower premiums for the insured.

The 'responsibilization' of the insured as an agent of prevention is exemplified in the field of automobile insurance. Some automobile insurers have substituted the word 'crash' for accident. 'Crash' connotes something that has a cause and can be avoided, whereas 'accident' suggests that the event was unanticipated and not attributable to a cause or fault. Where there is a cause and intentionality, there can also be attributions of responsibility and a basis for governance. The dominant theme in the insurance organization of crash reality is that drivers are taking too many risks and therefore are justifiable targets for engineering, education, and enforcement efforts aimed at prevention. Drivers can be made responsible for preventing crashes because of a declaration of causality: they are culpable not because of motivation and will per se, but because they should be knowledgeable about crash risks and the consequences of miscalculating them. In some cases, driver responsibility is attributed in a strict liability manner simply because it is the easiest way to render ambiguous accidents unambiguous crashes. The bottom line is how the moral utilitarianism of insurance loss ratio security can be met through the moral determination of individual responsibility.

This approach is related to the wider political and social culture, in particular, the victims' movement, which declares unequivocally that individuals who harm others are culpable regardless of their ignorance, miscalculations, or mistakes. Ironically, a strong blaming the victim component results. People who are deemed to be not responsible enough about risk taking because of ignorance or poor judgment are to bear the brunt of education and enforcement for prevention. Everyone is suspected to the degree that they are deemed to be contributing to a more risky environment.

In this context, insurers fund advertising campaigns, foundations that promote 'smart risk,' school-based driver education programs and the like, to make each individual act as if she is responsible for crash reality. These efforts in turn encourage traffic enforcement campaigns that seek behavioural change through surveillance. Enforcement for behaviour modification of the insured is the goal, and social advertising and education are part of the enforcement strategy.

Ironically, while automobile insurers participate in smart risk campaigns that declare that they are taking as much risk as possible out of driving, they must leave some risk in the insurance contract as an incentive to drive carefully. The insurance contract is seen as a tool of behaviour modification, passing risks to the driver in order to control her moral risks. The extremes in this regard are represented, on the one hand, by a no-fault system with full insurance coverage, which may make people less smart and less responsible about their driving behaviour. On the other hand, where insurance is not compulsory, which was the situation in Canada until about thirty years ago, people driving without insurance suffer lasting financial consequences from an accident and therefore have an incentive to be smart about their risk taking.

Suspicion of the insured crystallizes in the claims process. We documented a presumption that people will inflate the harms they have suffered and otherwise adjust their claims story to suit their interests. The claimant's moral neutralization of fraud is seen as opportunistic. Since the insured has been paying premiums over time – which have swelled the investment coffers of the insurer and been distributed to others in the pool who have suffered losses – a payback of extra magnitude is justifiable in the event of a claim. Claims adjusters and investigators work on the assumption that everybody commits fraud. They are confronted with fraud on an everyday basis, knowing that it is institutionalized in the insurance relationship.

In claims processing, suspicion and service are always in tension. The claimant is interrogated with a smile, but the adjuster is always half-watching in terms of another show, that of red flag indicators of bogus claims. Indicators that can be scanned include the claimant's insurance record and history of claims; employment, income, and credit records; race and ethnicity as signs of the claims culture the person participates in; incongruity in claims storytelling; and demeanour, for example, focusing too much on benefits ('claims consciousness') or being too legalistic. Insurers have their own automated data systems that 'trigger' red flags as soon as the client calls the insurance claims centre to report a loss. They also datamatch to other systems that provide details not only on past insurance claims, but also on credit and other financial risk histories that might indicate the claimant is looking for a quick fix to financial problems through an insurance claim. In combination, these automated red flag systems place the claimant on a spectrum from pink to ruby, signalling whether further investigation might be fruitful.

Large insurance companies have in-house private police forces called Special Investigation Units, and these units expanded substantially in the 1990s. Competitive markets and state restrictions on underwriting criteria made premium revenues tight and led to a crackdown on claims to secure loss ratios. These units are typically staffed by former public police officers and conduct investigations of suspected fraud where substantial claims are involved and investigative pay-offs are likely.

There is extensive contracting with private investigation firms. Private security operatives have extensive networks in the policing community, and with informants. They are subject to few effective legal due process controls, and can focus on efficiency and summary justice in helping to produce evidence and deny claims. They are also somewhat distanced from the insurance company and its relationships to policyholders, so that if they make a mistake they can be blamed and their contract cancelled in favour of another agency.

Insurance investigators are information-dependent in the same way as other policing agents. Therefore they cultivate informant networks with claims service providers, such as auto body shops, and with individuals who regard it as good citizenship to inform on those whose fraud threatens the integrity of the risk pool. Insurers also use informant tip lines, and intermediaries, such as Crime Stoppers, to encourage policyholders to be like a good neighbour in this respect.

Prosecution and punishment of insurance fraud through the legal system are extremely rare. Summary justice may be effected through denying a claim, cancelling the insurance contract, or changing insurance contract conditions. Moreover, a great deal of fraud is tolerated for a number of reasons. First, there are often evidence problems. Second, 'nuisance payments' are often propitious for reasons of efficiency: the indemnity principle is sacrificed to expediency, in the knowledge that claims costs might be recovered in the future through altered contract conditions and higher premiums. Third, as part of relationship management with more wealthy policyholders, insurers are especially sensitive about alleging fraud that might be easy to visualize but impossible to prove. Again, they must keep an eye on the premium-generating side of loss ratios and how it might be affected by a tough approach to fraud enforcement. Overpolicing can impede the smooth flow of economic and social relations in the insurance business. Expediency in governance is the result.

The governance of claims fraud encapsulates many of the arguments made in this book. Claims fraud, as a moral risk, is a product of insurance relationships. Its nature and extent are a function of the governance processes through which claims investigators manage their company's loss ratio. As such, claims fraud occurs through the practices of governance. At the same time, there is governance through claims fraud. The moral risk of documented fraud is used to justify the expansion of policing operatives, informant networks, databases, and other surveillance mechanisms for governing insured populations more generally.

Insurance practices in defining and responding to moral risks are key loci for understanding how governance is organized in liberal risk regimes more generally, and the forms of hierarchy, inclusion, and exclusion that result from this organization. Insurance moral risk assessment involves judgments about human agency and responsibility, and is therefore central to our understanding of how freedom is governed. Insurance provides enormous freedom for people to take risks without having to fear the full financial burden of negative outcomes. At the same time, those unpooled from the preferred insurance populations, or excluded from obtaining insurance altogether, experience insurance as but another institution that keeps them relatively powerless. In this respect, our analysis of how insurance governs reveals not only the structure of the insurance industry, but also how that industry coheres with the liberal risk regimes of the state and other institutions in the structuring of our lives.

References

Abbott, A. 1988. *The System of Professions: An Essay on the Division of Expert Labor.* Chicago: University of Chicago Press

Abramovitz, M. 1981. 'Welfare Quandaries and Productivity Concerns.' *American Economic Review* 71: 1–17

Adams, J.G. 1995. *Risk.* London: UCL Press

Adams, J.R. 1990. *The Big Fix: Inside the S&L Scandal.* New York: Wiley

– 2003. 'Risk and Morality: Three Framing Devices.' In R. Ericson and A. Doyle, eds., *Risk and Morality.* Toronto: University of Toronto Press

Archer, M. 1988. *Culture and Agency: The Place of Culture in Social Theory.* Cambridge: Cambridge University Press

Arnott, R., and J. Stiglitz. 1991. 'Moral Hazard and Nonmarket Institutions: Dysfunctional Crowding Out or Peer Monitoring?' *American Economic Review* 81 (1): 179

Arrow, K. 1974. *The Limits of Organization.* New York: Norton

Association of British Insurers. 1995. *Risk, Insurance and Welfare: The Balance between Public and Private Protection.* London: Association of British Insurers

Atkinson, A. 1999. *The Economic Consequences of Rolling Back the Welfare State.* Cambridge, MA: MIT Press

– 2000. 'Can Welfare States Compete in a Global Economy?' In R. Ericson and N. Stehr, eds., *Governing Modern Societies*, 259–75. Toronto: University of Toronto Press

Babbage, C. 1826. *Comparative View of the Various Institutions for the Assurance of Lives.* London: J. Mawman

Baker, T. 1994. 'Constructing the Insurance Relationship: Sales Stories, Claims Stories, and Insurance Contract Damages.' *Texas Law Review* 72: 1395–1434

– 1996. 'On the Genealogy of Moral Hazard.' *Texas Law Review* 75: 237–92

– 2000. 'Insuring Morality.' *Economy and Society* 29: 559–77

– 2003. 'Containing the Promise of Insurance: Adverse Selection and Risk
   Classification.' In R. Ericson and A. Doyle, eds., *Risk and Morality*. Toronto:
   University of Toronto Press
Baker, T., and K. McElrath. 1997. 'Insurance Claims Discrimination.' In G.
   Squires, ed., *Insurance Redlining: Disinvestment, Reinvestment, and the Evolving
   Role of Financial Institutions*, 141–56. Washington: Urban Institute Press
Baker, T., and J. Simon, eds. 2002. *Embracing Risk: The Changing Culture of Insur-
   ance and Responsibility*. Chicago: University of Chicago Press
Bay, C. 1981. *Strategies of Political Emancipation*. Notre Dame: University of
   Notre Dame Press
Beck, U. 1992a. *Risk Society: Toward a New Modernity*. London: Sage
– 1992b. 'Modern Society as Risk Society.' In N. Stehr and R. Ericson, eds., *The
   Culture and Power of Knowledge: Inquiries into Contemporary Societies*, 199–214.
   Berlin and New York: Walter de Gruyter
– 1999. *World Risk Society*. Cambridge: Polity Press
Beck, U., A. Giddens, and S. Lash. 1994. *Reflexive Modernization: Politics,
   Tradition and Aesthetics in the Modern Social Order*. Cambridge: Polity Press
Beiner, R. 1992. *What's the Matter with Liberalism?* Berkeley: University of
   California Press
– 2000. 'Is Social Democracy Dead?' In R. Ericson and N. Stehr, eds., *Governing
   Modern Societies*, 225–241. Toronto: University of Toronto Press
Bennett, C., and R. Grant, eds. 1999. *Visions of Privacy: Policy Choices for a Digital
   Age*. Toronto: University of Toronto Press
Bentham, J. 1962. 'Pauper Management Improved.' In J. Bowring, ed., *The
   Works of Jeremy Bentham*. New York: Russell and Russell
Berlin, I. 1969. 'Two Concepts of Liberty.' In *Four Essays on Liberty*. New York:
   Oxford University Press
Blasingame, F., and P. Smeljanick. 1997. 'The Insurance Churning Victims
   Infopage' web site, 29 October 1997
Booker, C., and R. North. 1994. *The Mad Officials*. London: Constable
Boorstin, D. 1973. *The Americans: The Democratic Experience*. New York: Random
   House
Broadbent, E. 2000. 'Social Justice and Citizenship: Dignity, Liberty, and
   Welfare.' In R. Ericson and N. Stehr, eds., *Governing Modern Societies*, 276–95.
   Toronto: University of Toronto Press
Brun, S., D. Etkin, D. Low, L. Wallace, and R. White. 1997. *Coping with Natural
   Disasters in Canada: Scientific, Government and Insurance Industry Perspectives*.
   Toronto: Institute for Environmental Studies, University of Toronto
Burchell, G. 1991. 'Popular Interests: Civil Society and Governing "The System
   of Natural Liberty."' In G. Burchell, C. Gordon and P. Miller, eds., *The*

Foucault Effect: Studies in Governmentality, 119–50. Chicago: University of Chicago Press

Burke, K. 1989. *On Symbols and Society*. Chicago: University of Chicago Press

Canadian Life and Health Insurance Association (CLHIA). 1995. *Federal Financial Services Review: Perspectives of the Canadian Life and Health Insurance Industry*. Toronto: CLHIA (June)

– 1997a. *Understanding and Implementing the New Life Insurance Illustrations Guidelines*. Toronto: CLHIA (May)

– 1997b. *Standards of Sound Business and Financial Practices for Life and Health Insurers*. Toronto: CLHIA

– 1997c. 'Who We Are.' www.clhia.ca

Carriere, K., and R. Ericson. 1989. *Crime Stoppers: A Study in the Organization of Community Policing*. Toronto: Centre of Criminology: University of Toronto

Castel, R. 1991. 'From Dangerousness to Risk.' In G. Burchell, C. Gordon, and P. Miller, eds., *The Foucault Effect: Studies in Governmentality*, 281–96. Chicago: University of Chicago Press

Castells, M. 1989. *The Informational City*. Oxford: Blackwell

– 1996. *The Rise of the Network Society*. Oxford: Blackwell

– 1997. *The Power of Identity*. Oxford: Blackwell

– 1998. *End of Millennium*. Oxford: Blackwell

Chubb Insurance. 1996. *Annual Report*

Clark, G. 1999. *Betting on Lives: The Culture of Life Insurance in England, 1695–1775*. Manchester: University of Manchester Press

– 2002. 'Embracing Fatality through Life Insurance in Eighteenth-Century England.' In T. Baker and J. Simon, eds., *Embracing Risk*, 80–96. Chicago: University of Chicago Press

Clarke, M. 1990. 'The Control of Insurance Fraud: A Comparative View.' *British Journal of Criminology* 30: 1–23

– 1999. *Citizens Financial Futures: The Regulation of Retail Financial Services in Britain*. Aldershot: Gower

Culpitt, I. 1999. *Social Policy and Risk*. London: Sage

Dandeker, C. 1990. *Surveillance, Power and Modernity: Bureaucracy and Discipline from 1700 to the Present Day*. New York: St Martin's Press

D'Arcy, S. 1994. 'The Dark Side of Insurance.' In S. Gustofson and S. Harrington, eds., *Insurance, Risk Management and Public Policy*. Boston: Kluwer

Davis, M. 1990. *City of Quartz: Excavating the Future in Los Angeles*. London: Verso

– 1998. *Ecology of Fear*. New York: Metropolitan Books

Daw, J., and J. Ferguson. 1995. 'The Collapse of Confederation Life: How and Why It Happened.' *Canadian Journal of Life Insurance* 11 (62/63): 25–38

Defert, D. 1991. '"Popular Life" and Insurance Technology.' In G. Burchell, C. Gordon, and P. Miller, eds., *The Foucault Effect: Studies in Governmentality,* 211–33. Chicago: University of Chicago Press

Dillon, M. 1995. 'Security, Philosophy and Politics.' In M. Featherstone, S. Lash, and R. Robertson, eds., *Global Modernities,* 155–77. London: Sage

Ditton, J. 1979. *Controlology: Beyond the New Criminology.* London: Macmillan

Donzelot, J. 1991. 'The Mobilization of Society.' In G. Burchell, C. Gordon, and P. Miller, eds., *The Foucault Effect: Studies in Governmentality,* 169–79. Chicago: University of Chicago Press

Dornstein, K. 1996. *Accidentally on Purpose: The Making of a Personal Injury Underworld in America.* New York: St Martin's Press

Douglas, M., 1986. *How Institutions Think.* Syracuse: Syracuse University Press
– 1990. 'Risk as a Forensic Resource.' *Daedalus* 119: 1–16
– 1992. *Risk and Blame: Essays in Cultural Theory.* London: Routledge

Douglas, M., and A. Wildavsky. 1982. *Risk and Culture: An Essay on the Selection of Technical and Environmental Dangers.* Berkeley: University of California Press

Doyle, A. 2003. *Arresting Images: Crime and Policing in Front of the Television Camera.* Toronto: University of Toronto Press

Durkheim, E. 1964. *The Rules of Sociological Method.* New York: Free Press

Dworkin, R. 1996. 'The Curse of American Politics.' *New York Review of Books* 43/16 (17 October): 19–24

Ericson, R. 1975. *Criminal Reactions: The Labelling Perspective.* Westmead: Saxon House (D.C. Health)
– 1982. *Reproducing Order: A Study of Police Patrol Work.* Toronto: University of Toronto Press
– 1993. *Making Crime: A Study of Detective Work.* 2nd ed. Toronto: University of Toronto Press
– 1994. 'The Decline of Innocence.' *University of British Columbia Law Review* 28: 367–83
– 1998. 'How Journalists Visualize Fact.' *Annals of the American Academy of Political and Social Sciences* 560: 83–95

Ericson, R., P. Baranek, and J. Chan. 1987. *Visualizing Deviance: A Study of News Organization.* Toronto: University of Toronto Press; Milton Keynes; Open University Press
– 1989. *Negotiating Control: A Study of News Sources.* Toronto: University of Toronto Press; Milton Keynes: Open University Press

Ericson, R., D. Barry, and A. Doyle. 2000. 'The Moral Hazards of Neoliberalism: Lessons from the Private Insurance Industry.' *Economy and Society* 29: 532–58

Ericson, R., and A. Doyle, eds. 2003. *Risk and Morality.* Toronto: University of Toronto Press

Ericson, R., and A. Doyle, forthcoming. *Uncertain Business: Insurance and the Limits of Knowledge*. Toronto: University of Toronto Press

Ericson, R., and K. Haggerty. 1997. *Policing the Risk Society*. Toronto: University of Toronto Press; Oxford: Oxford University Press

Etzioni, A. 1993. *The Spirit of Community*. New York: Crown

– 1997. *The New Golden Rule: Community and Morality in a Democratic Society*. London: Profile

Evans, L. 1993. 'Medical Accidents: No Such Thing?' *British Medical Journal* 307: 1438–9

Ewald, F. 1991. 'Insurance and Risk.' In G. Burchell, C. Gordon, and P. Miller, eds., *The Foucault Effect: Studies in Governmentality*, 197–210. Chicago: University of Chicago Press

Foot, D. 1996. *Boom, Bust and Echo: How to Profit from the Coming Demographic Shift*. Toronto: Macfarlane, Walter and Ross

Foucault, M. 1977. *Discipline and Punish: The Birth of the Prison*. New York: Pantheon

– 1982. 'Is It Really Important to Think?: An Interview with Michel Foucault.' *Philosophy and Social Criticism* 9 (1): 38

– 1988. 'Social Security.' In L. Kritzman, ed., *Politics, Philosophy, Culture*, 159–75. London: Routledge

– 1991. 'Governmentality.' In G. Burchell, C. Gordon, and P. Miller, eds., *The Foucault Effect: Studies in Governmentality*, 53–72. Chicago: University of Chicago Press

Friedman, M. 1988. 'The Social Responsibility of Business Is to Increase Its Profits.' In T. Donaldson and P. Werlane, eds., *Ethical Issues in Business: A Philosophical Approach*. Englewood Cliffs, NJ: Prentice-Hall

Fukuyama, F. 1996. *Trust: The Social Virtues and the Creation of Prosperity*. Harmondsworth: Penguin

Gabor, T. 1994. *Everybody Does It*. Toronto: University of Toronto Press

Gandy, O. 1993. *The Panoptic Sort: A Political Economy of Personal Information*. Boulder, CO: Westview

Garland, D. 1997. '"Governmentality" and the Problem of Crime: Foucault, Criminology, Sociology.' *Theoretical Criminology* 1: 173–214

Gates, J. 1998. *The Ownership Solution*. New York: Basic Books

Giddens, A. 1984. *The Constitution of Society: Outline of the Theory of Structuration*. Cambridge: Polity

– 1985. *The Nation State and Violence*. Berkeley: University of California Press

– 1990. *The Consequences of Modernity*. Cambridge: Polity

– 1991. *Modernity and Self-Identity: Self and Society in the Late Modern Age*. Stanford: Stanford University Press

- 1998. *The Third Way: The Renewal of Social Democracy.* Cambridge: Polity
Glenn, B. 2000. 'The Shifting Rhetoric of Insurance Denial.' *Law and Society Review* 34: 779–808
Goodin, R., B. Heady, R. Muffels, and H.-J. Driven. 1999. *The Real Worlds of Welfare Capitalism.* Cambridge: Cambridge University Press
Gordon, C. 1991. 'Government Rationality: An Introduction.' In G. Burchell, C. Gordon, and P. Miller, eds., *The Foucault Effect: Studies in Governmentality,* 1–51. Chicago: University of Chicago Press
Gowri, A. 1997. 'The Irony of Insurance: Community and Commodity.' PhD dissertation, University of Southern California
Green, J. 1997. *Risk and Misfortune: The Social Construction of Accidents.* London: UCL Press
Gusfield, J. 1981. *The Culture of Public Problems: Drinking-Driving and the Symbolic Order.* Chicago: University of Chicago Press
- 1989. 'Constructing the Ownership of Social Problems: Fun and Profit in the Welfare State.' *Social Problems* 36: 431–41
Hacking, I. 1986. 'Making up People.' In T. Heller et al., eds., *Reconstructing Individualism,* 222–36. Stanford: Stanford University Press
- 1990. *The Taming of Chance.* Cambridge: Cambridge University Press
- 1991. 'How Should We Do the History of Statistics?' In G. Burchell, C. Gordon, and P. Miller, eds., *The Foucault Effect: Studies in Governmentality,* 181–95. Chicago: University of Chicago Press.
- 2003. 'Risk and Dirt.' In R. Ericson and A. Doyle, eds., *Risk and Morality.* Toronto: University of Toronto Press
Haggerty, K. 2003. 'From Risk to Precaution: The Rationalities of Personal Crime Prevention.' In R. Ericson and A. Doyle, eds., *Risk and Morality.* Toronto: University of Toronto Press
Haggerty, K., and R. Ericson. 1999. 'The Militarization of Policing in the Information Age.' *Journal of Political and Military Sociology* 27 (2): 233–45
- 2000. 'The Surveillant Assemblage.' *British Journal of Sociology* 51: 605–22
Haggerty, K., L. Huey, and R. Ericson. 2003. 'The Genocide Will Be Televised: Surveillance in Canada's Poorest Urban Neighbourhood.' Unpublished paper
Hannigan, J. 1998. *Fantasy City: Pleasure and Profit in the Postmodern Metropolis.* London: Routledge
Harris, C. 1998. 'The Mismeasure of Fraud.' *Canadian Insurance* (May)
Hawkins, K. 1984. *Environment and Enforcement: Regulation and the Social Definition of Pollution.* Oxford: Oxford University Press
Heimer, C. 1985. *Reactive Risk and Rational Action: Managing Moral Hazard in Insurance Contracts.* Berkeley: University of California Press

– 2001. 'Solving the Problem of Trust.' In Karen Cook, ed., *Trust in Society*, 40–88. New York: Russell Sage Foundation

– 2003. 'Insurers as Moral Actors.' In R. Ericson and A. Doyle, eds., *Risk and Morality*. Toronto: University of Toronto Press

Held, D. 2000. 'The Changing Contours of Political Community: Rethinking Democracy in the Context of Globalization.' In R. Ericson and N. Stehr, eds., *Governing Modern Societies*, 42–59. Toronto: University of Toronto Press

Hindess, B. 2000. 'Divide and Govern.' In R. Ericson and N. Stehr, eds., *Governing Modern Societies*, 118–40. Toronto: University of Toronto Press

Hirst, P., and G. Thompson. 1996. *Globalization in Question*. Cambridge: Polity

Hives, C. 1985. *The Underwriters: The History of the Insurers' Advisory Organization, the Canadian Fire Underwriters' Association and the Canadian Underwriters' Association, 1883–1983*. Toronto: Insurers' Advisory Organization

Huey, L., K. Haggerty, and R. Ericson. Forthcoming. 'Policing Fantasy City.' In D. Cooley, ed., *Policing in Canada*. Toronto: University of Toronto Press

Hunt, A. 1996. 'The Governance of Consumption: Sumptuary Laws and Shifting Forms of Regulation.' *Economy and Society* 25: 410–27

– 1997. 'Consumption, Choice and Regulation.' In M. Valverde, ed., *New Forms of Governance: Theory, Practice, Research*, 31–2. Toronto: Centre of Criminology, University of Toronto

Ignatieff, M. 1995. 'The Myth of Citizenship.' In R. Beiner, ed., *Theorizing Citizenship*. Albany: SUNY Press

Insurance Advisory Board. 1995. *To Wake the Sleeping Giant: Insurance Distribution in an Open Market*. Washington: Insurance Advisory Board

– 1997a. *The 'Retail' Revolution: Retirement Services in an Era of Self-Reliance*. Washington: Insurance Advisory Board

– 1997b. *Partnerships for Growth: The Rise of Collaboration in Insurer Business Management*. Washington: Insurance Advisory Board

Insurance Bureau of Canada (IBC). 1996. *Facts of the General Insurance Industry in Canada*. Toronto: Insurance Bureau of Canada

– 1997. www.ibc.ca

Insurance Corporation of British Columbia. 1996. *Motor Vehicle Insurance in British Columbia at the Cross Roads*. Volume 1. *The Case for Change*. Report prepared by KPMG, Exactor Insurance Services Inc., Eckler Partners Ltd. (19 December)

– 1997a. *Loss Prevention: Road Safety and Auto Crime Five Year Plan*. Vancouver: ICBC

– 1997b. *Automobile Insurance Review*. Report to the B.C. Minister of Finance and Corporate Relations, and Minister Responsible for ICBC (March)

Insurance Planning. 1997. 'Life Insurance Illustrations.' *Insurance Planning* 4, 4.

Jebens, K. 1997. *LAUTRO: A Pioneer Regulator, 1986 to 1994*. London: LAUTRO

Keister, L. 2000. *Wealth in America: Trends in Wealth Inequality*. Cambridge: Cambridge University Press

Kenworth, L. 1999. 'Do Social Welfare Policies Reduce Poverty? A Cross-National Assessment.' *Social Forces* 77: 1119–39

Klein, N. 2000. *No Logo: Taking Aim at the Brand Bullies*. Toronto: Knopf Canada

Klein, R. 1997. 'Availability and Affordability Problems in Urban Homeowners Insurance Markets.' In G. Squires, ed., *Insurance Redlining: Disinvestment, Reinvestment, and the Evolving Role of Financial Institutions*, 43–82. Washington: Urban Institute Press

Knight, G. 1997. 'What's Working: Insurance as a Link to Neighborhood Revitalization.' In G. Squires, ed., *Insurance Redlining: Disinvestment, Reinvestment and the Evolving Role of Financial Institutions*, 214–34. Washington: Urban Institute Press

Laframboise, D. 1998. 'Governments and Gambling: Long-Armed Bandits.' *Globe and Mail*, 21 February D1–2

Lane, R. 1991. *The Market Experience*. New York: Cambridge University Press

Lash, S. 1995. 'Reflexive Modernization: The Aesthetic Dimension.' *Theory, Culture and Society* 10: 1–23

Lemmens, T., and P. Bahamin. 1998. 'Genetics in Life, Disability and Additional Health Insurance in Canada: A Comparative Legal and Ethical Analysis.' In B. Knoppers, ed., *Socio-Ethical Issues in Human Genetics*. Cowansville: Les Éditions Yvon Blais Inc.

Life Insurance Marketing Research Association (LIMRA). 1997. *The Buyer Study Canada: A Market Study of New Insured and the Ordinary Life Insurance Purchased*. Hartford: LIMRA

Lindbeck, A. 1995. 'The End of the Middle Way?' *American Economic Review* 85: 9–15

Lippert, R. 2002. 'Policing Property and Moral Risk through Promotions, Anonymization and Rewards: Revisiting Crime Stoppers.' *Social and Legal Studies* 11: 478–502

Loader, I. 1999. 'Consumer Culture and the Commodification of Policing and Security.' *Sociology* 33: 373–92

Loader, I., and N. Walker. 2001. 'Policing as a Public Good: Reconstituting the Connections between Policing and the State.' *Theoretical Criminology* 5: 9–35

Lowi, T. 1990. 'Risks and Rights in the History of American Government.' *Daedalus* 119 (4): 17–40

Lowther, B. 1996. 'Maximum Coverage.' *Monday Magazine* 22 (46): 1, 6–7

Luessenhop, E., and M. Mayer. 1995. *Risky Business: An Insider's Account of the Disaster at Lloyd's of London*. New York: Scribner

Luhmann, N. 1979. *Trust and Power*. Chicester: Wiley

Lupton, D. 1999. *Risk*. London: Routledge

Lynch, W. 1997. 'NAACP v. American Family.' In G. Squires, ed., *Insurance Redlining: Disinvestment, Reinvestment, and the Evolving Role of Financial Institutions*. Washington: Urban Institute

Macpherson, C. 1973. *Democratic Theory: Essays in Retrieval*. Oxford: Clarendon Press

Magnusson, W. 2000. 'Hyperspace: A Political Ontology of the Global City.' In R. Ericson and N. Stehr, eds., *Governing Modern Societies*, 80–104. Toronto: University of Toronto Press

Mannheim, K. 1936. *Ideology and Utopia: An Introduction to the Sociology of Knowledge*. New York: Harcourt, Brace

Mantle, J. 1992. *For Whom the Bell Tolls: The Lesson of Lloyd's of London*. London: Sinclair-Stevenson

Marsland, D. 1996. *Welfare or Welfare State?* Basingstoke: Macmillan

McClusky, M. 2002. 'Rhetoric of Risk and the Redistribution of Social Insurance.' In T. Baker and J. Simon, eds., *Embracing Risk: The Changing Culture of Insurance and Responsibility*, 146–70. Chicago: University of Chicago Press

McMahon, F. 2001. 'Poverty Is Voluntary, So Let's End It: Social Programs Like Welfare Merely Subsidize Bad Choices,' *Vancouver Sun*, 9 August A9

McQuaig, L. 1998. *The Cult of Impotence: Selling the Myth of Powerlessness in the Global Economy*. Toronto: Viking

McQueen, R. 1996. *Who Killed Confederation Life?* Toronto: McClelland & Stewart

Melody, W. 1994. 'Electronic Networks, Social Relations and the Changing Structure of Knowledge.' In D. Crowley and D. Mitchell, eds., *Communication Theory Today*, 254–73. Stanford: Stanford University Press

Miles, M., and M. Huberman. 1994. *Qualitative Data Analysis: An Expanded Sourcebook*. Thousand Oaks, CA: Sage

Misztal, B. 1996. *Trust in Modern Societies*. Cambridge: Polity

Moss, D. 2002. *When All Else Fails: Government as the Ultimate Risk Manager*. Cambridge, MA: Harvard University Press

Nietzsche, F. 1974. *The Gay Science*. New York: Vintage

Novas, C., and N. Rose. 2000. 'Genetic Risk and the Birth of the Somatic Individual.' *Economy and Society* 29: 485–513

Nye, J., P. Zelikov, and D. King, eds. 1997. *Why People Don't Trust Government*. Cambridge, MA: Harvard University Press

Oakes, G. 1990a. 'The American Life Insurance Salesman: A Secular Theodicy.' *International Journal of Politics, Culture and Society* 4: 95–112

– 1990b. *The Soul of the Salesman*. Thousand Oaks: Sage

Offe, C. 2000. '"Homogeneity" and Constitutional Democracy: Can We Cope with Identity Conflicts through Group Rights?' In R. Ericson and N. Stehr, eds., *Governing Modern Societies*, 177–211. Toronto: University of Toronto Press

Office of the Superintendent of Financial Institutions. 1996. *Annual Report*. Ottawa: OSFI

O'Malley, P. 1991. 'Legal Networks and Domestic Security.' *Studies in Law, Politics and Society* 11: 171–90

– 1992. 'Risk, Power and Crime Prevention.' *Economy and Society* 21: 252–75

– 1997. 'Governing Thrift: Insurance Technology, Political Rationalities and Working Class Security.' Unpublished paper, School of Law and Legal Studies, La Trobe University

– 1998. 'Introduction.' In Pat O'Malley, ed., *Crime and the Risk Society*, xi–xxv. Aldershot: Dartmouth

– 1999. 'Consuming Risks: Harm Minimisation and the Government of "Drug Users."' In R. Smandych, ed., *Governable Places: Readings in Governmentality and Crime Control*, 191–214. Aldershot: Dartmouth

Ontario Insurance Commission. 1997. 'Request for Recognition of the Life Agents Council of Ontario.' Submitted by the Incorporating Board of Governors of the Life Agents Council of Ontario to the Insurance Commissioner, 17 January.

Ontario Ministry of Financial Institutions. 1986. *Ontario Task Force on Insurance*. Toronto: Ministry of Financial Institutions

Ontario Red Tape Commission. 1997. *Cutting Red Tape Barriers to Jobs and Better Government*. Toronto: Red Tape Review Secretariat, Cabinet Office

Ortony, A., ed. 1979. *Metaphor and Thought*. Cambridge: Cambridge University Press

Parker, L. 2002. 'Luck Be a Lady,' *Report on Business Magazine*, April.

Petrou, M. 2001. 'Bring Back Poor Houses, End Poverty: Economist.' *Vancouver Sun*, 9 August, A1–2

Porter, T. 1995. *Trust in Numbers: The Pursuit of Objectivity in Science and Public Life*. Princeton: Princeton University Press

Posner, R. 1973. *Regulation of Advertising by the FTC*. Washington, DC: American Enterprise Institute for Public Policy Research

Poster, M. 1990. *The Mode of Information: Poststructuralism and Social Context*. Cambridge: Polity Press

Power, M. 1994. *The Audit Explosion*. London: Demos

– 1997. *The Audit Society: Rituals of Verification*. Oxford: Oxford University Press

– 2003. 'Risk Management and the Responsible Organization.' In R. Ericson and A. Doyle, eds., *Risk and Morality*. Toronto: University of Toronto Press

Powers, D. 1997. 'The Discriminatory Effects of Homeowners Insurance Underwriting Guidelines.' In G. Squires, ed., *Insurance Redlining: Disinvestment, Reinvestment, and the Evolving Role of Financial Institutions*, 119–40. Washington: Urban Institute Press

PPI Financial Group. 1997. 'Illustrations: New Generation of Life Insurance Products Demand Full Disclosure.' Toronto: PPI Financial Group

Priest, G. 1990. 'The New Legal Structure of Risk Control.' *Daedalus* 119 (4): 207–27

Procacci, G. 1991. 'Social Economy and the Government of Poverty.' In G. Burchell, C. Gordon, and P. Miller, eds., *The Foucault Effect: Studies in Governmentality*, 151–68. Chicago: University of Chicago Press

Rayher, J. 1998. 'Governing the Future: Marketing Financial Security.' MA thesis, Department of Anthropology and Sociology, University of British Columbia

Reason, J. 1990. *Human Error*. Cambridge: Cambridge University Press

Reich, R. 1991. 'Succession of the Successful.' *New York Times Magazine*, 20 January, 16–17, 42–5

– 1999. 'We Must Still Tax and Spend.' *New Statesman*, 1 May, 13–14

Reichman, N. 1986. 'Managing Crime Risks: Towards an Insurance Based Model of Social Control.' *Research in Law, Deviance and Social Control*, 151–72. Greenwich, CT: JAI Press

Rigakos, G. 2002. *The New Parapolice: Risk Markets and Commodified Social Control*. Toronto: University of Toronto Press

Ritter, R. 1997. 'Racial Justice and the Role of the U.S. Department of Justice in Combating Insurance Redlining.' In G. Squires, ed., *Insurance Redlining: Disinvestment, Reinvestment, and the Evolving Role of Financial Institutions*, 187–214. Washington: Urban Institute

Rose, N. 1996. 'The Death of the Social: Re-figuring the Territory of Government.' *Economy and Society* 25: 327–56

– 1997a. 'Contesting Power: Some Thoughts on Governmentality.' In M. Valverde, ed., *New Forms of Governance: Theory, Practice, Research*, 6–9. Toronto: Centre of Criminology, University of Toronto

– 1997b. 'Comment.' In M. Valverde, ed., *New Forms of Governance: Theory, Practice, Research*, 33–4. Toronto: Centre of Criminology, University of Toronto

– 1997c. 'Between Authority and Liberty: Governing Virtue in a Free Society.' Paper presented to a conference on Civil Society, Communitarianism, Third Sector, Helsinki, October

– 1999. *Powers of Freedom: Reframing Political Thought*. Cambridge: Cambridge University Press

- 2000. 'Governing Liberty.' In R. Ericson and N. Stehr, eds., *Governing Modern Societies*, 141–76. Toronto: University of Toronto Press

Rueschemeyer, D. 2000. 'Democracy and Social Inequality.' In R. Ericson and N. Stehr, eds., *Governing Modern Societies*, 242–58. Toronto: University of Toronto Press

Rueschemeyer, D., E. Huber-Stephens, and J. Stephens. 1992. *Capitalist Development and Democracy.* Chicago: University of Chicago Press

Schor, J. 1998. *The Overspent American: Upscaling, Downshifting and the New Consumer.* New York: Basic Books

Scott, C. 2002. 'Private Regulation of the Public Sector: A Neglected Facet of Contemporary Governance.' *Journal of Law and Society* 29: 56–76

Seaboard Insurance. 1996. *Annual Report*

Searle, J. 1995. *The Construction of Social Reality.* New York: Free Press

Sedgwick Insurance. 1996. *Annual Report*

- 1997. *Insurance Market Trends and Development*

Shearing, C., and R. Ericson. 1991. 'Culture as Figurative Action.' *British Journal of Sociology* 42: 481–506

Simmel, G. 1950. *The Sociology of Georg Simmel*, ed. Kurt Wolf. Glencoe, IL: Free Press

- 1978. *The Philosophy of Money.* London: Routledge and Kegan Paul

Simon, J. 1987. 'The Emergence of Risk Society: Insurance, Law and the State.' *Socialist Review* 95: 61–89

- 1997. 'Governing Through Crime.' In G. Fisher and L. Friedman, eds., *The Crime Conundrum: Essays on Criminal Justice*, 171–90. Boulder, CO: Westview

- 2002. 'Taking Risks: Extreme Sports and the Embrace of Risk in Advanced Liberal Societies.' In T. Baker and J. Simon, eds., *Embracing Risk: The Changing Culture of Insurance and Responsibility*, 177–208. Chicago: University of Chicago Press

- 2003. 'Risking Rescue: High Altitude Rescue as Moral Risk and Opportunity.' In R. Ericson and A. Doyle, eds., *Risk and Morality.* Toronto: University of Toronto Press

Slater, D. 1997. *Consumer Culture and Modernity.* Cambridge: Polity Press

Squires, G. 1997. 'Race, Politics and the Law: Recurring Themes in the Insurance Redlining Debate.' In G. Squires, ed., *Insurance Redlining: Disinvestment, Reinvestment and the Evolving Role of Financial Institutions*, 1–26. Washington: Urban Institute

Staples, W. 1997. *The Culture of Surveillance: Discipline and Social Control in the United States.* New York: St Martin's Press

Stehr, N., and R. Ericson. 2000. 'The Ungovernability of Modern Societies.'

In R. Ericson and N. Stehr, eds., *Governing Modern Societies*, 3–25. Toronto: University of Toronto Press

Stone, D. 1993. 'The Struggle for the Soul of Health Insurance.' *Journal of Health, Politics, Policy and Law* 18: 287–317

– 1994. 'Promises and Public Trust: Rethinking Insurance Law through Stories.' *Texas Law Review* 72: 1435–46

Strange, S. 1996. *The Retreat of the State: The Diffusion of Power in the World Economy.* Cambridge: Cambridge University Press

Sullivan, T., E. Stainblum, and J. Frank. 1997. 'Multicausality and the Future of Workers' Compensation.' Paper presented to the Third International Congress on Medical-Legal Aspects of Work Injury

de Swaan, A. 1990. *The Management of Normality.* London: Routledge

Sykes, G., and D. Matza. 1957. 'Techniques of Neutralization: A Theory of Delinquency.' *American Sociological Review* 22: 664–70

Thompson, G. 1997. 'Where Goes Economics and the Economies?' *Economy and Society* 26: 599–610

Tillman, R. 2002. *Global Pirates: Fraud in the Offshore Insurance Industry.* Boston: Northeastern University Press

Turow, J. 1997. *Breaking Up America: Advertisers and the New Media World.* Chicago: University of Chicago Press

Walker, C., and M. McGuiness. 1997. 'Political Violence and Commercial Victims: High Treason Against the Political Economy.' Unpublished paper, Faculty of Law, University of Leeds

Weber, M. 1964. *From Max Weber: Essays in Sociology.* Ed. H. Gerth and C.W. Mills. London: Routledge and Kegal Paul

Weisberg, H., and R. Derrig. 1991. 'Fraud and Automobile Insurance: A Report on Bodily Injury Claims in Massachusetts.' *Journal of Insurance Regulation* 9: 497–541

– 1992. 'Massachusetts Bodily Injury Tort Reform.' *Journal of Insurance Regulation* 10: 384–440

Werner, S. 1992. 'The Movement for Reforming American Business Ethics: A Twenty-Year Perspective.' *Journal of Business Ethics* 11: 61–70

Wolff, E. 1995. *Top Heavy: A Study of the Increasing Inequality of Wealth in America.* New York: Free Press

Zelizer, E. 1979. *Morals and Markets: The Development of Life Insurance in the United States.* New York: Columbia University Press

– 1997. *The Social Meaning of Money: Pin Money, Paychecks, Poor Relief, and Other Currencies.* Princeton: Princeton University Press

Zimring, R., and G. Hawkins. 1991. *The Scale of Imprisonment.* Chicago: University of Chicago Press

– 1993. 'Crime, Justice and the Savings and Loan Crisis.' In M. Tonry and
  N. Morris, eds., *Beyond the Law: Crime in Complex Organizations*, 247–92.
  Chicago: University of Chicago Press
Zwiebach, B. 1975. *Civility and Disobedience*. Cambridge: Cambridge University
  Press

Index